The Pros

The Forgotten Era of Tennis

Frontispiece. *On the road with the pros' hire-wire act. Young Pro Champion Pancho Gonzales might be moving beautifully, but the ramshackle canvas court that the pros carried with them on tour has slightly rucked up beneath his right foot.*

The Pros

The Forgotten Era of Tennis

Peter Underwood

Foreword by John Newcombe
and
Afterword by John Clarke

"The Pros: The Forgotten Era of Tennis" is published by New Chapter Press (www.NewChapterMedia.com) and is distributed by the Independent Publishers Group (www.IPGBook.com).

ISBN: 978-1937559915

For more information on this title or New Chapter Press contact:
Randy Walker Managing Partner
New Chapter Press
1175 York Ave Suite #3s New York, NY 10065
Rwalker@NewChapterMedia.com

First published in 2016 by
Beyt Noir Press
4 Harwood Street, Hilton, Western Australia, 6163.

National Library of Australia
Cataloguing-in-Publication entry:
Underwood, Peter J., author.
The pros: the forgotten heroes of tennis/Peter Underwood.

Includes bibliographical references and index.
Professionalism in sports—Australia—History
Tennis players—Australia—Biography
Tennis—Tournaments—History.
Tennis—Rules—History.

796.3420922

Editorial Consultants: Michèle Drouart and Janine Drakeford
Designed by Louise Burch
Typesetting in Goudy Old Style 12.5pt font by Ian Chambers
YouTube™ is a registered trade mark of Google

FRONT COVER: *Pancho Segura, Bobby Riggs, Dinny Pails and Jack Kramer (left to right), ham it up on the 1947–48 tour. Riggs and Kramer were battling to be World Pro Champion. The place is one of the cramped, el-cheapo, indoor venues in which the pros were forced to play. (Photo: UPI)*

BACK COVER: *Ken Rosewall, who, as a pro, was banned for a decade from Wimbledon, shows what it meant to him to finally win a World Championship – here the 1972 World Championship of Tennis. And against Rod Laver, once Amateur, Professional and Open World Champion! (Photo: Melchior DiGiacomo)*

To my brother Roger and my sons Crispin and Jim;
heroes always.

Le style est l'homme même.
(Style is the man himself.)

Buffon
Discours sur le Style

FOREWORD

by John Newcombe

PETER UNDERWOOD'S story of eight great professional tennis players covers a period of almost 40 years prior to tennis going Open for professionals and amateurs in 1968.

Imagine being the best tennis player in the world, a hero in your own country through your exploits in the Davis Cup and the Grand Slam tournaments. You decide to turn professional, which means you are ineligible for all those events, so you find that at 23 or 24 years of age you no longer feature on the sporting pages and are, to a certain extent, a forgotten commodity.

So why do it? The simple answer is money! As the world's best in 1962 Rod Laver probably made about $5,000 following his winning of the four Grand Slams. His professional takings for the first year as a pro in 1963 were about $100,000. In 1967 I won Wimbledon and the US Singles, finished the year at No. 1 and made about $15,000, most of which came from under-the-table payments for appearing at tournaments.

Certainly, before the Open Era, to make an honest living – and of course to be decently rewarded for doing so – was the main reason why the top amateurs looked to leaving the great tournaments and joining the pros. But as Peter points out, in those days the very best players were pros, and spurred by curiosity and pride, the champions of Wimbledon and the Davis Cup also wanted to see how they stacked up against them. Peter quotes Laver, the Grand Slam behind him, saying that only by joining the pros could he 'find out how good [he] was'.

I turned pro immediately after the Davis Cup Challenge Round against Spain at the end of 1967, and the first open tournament was in April,

1968; the first major, the French Championships, followed in May that year. Then came the first Open Wimbledon a month later, where Rod *The Rocket* defeated fellow new pro – and my doubles partner – Tony Roche in the Final. So I only spent a short time in the pros, and that was when open tennis was on its way. As a result, I wasn't forced to suffer years of the hardships – and the injustices – of the old pro tour, all of which are spelled out in this book.

The names Peter has chosen to follow are Tilden, Vines, Budge, Riggs, Kramer, Gonzales, Rosewall and Laver. As I grew up I was a big fan of the history of the sport I had chosen to be a big part of my future life. My belief is that to truly love your sport you must have an understanding of its history and past heroes. Here we find out how these eight men grew up, and what inspired them to become champions.

This is an important task Peter has chosen to tackle and I think his book should be a must read for any aspiring young player. Certainly any sports lover born between 1930 and 1970 will devour it. These players were all national and international heroes in their time, and media stories following some of their epic clashes make for fascinating reading.

I wish Peter all the best for his book, which should be compulsory reading for budding young tennis players and tennis lovers in general.

John Newcombe

John Newcombe
February 20, 2015

Contents

Preface

I am now beginning to feel that, try as I might, the pros, who have already lived with me from childhood, will be indissolubly bound to whatever of my life remains.

Back in 2016, following a decade of work, and after receiving a bevy of rejection slips from local and overseas publishers, I published *The Pros* myself, without fanfare, in Australia. My earnest hope was that I could then devote myself to an entrancing new writing project.

However, despite such modest origins and minimal promotion, the book—then entitled *The Pros: the forgotten era of tennis*—crept out and about in the marketplace. And before long, sympathetic souls from around the world began to tell me that there was poetry in my story, and that this forgotten tale needed to be told more widely. Buoyed, I decided on a final go: I would try to find a real publisher in America.

As it happened, my trip to the USA in October 2017 coincided with an extraordinary event. A decade earlier, the Australian peace group, the Medical Association for Prevention of War—another major part of my life—had founded an international arm, the International Campaign Against Nuclear Weapons (ICAN). From beginnings in someone's kitchen, this tiny group had survived and grown—and, with others, eventually, managed to persuade the United Nations to promote a worldwide ban on nuclear weapons.

To everyone's astonishment, this effort was noticed, and in July of that year, our still miniscule band was awarded the 2017 Nobel Peace Prize.

Synchronously, my trip had found a second purpose: as well as trying to 'spruik' my book about an obscure band of sportsmen, I was now prevailed upon to promote ICAN's achievement, and the global movement in nuclear disarmament.

So, when I found myself speaking up and down the country, it was not only to members of tennis clubs, the media and publishers. My American audiences were also community groups and service clubs, and the subject was why nuclear weapons should be illegal.

In this often demanding, double pilgrim's progress across the USA, in venues salubrious and otherwise, I became haunted by a particular fear: one night or other, in the midst of speaking to, say, the members of the famed Los Angeles Tennis Club (the school and university of many of my pros), I would find myself over-tired, or the victim of that extra glass. Then and there, instead of elucidating the magic of Rod Laver's topspin backhand, I would suddenly discover that I was pointing out why the nuclear-armed states had been against 'our' Treaty banning nuclear weapons, and gone as far as employing skulduggery to undermine it.

Or, alternatively, I wondered whether the (to me, surprisingly sympathetic) members of the Wall Street Rotary Club, would be finding themselves bemused at a point in my talk to them on nuclear issues. Indeed, in my tortured dreams I could overhear them suddenly asking themselves: What in heaven's name is the relevance of Ken Rosewall's neglect as a true tennis great—a subject on which the speaker clearly holds passionate views—to the dangers of *The Bomb?*

Now it's true that on my return to Australia, one witty (and sceptical) mate of mine informed me that if I had in fact so mixed things up, the respective audiences might never have noticed the change; more, she thought, it's possible that they could have lapped up my whimsically adjusted speech and its startling interpolations with even greater enthusiasm!

As far as I know, her theory was never put to the test.

How much good I did for ICAN is hard to measure, but with the help of a number of newfound and generous friends—some of them real 'insiders' in a world foreign to me—I eventually began to close in on potential publishers. In this, three persons were crucial: David Kramer, son of the legendary Jack; Donald Dell, former US Davis Cup Captain and celebrated tennis entrepreneur; and Lawrence Jordan, innkeeper and literary agent.

So, after innumerable tries, I reached Randy Walker and his fine and thoroughly fitting New Chapter Press. The book you are now reading is the result.

It is my hope that this edition will now find its wider readership. Certainly, like Shakespeare's poor players, our tatterdemalion pros, while trying to make a living from their little hour upon the stage, wished to move their watchers. And, with wonder, lift them a little beyond the everyday.

For you, the reader, may the words into which their distant play is now transmuted do the same.

Peter Underwood

Perth, West Australia
2019

The Cast of Characters

The Pro Champions in Chronological Order

No. 1 **VINCENT RICHARDS**
Vinnie
American, born 1903, died 1959
Pro Champion 1927–28/9
Prodigy; showman; entrepreneur; master volleyer; won major doubles titles aged fifteen and forty-two; ever-loyal to the pro circus he helped found.

No. 2 **KAREL KOŽELUH**
The Professor
Czech, born 1895, died 1950
Pro Champion 1928/9–31
Lugubrious defensive master; played international football for two countries; pinched from Europe by Richards in 1928 for first head-to-head pro tour; could beat anyone, anywhere, except sometimes Richards and usually Tilden.

No. 3 **WILLIAM TATEM TILDEN**
Big Bill
American, born 1893, died 1953
Pro Champion 1931–34
Began as poor little rich boy; became maestro and multi-sided celebrity loved and hated; self-taught but unrivalled giant in every facet of the game; enjoyed nothing more than showing that he was; held pros together for two decades; life ended badly.

No. 4 **ELLSWORTH VINES**
Elly
American, born 1911, died 1994
Pro Champion 1934–39
One of tennis's most explosive stars and sweetest souls; reached the amateur heights; done in by the establishment; found himself again with pros, but no one noticed; retired early to become a pro golfer.

No. 5 **DON BUDGE**
The Fire Dragon or just *God*
American, born 1915, died 2000
Pro Champion 1939–46
Game like battering ram; celestial backhand but whole game flawless and aggressive; regal yet kind-hearted; ran out of luck when he needed it.

No. 6 **BOBBY RIGGS**
Little Bobby
American, born 1918, died 1995
Pro Champion 1946–8
Diminutive loudmouth; clown and gambler hatched in the Bible Belt, helpful cover for desire to become the world's best player, which he became; superlative defender and strategist; underrated master of every aspect of game; ended up as notorious celebrity.

No. 7 **JACK KRAMER**
Big Jack or *King*
American, born 1921, died 2009
Pro Champion 1948–54
Tough child of Depression-era Las Vegas; never gambled but obeyed odds in life and on court; masterful serve-volleyer; devoted boss of the pros for over a

decade; midwife to the Open Era, and his own pros' demise.

No. 8 **RICHARD GONZALES**
Pancho or *Gorgo* to the pros
Mexican-American, born 1928, died 1995
Pro Champion 1954–60
Lithe; gorgeous, recalcitrant; so swift exhausts epithets for big cats; serve and moves made in heaven; fearsome master who sent off every challenger for almost a decade.

No. 9 **KEN ROSEWALL**
Muscles or *Saint Rosewall*
Australian, born 1934
Pro Champion 1960–65
Like Bobby Riggs, small, dark, quick, super smart; unlike Riggs, shy, modest, natural left-hander; backhand and court-craft made grown men and opponents weep.

No. 10 **ROD LAVER**
The Rocket
Australian, born 1938
Pro Champion 1965–68
Left-handed wizard; almost unplayable combination of power, spin and angles: sensitive soul beneath mien of bush plumber; young and good enough to dominate Amateur, Pro and Open Eras, collecting two Grand Slams.

The Major Nearly-Pro Champions

FRED PERRY
British, born 1909, died 1995
A top pro 1936–55
Tough-as-nails English street fighter; acrobatic egotist; dream forehand; after three Wimbledon titles could beat anyone except Vines and Budge; never let on to anyone he couldn't.

FRANCISCO SEGURA
Pancho or *Little Pancho*
Ecuadorian-American, born 1921
A top pro 1947–70
Born on a dirt floor; bandy-legged from childhood rickets; magus and wit; at forty could still beat almost anyone; neglected master loved by spectators, revered by fellow pros.

FRANK SEDGMAN
Sedg
Australian, born 1927
A top pro 1953–62
Gorgeous volleyer and mover; doubles master; faced Kramer and Gonzales at their peak, then, towards the end of his career, Rosewall and Laver at theirs.

TONY TRABERT
American, born 1930
A top pro 1955–62
Built like a quarter-back; superb all court game; shade too slow, shade too nice to get to the very top of pros.

LEW HOAD
Australian, born 1934, died 1994
A top pro 1957–63
Background Sydney working class; with Ken Rosewall, the muscular half of the Tennis Twins; played and looked like a Greek God; liked a beer; held from supreme success by happy-go-lucky disposition, his own flawed frame and Pancho Gonzales.

Fig. 0.1. Here comes the circus! It's 1949, and the banners in Queens, New York, advertise the arrival of the pro troupe under entrepreneur Bobby Riggs. The 'world's greatest players' are there for the National Pro Championships, and apparently there's a stack of cash at stake.

Prologue

The Travelling Players

For it's my experience, every day, and I make no doubt it's yours,
That a third-class pro is an overmatch for the best of the amateurs.

A B 'Banjo' Paterson
'Saltbush Bill's Second Flight'

IT is now nearly forgotten that until the late 1960s professional tennis players were banned from competing in the world's major tournaments. Those who played openly for money could take no part in the Davis Cup, or in the Wimbledon, French, Australian and US Championships. These events formed the exclusive arena of the so-called amateurs. Apparently, amateur tennis players competed only for glory.

The divide between those who were paid to play and those who weren't had arisen by the early twentieth century – just when, with the spread of social tennis and the sprouting of tennis clubs and tournaments, tennis began to take on its modern form. By the 1930s and the arrival of the 'Pro Tour', the schism was entrenched – and would last for another 40 years.[1]

Though the pro/amateur split proved remarkably persistent, it ended abruptly. One cold day in April 1968, for the first time ever, an amateur and a pro stepped onto a tennis court to play each other before the public. The two who brought down the curtain were wondrously fitted to represent their rival traditions.

It was Bournemouth, England, and a sharp, early spring. The first of the two striding onto the windswept court was a youngster fresh from Cambridge University. In shining whites and a hand-knitted woollen sweater revealing university colours, and with his blonde curls and pink face, Mark Cox could not have looked more the part of the untainted amateur.

In contrast, a step behind him was the old pro, Richard 'Pancho' Gonzales. A black tracksuit, well worn, hid his tennis whites. By then Gonzales was 40 years old, a grisly, black-and-grey-maned veteran of a thousand one-night stands: *Gorgo*, as the other pros called him, owned the looks, the appetite and the temper of an aging lion.

Their confrontation was significant, not for who won or lost but for what it represented in the history of tennis. From this game forth, any 'professional' player could compete officially against any 'amateur'. In a moment, a new era had begun, the 'Open Era', which lasted to the present day.[2]

Before Open Tennis, professional and amateur tennis were worlds apart. Unmistakably, the pro's was the less glorious. Let's catch them, on the road, at a moment somewhere in the middle of their history.

In 1952, finishing a summer tour of Europe, the pro band had dwindled to only four performers.

Their leader was the Pro Champion, the man sometimes called King: Jack Kramer. Besides being the best tennis player in the world, Kramer was ringmaster and circus owner.

Desperate to usurp the King was the Challenger, the leonine Pancho Gonzales, then only twenty-four and, as always, angry and hungry.

The third of the troupe was Don Budge, the legendary ex-champion. Budge was past his peak, but he could still hit the ball with such command that he would draw the other pros out to study him – and wince to see a tennis ball struck with such sublimity.

The final member of the quartet was Francisco *Little Pancho* Segura, a tiny bandy-legged Ecuadorian, and so delightful a character that he was the favourite of every spectator who saw him. Although unknown as an amateur, the other pros saw Segura as a complete master: armed with one of tennis's most lethal shots – his double-handed forehand – they counted him the most underrated player since tennis began.

Only four performers, but wasn't this some show!

And yet, what was the fate of this tiny but extraordinary band? Says Jack Kramer:

> We were in Falkirk, Scotland ... and our next one-night stand was in a place in England called Harrogate. Then we were scheduled to double back the next night to a little town named Kirkcaldy. Well, we were all exhausted from touring and ... Don [Budge] suggested that we drop in to see the promoter [in Kirkcaldy] and cancel that date.
>
> The promoter was crestfallen ... We were the biggest thing to hit Kirkcaldy in years. Why he had already sixty pounds [then about US$240] in the till ... And so, regretfully, we promised we'd be back to honour our commitment the next night. We drove all the way to Harrogate, played two singles and a doubles from around 7 pm to midnight, caught some sleep at a bed-and-breakfast place, and then the next day, drove the hundred and fifty miles back over the winding Scottish roads to Kirkcaldy. And we played all evening there.
>
> When I went to settle up with the promoter, he was ecstatic. The sixty pounds advance sale had only been the start. We had drawn so well at the gate that our cut was ninety-two pounds, about $400 in those days. 'But laddie,' he said as he gave me the money, 'you and the boys played so well, we want to give you this.' And he slipped me eight more pounds, bringing it up to an even hundred. Three figures!
>
> I went out to the car where the other three were waiting.
>
> 'How'd we do, Jack?' Budge asked.
>
> 'Great,' I said. 'We got a tip.' And we all laughed ourselves silly and sat there like a bunch of two-bit hoods who had just robbed a gas station, divvying up a hundred pounds — minus the gas money and other expenses that had to come off the top.[3]

Kramer concludes ironically: he asks the reader to visualise the present superstars of tennis. Could we imagine them splitting a few measly bucks, in the middle of nowhere, to which they'd just driven a hundred miles, and in one hire car? For a start there wouldn't be room enough for their psychologists.[4]

Yes, although the pros' top performers were famous stars, the fans and media reserved their attention for the amateur champions who dazzled the crowds at the great fiestas of Wimbledon and the Davis Cup Challenge Rounds. To them, this glamorous coterie in shining white were patriots, playing not for themselves, but for their country – and surely above mammon.

If we turn briefly to Australia, we discover more of the contrary world confronting a top amateur when they joined the travelling players.

In his modestly swashbuckling style, Frank Sedgman spearheaded an Australian tennis renaissance after the war, and by the 1950s had become a national hero. But when he 'turned pro' at the end of 1952, the move engendered such ill feeling that the old guard who ran the amateur show could almost brand Sedgman as a traitor to his country.

On one occasion, when Sedgman was on a break from the pro tour and back in Australia, a mate invited him for a game of golf at his swank golf course. On their arrival, the club's President accosted Sedgman. On the spot, he banned him from playing on the course.

'The reason?' asked the hapless tennis player, celebrated for his sportsmanship.

'You're a professional – we don't accept them here,' was the explanation.[5]

Why was the game ruled by such attitudes? Some answers can be found in Lowe's Lawn Tennis Annual 1934.[6]

If you leaf through my tattered copy you will find that this book speaks to the inhabitants of a gracious world, now long past. The Annual begins with pages of advertisements for hotels with attractions irresistible to the upper classes – of course tennis, as well as hunting, shooting and fishing, to say nothing of betting.

The editor, Sir Gordon Lowe, nonetheless concedes a place in his book for a colonial, albeit one with a title. Eighty years and an age later, the comments of the Honourable E. B. Fisher remain of interest.

By 1934, the New Zealander had been playing good tennis for 50 years, and could speak with authority on the game's evolution. The, to me, increasingly likeable Hon. Fisher, arrives head-on at a problem so serious he believes that it could kill tennis: the failure of the Lawn Tennis Associations (LTAs) to provide for the players in their charge. Unless independently rich, to continue playing at top level the best players must become either professionals, who can officially accept payment for playing and teaching, or what he calls 'shamateurs'. These, he indicates, are in fact paid – but under the table.

Fisher then feigns a dialogue to explain his case.

He describes the situation facing a leading amateur who, although 'without private means', is required to represent 'his country' for nothing. He ends with the player's words: 'I cannot take a job ... If any cash proceeds arise from my playing, the LTA gets them ... I get nothing ... I must remain a pure lily-white amateur ... [and let them] ... appropriate my share. *Else I make some other arrangement.*' [My emphasis]

These could be the words of Frank Sedgman – 20 years later, and in another country – as he contemplated his future as an amateur.

But what allowed the LTAs to 'appropriate' the players' share and to keep the worker-players underfoot? As it happens, the prescient Hon. Fisher slips in the answer: he describes the 'purple indignation of the Victorian father who, upon being asked if he would permit his daughter to play at Wimbledon, answered: "Play tennis in public! My God, no sir, no sir." '

If this gentleman viewed playing before the public as distasteful, imagine his opinion on being paid to do so! It appeared to Fisher – and it appears to me – that it was the descendants of this 'Victorian father' who, living off the players, ran international tennis for generations.

Fred Perry, English and a triple Wimbledon Champion, adds a relevant story.

Perry explains that despite his amateur pre-eminence, because he was the son of a Labour MP from the wrong side of the tracks the tennis hierarchy could not bear him. When he first won Wimbledon, he overheard (from his bath after the match) a Wimbledon official congratulating his defeated opponent. 'For once the best man didn't win,' remarked the man, who then went out, leaving Perry a Wimbledon Club tie draped over a chair to mark his victory. When Perry turned pro, the club took it back.[7]

So the tenacious hierarchy of social class was a major reason why, despite what most of the younger generation believe, tennis was not always a game like golf, where the best have always played each other for money. Nor was it like cricket, where eventually – but much sooner than in tennis – pros and amateurs were permitted to play together, if at first required to enter the field through different gates.

At this point we must ask: Why tell the story of the pros? To the present age, reared on the now, the megastar and the dollar, all concocted for and by television and advertising, the history of players whose battles went unnoticed and were fought for peanuts might appear trifling. But to lovers of the game, this period of tennis history is worth the telling.

For a start, this was a circus of star sportsmen at their best. Further, as players and showmen/entrepreneurs, these men made a career and a living from the game – and thereby created modern tennis. But I also believe that the pro/amateur split spawned a host of injustices that, if uncorrected, will continue to distort a fair telling of the game's history.

Jack Kramer brings these out in his wonderfully honest autobiography.

In a chapter entitled 'The Way It Wasn't', Kramer says that the real 'fix' in tennis during the divided era was in 'the championships' – because the real champions, the professionals, couldn't get into them. Kramer then proceeds 'for the sake of justice' to rewrite history, and he lists those who would have won Wimbledon and the US Championships 'if the real champions had been allowed to play'.

Although fanciful, his words are worth including.

> ... a lot of things happened quite differently. Fred Perry would have won only one Wimbledon, and so I, not Fred, would have been the first modern player to win three Wimbledons in a row ... Budge would have won six straight Forest Hills [US Championships] ... Gonzales also would have won seven Forest Hills and six Wimbledons too, giving him the modern record of thirteen. And little Rosewall — not only did he get a Wimbledon title, he would have gotten four to go with his five Forest Hills.
>
> Oh it would have been very different ...[8]

I have a further motive in writing this book: it arises from the nature of the pros' individual confrontations.

For most of the Pro Era, the core of the company consisted of less than half a dozen elite players. By the early 1930s a specific pattern had emerged, which lasted into the '60s. A promoter would pull the group together to 'do a tour'. He would find the players, and arrange some financial guarantees, a format, itinerary and provisional venues. For the next months they played each other day-in and day-out (though 'night-in and night–out' is more accurate).

During most of this period, the keystone of the show – the high trapeze act – was a head-to-head between the champion and the contender. Preferably, the contender was the top amateur, or someone as close as possible to that position, fresh from triumphs in the great championships of the world. Over an extraordinary hundred-or-so matches, lasting months and cast in a half-dozen countries, the battle was joined. Eventually a victor emerged ... to become the Professional Tennis Champion of the World.

Supporting the star act was the rest of the troupe, usually made up of former champions and former contenders – though a place was sometimes found for a marvellous maverick like Pancho Segura.

The pros also ran fixed tournaments, if infrequently: here the competition among the top touring players was bolstered by a somewhat larger group drawn from among the best, usually local, teaching pros that the promoter signed up for the event.

This intense competition among a handful of champions offered a unique opportunity: the chance to play and study the best, and then to demonstrate the fruit of this education over months and years. 'Until I turned pro, I didn't know a bloody thing about tennis,' the one and only Lew Hoad used to admit with characteristic bluntness. This book examines how these men, immersed in the pro cauldron, learnt, confronted the best and turned themselves into masters.

Rod Laver, in a touching letter to me, considers that he was 'very fortunate' to have participated in, and survived, three eras – the Amateur, the Pro and the Open. Doing so, he said, was 'character-building'.[9] Tony Trabert adds bluntly: 'There was no charity in pro tennis.'[10] Survival among the travelling players of the old pro tour certainly required that Laverian quality of 'character', and it is the way this quality played out that I explore in these eight individuals.

The more the pros, with their funny wooden rackets and white clothes, begin to fade into history, the stronger appears their link to our group and the generations of travelling players that preceded them. And as we look back into history, it is now clearer how exceptional was any any individual who joined an itinerant group of performers. Why? Because from ancient times every novice player taking to the road had to trust that their act was sufficiently extraordinary and appealing to allow them to extract a living – no matter how transient or meagre – from the settled folk who grow, make, or sell things.

Of these uncommon persons, a few possessed even rarer qualities: the drive and talent to take their act beyond sufficiency to mastery. The tennis pros were such individuals. To make a living, they chose the life of the wandering performer; beyond survival, they laboured to become masters of their craft. Indeed, by testing the limits of mind and body, the pros challenged many in the watching crowd; sometimes, in the way of the great artist, they asked of their imagination, and changed them as a result.

Such is the stuff of heroes. In the days of the oral tradition, heroes became the font of epic poems and songs of praise.

This book offers such a song for our times.

Notes

1 I have drawn heavily on Joe McCauley's 2000 book on the history of the pros, now supplemented by Ray Bowers, who has used primary sources to detail the first half of the Pro Era. McCauley, Joe. *History of Professional Tennis*. Short Run Book Company, Berkshire, 2000. Bowers, Ray. *Forgotten Victories: History of the Pro Tennis Wars* 1926–1945. In *Between the Lines* by Ray Bowers, in http//www.TennisServer.com

2 I take poetic licence here: the very first match in this first Open tournament was between two virtual unknowns, a teaching pro and a minor amateur. But the match between Gonzales and Cox, which followed, was the first between a top pro and a top amateur, and so has been generally acknowledged as the match that ended one era and began another.

3 Jack Kramer with Frank Deford, *The Game: My Forty Years in Tennis*, André Deutsch, London, 1979.

4 Andre Agassi indicates the requirements of a top player of today. The standard entourage would consist of: agent/manager, coach, fitness and strength coach, hitting partner, racket stringer, shoe and clothes endorsement representative, masseur, psychologist, spiritual adviser/guru (optional), and family and family friends. Andre Agassi, *Open: an autobiography*, HarperCollins, London, 2010. And Andy Murray now adds web manager to his touring team!

5 Interview with Frank Sedgman, *The Fifth Set* (television documentary on the Davis Cup), dir. Sue Thomson, ABC, December 6, 2000.

6 *Lowe's Lawn Tennis Annual 1934*, ed. Sir Gordon Lowe, Eyre and Spottiswoode, London, 1934. The excerpts are from the article by E B Fisher entitled 'Looking forward and back'.

7 Fred Perry, *Fred Perry: An Autobiography*, Arrow Books, London, 1984.

8 Kramer, *The Game*. Kramer shows how, in the sixties, Roy Emerson could amass 12 Grand Slam titles without beating the best half-dozen tennis players in the world, Gonzales, Rosewall, Hoad and Laver included. In describing himself as 'a high class hacker', the likable Emerson understates his abilities, but when facing the true champions in open competition, Emerson never won another major. See Banjo Paterson's epigraph to this chapter, from a century earlier!

9 From a personal letter to the author from Rod Laver on April 25, 2005.

10 Tony Trabert, 'Doubles', Chapter 9 of *The Art of Tennis*, ed. Alan Trengove, Hodder and Stoughton, London, 1964.

Fig. 1.0. A majestic Tilden at the end of his career as amateur. Though way into court, the follow through is typically full and sweeping.

1

TRAGEDIAN – TILDEN

For all my career I have loved the brightness,
and I long for it again.

Bill Tilden
My Story: A Champion's Memoirs

IN 1967, immediately after his first Wimbledon victory, a young John Newcombe was asked by a reporter, 'From whom did you learn most?' He replied, 'Why, Tilden of course.'

Although 15 years had passed since Tilden's death, his influence remained unquestioned. But after a further five decades, most of today's tennis players and followers would not, as Newcombe did, take for granted Tilden's unique contribution to the making of modern tennis. Despite one of sport's outstanding biographies – *Big Bill Tilden: The Triumphs and the Tragedy* by Frank Deford – many would hardly have heard of him.[1]

Tilden is a challenge to the biographer not only because he is becoming forgotten: his gifts to the game arose from his several, often contradictory, selves. Not just a tennis champion, he became a celebrity, loved and vilified, and an entrepreneur and actor who wrote plays and novels.

We begin with a glimpse of this many-sided man at the end of his career.

The veteran: two contemporary snapshots

Joining the aging *Big Bill* and his band on tour, let's hear what two of his greatest contemporaries have to say about him.

At a point in his autobiography, Fred Perry takes us to America and a mid-summer day in 1941.[2]

On this occasion the pro caravan arrived late in the morning in the little town of Independence, Kansas, straight from their previous night's performance nearby. The heat was 'fierce.' Perry checked into his hotel.

Before long, he got a call. It was Tilden.

'Hey Fred,' said *Big Bill*, 'what're your plans for the day?'

Perry replied that he might 'sit under a tree, relax, and smoke my pipe'.

But Bill had other ideas: he wanted Perry to 'hit a few balls' with him.

'For crying out aloud,' cried the exasperated Perry, 'we've been playing daily for two months and we've got a match tonight. You want to go out in this heat and hit? You're crazy.'

But *Big Bill* insisted. There was something he had to show him.

Despite everything, Perry was intrigued. Out they went.

Out on court, in the blazing heat, Tilden asked Perry to feed him a few balls, 'wide and low,' to his forehand.

Immediately, Perry saw it all – Tilden had got himself a new shot. He was returning the ball with a new style, now with a different grip to the Eastern he had championed for his whole career. Turning the palm a quarter turn anticlockwise, so it is not behind the handle but partly on top, the old master was hitting 'a perfect' Continental forehand, so mimicking one of the legendary strokes of tennis – Perry's own forehand.

Perry wondered: *What is the old trickster up to?*

Tilden explained.

While studying Perry over the years, he'd come to see the advantages of the Continental grip, particularly for low balls. It allowed the ball to be taken earlier, and with more wrist and concealment. The result was the surprise, the 'quickness' of those master forehands of the slick Continental artists like Cochet, and Perry himself (and, later, Hoad and Laver). The strategist Tilden also saw how the shot could be seamlessly choreographed into a play – the fleet swoop into a ball a few inches above the turf, the forward momentum to commandeer the net, then the jugular put-away.

Tilden told Perry that here the Continental was best. And added, 'I felt I wouldn't be the complete player unless I had mastered it ... [so] I could use it in match play if I wanted to.' Now this was the man who had often dismissed Perry, calling him a player so truncated as to be 'nothing more than his forehand'. Then adding salt to the wound by concluding that the famous Perry forehand itself was 'badly produced, wristy and unorthodox'!

Our second snapshot catches the veteran at about the same time. Originally from Don Budge, Deford re-tells it in a chapter enticingly called 'Please boo me all you will between points.'

By 1940, top dog Budge had conquered Vines, then twice convincingly beaten Perry on tour. So a desperate promoter dragged out Tilden, 47 years of age but hopefully still a crowd-puller, for a short tour against the Champion. Tilden was still competitive, but on a night-after-night tour he was no match for Budge, twenty years younger and at his peak.

On the occasion in question the pros had made it to the big smoke: Montreal. By then, with his irascible and many-sided nature rumbling closer to the surface, *Big Bill* had shortened 'J Donald God', Perry's name for the invincible Budge, to his own equally sarcastic 'Mister God'. On this particular evening a linesman had started making a succession of bad calls. It was hard enough trying to match divinity: add poor umpiring, and Tilden had become rattled.

Though most of the bad calls had been in his favour, *Big Bill* suddenly stopped playing! Walking up to the umpire, he demanded the linesman's removal.

Following the resumption of the match, Budge recalled that 'the crowd got onto Tilden, and began booing him ... even during ... points.'

After a little more of this, Tilden had had enough. In the middle of a game, he held up his hands, and again stopped play. Once more he walked over to the umpire's chair, this time abruptly seizing the microphone from the awestruck official.

Enthralled, Budge watched. Though he knew *Big Bill* was 'glib enough to get out of it', Budge 'sure didn't know how he was going to manage it this time'.

Tilden looked around. Nothing in the crowd moved.

Tilden spoke calmly:

> Ladies and gentleman, I believe you will observe the British way of letting a man defend himself before you condemn him. It is you, not I, who suffer the most from these bad calls. Mr Budge is now the greatest player in the game, and you have paid good money to watch me try to put up a match against him. If I am to be disturbed by bad calls, I cannot play my best, and if you razz me or boo me during a point, you will only make it more difficult for me. Please boo me all you will between points. I have endured that all my life and I am quite used to it, but if you wish to obtain the most for your money, hold off while I try to play the best player in the world. Thank you.[3]

For the remainder of the match the crowd was silent.

These two vignettes reveal at least three of Tilden's traits.

Perry shows us the contradictory but indefatigable perfectionist, the artist who never gave up studying his calling, and was driven to display every aspect of it. Budge then lets out the charismatic, yet tetchy and narcissistic showman who could never leave the illusory world of the bright lights. Hovering alongside this figure is the sportsman, proud yet magnanimous and humble in defeat.

And there is a fourth. Slipping out from the Tilden monologue is the long-suffering victim. One more time, he implies, I've had to don the mask, and one more time strut my wares upon this shining stage before a hungry crowd ...

Let's pause briefly to picture what exactly the 'hungry crowd' – or Tilden's younger opponents such as Budge, Perry or Bobby Riggs – might have seen when the veteran Tilden stepped out to play them.

As the pros make their one-night stop in some little town, let's first imagine what the impresario has to say as, one by one, he announces the performers.

The MC leaves till last the man whose years as the king of the high wire were years past. He waits, the crowd hushes, then he begins, so we suppose:

'Ladeeeez and Gennelmen! In this galaxy of champions, I am pleased to introduce to you ... the last of tonight's great champions! Now, here in front of you,

is the greatest of them all! The incomparable! The one and only! The champion of champions! The Legendary Lion of Tennis! Big ... Bill ... Tilden!'

Into the glare steps a tall, gaunt man with coat-hanger shoulders and a lop-sided smile.

Approaching 50 years of age, he is greying now and thinner than ever. But the crowd – often country folk, sparsely packed into a local hall – have not forgotten him. Their salute is more explosive than that given to any who preceded him. To them, Tilden is the star of the show.

The veteran pauses courtside, but does not bow or beam. As if by right, with the ghost of a smile, he bends his head to their ovation.

Perhaps, however, those seated in the front rows might wonder about such kingly condescension. From close-up the former fashion plate is cracked: his clothes are far from spruce, and his too-short shorts and almost mincing gait add a brittle feel to this long-legged creature. Some may sense that here, behind the public face, is an old queen of an actor, down on his luck.

Yet the veteran could still play! Despite the cracks, two decades past his prime, even that superlative trio of Budge, Perry and Riggs couldn't take 'the old man' lightly. Their in-joke – *for one set, Big Bill is still the best* – mixes a little derision with relief and respect. On court that night – and every night – he would be no pushover. [4]

Let's find out how Tilden started the game, and became a champion.

A stumbling apprenticeship

Tilden was far from a prodigy. Born into money, he had started tennis at high school and continued playing a little at university – there, says biographer Deford, he wasn't good enough for the 'very ordinary' university team. Following a couple of desultory years – coincident with a series of family traumas to be explored later – he began playing the local East Coast tennis circuit to fill in time.

Then came a crucial turning point.

Overnight, tennis became his life. By now aged 22, in what appeared an inexplicable about-face, he was entering 'every rinky-dink tournament that would have him'. And playing every day. To mark this metamorphosis, he changed his name: christened 'William Tatem Tilden Junior', he became 'William Tatem Tilden 2nd'.

During the five years from aged 22 to 27, the young patrician embarked on an extraordinary quest – to become a tennis champion. And his first step was to make a bottom-up analysis of the whole game. Before long, Tilden was telling anyone who would listen how tennis should be played.

For a start, he classed players into three broad groups according to their style.

First was the 'net rusher,' who aims for the net as soon as possible after serve or approach, attempting to finish off the point by a volley or smash. Second was the 'baseliner', who stays back and outmanoeuvres, or who passes or lobs opponents if they attack the net. Last was the 'all court player' who, depending on circumstances, does both.

To this day, the three categories remain useful. For instance, the flowering of champions Rosewall and Gonzales required a transition from one style to another. Though Gonzales moved from net rusher and Rosewall from baseliner, both ended up as all court players. More recently, McEnroe and Sampras were net rushers, Nadal and Djokovich baseliners, and, by the end of his career, Federer an all court player.

Tilden's analysis began by noting that, deplorably, the choice of style was usually governed by fashion, not effectiveness. He himself had seen fashions come and go. When Tilden began his analysis, both the net-rushing and baseline style had had their day. The teenage Tilden, coming up in the century's second decade, had watched net rushers like Maurice McLoughlin, the 'California Comet', sweep all before them. Just a few years later, it was their turn to be fossilised – and back came the baseline game.

Tilden concluded that a game centred purely on net or baseline was for fools. His response? He began championing a method that would possess the virtues of forecourt and backcourt games, without their defects: the *all court* style.[5]

Tilden also scrutinised the mechanics of the champions' strokes. As a result – and typical of a man in love with extremes – the complete ideal he came to espouse was *all court, all stroke, all speed*. Here, his true tennis player aimed to possess more than control of net and baseline. They also needed to master *spin* – whether topspin (hitting over the ball) or slice (hitting under the ball) – and *pace*, which meant allowing the shot or rally to be conducted at any speed from fast to slow.[6]

In his resonantly titled 1928 classic, *Match Play and the Spin of the Ball*, Tilden explains that as night follows day, his multi-sided maestro, the 'Tennis Player', will always triumph over those hoi polloi who can only drive or only volley, or who employ one pace or one spin. Indeed, in Tilden's eyes, such one-dimensional souls seem to inhabit a lower moral universe. Further, unless they see the light, Tilden's light, they are likely to languish there forever.

From humble instructor, in his own eyes he has become Messiah.

Yet for many years, try (and talk) as he might, his ideal remained beyond him. Worse, he realised that his less-than-authoritative performances and know-it-all opinions made him an object of derision – more reason for him to assume the mantle of martyr.

However, during the latter stages of his uncomfortable apprenticeship, Tilden had taken one crucial leap on his road to mastery. In 1919, on his fourth attempt at the US Singles, Tilden had reached the final for the second time. But once again he was mauled. His nemesis was William O. Johnston.

To the adoring public, Johnston was *Little Bill* to Tilden's *Big Bill*. Although of small stature, Johnston possessed a huge western-grip topspin forehand. The contrasting styles of Tilden and Johnston, the owners of two of tennis's legendary forehands, are beautifully shown in Figure 1.1. Johnston would whirl into his shot, and then crack the ball so hard that at follow-through his feet would leave the ground. And he knew where to put his firecracker – straight into *Big Bill*'s weaker backhand side. As an early exponent of the all court style, *Little Bill* would follow this crunching drive into net – and volleying surely, finish off the point.

Though by then Tilden was equal to the smaller man in every other department of the game, this sequence sealed Tilden's fate.

After this defeat of 1919, Tilden decided that he had only one chance left. What he needed was a backhand that could fight fire with fire. If he added an attacking backhand drive to his growing arsenal of style, stroke, spin and pace, he might realise his ideal. And beat *Little Bill* too.

In one of the most famous moves in sport, Tilden stopped playing competitively for six months. He located an indoor court, found a couple of sparring partners and rebuilt his backhand from scratch. When he emerged a half-year later his new stroke was fireproof.

Tilden's choice of action is doubly astonishing to our own age: we bow to his humility before his craft and we are astounded to discover a player in the top ten taking himself out of the circuit for months in order to perfect one stroke. How much more leisurely, how much less commercial, was the age of Tilden.

Fig. 1.1. Power strokes: the contrasting forehands of Tilden and Johnston. Above, Big Bill's *eastern grip and flatter stroke would appear more modern – at least until today's fashion for extreme topspin; below,* Little Bill's *western grip imparts huge top-spin;*

Breakthrough at Wimbledon

At the beginning of the northern summer of 1920, his retreat behind him, Tilden had reason to believe that mastery was within his grasp. Nevertheless, it was not until the Wimbledon of that year – in fact on the last day of that Wimbledon – that Tilden managed to validate his years of struggle. Earlier I described the 22-year-old Tilden's overnight change of attitude to tennis – from diversion to life focus – as a crucial turning point. Five years later came his second.

Frank Deford provides a luminous description of what happened on that particular day on the Centre Court.

The biographer prefigures this moment by telling us that he believes that 'for any (great) artist ... there must be one moment, an instant, when

Fig. 1.2. The US team at Wimbledon, 1920. Tilden, in a pose, is far left, Johnston far right. Baseballer Ty Cobb expostulated, 'Who is this fruit!' on first seeing Tilden play.

genius is first realised, when a confluence of God's natural gifts at last swirl together with the full powers of endeavour and devotion'. For Tilden this moment was more remarkable: his fateful coincidence was 'isolated, forever frozen in time. He knew precisely when he had arrived, and, thoughtfully, he revealed it.'[7]

The Wimbledon Final of 1920 was between Tilden and an Australian, Gerald Patterson.

Patterson was confident. He was a star, out of a stable of stars. The nephew of one of the world's greatest opera singers – the famous Dame Nellie Melba – he was defending Wimbledon champion and lynchpin of the Australian team that held the Davis Cup. Patterson was tough, at his peak, and fighting to keep his crown.

In the way stars are expected to shine, so shone Patterson: he breezed through the first set, 6–2.

His opponent was a little-known, 27-year-old American. William Tatem Tilden 2nd had never got close to winning a major singles championship. Now he had scrambled into a final of a very big one, was a set down, and being 'clobbered by the best player in the world'.

Then it happened. Biographer Deford gives the picture as seen by Peggy Wood, a spectator in the gallery's front row.

Changing ends after the second game of the second set, Tilden caught sight of Ms Wood. Typically, she was an actor friend, present by courtesy of a ticket *Big Bill* himself had provided.

As Deford tells it, Tilden caught Ms Wood's eye and threw her a special glance. To this he added 'a reassuring nod, the kind delivered with lips screwed up in smug confidence'. This 'signalled to her that all was quite well [and the match] was in the bag'.

The recipient of the coded signal, Ms Wood, admitted to being astonished. Indeed, this perplexity – how could the challenger be so confident? – remained with her for the rest of her life. Nor did she ever forget what followed. She told Deford: 'Immediately, Bill began to play.' The biographer explains that there was such wonder in her voice that she seemed to imply that 'magic was involved'.

The challenger proceeded to win the next three sets straight – and the championship.

Can the 'magic' ever be explained? The superficial best that can be said is that following the first set, Tilden was better, Patterson worse. But the reason was deeper: during the losing first set Tilden had worked out Patterson's game. He had then devised a response, and carried it out.

The man himself helps us to understand more of this process.

At the time, the budding master was engaged on the first of his several books of tennis instruction. In *The Art of Tennis*, Tilden states his credo pithily: 'the primary object in match play is to break up the other man's game.' As it happened, Tilden had so exposed Patterson's powerful but lopsided game that towards the end of the match the correspondent for *The Guardian* noted dryly: 'the Philadelphian was ... [making] rather an exhibition of his opponent.'

Fig. 1.3a and 1.3b. At his peak: Tilden graces Wimbledon in 1920. Beautifully balanced, on the left he moves into a half volley; on the right he leaps for a high backhand volley.

The action photographs taken at the time, and included here as Fig.1.3a and 1.3b, allow us to glimpse the power and grace Tilden's game had attained by this point.

Yet the essence of his progression to maestro was more than the incremental acquisition of skill. Writer Henry Miller speaks of moments of integration such as Tilden's, and of 'the grand tuning of the instrument' that precedes them. By the Wimbledon of 1920, the means came together to make great music.

From then on, the transformation to 'readiness' was so deep that Tilden saw himself – and generations of observers came to see him – as a different person. During a playing career that lasted until the day he died, Tilden believed he was mentally superior to any opponent: he felt that he could always out-think them. During his long peak – and even when age caught up – he also held an unchallengeable faith in his physical arsenal to exploit the weaknesses detected. When he lost – even 'when [in a rally] I don't return a shot' – he tells us that he invariably found himself 'surprised'.

Here, then, is a picture of the emerging master that Patterson would have seen opposite him in the 1920 Wimbledon Final.

Tilden's serve was magnificent, with all three variations of the cannonball, slice and twist. His ground strokes were impeccable in attack or defence, and various with spin and speed. On either wing he could hit out hard for a winner, or abruptly change pace, returning the ball deep with a hanging tantalising slice. Then there was one of his pets: softening up the net rusher with a ball sveltely rolled or chipped gently across their body and into their feet. His net game was sure, his court-craft velvet and his stamina such that, when not in a tournament, he would play five sets of singles in the morning and five in the afternoon. *All court, all stroke, all speed*: his game was complete. And he knew it.

The result? Deford puts it neatly: 'Playing for himself, for his country, for posterity, he was invincible'.

Colossus and change-agent

After Tilden's apotheosis at Wimbledon, the rest, as the saying goes, is history.

And what history! From 1920, at the age of 27, until 1926, at 33, he won at will. In that period, he never lost a single match of any significance. He took the US Nationals, the championship he considered the most important, every year for six years from 1920 to 1925, and then again in 1929. In the Davis Cup he led the US team to victory from 1920 to 1926.

It was not until the later twenties, with Tilden well past thirty, that his star began to wane. Crucially, this was coincident with the rise of the three great French stars Lacoste, Cochet and Borotra. By a cooperative act, the so-called *Three Musketeers* – abetted by a fourth, the master doubles player Brugnon – had devised a policy to wear him out and bring him down. Eventually, in 1927, the tide turned and the Davis Cup crossed the Atlantic to France.

Tilden never lost a big match against the third *Musketeer* Borotra, whom he despised. Deford quotes Tilden as saying: 'I never lose to someone I hate.' And Tilden damned Borotra as achieving 'first class results with second class technique' and 'the enchantment, the colour, the charm, and most important, the insincerity of Paris'.

However, although Tilden had several great victories against Lacoste and Cochet, these two champions began to get on top of him from 1926 onwards. As Deford explains, when asked how they had managed it, Cochet generously admitted that they were not only younger and fitter, but, 'Arr! We had Tilden to teach us'.

In 1930, ten years after his first triumph over Patterson, the 37-year-old Tilden won Wimbledon for the third and last time. For *Big Bill* there was a blunt lesson in the Wimbledon victory: along with the burdens of age and injury, he had had enough of the amateurs and their hypocrisy. For years he had feuded incessantly and often publicly with their Pooh-Bah administrators. Thus, despite loftily disparaging professional tennis throughout his entire amateur career, he abruptly announced his retirement from the amateur ranks and a change of status to professional.

Typical of this wilful man, the reason given for his change of status was not the obvious. It appeared that drawing him from the bright lights was neither the lure of being his own man nor the potential gold of the fledgling world of the pros and their pay-for-play game. When we appreciate that Tilden always saw himself as an actor, it becomes clearer what that lure might be: Hollywood. Tilden had signed an apparently lucrative contract with movie giant MGM. Even the first stage of that contract, an instructional film on tennis, contravened the rules of the amateur tennis world.

With an attempt at good grace, but with what must have been huge relief, the various national Lawn Tennis Associations of the amateur world bade farewell to the colossus who had bestrode the game for the previous decade.

Apart from personal triumph, by the time Tilden turned pro in 1930 what had been his contribution to tennis?

When Tilden began to play tournaments, tennis was much like the world of the upper crust country house described in the Prologue. The game was a diversion of the rich. From society's top drawer and possessing private means, Tilden remained contemptuous of the game's first professionals – the working pros who had to teach the game to make a living. As ever capricious, Tilden was to retain this depreciating attitude to the 'lower classes' while despising the elitist world of tennis and devoting his lifetime to overturning it.

His ascent to champion confirmed such views: once Tilden had formed his vision of tennis he believed that he had to work it all out, and get to the top, entirely on his own. 'I began tennis wrong,' he said later in the aptly titled *The Art of Tennis*. (Deford notes that his English was usually more correct than this.), 'My strokes were wrong and my viewpoint clouded.'

When he had arrived at the technically perfect game, his dominance – and his celebrity status – mushroomed. As it happened, a contemporaneous change was taking place in tennis itself. Great social forces were at work giving leisure time to the workers and middle classes; change-agent Tilden took note, and assiduously began bending these forces to his purpose. Little by little, tennis was being loosened – if not released – from the grip of the idle rich.

With more help from the perceptive Deford, the Tilden gestalt can be better understood through a quotation from a character in one of his novels.

In the wondrously titled *Glory's Net*, Mary Cooper says to her husband, David: 'you must play ... You owe it to your country, to the game, and to us ... You are an artist ... Any artist belongs to the country and to the world.' Tilden, player and person, saw tennis as the fictional Mary saw it. [8]

And true artists are there to stir emotion. So Tilden would rail and prance his hour upon the stage and, on many occasions, allow a lesser opponent to get ahead. But then, after throwing a jug of iced water over his head, *Big Bill* would 'begin to play'. And the hapless opponent could but watch.

At times the actor upstaged the player. Thus, on the point of victory, *Big Bill* might turn his last game into an apotheosis of his performance. By elaborating a scene from Deford's biography, we can imagine how Tilden might appear, serving for the match.

At 15–Love, he raises his fingers to call for *four* balls from the ball boy. He takes them, all four, in his large left hand. Caesar before the Senate, he holds them up to the crowd.

Then he slams down three aces. Bang. 30–Love. Bang, 40–Love and match point.

Bang.

'Game, set and match Mr Tilden.'

Then, abruptly – oh he is so tired – he turns away.

But with a gesture of infinite weariness, he suddenly discovers the fourth ball in his hand!

Mixing despair with bittersweet triumph, the exhausted warrior ends it all – and tosses this now-useless thing to the ball boy.

Deford is so right: this final gesture, the throwing away of that fourth ball, provides the dramatic frisson, stamping *Big Bill* as both actor and sporting champion.

Player, artist/actor and celebrity, also became scholar and teacher. We will soon discover how Mr Robert Rosewall used the flowing strokes of Tilden as the model for the earnest, dark-haired son to whom he was teaching the game in the early years of the Second World War. A few years later, even in outback Queensland, a generation of teachers like Charlie Hollis drew on the body of knowledge that Tilden had tirelessly expounded. Taking aside his latest pupil – a red-headed, freckle-faced, left-handed runt of a fellow – for sessions on the game's legends and lore, Hollis would highlight the Tilden legacy, and use the master's analysis as the bedrock on which the education of a tennis player rested. And Rodney George Laver, the last Pro Champion and number eight in a direct line from Tilden, never forgot that lore or its source.

From the time Tilden walked onto the court – exploiting his undoubted charisma with a carefully rehearsed ritual – his focus was to dominate, to hold the cards, to be in all-knowing control. He tells us something of this aim of psychological domination in his *Match Play and Spin of the Ball*, where he states, 'I may sound unsporting ... but it is my ... belief that no man is defeated until his game is crushed'.

And how it worked! Deford quotes one opponent as saying the real problem was that 'you never fully knew what he [Tilden] was doing to you'.[9]

So the legend grew. Even to the present age, besotted with celebrity, it is hard to imagine how much the amateur tennis world was dominated by Tilden's chameleonic persona. The cartoon of Figure 1.4 wonderfully caricatures Tilden as a caped tragedian almost too great for his stage – and the stage, Shakespearian-like, could be the great globe itself.

Helped by this larger-than-life figure, by the 1930s and Tilden's departure from the amateurs, tennis was taking on its modern, international form. While far from democratic, and split between pros and amateurs, the game had reached beyond the country house into the state schools and public parks of the masses.

There was a further triumph of Tilden's, not celebrated but highly significant.

In 1922, at his top, he suffered an injury that nearly killed his career. In a minor game, Tilden crashed into the backstop, cutting the middle finger of his right (racket) hand. With his aversion to greens and vegetables, Tilden was susceptible to bacterial infections, and an apparently trivial injury turned septic. In this pre-antibiotic era, surgery was required to save his hand and, perhaps, his life. His finger was amputated just above the first joint above the knuckle. It left what Deford calls a 'rather grisly' stump.

Fig. 1.4. Tilden as heroic actor. This contemporary caricature of Tilden as caped tragedian towering over the stadium, named him as 'The Edwin Booth of Tennis' after a then famous actor.

Tilden's career appeared to be over. But before long he was back on the practice court. Then, to everyone's astonishment, with only a minor modification to his grip he was as good as ever.

Certainly, William Tatem Tilden was a survivor – but as player, teacher and celebrity he had enjoyed 'the brightness' and given gloriously to the game he loved. What then of his future? Surely, after such achievement, a graceful decline was beckoning?

Not so: *Big Bill*'s waning from his amateur triumphs turned out to be anything but 'graceful'.

Tilden takes up the pro world

Dramatically, Tilden declared his change of status on the very last day of 1930: apparently he was off to star in Hollywood.

However, not very long after his sudden exit, there he was back again on his 'real stage' – playing tennis as a pro. On February 18, 1931, he made his professional debut at Madison Square Garden in New York, a venue already taking on a special cachet for the pro tour. This was the opener of a series to establish the World Pro Champion. His opponent was one Karel Koželuh.

A response of 'Karel who?' from most readers would be understandable. Who was he? And where was pro tennis when Tilden strode onto the huge Garden stage to play him? A short diversion is needed to answer these questions.

In his labour of love, *The History of Professional Tennis*, Joe McCauley explains that professional competitive tennis, as distinct from teaching tennis as a paid job, began in Western and Central Europe just after the turn of the twentieth century.[10] More recently, in his *Forgotten Victories: A History of Pro Tennis 1926–1945*, Ray Bowers adds crucial detail to this early period.[11]

By the end of the first decade, McCauley and Bowers explain, pro championships were more or less fixtures in several European countries, and the top players, usually teaching pros attached to private clubs, would travel to compete at them. By the mid-twenties, the Czech Koželuh had become recognised as the top player in this unassuming circuit, a poor relation of the glorious amateur championships of the major western countries inside and outside Europe.

Then came a dramatic development, and an upping of the stakes. Typically, it came from the land of entrepreneurs across the Atlantic. Charles C. Pyle was an American millionaire whose fortune was based on a retail chain. He preferred to be called *Cash and Carry* Pyle after the name of his empire.

Now this pragmatic merchant just couldn't see why one tennis player shouldn't play any other. Didn't they live in God's freest country? So if the public wanted to see any of them play their game, and were ready to pay for the privilege, why shouldn't they play, and take their cut?

Pyle first organised a series of matches between former amateurs, in which they received payment from the gate. Then he began to conceive of a pro circuit, including men and women. Businessman Pyle calculated his innovation could yield a decent profit – both for the players and for him.

In 1926, old *Cash and Carry* put together the first-ever pro tour. Pyle went straight to the top, and immediately snared the world's best female player – and tennis' darling – Suzanne Lenglen. Then he went for Tilden.

But *Big Bill* was in love with the brightness. After that it was the next best, but *Little Bill* Johnston was a patriot tied to playing for his country.

However, Pyle found someone close to the top of the amateur tree. Ready for something different was Vincent Richards, a one-time tennis prodigy and Tilden protégé.

It was true that Richards had never won a major. But he'd come close, and was a magnificent Davis Cupper. Tennis was then an Olympic sport, and Richards was the reigning Olympic Champion having defeated the legendary Cochet in the final. With a game based on brilliant net play, Richards was ebullient in character and style. Crowds loved him. Figure 1.6 shows his lovely form, here winning the US Doubles – at 15 years of age! And who was the wunderkind's partner? None other than *Big Bill* himself!

Not long after delivering Richards to the pro troupe, with some difficulty he proceeded to fill up the field.[12]

Beginning in late 1926, a tour through the States followed. Although it went well at first, the cash flow stuttered. There was one major reason: Richards and Lenglen were a class above the rest of the troupe. Nevertheless, there was still encouraging talk of 'open' tournaments where, as in golf, amateurs and pros could compete against each other. But the establishment closed ranks. Bowers quotes one influential figure, S. Wallis Merrihew, in his editorial in *American Lawn Tennis*. Under the headline 'The Rubicon

Fig. 1.5. Entrepreneur C. C. Pyle and friends. Shown with baseballer Red Grange (left) and French star Suzanne Lenglen, Pyle formed the first pay-for-play pro tour in 1926.

is Crossed', he writes: 'They [the pros] have made their bed. Lie on it they must, however hard it may become ... '

No one was to know it, but at this point the pros' hopes for a genuine alternative to the amateurs were dashed, and 40 years of struggle began.

Yet the newborn survived. After winning the first US Pro Championship in 1927, as king of the tiny, stop-go circuit, Richards had a brain wave. He began to think big, and look further afield. He went to Europe, and took in the pro scene. Richards was impressed, especially with his opposite number on the Continent, Koželuh. After much bargaining, Richards signed the Czech, and in late 1928 they began the first-ever head-to-head tour. It began in Europe, and ended with a sweep of the US.

From Bowers' assiduous research, the European champion and defensive master Koželuh was fairly evenly matched against attacker Richards, so making it hard to say who was the World Pro Champion in the two years that followed. Bowers believes that Koželuh won the tour against Richards, but then lost to him in the second US Pro Championship in 1928, and beat him for the third in 1929.

Fig. 1.6. A master in the making. Aged 15 years, Vincent Richards makes a sweet and urgent volley along the way to winning the US Doubles of 1918. His partner is Tilden, then age 25.

However, after again beating Koželuh in the fourth US Pro Championships in 1930, Richards suddenly announced his retirement. (His 'retirements' were to be revoked and re-issued on several occasions subsequently.) Since Koželuh was now indisputably the top player, it was he who faced Tilden on a winter's evening in New York in 1931 – the start of a tour to settle the newly minted crown of World Professional Champion.

Although today virtually forgotten, Koželuh – nicknamed 'Professor' for s his studious and lugubrious manner – began as a master of defence and the clay court. But on the faster courts outside Europe, he was soon showing that he could compete against any of the top players of the day, pro or amateur, on any surface. Nevertheless, in their first clash of February 1931 in the Garden, Tilden managed a fairly comfortable win. To many astute observers, despite his age – or because of it – *Big Bill* had finally learnt the key to handling a master defender such as Koželuh: attack. In the following long tour to settle the title, most of which was played on fast indoor courts, Tilden beat the Czech decisively, 63 matches to 13.

After that, with some ups and downs, Tilden held the position of top pro for the next three years. Before long he'd also taken over the management of the pros; in the subsequent decade, Tilden was to lay down the blueprint for the pro era.

Big Bill built on the steps of the European pros and of Pyle and Richards. Pro tennis was internationalised, with tours and tournaments run in the Far East and South America as well as in the US and Europe. Further, the three national pro championships – the US, French and British – became annual fixtures, and attempts were made to develop national pro teams competing along Davis Cup lines.

Fig. 1.7. The players' stage. Carried with them, the canvas court was laid down on whatever surface they could find, and tightened with guy ropes. Here covering the Madison Square Garden wooden stage, with Richards and Koželuh chasing the 1928 US Pro title.

Fig. 1.8. The master shows how. As pro in 1932, Tilden gets across to a make a backhand drive. Note the triumphant follow-through.

He was indefatigable. Deford and McCauley discovered that in his first seven years as a pro, Tilden played over 1500 matches, or two competitive matches every three days! And in those seven years, he missed only three from injury.

Despite such energy, the whole set-up never got past being another tiny, down-at-heel travelling circus. Sometimes the pro band had a good run, but often they were scratching out a living from any old place on offer – and always they were outcasts. McCauley quotes the progenitor of the line, Vincent Richards,

Fig. 1.9. Tilden the actor. 'Tilden keeps his amateur status' was the verdict of one critic after Tilden's only appearance on Broadway. But it never put Big Bill *off from pursuing an acting career.*

Fig. 1.10. Among the superstars. Big Bill *mixes it with the celebrities he loved: from left, Charlie Chaplin, Tilden, Douglas Fairbanks, Mary Pickford, Spanish tennis star Manuel Alonzo and Tilden protégé Alex Weiner (far right).*

reminiscing about his days as Pro Champion: 'There was a ... stigma playing for filthy lucre ... As an amateur, you were showered with hospitality by the social colony ... As a pro, you were ignored.' Forty years later, Rod Laver was saying the same thing.

However, if Tilden's drive had launched and then sustained the new Pro Era, beneath the surface the old trooper was in trouble. By the time he had joined the pros – and soon had turned forty – *Big Bill* was becoming increasingly singular, rootless and febrile.

Although a terrible businessman, in his first decade as a pro he'd made a lot of money. But he spent it as fast as he earned it. Whether it was in New York or in Independence, Kansas, he stayed in the best suite of the best hotel. With his family inheritance long gone, as the years rolled on the man was adding poverty to that cruel duo of aging and loneliness.

Contributing to his financial stress were his theatrical ambitions. From early adulthood he tried repeatedly and desperately to make a career in the theatre – and lost a fortune. In fact, he always claimed that tennis ranked third for him: music and the stage were his greatest loves and preferred careers. But he had no musical ability, and little as a stage actor. Even in the role of Dracula – which he played for a short season on Broadway – his flaw of overacting was fatal.

He also tried hard at writing fiction, but as Deford points out, any eminence he achieved in the literary arena was as a character in another writer's novel. 'In Nabokov's *Lolita*,' writes Deford, 'the nymphet takes lessons from a former great player who has a "harem of ball boys." The wrinkled old coach's name is Ned Litam. Backwards, Ned Litam spells "Ma Tilden." '[13]

About mid-way through his life, Tilden's personal demons began nosing their way from the private into the public space. A decade after his entry into the pros, a chasm lay between the performer and the person behind it. Who was behind Tilden's many masks?

Nabokov's invented character suggests the answer: *Big Bill* Tilden, champion male athlete, was not only single and deeply alone, but homosexual and with a predilection for boys. Increasingly, he found this difficult to keep quiet. Finally, the inevitable: in 1947 Tilden was nabbed with a teenage boy, hauled before the court, charged with indecency with minors, found guilty and sent to prison.

Now fame and honours meant nothing. Gone was the caped hero strutting the world stage; instead was a tired old queen, broke and ostracised by the society that had lionised him. In his glory days *Big Bill* surrounded himself with people; in truth, he was always a loner. Now he *was* alone. And worst of all, banned from tennis, he could no longer practise his only creative outlet.

Where lay the seeds of such a fall? To appreciate the sad majesty of the aging pro, we need to delve into Tilden's family.

Childhood and the making of a tragic hero

William Tatem Tilden Junior was born at the end of the nineteenth century into a rich Philadelphia family. William's early life had all the appurtenances of comfort and security, including servants and horses. His father, William Tatem Senior, was a successful merchant; his mother, Linie, also of good family, a fine musician.

Yet by the time young William arrived in February 1893, the calm and security of the household had already been sundered.

William Senior and Linie Tilden had commenced a family some 13 years before the birth of William: the first child, Elizabeth, was born in 1880, to be followed by Harry in 1881 and then Williamina in 1883. From all accounts, family life was that of a normal, privileged family.

Then in 1884 tragedy struck.

It took the form of the second horseman of the Apocalypse: Disease. In a period of less than three weeks, from November 29 to December 15, all three children were taken off with diphtheria. In a stroke, the parents had lost their family. Furthermore, the grief-stricken Linie never recovered her emotional stability.

So it was into a haunted family that the second batch of children emerged. First, in 1887, came William's older brother Herbert; six years later, in 1893, arrived the present hero, thereafter known in the family as 'Junior'.

This was now no normal family. From his birth, William's ravaged mother spoiled, overprotected and terrified the young boy whom she had desperately wanted to be a girl. Although the disturbed Linie inculcated into young William a dread that others were primarily a reservoir of contagion, she attached a particular fear to the female. According to biographer Deford, 'the only sex training Tilden ever received' was that women were a source of (venereal) disease.

Isolated, terrified by the dangers of human contact, yet mollycoddled and indulged, the boy was raised as a fragile sickly creature. No wonder he grew up proud and superior, but incapable of warm human contact.

If this was not enough, more tragedy followed: the musical mother he doted on developed a chronic kidney condition. By the time Junior was 15 years old, she was an invalid in a wheelchair. As a result, the younger son was moved into the nearby home of his maiden aunt.

For the next 33 years, it was Junior's only home. From there, says Deford, the teenager would dutifully walk over to the ghost-filled family home to visit his dying mother. He sat beside her on the terrace, with only a nurse hovering in the background. Sometimes they would listen to music. When she died three years later, the 18-year-old William was inconsolable.

For the next four years, the young man struggled and drifted. There was an aborted attempt to study at the University of Pennsylvania, some teaching of tennis at his old school and part-time journalism for a local newspaper. Then, once more, the Horseman re-appeared: in July of 1915, his father, always distant – and virtually absent since Linie's death – died suddenly of heart disease.

Fig. 1.11. The aging pro in practice. After long trousers, Tilden went to short shorts. 'For Tilden's legs I would give anything', said movie star Betty Grable.

Fig. 1.12. Tilden's last title. With a portly Vincent Richards, after winning the US Pro Doubles Championship in 1945. Fig. 1.6 on p.29 shows Richards, thirty years younger, winning the US Doubles, again with Tilden.

Two months later, it was the turn of the last of the family: William's elder brother, Herbert. The person who had introduced William to tennis, Herbert was a man's man – extrovert, a drinker and keen on the ladies. One day he caught a cold. Three days later he was dead, presumed from pneumonia.

At 22 years, William Tatem Junior *was* the family.

For months, immobilised by despair, tennis saved him.

This young man, his family eradicated, came to see that there was only one way to give meaning to his life: to discover a cause. Deford helps us see that, in Tilden's eyes, the cause had to be bigger than he was and a creative engagement to which his love for his lost and musical mother could be tuned.

Survival would have been an achievement for one in his position. Yet the young man, bereft of family, did better than survive: he reached the top of his chosen career.

The force of the loss seems to have focussed the young man's energy, but the past never let him go. Though Tilden had always been homosexual, the drive had been more or less hidden, and eclipsed by the adulation of the triumphant years. And Tilden was not only homosexual, a difficult enough fate in an era that criminalised homosexuality: he was drawn to teenage boys, which is a different matter.

Even during the 1920s and Tilden's ascendency, the players and officials knew, but kept quiet, and the man himself was discreet. By the time he had turned pro, discretion was falling away.

To the other pros it was something they had to know about, not least to protect the tour. For instance, though loyal Budge and Perry say little, what they say is enough. Perry tells us that to avoid irate fathers, the pro band would often have to change cars and get out of town fast, while Budge mentions that *Big Bill*'s escapades on the road would be hushed up by making sure certain towns were avoided from then on.

Alas, even the transient measure of comfort such liaisons might be expected to provide was absent. Deford says of Tilden that 'even his homosexual experiences were surface in nature'. With sadness, but luminous clarity, the biographer concludes: 'More than any man, Bill Tilden diverted his sex drive to the arena, to a clean, bright place.'

But the edges of the old pro tour were hardly clean and bright.

Free fall – the last years

By the time Tilden was forty he was leading a double life: one on the tennis stage with remnants of glory, the other off it – and inglorious. In the latter place he was to be found pursuing a string of older boys and teenagers in a demimonde of furtive, risky, illegal and profoundly unsatisfactory liaisons.

As I dwell on Tilden's fate, I recollect a line from Shakespeare's *Hamlet*: 'Fortune? O, most true; she is a strumpet'. Barry Unsworth's haunting novel, *Morality Play*, about a troupe of medieval players also comes to mind. Unsworth gives these lines to one of the novice actors: 'Now it came to me ... the player is always trapped in his own play but he must never allow the spectators to suspect this, they must always think that he is free. Thus the great art of the player is not in showing but concealing ... '.[14]

Bill Tilden was trapped in his own play while trying to convince the audience he was free. But the trap was closing and his efforts to convince rang more and more hollowly. For this player was doubly bound – as performer on stage and performer off it. *Big Bill* could never really come to terms with himself and who he was. Says Deford so aptly: it was as if he was simply just 'a wrong call'.

Eventually, Tilden became a man whom he himself despised; so much so that soon he couldn't care for himself. Then, banned, he was unable to play or teach. Who wanted an ex-con paedophile who smelled bad? Thus he was denied his tennis – the only thing he loved, the only thing imparting meaning to his devastated internal world.

Here are excerpts from two letters. They were written when, for once, the mask had slipped a little from the face of this pitiful giant, the first and most tragic of our pro champions.

Biographer Deford located the first, written just a few weeks before Tilden died in 1953. It was to Vincent Richards. The first Pro Champion, Bill's old doubles partner, *Vinnie* (to his friends) had remained one of Tilden's few friends.

Tilden writes: 'Vinnie, could you please send me a couple of dozen balls and a racket or two? If I had them I think I could get some lessons ... I need the money badly.'

The second letter from Tilden surfaced recently, and dates from a few years earlier than the first. It was addressed to his then current young buddy, Arthur Anderson, aged 16. (Tilden dedicated his final book, written just before he died, to Arthur.) The notepaper is headed Hotel Fontanelle, Omaha, and the attached envelope is franked Omaha, Nebraska, and dated February 10, 1946.

Tilden, then fifty-three, was on tour, in the freezing sticks.

> Dearest Stinky, I am crazy about my beautiful shirt and thank you very much. Your letter was here when I arrived and was welcome for I was missing my brat. I wish you had been here last night. We had quite an evening. We were playing on wood under bad lights & I'll tell the world it's tough. Carl Earn went crazy against a bad Riggs & nosed him out in a very excellent match 7/5, 6/8, 6/4. Riggs was lucky to win the 2nd set but then had the match in hand at 4/3 40/30 on his own serve in the third set but blew it. Earn really played well. Riggs underestimated him. Bobby Harman had me in serious trouble in our match. He won the first set 6/2, had me down 0/40 at 1 all in the 2nd, and had 15/40, 0/30 & 30/40 on my next four service games but I was getting better

> & I won 2/6, 6/3, 6/2. Semi Finals Singles & Doubles today. Sabin beat Faunce again. Give my love to the family. I'll write soon. I miss you, Stinky. Play lots of good tennis. Love always, Your old man Bill.[15]

The reader of such a letter is moved to ask: how much did this person – described by a fellow pro as 'this strange man whom no one understands' – have to bear for the loss of his family? And how much did he rue never having a son?

Bill Tilden died on June 6, 1953. He was the same age – sixty years and four months – as his own father when he died.

However, despite all that savaging by that strumpet 'fortune', in those last June days before *Big Bill*'s great heart finally gave out, things were looking up. In his autobiography, probably written in gaol just a little earlier, Tilden tells how much he still longed for the brightness. At least now he could see a patch of it.

For the first time in years, he had been accepted into the US Pro Championships. Furthermore, before play started a couple of weeks later in Cleveland, he had managed to snare some exhibitions and paid teaching sessions along the way. This is why he had so desperately needed the balls and rackets from Richards. He had already started practising. The stage! His art! His loves were beckoning. *Big Bill* was raring to go.

By then Tilden was living alone in a tiny rented apartment in Los Angeles. The loyal Anderson family kept an eye on him, and after he had practised in the morning with young Arthur, they had invited him to dinner for the following day. But the next evening he hadn't appeared, so Arthur went to his apartment to find him.

Amongst other personal idiosyncrasies, Tilden had a habit of getting ready early. Then, fully clothed, he would lie on his bed awaiting his departure. When that moment came, he would put on his shoes and, if it was winter, add his famous, but now reeking, camelhair overcoat, before leaving for his appointment.

It was thus, stretched out dead, that they found him.

Beside him was a small bag, packed and ready with his tennis gear. His two rackets were beside it. They were his only rackets; the gift of Richards, sent to him as requested a few days before.

Once again, *Big Bill* Tilden was ready to play.

Then his heart gave out.

Notes

1 Frank Deford, *Big Bill Tilden: The Triumphs and the Tragedy*, Victor Gollancz, London, 1977. This chapter quotes freely from this fine biography and is deeply indebted to it. The Tilden epigraph is from *My Story: A Champion's Memoirs*, published by Hellman, Williams and Co., New York, 1948. I also draw from several other books by Tilden, particularly: William T Tilden, *The Art of Lawn Tennis*, Methuen, 3rd edition, London, 1921; *Match Play and the Spin of the Ball*, Methuen, London, 1928; and *Tennis A–Z*, Victor Gollancz, 3rd edition, London, 1952.
2 Perry, *Fred Perry: An Autobiography.*
3 Deford, *Big Bill Tilden.*
4 Bobby Riggs, *Tennis is My Racket,* Stanley Paul, London, 1949. Part Three. Riggs explains the difficulties even the middle-aged Tilden put in the way of his opponent. He describes playing Tilden when, as the world's best player, he appeared about to be beaten by a man 25 years his senior. Riggs got out of the match, but only by drop shotting and lobbing his opponent to exhaustion. Riggs concludes that you just had to take Tilden seriously, and he never saw his equal.
5 If Tilden could witness twenty-first century tennis, no doubt the old maestro would feel dismay, if tinged with relish. For today's fashion declares net-rushers are passé, and the baseline style the very thing. Indeed, many of its finest exponents, players like Andy Roddick for instance, looked out of place when they found themselves at net; they appeared embarrassed – as if they had turned up at a bordello when expecting to be at the opera.
6 Alas, the modern singles game is dominated by one kind of spin: topspin, and one kind of pace: fast. Of the top players, Federer is something of an exception: he uses a slowish, deep, sliced backhand, particularly on return of serve, to break up the opponent's fierce topspin from the backcourt. Tilden would have loved it. Federer also takes another leaf from Tilden's book. Like Tilden – although Tilden never advocated it – in order to hit down on high forehands, Federer moves his usual Eastern grip around to Western.
7 Deford, *Big Bill Tilden.*
8 Tilden's books sound surprisingly modern: in a prophetic gesture to the modern notion of Zen in the art of tennis, in *Match Play and the Spin of the Ball* Tilden tells us that the ball is 'an individual, and the third party on the court'.
9 One of Tilden's opponents did know what he was doing to them, and even turned the tables on him. The French champion René Lacoste secretly perfected a wide slice serve backed by a net attack. At a key moment, he unveiled the tactic. Only after the event, Tilden caught on – to the end of his life he regretted that his error had been to 'fundamentally underestimate' his great rival.
10 Joe McCauley, *The History of Professional Tennis.*
11 Ray Bowers, *Forgotten Victories: History of the Pro Tennis Wars 1926–1945.*
12 Like Tilden, Lenglen, the most famous female player of the era, was 'highly-strung'. If Tilden had joined Pyle's first-ever pro tour, it is unlikely that he would have cooperated with Lenglen: he loathed her, and the feeling was mutual. Once, when both were at their peak, Lenglen finally lured Tilden to face her on court. Later she was asked how the match

had gone. 'I don't remember,' she answered, 'but one of us won easily.' Tilden had won the one set they played 6–0.

13 Vladimir Nabokov, *Lolita*, Vintage Books, New York, 1955.

14 Barry Unsworth, *Morality Play*, Penguin, Harmondsworth, 1992.

15 Quoted with thanks by permission of the letter's then-owner: Alan Chalmers of Tennis Bookshop in the UK (www.tennisbookshop.com). With McCauley's help, I have pinpointed this tournament in Omaha. On the evening the letter was sent, Tilden lost, just, to the tournament's eventual winner, Fred Perry.

Fig. 2.0a and 2.0b. Far from Wimbledon, but still majestic: Vines (top) and Budge (below) rough it as pros. On forgotten, makeshift, indoor courts, they display their masterstrokes.

2

MODEST EMPERORS – VINES AND BUDGE

When Elly was on, hell! You might as well have stayed home.

Don Budge

Interview in *Kings of the Court*

Except in bursts, no one in tennis ever hit with such controlled power. But Don, well, he was just never off.

Ellsworth Vines

Tennis: Myth and Method

AMONG friends, late at night, sometimes we little people like to talk of greatness in others. Though we may bicker about the question of what *is* greatness, or about which individual heroes make up our own pantheon, for a few extraordinary individuals we usually shelve our differences. Then together we sigh, and with homage tinged by envy, look up, and marvel at the glory of their achievement.

Sometimes, too, the talk turns.

First we note the disasters so often strewn about the extraordinary person's family and colleagues. Then we begin to ruminate on the costs of singular achievement in a human life. We ask: Is the damage to those around them the price of the great achiever's ruthless pursuit of excellence? And, in the grand scheme of things, was the price worth it?

As a consequence, we may find ourselves reining in our adulation, even throwing doubt on the idea of greatness as public achievement. In doing so, with fresh eyes and renewed respect, we take a second look at those like us – the great anonymous, the mass of our human tribe, un-storied now and ever.

Then, again, we ask: If our own achievements seem paltry, unmarked today, forgotten tomorrow, have we not still made a worthy life? For sure, we have not written *War and Peace*, and only in our dreams rifled back a Gonzales serve, or flat-footed Nadal with a drop shot. But can we not claim to have distributed, more or less fairly, some kindness about our little band of family and associates? And isn't it also true that thus far our attainments – flimsy and ephemeral as they may be – haven't depended on the emasculation of others' talents and achievements? And who knows – now we are slapping each other on the back, calling for another glass – what staggering heights we might have realised if we hadn't been so ... ordinary and caring ...

However, a few men and women appear to fall into a select category. In the midst of a celebrated, triumphant and public life, they appear to have added regular increments to the sum of everyday human kindness. Further, in attaining pre-eminence in their chosen field, these persons seem not to have used others to get there. Such great achievers remained, simply, good people.

The two men who followed Tilden as the next pro champions, Ellsworth Vines and Donald Budge are, I believe, examples of this rare breed. Their honesty and generosity shine through in the two epigraphs to this chapter. Budge, speaking in the television documentary *Kings of the Court*, gives us an idea of what it was like to play Vines when Vines was having a good day.[1] Then Vines, in his book *Tennis: Myth and Method*, provides a picture of Budge at *his* peak.[2] Their mutual admiration is neither grudging nor self-serving. They were fierce competitors, and while at times it may be useful to applaud a rival, I hope these next pages will reveal that in both cases the praise was genuine and a reflection of the man offering it.

Virtues of this kind can pose a problem for a biographer. As a legion of successful authors assert, flawed characters engage readers best – the wickeder, the more intriguing. Lytton Strachey's biography of Florence Nightingale, for instance, brings forth the demon beneath the Lady of the

Lamp and, while it makes the lady of legend 'less agreeable', his Nightingale is decidedly more 'interesting'.[3]

Nevertheless, despite the wholesomeness associated with our next two heroes – or because of it – the trajectories of their lives were far from smoothly ascendant. Indeed, I believe their stories contain sufficient dashed hopes, unrealised goals and poignant human failure to redeem them from the blandness of Pollyanna's curse. Perhaps, too, the reader may finish the present account believing that if Vines and Budge had been more ruthless human beings, the steely gaze of history – though not of their family and friends – might have judged them even greater figures.

The first of the good men, Vines, poses a further problem. As far as we can see, he alone of the eight pro champions has not been the subject of any extended memoir, biography, or autobiography. Vines' period at the very top of the amateurs was cut short: consequently, and given the scarcity of biographical information, this gentle character has become the most elusive of our eight. Yet, apart from instructional works, he produced one masterly book, *Tennis: Myth and Method*, written with Gene Vier. Although not an autobiography, this book provides a wealth of information on what Vines thought about tennis, and allows the man to show through as intelligent, sensitive and reflective.[4]

The accepted view of Vines – derived from the historical vantage point that relegated the pro band to a ragtag – is that his career shone brilliantly but briefly, that it flared up and burnt out. The truth is different. Though Vines' star exploded across the sky then seemed to self-destruct, in fact it made a lovely, double apogee. After a fleeting efflorescence as amateur, Vines was restored as pro, and marvellously. This wider view also shows that when his star did recede, it was not in a shower of sparks, but graciously, leaving a generous after-glow.

The Budge story has intriguing similarities. Although Budge's rise was less explosive and steadier than his predecessor's, and he was longer at the very top, his exit from the limelight was also abrupt and painful. Further, he tempered his decline with honourable if unspectacular achievement.

Now to the first of our two kindly, if often misread, souls.

A new star or a flash in the pan? Vines as amateur

From the outset of his career Ellsworth Vines was seen as an enigma, and as a player whose description required stellar imagery. From humble beginnings in the public parks of Pasadena, Vines rose so fast that he was only a teenager when he found himself – after the explosive Maurice McLoughlin of 20 years before – hailed as another *California Comet*. This *Comet* also based his game on uncompromising power, and shot to the top of amateur tennis in the US by the time he was 19 years old.

Yet even this rise was not as straightforward as it seemed. The wonderful Allison Danzig, doyen of twentieth century tennis writers, gives a striking

Fig. 2.1. A lean young Vines unleashes his lethal forehand, the power lifting him from the ground. Unlike Laver, as shown in Fig. 7.4, Vines has struck the ball flat – a characteristic of the Vines stroke.

picture of the whipcord-thin 19-year-old halfway across America and more than halfway up the first arc of his fame. Writes Danzig in September, 1931:

> Somewhere west of Chicago, on a transcontinental Pullman clicking the rails towards California, is a sandy-haired, hazel-eyed young man, dangling his long legs over the seat and watching the world go by through rose-coloured glasses. Telegrams are scattered all about him and likenesses of his thin, solemn face look up from newspapers beside him. H Ellsworth Vines Jr., of Pasadena,

> California, just another youngster with a tennis racket fifteen months ago, is homeward bound, the greatest amateur player in the United States.[5]

But a year before Danzig's hosanna to Vines' capturing the US Championships as a teenager, journalist Bud Collins had caught him in a different frame of mind. Collins discovered the young man 'on a rocking chair on the porch of the Peninsula Hotel in Seabright, New Jersey, looking out to sea, and thinking his tennis dreams were shattered'.

'I guess I'm just a flash in the pan like they say,' were the lad's thoughts as he rocked away – or so Collins tells us.[6]

At this time of apparent collapse, Vines had just got his second chance at the prestigious Eastern US grass court circuit. At first, the youngster who had ridden out of the west with the 'kick of a mule' in his cannonball service, had begun laying all before him. He might have been serious, shy and lanky, with a characteristic shambling gait (he 'ambled along mournfully like slow molasses', croons Collins), but on the court his play was devastating, his sportsmanship impeccable and, when he allowed himself a rare smile, his face was all crinkles. The press and tennis public couldn't get enough of him. Here was a new star – and a regular guy.

Still, at Seabright – not a major tournament, but a part of the Eastern circuit – the meteor's rise had been checked. After crushing two of the nation's very top players, Vines had come up against a crafty Sidney Wood, who soft-balled the young powerhouse to an agonising death. And if there is one thing the press love more than a rising star, it is one on the point of falling. As the writer Cyril Connolly put it, what the critics had lauded as 'promising', they could now damn. Certainly, in Vines' case, some doing the damning claimed that the new *Comet* had already burnt out, while others could never resist labelling him another 'flash in the pan' at every opportunity from then on.

How did Vines respond to this setback? He bravely shrugged off the humiliating defeat, and the name-calling, and went back home to California to work on his game over the winter. With the help of good coaching, he understood that he had to make his game less subject to hot streaks and more resilient and flexible. In particular, Vines devoted time to learning the skill of handling 'junk', the pros' term for slow, high balls designed to throw off the opponent's timing and pace, and a useful ploy against big hitters who thrive on speed.

What a contrast is emerging between this picture of the dedicated student and the media-driven image of the febrile meteor!

The next year, 1931, Vines again went east. Now he was unstoppable. Seeded only No. 10, he went through to the semi-finals of the US Nationals like a train. There he came across someone we have already met in this narrative – the British star Fred Perry.

A little older and more experienced than Vines, Perry was one of the fastest, fittest and hardest athletes in tennis history. Perry got Vines two sets to Love down – and still lost.

In the Final, Vines came up against another tough and heady veteran, George Lott. Once more dropping the first set to an inspired opponent, he ambled and shrugged. Then he lifted his game – and ran out the next three tough sets for the championships.

Fig. 2.2. Vines' serve: explosive, yet sinuous, simple and elegant. In the 5th still, one can catch Vines' famous split-second wrist snap, which provided extra power and deception.

The six months of reflection, practice and study had paid off. At once Vines was ranked No. 1 in the US, and marked out as ready to take on the world.

The following year, he did so, and triumphed. In the Wimbledon Final of 1932, he faced the British star Bunny Austin, a player with no big weapons, but highly experienced, and the possessor of a complete game. Vines demolished him.

The final point – a blistering service ace from Vines – became the stuff of legends. To his dying day, Austin claimed the serve was so fast and so well concealed that he had no idea on which side it passed by. Apparently the first he knew of it was when he heard a crunch – it was Vines' serve striking the backstop behind him.

The crowd was captivated. Immediately after the match, only the most parochial were not touched when the new young champion, at the moment of his success, rushed to comfort the loser.

In September of that year, the young man again reached the Final of the US Championships. His opponent was the man who had given Tilden so much trouble – the French star, Henri Cochet. This time, to retain his title, Vines took the match in straight sets and in under an hour. And though, after a grossly unfair confrontation in Paris, the US failed to retrieve the Davis Cup from the French, Vines had become the lynchpin of the team.

In the world that counted, the amateur world, Vines was top dog. To boot, he was the tennis public's darling.

Writes Danzig:

> The praises of this Pasadena stripling have been sung continuously ... The whole tennis world [knows] he has the most devastating drive in amateur competition [and with] his meteoric speed off the ground, his annihilating service and smash, he combines a repertory of strokes second to none ... During the last decade no one has so fired the imagination of the tennis public ... [He is] close to a national idol. [7]

Danzig then continues with some perceptive remarks on Vines' personality, which he felt had much to do with the popularity of the 'stripling' – and with his success.

Danzig began by noting that Vines' appearance on court was characterised by two qualities: youthfulness and solemnity. In Vines these usually contradictory qualities complemented, even accentuated, each other. Danzig also picked up that the dour mien was no affectation. Rather it indicated a reservoir of purpose. If Vines was in trouble, he could draw on it.

Off court the seriousness persisted, and yet there was another side to the young man that shone through. He had such a good sense of humour that Danzig thought it was one of Vines' most 'winning qualities'. In short, apart from 'the magnetism of his strokes', his appeal arose not from 'temperamental pyrotechnics', but from the 'compelling force of his personality and simplicity'.

History shows that Danzig overstated the case: he concluded that Vines was 'imperturbable', and nothing could 'distract his attention from his goal' or 'stampede him out of his self-possession'. As the story unfolds, we will discover that if young Vines might have been precocious in wisdom as well as talent, he was also the sad-faced clown. His thin, almost gloomy demeanour was the outer reflection of a tender soul, and one increasingly troubled by the rising din about him, and by the insincerity and machinations of the camp followers who lived off his exploits. Before long he came to see that though they were his dependants, they would be satisfied only if he gave them the world. When he delivered, they fawned; if the flow stuttered, they derided. Worst of all, he realised that he was bound to them, and to their masters who ran the great tennis associations and tournaments.

Such insight boded trouble. And trouble, for this talented young man, was around the corner.

Things began to unravel towards the end of 1932 – at a time when the world's best amateur tennis player, holder of both the US and Wimbledon titles, was still only 21 years of age. Some point the finger at one particular day in September of that year. After Vines' second victory in the US Championship, we can guess who was the first to call on the young dazzler with the world at his feet. Rocking up at the Forest Hills locker room was none other than a tall, gaunt man with a funny smile. Long gone from the amateurs, *Big Bill* Tilden was now representing the mob from the other side of town. Yes, he wanted to have a little chat.

Then master of the pros, *Big Bill* saw that Vines was the goods, the sort that comes along once in a decade. So when he put his offer to Vines to turn pro, it was 'highly attractive'. Though very young, Vines was receptive, but he was also a bit worn down, as well as in love and about to be married. At the time, a murderous night-after-night pro tour through the backblocks of America was not what the young man had in mind.

Soon news of their 'little chat' was everywhere; before long everyone in the amateur world knew the pros were after their man, and that their offer had not been refused point blank. Without a doubt, the brilliant young champion was considering leaving the glittering scene of his triumphs for the play-for-money game of the renegades.

While well-wishers were besieging him with conflicting advice, the nabobs who ran the show became incensed. And the press jumped on the bandwagon. The outcome? An apparently unanimous hostile reaction against Vines from the public, the press and the game's administrators.

Vines was astonished at the reaction. Rattled, he decided that the best thing for him to do was to sit on the offer. So he told Tilden that he was saying neither yes nor no, and after a decent while he would make up his mind and tell him his decision. Meanwhile he would stick with the amateurs.

Following this shemozzle, things got worse. After only a short break – and when Vines might have been regaining his zest during the northern winter – the authorities pushed him into a tour of Australia.

Already, Vines was beginning to feel sick of fame and the tennis grind. From the start of the Australian tour of 1932–33, which involved a double sea journey and a long absence from wife and hearth, nothing went right.

Finally, in an early round of the Australian Championships, Vines came up against the young Vivian McGrath, the possessor of a powerful, unorthodox game including a potent and then rare two-handed backhand. Playing out of his mind, McGrath upset the US and Wimbledon Champion.

In *Myth and Method*, Vines gives us enough hints about his feelings at the time: all he wanted to do was go home.

Now the knives were well and truly out. With renewed venom, back came the old label, 'flash in the pan'. This time, when Vines dangled his long legs and surveyed the newspapers, he discovered the pundits had drawn their conclusions: his once irresistible character was so flawed that his stellar genius was fast fading away.

Shaken, he returned to the States to prepare for a European tour, the Davis Cup and his Wimbledon defence. Then came a knock on the door. Here was a second visitation from the other side. It was *Big Bill* with his chequebook.

Tilden pointed out to Vines that while Vines had not given a final yea or nay to the earlier pro offer, he'd provided an understanding: before a final decision, Vines said he'd give pros and amateurs equal consideration. So Tilden had this question for the young man. For once the wily promoter, he asked, 'Elly, if you win Wimbledon and the Davis Cup, the [US Lawn Tennis] Association will do everything to get you under contract. Will you [then] keep your engagement with us?'

'And if I lose both?' replied the thoughtful and disarmingly modest young man.

On that, Tilden merely offered his hand. A deal was sealed.[8]

Struggling with all his might and desperately unlucky, Vines' worst fears were realised. He ended up losing both the Wimbledon Final and his key singles in the Davis Cup. The latter was against the same Austin he'd annihilated the year before in the Wimbledon Final.

By then, the leaders of the United States Lawn Tennis Association (USLTA) were more than furious – they were out of control. At the worst moment, just before Vines started his defence of his US crown, the association decided to hold an investigation of the young man's 'status'. They asked: by simply talking to Tilden, had Vines already sullied his amateur halo?

This was the final straw. Although exonerated by the kangaroo court, by the time the championships got going, Vines was right off kilter. Even before the final rounds, the troubled young man found himself thrown out of the tournament. His conqueror? *Bitsy* Grant, a tiny retriever of 5 feet 3 inches (160 centimetres) who would normally count himself lucky to scratch a few games from a confident Vines.

Inarguably, Vines was a star fallen.

Part of the explanation given for the fall was the 'high risk' game that Vines had put together, one that might be expected to run cold as well as hot. Vines' detractors would opine, with some accuracy, that his game depended on power and his penchant was to use that power to hit out and win quickly. Moreover, all his shots were struck with little controlling spin, so that to stay in court these projectiles from a cannon passed dangerously close to the net. Indeed, the famous Vines' forehand was said to be so flat and low that a keen-eyed spectator in a front row could pick out the name of the maker on the ball as it passed by shaving the net cord. And when Vines landed one on the line, it dug out such a storm of chalk that Dr Heldman – that maestro of analysis – said another 20 years was required before the advent of an equivalent skimmer and gouger: Ken Rosewall's flat-slice, down-the-line backhand. As with Vines, on games played on chalked grass, the propulsive, gripless weight of Rosewall's masterstroke was capable of blinding, as well as demoralising, a hapless opponent.[9]

However, from remarkably early on Vines had got down to the grind of building consistency in all his shots. To prove that his power could be coupled to steadiness, by 1931 Vines had triumphed on the slow surface of the National Clay Courts. And time and again, when down, he focussed, thought it out and reduced his errors. And won.

In summary, beneath his languid movements, easy athleticism and awesome power, the exceptionally modest young man possessed three less-than-obvious attributes: a fine match temperament (with the champion's capacity to rise in adversity), a tenacious work ethic, and a keen tennis eye and brain.

Further, unlike his fellow Californian – the rebel Gonzales who was to emulate many of Vines' achievements – Vines knew how to use good teachers. One such was Mercer Beasley, who is credited with discovering the 14-year-old future champion and helping him develop his power game through the early days. And Vines was able to benefit from the famous coach in his later amateur years as he worked on accuracy and consistency.

Clearly, there is more to explain Vines' fall of 1933 than was commonly supposed. If the pro offer had unsettled Vines, the response from the hysterical mossbacks of the USLTA had made it worse. To most of us, one of life's most appalling spectacles is the sight of the wealthy in shrill defence of what they have appropriated. To the USLTA, the young star Vines had become 'their' property. Apart from Tilden and Vinnie Richards, they had never lost a serious meal ticket to the pros. Secretly, they were overjoyed to see Tilden go, while Richards, never right at the top, was also becoming a thorn in their side. Now, when they saw their young star Vines about to decamp ... they were enraged.

The rage had made Vines' life impossible. By the time he reached Europe, the pressure arising from what tennis historian Gianni Clerici aptly calls 'the inquisition' had reached ludicrous proportions. On hearing Vines had received a letter from Tilden, they demanded Vines turn it over to them – or they'd ban him. Vines complied: it contained only *Big Bill*'s best wishes for success at Wimbledon.

By the time of the US Championships, the leaders of the USLTA seemed unaware, or didn't care, that their behaviour was damaging the precious goods they were meant to preserve.

So Vines was hounded. A gentle soul, he was learning that the crown he wore was not just hollow, but rented.

Kramer, many years later, offers more insight concerning Vines' precipitate decline, a fall that saw him, in 1933, become a shadow of the all-conquering hero of the previous year.

Writing an introduction to Vines' *Tennis: Myth and Method*, Kramer has this to say of the man he revered: 'Elly is probably the most unassuming and least egotistical of all the great champions'. He notes that as Vines strove to the top, this shy man had all the challenges he needed – and took them up and beat the lot. Then there were 'no more worlds to conquer'. Kramer adds perceptively, 'further, when a player has the heavy guns of a Vines, there is ... a temptation to feel you can pull out of a match at any time'. Such a view, he says – and this explains as much about the ruthless Kramer as about Vines – is fatal to the champion who wishes to stay on top.

It seems fair to say that the Vines' game of 1932–33 remained something of an explosive mix, that his incentive and killer instinct may have softened a little, and that he may not have recognised how different the challenge of staying on top was from the challenge of getting there. But I suspect a more directly emotional element is operating here, and one that helps us comprehend his near collapse.

Vines was still very young, and after what seemed to him only minor blemishes, the camp-followers had taken him apart. Relatively powerless, amidst a rising welter of blame and manipulation created by the press and officialdom, he must have become deeply hurt, confused, and lost.

And what does Vines have to say about his fall after his year of triumph? Not much, but, as seemed always the case with this wise man of few words, those he chooses count. In *Tennis: Myth and Method*, he says he was stale, and when he needed a break it was more pressure and higher expectations, and at the time he couldn't take it.

Tilden put it succinctly: the truth was 'the poor guy had had it up to here – ad nauseam.' In more modern and more medical parlance, the likely cause of the trough of 1933 was that the young man was significantly depressed.

As Vines was towelling down in the dressing room after his miserable exit from the US Championships – and just as the critics were preparing to roast the ex-champion in the next day's papers – Clerici tells us that the old ghost, *Big Bill* Tilden, once more 'slipped into the dressing room, and put last year's contract before his eyes'.

This time, 'Elly signed it without a word.'[10]

No one had won both the US and Wimbledon at the age of 20, become the world amateur champion and then, after a disastrous season, joined the professionals before he was 22.

Elly Vines had decided that only as pro could he be a champion – and be himself.

Once more unto the breach – Vines as pro

The forthcoming pro tour pitted the reigning Pro Champion, Tilden, aged 40, against the fresh-faced Vines, just 22. The opener was of course in Madison Square Garden, New York. One winter's night in January 1934, 16,000 fans, then a record crowd for a tennis match in the US, found the event irresistible. How could they not? Here was their new darling, facing their old.

It was a terrific contest. But the wily old king, *Big Bill*, pulled out his every trick, and put the young contender in his place in straight sets 8–6, 6–3, 6–2. Tilden had been winning tournaments when Vines was in primary school, and on that night his game was complete. Apart from his pinpoint passing shots, what most astonished the crowd was his – oh those Tilden legs! – tireless retrieval from the backcourt. Vines was discovering that, at this level, there wasn't an easy point to be had.

Taking in the match for *The New York Times* was Danzig. Despite the score, this sharp observer noted that the new boy Vines had played well. He appeared a more solid, and a more spirited tennis player than the one left behind in his amateur doldrums. For the younger man, said the wise critic, the omens were good.

Like all the tyro pros, Vines was handicapped by his lack of experience in playing under lights on fast indoor surfaces. However, this young man was ever the good student, and patient. In the tour through the US that followed, Vines got to know the ropes so fast that before long he had established a lead. He was to run out the tour a convincing winner, 47 matches to 26. By the age of 23, Vines was the new World Professional Champion.

The surprise was that 'circus' life suited him! Immediately the new champion recovered his keenness and his equanimity. Ironically enough – just like the young Kenny Rosewall a quarter of a century later – Vines found the grind of the pro tour liberating. The little troupe, admittedly a bit tatty around the edges, had no worry about national pride, and made their own decisions on their playing lives. Shorn of the two-faced retinue, Vines prospered.

Like all the masters who followed him into the pros, Vines rounded off his game. After 73 matches against maestro Tilden, he had added new measures of strategy, defence, consistency and flexibility to his attacking game.

In contrast to the images taken from his amateur days, Figure 2.0 on page 42 shows Vines as the fully mature touring pro. He is captured on what looks like a rough indoor court, somewhere in the sticks. Now thicker of frame, Vines shows little of the languid and the imperious. Yet, as he gets across to a wide ball, the more compact and almost grim master generates a reply with fierce interest. For those with eyes to see, a star has been restored to the firmament, more dazzling than ever.

For the next five years Ellsworth Vines was the undisputed Pro Champion. The highlights of this period were to be Vines' great battles with the previously all-conquering Fred Perry, and his final showdown with Budge.

As the Tilden chapter revealed, during Vines' reign from 1934 to 1939, the pattern that Tilden and others had built up was consolidated. At times, it looked reasonably strong. To embellish the troupe of experienced pros, the great Henri Cochet was poached from the amateurs. The band was also strengthened by a little-known though excellent German pro, Hans

Nusslein. Alongside were the veterans: Tilden, Karel Koželuh and Vinnie Richards (as ever in and out of retirement). With Vines winning the ones that mattered, including re-establishing his amateur superiority over the brilliant Cochet, the troupe toured the world, including Asia.

Then in 1936, just when they desperately needed a new challenger, they snared the big one – Fred Perry.

Perry, a Londoner, was two years older than Vines. However, after some great amateur battles with Vines, he stayed amateur after Vines' precipitate departure to the pros. By winning Wimbledon in 1934, '35 and '36 for what was then a record three successive times, as well as the US Championship in 1933, '34 and '36, he had become the undisputed No. 1 world amateur.

Before he became really serious about tennis, Perry had been the world table tennis champion, so his hands and reflexes were like lightning. His game was based on this quickness plus court speed, allied to his toughness, both physical and mental. The whole fitted into a radical style based on one masterstroke.

What does Vines have to say about the man he faced in two tours and who brought out the best in his game?

In his *Myth and Method*, Vines calls first on Budge's observations on Perry: 'He was so fast, both afoot and with his racket that I came to feel like a street brawler, who, floored, would climb to one knee, and then get knocked down again.' Describing Perry's famed Continental forehand, Budge adds: 'He could do so much with the shot, change direction on it so quickly and deceptively ... He could put you in trouble, almost in one motion, by flipping his forehand on the rise ... and then following it into the net.'

Vines builds on Budge's descriptions. Perry was never caught off balance, he says, and, 'like all the leading players of his era', possessed a masterful service return. Even his backhand, his weaker side, would be 'the envy of most top players'. His technical repertoire was complemented by a mental and physical resilience that set him apart.

Vines concludes: 'Perry had no weaknesses. He was a peerless net player and half volleyer, his overhead was deadly, and if his serve and backhand could only be described as first rate, then his forehand was ... the finest Continental stroke in history.'[11]

How then did one beat him? Only one way, says Vines: you overpowered him.

It took a while for Vines as pro to remember how – but, eventually, that's what he did. In their first tour of 1937, Perry, fresh from his amateur triumphs, thumped Vines in their opener and convincingly won the first three matches from an off-colour Vines. While the final outcome of the head-to-head was 'so close most ... can't recall who won', says the ever-modest Vines, the incumbent eventually got his nose just in front of the challenger, 32 matches to 29.

If his first pro head-to-head against the great master Tilden had taught Vines a lot, the brilliant and ruthless Perry had made him lift his game even

Fig. 2.3. Vines moves sweetly into a backhand drive. It was said that Vines 'never knew what it was to move back'.

further. By the time the pair fronted the next year for a second match-up, Vines pulled further ahead, winning 49–35.

By then Vines had marvellously achieved the goal he had set himself as a reflective teenager – his power was under control, and relied on strokes in which he had complete confidence. Further, in handling the tough-as-nails Perry, Vines should have expunged any doubts about his mental strength.

By the end of his roller-coaster rise to mastery, what did Vines' game look like?

Ellsworth Vines was a brilliant natural athlete who excelled at any game he took up. At college, Vines had been such an outstanding basketballer that he could have made a career in this sport. To tennis he brought some of the moves – the swift, sinuous and effortless turns and leaps – of the gifted centre. It was from basketball, says the perceptive tennis writer Julius Heldman, that Vines also learnt how to use his body, 'moving and stretching for volleys but still keeping his hard, flat approach.'

I love Heldman's exotic description of Elly's serve, certainly one of the finest deliveries in the history of the game.

> I ... [liken] Elly's wind-up action on the serve to a writhing snake. His body seemed to amass energy as he stretched up to maximum height for the ball. Think of the Indian fakir piping a snake into standing erect and you can visualise Vines climbing up to the top of his swing. It was a beautiful motion which was followed by a stinging heavy whip of the ball.[12]

Heldman tells us that at 12 years of age he once ball-boyed for Vines. He vividly remembered catching a Vines ace that had whizzed past his opponent. It was so 'leaden, heavy and hard', his hand hurt for an hour. Later Heldman played against all the great servers, including Kramer and Gonzales. None, he judged, had the same weight on serve, the same combination of speed and spin.

Although Vines was an Eastern stylist, turning his hand a good quarter-turn from forehand to backhand, he modified this grip in an individual way. At times he would move his hand down on the racket so his little finger would slide off, leaving the butt of the racket more in his palm. Though this four-fingered grip was part of the secret of Vines' extraordinary whip, it must have contributed to his occasionally erratic play.[13]

As noted already, Vines attacked most balls from both wings. While his shots were hit very hard and largely flat, he perfected a killer down-the-line forehand that was to become one of the game's greatest and most influential strokes. In this shot he could maintain awesome speed, while striking the ball flat, but slightly outside in, to impart a measure of sidespin. This helped to 'bury' the ball and to provide the pulverising heaviness described by Heldman. As well as a vicious baseline drive, this was a superb approach shot – one to be taken to new heights by Vines' pupil Kramer.

In his excellent *Tennis: Myth and Method*, Vines clearly outlines his philosophy on tennis: consistent ground strokes form the nub of an impenetrable game. These should be so solid that the players 'know when they are set ... they won't miss'. For him, this insight was a given from the beginning.

Vines was one of the greatest servers in tennis history, but in keeping with his emphasis on all court tennis, he attacked the net selectively. To the following generation of players this may have seemed strange, for his masterstrokes of serve and forehand were backed by a superb net game and great smash. In essence, Vines simply played a more aggressive version of Tilden's all court style, with its acknowledged bedrock of ground strokes. Tennis historian Clerici quotes Vines in mock travesty of his own style: 'What I did was smack the ball crosscourt, then if it came back really whack it back crosscourt once more – and if it still came back again, belt the living daylights out of it crosscourt one final time!' On hearing this, someone once asked him, 'And what if it came back again?' Drawled the charming Vines in reply, 'Well sure as Hell, I reckoned I was then up against one helluva tennis player.'[14]

However, beyond this potent and balanced armoury and the lovely movement of the champion basketballer, Vines – like a tiny handful of other supreme naturals in the history of the game – could, on occasion, take his game to another level. Then, says Heldman, Vines would slide *another* finger off the racket for a three-fingered grip! At such times Kramer believed that the only chance the poor fellow on the other side of the net had of 'getting a decent look at the ball was when [Elly] took it to serve'.

Kramer, in his autobiography, draws this conclusion on his mentor Vines: if he had to choose a team to represent the Earth in a Universe Davis Cup, he would have to nominate Vines for the singles berth. With

Fig. 2.4. A great athlete under pressure. The racket head never falls away as Vines volleys beautifully on his way to the net in the US Final.

humanity's fate riding on the choice, Kramer lets us know what he thinks of the received opinion that Vines' game was unstable!

Such, then, was the master confronting a succession of contenders – champion Perry included – during the years 1934 to 1938. By 1939, he would be up against the next pretender to his throne, and who hailed from Vines' own patch, California. And this new arrival was fresh from amateur triumphs even greater than Perry's.

It was none other than J. Donald Budge.

To have an idea of how these acknowledged titans squared up, one can do no better than hear what Vines himself, in *Tennis: Myth and Method,* has to say about their respective games.

As ever, Vines is both astute and modest (indeed so modest that readers would do well to substitute 'better' for Vines' words 'as good' in the following analysis).

Says Elly: 'I had a harder first ... and a better second serve to follow to the net ... my forehand was at least as good, and I was ... as good at the net. [But though] my backhand was good, his was something else'. Vines goes on to say that not only did Budge 'kill a high backhand with his famous leap' (and in doing so negate Vines' terrific twist service), but also 'caught his backhand earlier, saving him vital steps'. Since Vines was 'at least as fast' as his opponent, this was a crucial compensation. And even more – the Budge backhand possessed a unique flexibility 'comparable to an outstanding forehand'.

In fact, said Vines, what separated the two was not just his opponent's backhand masterstroke, but one component of it. Budge possessed the rare capacity to make one of tennis's most difficult shots – the hard, down-the-line backhand drive off a pressing serve, approach or drive. Crucially, he could also 'keep his opponent honest', and go crosscourt whenever he chose!

In *Don Budge: A Tennis Memoir*, Budge lets us in on a lovely interchange between the two masters. After the second tour with Budge – it had to be then, after which Vines retired – Vines told Budge: 'Don, it was your damned backhand down-the-line that killed me!' On hearing that, Budge mused, 'I wish he'd let me in on that earlier!'

The first head-to-head tour between the two was surprisingly short. Although close and brilliant, it hid a scar concealed from public view.

Surprisingly, Budge won their Madison Square Garden opener fairly easily, and then in Boston got two up over the under-prepared and by now slightly overweight champion. But Vines got back, winning the next four matches straight to run to a 4–2 lead.

The Champion then suffered a muscle strain to his right side. Despite the injury significantly affecting Vines' serve and overhead, this marvellous sportsman never refers to it. Vines then lost the next eight matches. And though he came back again, winning 14 to Budge's 11 of the last 25 matches, he could never get his nose in front.

So the red-head from Oakland, California, ended up winning the tour by just a few matches – only three in McCauley's final count of 21–18. If Vines had salvaged these three from the eight he lost on the trot when handicapped (and when Budge was the neophyte pro), he would have kept his crown.[15]

After that Budge took on Perry in a second head-to-head, and crushed the man who had given him so much trouble as amateur. Now there was a new king of the pros. Moreover, with this sort of competition, the newly crowned monarch was still improving. On a second and even shorter 20-match tour against Vines, the now unbeatable Budge increased his margin by winning 15 to 5. Then he dismantled Perry on their second tour.

It was then that Vines decided that he had had enough: abruptly he announced his retirement. In part explanation, this still-young athlete (Vines was just 28 and at his peak) added that he was taking up golf. However, privately this modest yet proud man admitted, 'I didn't want to hang around like Tilden and be second best.' Before long, he had become a golfer good enough to play in and win some significant professional tournaments.

This time without sparks, the meteor subsided from the firmament. The geniality of this lovely man is beautifully shown in his throwaway to Allison Danzig. Budge tells us that Danzig once asked Vines why on earth he needed to retire when still at the height of his powers? Replied Vines:

> Look, tennis used to be a lot of fun for me. I'd stand in one place and hit the ball from one side to another and watch the other guy chase it back and forth until finally he couldn't catch up with it, and I'd win the point. It was a marvellous game and I loved it. Now, unfortunately, about halfway through the tour with Budge, it occurred to me something wasn't quite the same … all of a sudden, I was the other guy … he was standing in one spot … I was … running back and forth. That's when I decided … to retire.[16]

When told of Vines' explanation Budge was flabbergasted. He began by asking why, when playing one of their matches, and 'while apparently standing still, I would lose nearly half a stone [over a kilo] in weight?' Nor does Vines' self-depreciating description tally with the losing margin of three in the first Vines–Budge tour of 39 matches. And let's not forget that, in eight of the 39, Vines had carried a significant injury!

What then can we infer from Vines' so-modest account of playing Budge?

For the first time in his life, Elly had found someone whom he knew he couldn't beat consistently, and this was enough. After that he didn't retain the fire to stay with the elite. Besides, for him, golf provided a much easier way of making a living than the rough-and-tumble pros.

However, in the tennis heavens he'd so swiftly vacated, Vines retained a glow, for despite his side-road as pro golfer he still taught tennis. To understand Vines' influence on the game, let's locate a match buried in one of Vines' pro tours.

This time it was the Vines–Tilden tour of 1934–35. Catching up with the pro show was an unknown schoolboy. One look at Vines changed the lad forever.

The boy's name was John Kramer. Later, he would be known as *Big Jack* and the best tennis player in the world. In the intervening years, Vines became more than the young player's teacher, friend and mentor: he was his model.

At this point, it seems right to complete our picture of our misunderstood good man not as the dazzling star he twice became, but as this boy's teacher. Here, the Eastern tradition of master and pupil in the arts and crafts is relevant.

Many Eastern cultures view the lineage of transmitted knowledge as crucial. The most skilled practitioners become teachers or 'masters'. It is believed that when the material things they make or the skills they display are long gone, the teachers' energy remains: it still flows through the hands of their students and their students' students, a part of the energy behind all things.

With a bow to such a connecting tradition, we leave the first of these modest emperors as pictured in the eyes of the boy who would become his apprentice. As young Jack Kramer looked down from the stands, his imagination took an imprint of this swiftly moving figure in white. Though in itself but a wisp of energy, as boy became man the heroic image endured. Over time it would be transmitted to others – to transform them, then to be passed on again.

So we can believe that, despite the Sturm und Drang of his early years, by later life this unassuming man must have felt quietly satisfied: Elly Vines, once the master of his craft, had become a master teacher, a teacher of masters, and one in the line of the game's greatest.

And as for the shrill critics who from first to last never cease writing Vines off, by then the man himself gave them hardly a glance.

'As sure as God made little apples,' we hear him say, his smile all crinkles, 'they just never knew any better.'

The wide empire of J. Donald Budge

Although also a modest man, the person who succeeded Vines was not quite as disinclined to blow his own trumpet. For a start, unlike his predecessor, John Donald Budge has given us a detailed description of the makings of a champion. Once again with help from Frank Deford, in *Don Budge: A Tennis Memoir*, Budge painstakingly describes his trajectory towards the level of mastery required to dethrone his friend Vines as Pro Champion.

Budge's story is remarkable, and in some ways reminiscent of Tilden's, for the progress of both men to virtuoso was a relatively slow curve in which laborious periods of semi-stasis were punctuated by forward spurts. As useful hooks on which to hang this tale of the rise of pupil to master – or poor boy to emperor – let's isolate four of these leaps.

The rise to master – 1: learn to swing a club

Budge tells us that he never would have been a tennis player – of any sort – if it were not for two events, widely separated in time, and on which he had no influence at all.

The first involved his father. Don's ancestry on both parents' sides was Scottish, and Highland Scottish in particular. Like generations before him, father John moved south from Scotland's poor north in search of work.

Budge Senior was small, wiry, and a gifted soccer player. In fact John Budge was so good at football he soon decided he might have a chance to make a living at the game he loved. When the famous club Glasgow Rangers took him on, he became a professional athlete. Rising fast, he established himself in their first division. But before long, a freak accident finished him as a sportsman. In the aftermath of being knocked unconscious in a practice match, he learnt that his lung was irreparably damaged. The doctors told him to find a less demanding job, and a warmer climate.

And so it was in sunny California, on June 15, 1915, in Oakland (on the outskirts of San Francisco), that one John Donald was born into a struggling yet strenuously happy household. Without the accident, the Budges would have remained in Scotland. Like his father, the gifted son came to depend on a game to make his daily bread, but he chose a game he would have had little chance of playing if he had stayed in the land of his fathers. Later, with his hallmark generosity of spirit, Budge made an astute reflection on this paradox. 'In a way,' he said, '[I had] picked up my father's interrupted career ... There is a certain misplaced justice – or irony – in my success, for perhaps it was meant to be realised ... earlier in another land.'

It was just 13 years after Don's birth that a second external twist of events again changed the course of his life. Don's brother Lloyd was six years older, and tennis mad. Soon Lloyd began hassling Don to give him some practice. Although the boy was skinny and small, he relished all sports, especially baseball, and excelled at them, but he knew what he liked, and he had decided that tennis was both dull and sissy. He kept resisting his big brother's urgings.

Lloyd, keen on improving his game and desperate for someone to hit with, kept harassing. Eventually the younger boy relented, and one day the pair ended up on the dirt courts at the public park down the road.

On arrival, big brother Lloyd thrust one of his heavy adult rackets into the little kid's hand and showed him how to wield it. At once, Lloyd discovered that his new pupil was unusual. Says Don later:

> I am more or less ambidextrous, even down to my feet — I can punt a football farther left-footed, though I am more accurate with my right foot. My mother was left-handed, and ... there are many things I can do better with my left. When I first started playing baseball, I began naturally as a left-handed batter ... And in the same way ... because it felt right [when Lloyd handed him a racket] ... I picked it up with my right hand.

So it was that when the tiny but ambidextrous youngster was turned to his left or backhand side, to his own and his brother's astonished delight, he already possessed the makings of an easy tennis swing. Here was a more or less straight copy of his left-sided, double-handed, baseball swing.

As he got older Budge dropped the left hand from the racket just before hitting the ball. However, the basic pattern of the swing retained its direct model from baseball – compact yet free, delivered largely wristless, but with a slight roll from below the ball's flight to just above it to produce topspin. From day one, the blueprint shown in Figure 2.5 hardly changed, and formed the basis of one of tennis's most feared shots.

For two years from age 13, the skinny little tyke hardly grew – in size or inclination to play tennis. Nevertheless, his brother could occasionally manage to drag him out for a hit on the local Bushrod Park courts. Says

Fig. 2.5. The origin of the Budge backhand. The shot was clearly modelled on his two-handed, left-sided baseball swing.

Budge, 'when Lloyd ... could find no one else, he would hunt me down, hand me one of his old rackets, and ... utilise me as a human backboard.' For despite being scrawny, the kid could run, and before long, scramble back most of his older brother's much stronger shots.

So the youngster learned to swing a club – if swung reluctantly.

The rise to master – 2: decide to be a master

One fine day, a couple of years later, came the second turning point. Says Budge: 'My scuffling tactics [must have been] somehow appreciated by Lloyd ... for one night he started the dinner-table conversation by declaring I could win the upcoming California fifteen-and-under championships. My first reaction ... was ... a "so-what" shrug.'

But the older brother knew his boy. Lloyd began 'razzing me ... calling me lazy'. The younger took the bait. 'Lazy, hey?' He would show the big bully what he was made of. This, of course, was exactly what Lloyd wanted.

Father John was present at the dinner table, and listening hard. Suddenly John upped the ante. If young Don gave it a go, well ... father would agree to buy the youngster some proper tennis kit.

Then the clever father added a crucial rider: Don would get his gear, but only after he'd played his first round match, and only after he'd won it.

So, young Don was hooked. With a newfound keenness that surprised everyone, including himself, he immediately started practising every day. Budge tells us that it was as if 'it was a new game'.

By the time the tournament arrived two weeks later, the lad had improved out of sight. Nevertheless, his two main attributes – perhaps his only attributes – remained the same: his baseball backhand and his ability to run all day.

Although pitched against the No. 1 seed in his first round match, Don wasn't fazed. Despite an unlikely outfit consisting of 'dirty sneakers, a T-shirt and tan corduroy trousers', the one-shot wonder kept getting the ball back. Eventually he got so many back he ran out the winner.

Now he was entitled to receive his new kit from his father. Appropriately spruce and white, he was then ready to complete the second part of the deal – the bet with his brother on winning the state trophy.

One by one he got through the next rounds, right up to the final. Then he won that too. The kid had collared the first tournament he had entered!

In surviving to the very end, the new Under-Fifteen Champion of California discovered the world looked different. In one of those mysterious inner shifts that alter us forever, he decided that tennis would be his game, and he was going to become very, very good at it.

In his memoir, Budge adds something significant to his account of this astonishing decision made at age 14. He says there was something distinctive about the idea of devoting himself to tennis. In his words, the decision was as much 'objective' as emotional, and prompted by his belief that he had a better chance to 'get further' – that is, build a paying career – in tennis than in baseball.

In this description of a youngster carving out his future, Budge comes across as surprisingly cool and calculating. However, a glance into Budge's Oakland family of origin makes his thinking more understandable.

At home, by day or often during a seemingly endless night, the son found himself an unavoidable listening-post to his wounded father, coughing and labouring for his every breath. If we combine this distressing glimpse with the words quoted earlier – when the mature man reflected on the ironic completion his success had provided to his father's life – we are offered an unequivocally fervent motive behind the decision that pushed the boy on. As he surveyed his future the son might have then been thinking out the implications of the following question: *One day perhaps, if I am good enough, might I not have the chance to realise a kind of justice, a re-balancing of the scales, for my loved and damaged father?*

In short, here was a unique opportunity for expressing love.

At first such ambitions seemed mere fancy, for the diminutive youngster hardly grew, and his game remained almost entirely based on a terrier-like retrieving. Nevertheless, to the experienced observer, there was little doubt about young Budge's talent, or the dedication behind it. Despite the handicap of his size he was soon filtering towards the top of the junior tree. Then, still unranked, young Don crossed the country to compete in the national junior championships. To the surprise of many, he won.

Of course, watching the lads from the stands and taking it all in was the old maestro himself: *Big Bill* Tilden. 'The future of American tennis,' wrote Tilden portentously in one of the major newspapers, 'rests with Frank Parker, Gene Mako and possibly Don Budge.'

Despite being singled out, little Don was infuriated by Tilden's remarks! What was meant by that cheeky word, 'possibly'? After all, hadn't he just beaten Mako in the Boys' Final?

By taking such praise as a slight, young Budge reveals how he was coming to regard himself: he was already 'a somebody', one with a big future.

Then something else happened: he started growing.

The rise to master – 3: become strong

One reason that Don's winning the US Juniors was a surprise to many was that he was so small in stature. In fact, during the whole of high school he hardly grew at all. No matter what he ate, he remained stuck on just over 5 feet 6 inches (169 centimetres), and under 100 pounds (45 kilograms).

Then, on turning eighteen, he left high school. And to everyone's astonishment the squirt suddenly started sprouting – he was to grow six inches (15 centimetres) in a single year! Overnight the diminutive boy became a tall young man. Further, his tall frame steadily filled out, if less prodigiously.

Equally suddenly, Don's tennis changed. As he became bigger and stronger, he began to put together an increasingly powerful all court game. From then on, in a tennis sense, no one could ever throw sand over Don Budge.

Ironically, the master himself came to see this belated ascent to physical maturity as a blessing in disguise. In his memoir, Budge says:

> It was no consolation to me at the time, but as it turned out, being small for so long was a distinct advantage for my game. It forced me to learn an entirely different game from the one I would have played had I been a big kid who could just get out on the court and huff and puff and blow everybody down ... I was really too small to beat everybody. I had to get the big kid across the net to beat himself.

To survive, little Budge had discovered the first rule of tennis: get the ball back. When he started growing, he could add power to his bedrock of control and consistency.

Control + power = controlled power.

No player in tennis was to exceed Budge in perfecting this equation.

The rise to master – 4: despite current achievement, look to your master, and seek perfection.

After reaching physical maturity, we can isolate three further insights responsible for major developments in his game. They fascinate because each involved the kind of scrutiny – and sweat – required to lift a player from very good to world-beater.

The first arose when Budge was a top junior and found himself for the first time playing away from his native California, and on grass.

Brother Lloyd had taught the 13-year-old to hit his forehand using the Eastern grip, with the wrist firmly locked behind the handle in the shake-hands position. But after a couple of years – as Budge moved into the teens but hadn't grown – he had a chance to study the top players who came over to California. He noted that some of them were crunching back forehands using the more extreme Western grip, with the hand now shifted further behind the handle. Clearly this was great for balls bounding high off the asphalt and cement courts of California. Further, while he was still a short fellow mainly hugging the baseline, the Western would give him a better chance to 'kill' a shoulder-level ball.

So at sixteen he made a decision, and began hitting his forehand with a Western grip. Despite immediate advantages, this was a decision he came to regret.

Although the Western grip necessitated an awkward switch from Budge's right side to his natural Eastern backhand – or from ground stroke to volley – Budge could have persisted with it. He was already a National Junior Champion, and he knew that *Little Bill* Johnston – Tilden's one-time nemesis and also from the San Francisco area – had made his Western forehand a masterstroke. However, when in his later teens he progressed to play on grass, Budge found that the ball would come through lower, even skidding through on a heavy or damp court. Soon the teenager began to doubt his change to the Western.

At that point, Don Budge knew exactly what he wanted to be: as close to perfect as any tennis player could be. On grass, where the biggest tournaments were then played, with a Western forehand he was not likely to reach the degree of perfection to which he aspired. As well, the lad was fast growing taller, and so getting fewer high balls.

He put all of this together, and decided that if he re-developed his Eastern forehand, he would end up the more complete and balanced player.

By then he was just 20 years old. Yet in full recognition of how tough it was going to be, he made the change. And after arduous practice over winter with his dedicated coach, Tom Stow, he had a new Eastern forehand. He admits it took *a further two years* to perfect the stroke. However, as the ever-astute commentator Heldman succinctly noted, following the growth spurt and the switch in grip, 'it was only a matter of time' before Budge would 'win the world title'.

The second and third insights both relate to Fred Perry.

In Budge's 21st year he reached the final of the 1936 US Championships – and faced Perry. Serving at 5–3 in the final set, playing for his country's national championship against the No. 1 amateur player in the world, Budge knew that 'all I had to do was hold my serve one more time'. But his serve was a 'dishrag'. Perry broke serve, took the set 10–8, and the match.

Shocked, Budge realised that he'd lost for one reason: he wasn't fit enough. On his return to Oakland, this time his aim was to strengthen not his strokes, but his body. Instigating a rigorous diet and exercise program, he worked on sprint and long-distance running, as well as conditioning the back and stomach muscles that had 'failed so disastrously against Perry'. After this off-season – 'the most important winter of my career' – Don Budge was, simply, 'a stronger man'.

Perry's second lesson for Budge was buried in a pro tour that took place a little later. Let's exhume it from Budge's memoir.

It was January 1937, and Vines was playing Perry early in their head-to-head tour to settle the Pro Championship. This evening they were in freezing Chicago. As with all travelling troupes, promoter Tilden was on the lookout for anything to spice up the bill. And Wow! Right here in Chicago was a gimmick that might lure a few more paying customers from the warmth of home and hearth.

It happened that one Don Budge, then near the top of the amateur world, was visiting the Windy City. In a little marketing coup, they pulled in the young champion. Of course, as an amateur Budge couldn't step on the court to play, but there was something he *was* able to do: he was invited to take on a unique role in the proceedings – as the umpire!

We can imagine the MC announcing the match about to follow: 'Ladies and gentlemen, how ... lucky ... are ... you! Why, right here, among the two players and the umpire, are a dozen Wimbledon and US crowns! And all three are still young men!'

The ring-in, Budge, believed that he knew the games of Perry and Vines backwards. Immediately after Vines' premature departure to the pros, as an amateur Perry had ended up supreme (and just ahead of the rising Budge). Nevertheless, Budge knew that Vines had the edge on Perry when both were amateurs. He also knew that since turning pro Vines had got his power game, and his head, even more sweetly together. Thus Budge considered that despite Perry's undoubted brilliance and toughness, the Vines' power would now 'crack the Englishman apart'.

But no!

From the first, the young man sitting high up in the umpire's stand was astonished to see that the match was not turning out as he had predicted. He had expected that Vines' huge shots would be making Perry 'scurry all over the court'. But Vines was doing as much scurrying as Perry. 'It made no sense to me,' says Budge. 'How could Vines, who was hitting a much heavier ball, fail to control the play?'

Then came Budge's Eureka insight.

He 'caught on' that Perry was taking the ball 'hardly six or eight inches after it had bounced', while Vines was letting the ball take a 'comfortable bounce'. The outcome? Though Vines was hitting harder, he took longer to do it, and had to hit the ball farther. Perry made up for lesser power by striking sooner. While he sat up there, his head 'swinging back and forth' in the attempt to keep the score, the young man's sharpened perceptions were widening the tiny interval preceding the impact of each shot. Split seconds seemed to become minutes. Perry was scooping, Vines rocking.

Then and there a question formed in Budge's mind: *What if a man could hit as hard as Vines, and take it as early as Perry? His next thought was: Could I be that man?*

With this vision uppermost in his mind, once more Budge returned to California – to the drawing board and more arduous practice.[17]

As it turned out, this even more aggressive approach happened to slot perfectly into the latest plan being hatched by Budge's master-teacher, Tom Stow.

As Stow saw it – like the opponents of the then all-conquering world heavyweight boxing champion, Joe Louis – the unfortunates who would have to play the new Budge were in for a hard time. By combining technique, match play tactics and mental strength, Budge would drive a wedge between himself and his opponents. They would soon come to recognise the relentless pressure they were about to face, and this foreknowledge would unnerve them before, during and after the confrontation.

'Playing you,' said Stow to the unequivocally genial young man, 'is going to be an unpleasant experience.' In short, it would be the tennis equivalent of doing twelve rounds – or five or two or one – with Joe Louis.

So these were the goals of the two conspirators after the two Perry matches of 1936 and 1937: first, supreme fitness; second, hitting the ball earlier; third, integrating these into a rock-like and frightening belief in Budge's invincibility.

With these changes in style, the transition was far from smooth. Budge's description of the process is irresistible.

> My game was not pretty ... but then I did not concern myself with accuracy. It was long before I was even able to get the ball [regularly] into court. This is in direct contradiction to my first rule of keeping the ball in play, but I was making a major adjustment to my game ... and Stow and I felt that the priority in this exceptional case must be in perfecting the stroke ... [The] control ... was to come later.

By the end of this training period in the early part of 1937, the game of the twenty-two-year old was quicker, the power was there, and the control had arrived. After 10 years of toil, demanding insights and more toil, Don Budge had realised his ideal mix.

He was ready.

Lord of all he surveys: the amateur champion

In the two years that followed the leaps described above, Budge did more than reach No.1, he became to amateur tennis what Joe Louis was to boxing.

In the period of Budge's ascendancy in 1937–38 we hear about the feelings of fellow players – wryly confirmed by our hero himself – when they had to confront him. When the draw for a major event was nailed up, his competitors crowded around it and, using the term they had coined for him, only one question emerged: 'Who's the first to be fed to the *Fire Dragon*?'

How did the *Fire Dragon* himself react to this hullabaloo? He tells us he made a point of never looking at the draw. He just found out who was to be his next opponent. Then, 'playing one match at a time', he went on in the same way until he won the tournament or lost a match.

Stow's strategy of intimidation had worked: in one way or another the young master appeared to have reached a level of dominant self-belief that would have been arrogance in anyone else.

In 1937, with Perry gone to the pros, Budge was undefeated on grass, and didn't lose a singles match on any surface until mid-September, when he lost in a minor tournament. By then he had won Wimbledon and the US, and helped return the Davis Cup to the US for the first time in 11 years. That year he received the Sullivan Award, presented annually to the world's outstanding athlete. It was a first-ever for a tennis player.

Then, in 1938, Budge reached new heights. By winning the four national championships of Australia, France, Great Britain and the US in one year, he took out what had just been christened the 'Grand Slam'. Here was another first ever: it would take a quarter of a century, and Rodney George Laver, to bring off this feat a second time.

Fig. 2.6. Budge unleashes his backhand. Note the power generation in frames 2 and 3. Here's the down-the-line cannon that Vines said became his nemesis.

For a full understanding of what Budge had to offer the world of tennis, let's take a closer look at the game of this still young man, whose complete dominance among the amateur players had been previously equalled only by Tilden.

Ellsworth Vines' picture (given earlier in this chapter) of the man he faced for his pro title, reveals the extraordinary virtuosity of the Budge backhand. With its flair and flexibility coupled with a kind of rock-like invincibility, no matter what you threw at it, from the left side he would reply aggressively and with interest.

But, according to the perceptive Heldman, if Budge's backhand was unrivalled, his forehand must have been the most under-estimated shot in tennis. Heldman provides a lovely description:

> Technically it was flawless ... It was mechanical in that it was not original with him, but though it did not have the personal flair of his backhand, it was a magnificent, forceful weapon. Of all the strokes of the great champions, this was the one that was always hit properly ...
>
> Budge's forehand was a relentless bludgeon ... He gracefully two-stepped into position, pivoting as the wind-up started. His backswing was a compact semi-circular motion, the hit was wristless ... [With] a slight amount of overspin (imparted by the follow through), the overspin was heavier on the crosscourts so [he was] one of the few men capable of hitting a sharp cross court with a lot of pace ... The racquet head never dropped ... he hit so well on a short ball that he seldom had to hit anything but a set-up.[18]

There were two further features that combined to make the Budge ground strokes overwhelming.

First, along with his natural power and rhythm, was the actual weight of his 'bludgeon': Budge's racket was the heaviest of any ever used by a top player. His preferred 16 ounces translates into an extraordinary 454 grams in modern terms! (Today a heavy racket is around 280 grams.) Yet, with his superlative timing, this war-club was wielded so dextrously, indeed so elegantly, that its 'strike' was the envy of every player who watched it.

The second of Budge's backcourt characteristics was the less obvious 'three-shot build-up.'

Unless his opponent was attacking the net, Budge stepped up the power shot by shot. With the *Fire Dragon*'s breath getting hotter incrementally, he only reached a cruel full power by the third time he struck the ball. To the opponent, the combination of sheer weight of shot and stepped-up power was like facing a battering ram. Worse, this one was so well directed, and so well tuned, it seemed to keep reserves at hand – until it forced a crack.

Budge's unequalled return of serve must be highlighted.

When receiver Budge took up a position on or just inside the baseline, to the server he appeared awe-inspiring: following a bum waggle he copied directly from Vines, his trunk would bend only slightly forward, to coalesce into his monumental and characteristic, almost erect, wide-legged stance. When the serve arrived, he seemed always on balance. With his weight

Fig. 2.7. Budge's famous service return. Taken from Budge's autobiography, the photo shows that the veteran can still jump a backhand return of serve. But it appears that Don is (mistakenly, if elegantly) left-handed – from the inversion of the original photograph, not corrected in printing his memoir.

moving forward in this fairly open stance, from either wing Budge was capable of taking the hardest serve early. As with the more recent service return of Andre Agassi, his was a power-stroke, not a block.

Now Jack Kramer was a man not easily overawed – especially when serving. But *Big Jake* needed to call on more demonic imagery when trying to explain what it was like serving to Don Budge. He admits that when he looked up at Budge's expansive shape awaiting his delivery, he felt he was looking into the mouth of 'a devouring dragon'.

How good was Budge's volley? Vines tells us his backhand volley was superlative, his forehand almost as good, and he hardly ever missed on either side. As for his serve, Heldman tells us it was 'a great serve ... heavy,

Fig. 2.8. Tall, yet deceptively fast, Budge moves wide for a backhand volley. This shot usually ended the point.

deep and well-placed' and 'there were no double faults'.

In short, at its peak the whole Budge game was technically flawless.

To finish, here is a note on the Budge strategy and tactics, and the court personality from which they arose.

Although his serve was tough, like Vines, Budge followed it in selectively; more often on grass or fast courts, or on key points, or sometimes to surprise or attack a weaker wing. Usually starting from the baseline, in a rally he built up the power, and moved and bruised his opponent into making a weaker return. Then Budge pounced, with either a whipped ground shot winner or heavy approach shot. Inevitably following in anything a little short, he would witness surrender then and there or finish the point with a killing volley or overhead.[19]

This meant that the Budge style – so elegant and sure that Heldman said he never once saw Budge play an ugly or false shot – lacked some of the nuances of other masters. In the Budge game there was little room – or need – for the lob, which in singles he only used in extremis, or for the change of pace, drop shot or drop volley.

But in one of what Tilden longingly called Budge's 'quieter moments', Budge would sometimes allow himself an indulgence: 'One of the great joys of tennis,' Budge tells us with palpable relish, 'is hitting a little roll topspin backhand crosscourt – the sort that gives you a great angle and dips below the net, forcing your opponent to volley up, assuming he can even reach the ball.' [20]

This picture would be incomplete without a look at Budge as doubles player.

He himself explains that he was an even later developer at doubles than at singles. In fact, Budge was already a singles champion and a pretty successful doubles player before his eyes were opened to the nuances of the double-handed game.

One day, after watching Budge play doubles, the veteran doubles master Wilmer Allison took him aside.

'Listen to me!' cried Allison. Then he proceeded to tell him, bluntly, that although Don was 'one helluva tennis player', he was the 'stupidest' doubles player he'd ever seen!

After that, Allison gave him a few tips. In particular, Budge was informed of the basic doubles ploy of setting up winning angles, often by first hitting down the centre and/or moving the opponents out of position.

To receive such advice at this point in one's career seems strange to Australians, who absorb doubles with their mothers' milk. But to Budge, Allison's advice was a revelation. Yet he took such profit from it that he became a master of the two-handed game. Further, those lucky enough to witness the mature Budge play doubles would have been able to see more than the impenetrable and relentless all court power of his singles game. Here was a chance to savour more of Budge's 'quieter moments': the lob (top- or underspun), the angled drop volley, and the soft dipper. With these came the manipulation – rather than the bruising – of his opponents.

In 1953, in the British Pro Championships at Wembley, somehow or other Frank Sedgman, a supreme doubles artist, found himself fortuitously partnered with Budge in the doubles event. Budge was out of shape and nearly forty, and the two had never played together. Nevertheless, the scratch pair decided they were going to have one heck of a time.

Putting Budge in the right court, they proceeded to waltz through the tournament. In the final, they faced the formidable Gonzales–Segura team at their peak, and thrashed them 6–3, 6–3, 6–2. Years later, when Kramer selected his best ever doubles team for his imagined 'Universe Davis Cup', it is Budge who takes a doubles spot, with that wizard John Bromwich beside him in the right court.

Budge's story cannot be concluded without a last look at the Budge court persona. For here, concealed in his apparently flawless self-image, lies a strange paradox.

Budge believed that he had to play hard, fast and ruthlessly. This was because this method worked in itself, and because it destroyed his opponent's *savoir-faire*. But, crucially, Budge considered that he had no option but to play that way.

In an almost throwaway line in his memoir, he admits: 'Early on ... [I decided] that I would not let up on my opponent. I found that however slight the competition, I could not relax, for I possessed the type of game that could fall apart at an instant and, like Humpty Dumpty, could not be put together again.' This fragility, paradoxical in an apparent iron-man, seems to have arisen from his style, which he called 'hard, driving, attacking ... [one] that demands a groove.' This rhythm was so relentless and insistent that he felt he couldn't 'turn it on or off like a light switch'.

In his memoir, Budge then offers a significant aside on a man who was to become his *bête noir* – Bobby Riggs. Riggs, he says, toyed with lesser opponents, and could 'raise and lower his game at will'. Budge explains that, even if he wanted to, he could never have played that way, for 'too much of my edge lay in power, *and, if you will, fear*'. [My italics.]

With this revelation, the fear present on court during a confrontation with Budge can now be seen as strangely double-sided. Budge had to instil one fear – in the opponent; then he had to protect and hide a second – his own. Once he let his opponent think he'd got a real chance against him, Budge felt weakened, as if (he said later, using a golfing image), he had been made to 'show his hole card'. It seemed the last thing he wanted was to allow his opponent to glimpse his secret terror of 'falling apart'.

Perhaps underlying Budge's fear of collapse lay a deep identification with his poor father. John had been left unconscious on the freezing soccer pitch, and was never the same again. The young man might have wondered:

Could not everything, in a flash, be forever taken away?

Doubtless it was mentally tough out there on court playing Don Budge. But if it was tough for the opponent, in a different way it was equally tough for Budge, the man thought imperturbable – and so immaculate that the fearless pair of Fred Perry and Bill Tilden called him 'God'!

So at the heart of the Budge invincibility lay a paradox – and a strange kind of vulnerability. But the vulnerability was so well hidden that it took years before anyone noticed it. Then along came a funny little gambler, who 'looked as if he came in from the rain', but was as smart as a barn full of owls.

But our story is getting ahead of itself ...

Rise and fall – Budge as Pro Champion

When Budge took on Vines and then Perry, two truly great champions, and defeated them one after another on the pro tour, his already complete game got even better. By then, no major changes were needed. He just tuned up his singular equation linking power and control, and became even more consistent.

Vines tells us that although Budge sometimes played a little better and sometimes a little worse, in their first tour of 39 matches Budge was 'never once off' – his power game was immune to hot or cold streaks. Tilden, for some reason always a little snide about Budge, concedes this unwavering impregnability. 'Over 365 days of the year,' he tells us, 'Don Budge was the best ever.'

What happened to Budge as pro?

First, with some difficulty, he disposed of Vines. Then with increasing ease, it was Perry's turn. From then on, Don Budge was unchallenged as top pro until war intervened in 1942. In those nearly four years, he beat everyone, including the old, as in Tilden, and the new, as in Bobby Riggs, the latest champion drawn from the amateurs.

When the US entered World War II, everything changed. First, for three years there was little tennis, pro or amateur. Then, when the war was over and tennis started up again, something had happened to the Achilles we had left standing on top of the world: he had developed a sore heel.

Actually it was not a heel, but a shoulder, and the crucial right one.

Budge had been called up in the army, and in 1943 found himself in a training camp in Texas. One freezing day, his company was thrown into a tough obstacle course. While jumping for a rope across a fence he tore his right shoulder. The pain was excruciating. Although it remained painful, he was able to carry on with his army duties. Since the brass had decided he would be more useful away from the front as a supervisor of conditioning programmes, these duties were not arduous.

Fig. 2.9. War and tennis in the Pacific: the Army/Navy matches of 1945, here in Guam. Budge and Parker, front, versus Riggs and Sabin, rear. With Parker still an amateur, here's open tennis 23 years before its time. As ever, Riggs is lobbing Budge.

Healing was slow, but towards the end of the war the injury had improved enough for him to start some tennis. As detailed in the next chapter, Budge and Riggs then found themselves matched in an inter-service competition.

At this point, a strange conjunction occurred. Our Achilles had not only developed his flaw, but a fellow warrior blessed with ability, insight and ambition, had noticed it. This was to spell the end of our hero as king.

Riggs did so well in the wartime mini-series that immediately after the war ended it seemed fair to everyone to kick off with a head-to-head between incumbent Budge and challenger Riggs – and, after years of disruption, to get the show on the road as soon as possible.

At once, Budge saw he had problems. As a result of the shoulder injury, his serve had been hurt. Nevertheless, possessed by what was to prove a fatal confidence, he was hardly fazed. Against 'Little Bobby' Riggs he was 'positive' he could win anyway.

However, Little Bobby had suddenly stopped being frightened of Big Don. What then followed was exactly what Budge had secretly dreaded. Now that his opponent's fear of him had evaporated, out stole the other fear – his own of himself. It was but a short step until the well-oiled perfection of the Budge machine began to seize up.

For Budge, from the start the tour went badly. His first response to Riggs getting on top was to hit himself out of trouble. To the wonder of the tennis world, that made things worse. Then the full realisation hit him: he was playing sudden death for his title, and he was falling behind, handicapped, in pain, and newly fearful. Thus Budge decided then and there that he had only one hope left. He had to give up the very essence of his dominance – his apparently natural, aggressive game. He must return to his original style as a tiny teenager before he grew – and get everything back.

But it was too late.

Starting from a deficit of 13 matches to 1, Budge made a supreme effort: in the tour's last 32 matches, he managed to win 21 to Riggs' 11. But, by tour's end, Riggs was still in front, if only by two matches, 24 to 22.

The world was astonished. Bobby Riggs was the new World Pro Champion. And to become so, he had vanquished one of the greatest tennis players ever.

To understand what had happened, it helps to return to a decade earlier: it was 1937, when amateur Budge had played what has often been considered 'the greatest tennis match ever'.

Budge himself thought it was *his* greatest-ever match; certainly, this Inter-zone Davis Cup Final between the US and Germany had everything. As well as deciding the tie – and the probable winner of the Davis Cup – the singles between the two No. 1 players, Budge and Gottfried von Cramm, held something beyond tennis rivalry. This contest reached directly into the world of international relations, and that world was tottering on the brink of war.

Even before the match began, the drama had started. Immediately before the pair walked onto the famed Wimbledon Centre Court for the match, von Cramm – an aristocrat and sporting champion both by birth and by nature – had been called aside. An agitated official informed him that there was a phone call for him.

It was the Fuehrer. Over the phone Hitler commanded von Cramm to win. He was told: *Victory for the Fatherland!*

After three hours of superlative seesaw drama, in the fifth set Budge had fallen behind. Von Cramm had only to hold serve to win the match, the tie, and the Fuehrer's seal of approval.

Staring at defeat, down 4–1 and a break, Budge decided that if he was ever to come out on top, it was time to throw caution to the wind. Succinctly he tells us: 'I had to get lucky and I had to make my own luck.'

Attacking everything, following even his service return into net, Budge drew back to 4–4, and then edged ahead to 5–4 and match point.

After a strenuous rally Budge was forced way off court into a do-or-die return. At full pace he completed the shot – then fell, and lay hopelessly sprawled on the turf.

Stunned, he heard a roar.

He looked up. His shot had passed his opponent and landed an inch inside the line.

Budge and America had won.[21]

A few years later – twice, crucially – the luck that Budge had kindled on that great occasion ran out. The first was in 1943, on that icy, wartime dawn when he was injured; the second, in 1946, when he had allowed himself to be pushed into a tour while hurt, against an opponent he had underestimated.

After the disastrous loss to Riggs, Budge did what he should have done much earlier: he took time off and, with the help of a good pro, dissected his game. After viewing slow motion films, a technique rare for those days, Budge was appalled. Gone was the whole once-fluid motion of his serve. They began rebuilding.

Although his shoulder healed and his serve and the rest of his aggressive game eventually improved, the king, seen as indestructible, never wrested back his crown. He came close, but, no matter how hard he tried after these two unlucky falls, Don Budge could never – to use his own words – put Humpty Dumpty together again.

Postscript – farewelling the Fire Dragon

After losing his title, unlike our other great achiever and good man, Elly Vines, Don Budge didn't retire from the game. A few years later, that astute old maestro Tilden watched Budge as the fifties began. All the strokes were there, noted *Big Bill,* and were such that they could annihilate anyone not of the very first rank. But what had gone was something more than the legs. Though in years 'still a young man', Don Budge, Tilden felt, had got old before his time.

It seemed that this particular hero was now tired of having to screw himself up into the *Fire Dragon* of his glorious youth and young adulthood. And so he never gutsed his way back to his rightful place at the very top.

Jack Kramer also knew that it was not age, but a mental change that kept back the older Budge. As Kramer saw it, what precipitated this change within Budge was the sudden disappearance of an often forgotten but essential ingredient of success: luck. Hence the unhappy confluence of war, Budge's injury, and Bobby Riggs. Yet like Tilden, Kramer also believed that if the former champ could only be fired up as he once was, even in 1954 he would still 'win the whole tour in a breeze'.

Budge's response to Kramer's optimistic prediction is significant. Wistfully, as if to himself, Budge reflected in his memoir, '[Of that] I have no doubts.'

Nor should any of us. Don Budge, the unlucky good man, didn't want to have to get mad at anyone anymore. He believed that he had done well already, and if the gods had diverted some of their blessings, it was a fleeting thing, for his days at the top had been truly fortunate. And by failing to be embittered, he believed that he'd turned downfall into a sort of victory.

I believe he had also concluded that during those glory days he had realised his boyhood dream. Once he'd hoped that if he ever became a champion, he might be able to repair some of the damage done to his poor father. As veteran pro looking back, he believed that the son had indeed managed to recoup and redistribute the blessings so cruelly withdrawn from the father.

But for those who wanted to find out how to strike a tennis ball, the veteran was always ready to show them – and perfectly. In so doing, this

Fig. 2.10. Imperious: the Budge backhand. Now the stands are empty and Budge an ample veteran, but the backhand is all majesty.

kindly soul hoped he would encourage them to become as content with the world as he was.

As it happens, Don Budge's tennis story has a lovely postscript.

It was September 1962. By then Don Budge was forty-seven, and a quarter of a century had passed since he'd won the Grand Slam. That year a brilliant young Australian had only to win the US to repeat Budge's feat.

When Budge came down to New York prior to the US Championships, he found the shy young man in something of a funk. At once he realised that he could be useful. So he took Laver out of the hothouse of New York. In the quiet of the Catskill Mountains, the pair played a little tennis, talked some, and relaxed. After a while, he told Rod that if he steadied, the Slam was his.

Laver went out and triumphed.

When Don Budge saw that his great feat had been equalled, the second of our two good men felt only one sentiment: delight. How fitting was this! The only previous winner of the Grand Slam had been given the chance to keep the torch burning, and to pass it on.

So, after all, wasn't he, Don Budge, the god-dammed lucky one!

Notes

1 *Kings of the Court: The ten greatest tennis players of all time*. Video documentary. International Tennis Hall of Fame, Newport R I, 1997.
2 Vines and Vier, *Tennis: Myth and Method*. I am indebted to this book for much of this chapter.
3 Lytton Strachey, *Eminent Victorians*, Oxford University Press, Oxford, 2003.
4 Vines and Vier, *Tennis: Myth and Method*.
5 Allison Danzig, *The Fireside Book of Tennis*, ed. Allison Danzig and Peter Schwed, Simon and Schuster, New York, 1972.
6 Bud Collins with Zander Hollander, eds, *Bud Collins' Modern Encyclopedia of Tennis*, Doubleday, New York, 1980.
7 Danzig, *The Fireside Book of Tennis*.
8 This account is drawn from Danzig, above, and from Gianni Clerici, *Tennis*, Octopus, London, 1976.
9 Heldman draws brilliant portraits of past and contemporary champions. Julius Heldman, 'Styles of the Greats', in Will Grimsley, *Tennis: Its History, People and Events*, Prentice-Hall, New Jersey, 1971.
10 Gianni Clerici, *Tennis*.
11 Vines and Vier, *Tennis: Myth and Method*.
12 Heldman, 'Styles of the Greats', in Grimsley, *Tennis*.
13 Vines' pupil Jack Kramer admits to something similar. When he was really 'on' with his serve, *Big Jake* tells us he would slide his hand down the handle so the butt of the racket rose up his palm a little, giving him an extra degree of leverage for more spin or power.
14 Gianni Clerici, *Tennis*.
15 Ray Bowers mentions the injury but doesn't emphasise the string of losses in his account of the Budge/Vines tour, and gives the final tally as 22–17. Jack Kramer once pointedly asked Vines whether he'd carried a significant injury early in the tour against Budge. According to Kramer, Vines 'just shrugged and turned away'. Kramer, *The Game*. Bowers, *Forgotten Victories: The History the Pro Tennis Wars 1926–1945*.
16 Donald Budge, with Frank Deford, *Don Budge: A Tennis Memoir*, Viking, New York, 1969. Except where otherwise stipulated, the Budge quotations in this chapter are from Budge's excellent memoir.
17 Andre Agassi, in his moving autobiography, describes how he was taught to take the ball on the rise. If his account uncannily resembles that of Budge's hours with Stow, young Andre's experience was more brutal: his father set up a huge ball machine over the net, nicknamed *The Dragon*, to fire thousands of balls at the hapless child. Andre Agassi, *Open*.
18 Heldman, 'Styles of the Greats', in Grimsley, *Tennis*.
19 From each of this story's six heroes who have left this life (and with sympathetic echoes from the two of them still here), there surely is a gnashing of teeth every time modern baseliners (like Lleyton Hewitt, who can actually volley well) receive a short ball, return it, and scamper rabbit-like back to the baseline. Despite improved rackets and slower courts, both of which have worked against the net game, a few modern champions, including Roger Federer, follow the old pros' dictum: *Never waste a short ball – it's a gift for the net*

and the surgical kill. I take comfort from one modern master coach, Brad Gilbert, who recommends the same.

20 Donald Budge, 'Be offensive with your backhand', in Chapter 3, 'The Backhand', in *Tennis Strokes and Strategies*, Tennis Magazine – Simon and Schuster, New York, 1975.

21. The Fuehrer was not happy. Not long after this marvellous match, von Cramm, who was no Nazi, was arrested and imprisoned on trumped-up charges. Though only twenty-two and uninterested in politics, Budge bravely supported his friend, refusing against great pressure to play in Germany until the Baron was exonerated.

Fig. 3.0. Riggs shows perfect form. In his autobiography, Riggs captioned this: 'Although I don't think I possess more strength on one side ... my pet is my forehand.'

3

THE GREAT ROBERTO – BOBBY RIGGS

Riggs was remarkable, beautiful to watch, a classic stylist who did everything right.

Ellsworth Vines
Tennis: Myth and Method

BIG BILL TILDEN'S assumption of the mantle of tennis mastery appears to have occurred in a few minutes. In a Wimbledon Final the mental and the physical coalesced – and a good player became a great one. Remarkably, for a man who was his opposite in physique and style, something similar happened to Bobby Riggs.

Physique and style were not the only difference: Tilden, the imposing patrician from Philadelphia, discovered his tennis genius on the famed Wimbledon Centre Court; Riggs, the short, scrappy loudmouth from the West Coast, discovered his on a tiny island in the North Pacific. Far from the hallowed turf of the world's greatest tournament, this conversion occurred on a makeshift hard court, in the midst of a world war. And watching were not the wellheeled cognoscenti of Wimbledon, comfy with strawberries and cream, but a couple of hundred noisy GIs chewing gum and, for a few hours, escaping the horrors of battle.

How so?

Winning the world: prelude on crushed coral

It was 1944. Riggs, aged 26, had been in the US Navy for nearly two years. After the shock of immersion, for him World War II was working out very nicely; by mid1944, he could play as much tennis as he wanted.[1]

From childhood Riggs had perfected the mien of antic clown; beneath it he was hard, deadly serious, and shrewd. When the US entered hostilities, Riggs was already well into his tennis career. In the years preceding his call-up, he had first reached the top of the amateurs, and then, for a brief period, joined the pros.

Despite appearances to the contrary, soon after enlistment Riggs began to suspect that war and the US forces might have given him an extraordinary gift.

For a start, the top brass, who liked his tennis, kept him so remote from the fighting that he had a good chance of survival. Moreover, we will soon see how Riggs – removed from the grind of the pro circuit and apparently fighting a war – actually connived to make space to practise his tennis. Thus, after only a few months in the navy, he'd dissected both his game and his tennis personality, and plotted an ambitious future.

As sailor Riggs made his odyssey from the States to Hawaii, then across the Pacific, little by little he realised that this future depended on three interrelated progressions.

First, he had to think differently. From boyhood he had wanted to be the best player on the planet, but now he saw that to *be* the best, he had to believe he *was* the best. By the time he entered the US Navy he had been close – one down from the top. To take the next step, required a self-belief that told him: *I can beat anyone.*

Second, aware that he needed to raise his game to another level, he'd started a renovation of his whole playing strategy and technique.

Third, in his path was a mountain – simple, awesome. It was called J. Donald Budge.

Budge hailed from Riggs's backyard: California. Three years Riggs's senior, Budge had moved stage by stage from the position of California's top junior, to the World No. 1 amateur. In 1938, with Budge aged 22 and Riggs 19, Budge's season became tennis history, and the first ever Grand Slam.

Behind this meteor trailed *Little Bobby* Riggs. As a result, throughout his amateur career Riggs had never been granted a moment's respite from the hot breath of the so-called *Fire Dragon*.

Then came his chance. At the end of 1938, Budge departed from glory, and joined the pros. Within two years Riggs had begun to get his feet into Budge's huge and recently vacated shoes. Despite disruptions from the impending war, eventually he was confirmed as the world's No. 1 amateur.

Although he had reached the top of a glamorous world, the pugnacious and rebellious Riggs remained forever disillusioned with amateur tennis. To him, it was phoney. So, just before the US entered the war in 1942, Riggs also forsook the amateurs and joined the pros.

With that switch, the interval at the top came to an abrupt end.

It was bad enough that he came up against the trials that beleaguered every new boy joining the pros. Now he was thrown straight back into Budge's shadow. Worse still, his former nemesis had become deadlier. For Riggs, Perry and the rest of this highly talented troupe struggling along on the wartime tour, the only fight was to see who would catch the light first behind the massif that was the reigning champion.

Then the US joined the war, the call-ups began, and it appeared that for a good while there'd be little tennis for anyone. Despite this, as the Allies battled their bloody way across the Pacific towards Japan, our camp-follower hero played the role of entertainer/tennis player by day, and gambler by both day and by night, and thus trailed quite productively in the wake of the frontline soldiers, sailors and airmen.

One day, the commanders of the vast force in the North Pacific noticed something. Right here, in the army, was Don Budge, and over there, in the navy, Bobby Riggs. Then a brain wave: *Hey! Between us, don't we own the best two tennis players in the world?* So, in order to divert the battle-weary soldiers and sailors, they hatched a plan. What about some top-draw matches between the best tennis players around?

As soon as the idea was mooted, Riggs saw that here was his God-given chance. He thought: *Despite this crazy war, if I can match Budge the scales will tilt, and in my favour.* When the war ended, Bobby would resume the pro tour at a different level. Not only would this mean a jump in his earning power but, more importantly, he could demand a head-to-head against the incumbent – with a chance to snatch the crown.

Riggs and Budge were not the only world-class tennis players hanging about the Pacific at the behest of the generals. The navy was also the temporary home of Wayne Sabin, a boyhood champion and buddy of Riggs. By the time the US had entered the war, Sabin had become a competitive touring pro. Also, serving in the army ranks alongside Budge was Frank Parker, who had just won the (amateur and depleted) US Championship held in 1944.

Revealing a power of imagination rarely associated with the military, the service chiefs brought inter-service rivalry into the mix: using top players, they would match the US Army against the US Navy. And how much better if the contest was drawn out over a series! There were to be five rubbers in total, each run in the style of the Davis Cup. Every rubber would consist of singles and doubles. They were planned for various island locations, stretching across the North Pacific.

The first of the series took place in August 1944 on the island of Guam.

Immediately, Riggs got a shock. When the world's best two players got down to it, the *Fire Dragon* seemed as indestructible as ever. With a straightsets win for Budge, it was as ever – Big Don versus Little Bobby. After this firstup drubbing, it appeared to a despondent Riggs that his grand plans might as well have been hot air.

For Bobby, this was bitter. Not only had he played far more wartime tennis than Budge, but during that time he had painstakingly re-built his game. Further, Seaman First Class Riggs knew that his own lucky war had been less kind to the world champion: Lieutenant Budge was carrying an injury to his key right shoulder. Despite all of this, Riggs had been crushed.

A week later, on the island of Peleliu, came Riggs's second inter-service clash with Budge. Though almost no one noticed, it was there that Bobby Riggs's world turned over.

With help from the wartime photograph shown in Figure 3.1 we can picture the scene of Bobby Riggs's unlikely beatification. Before us is a coralfringed atoll, a throng of palm trees, and one tennis court, coloured the dull grey of crushed-up coral. The air beats down with tropical heat and humidity. A few hundred loosely uniformed servicemen are spread about the perimeter of the court. Smoking, barracking, they lounge, or sit spread-eagled across their service jeeps and trucks ranged alongside the court.

Fig. 3.1. Prelude on crushed coral. The court in Guam, 1944, where Riggs practised and schemed against Budge.

On this second occasion, the singles between the world's best two players was a good one. Each of the two sets of the best-of-three-set match had been close. But in both, Budge was too tough.

In his autobiography, *Tennis is My Racket*, Riggs lets us into his thoughts as, exhausted and despondent, he was towelling down after the match beside the court. The gist was: *OK, this one was close, but losing the first two in a best-of-five match series ... well, it just goes to show how second-best I am.*

Right then Budge's partner, Frankie Parker, sidled up. Compulsively, and along the lines of 'It's no use – I'll never beat the bastard', Riggs started unburdening his woes to Parker.

But Parker stopped him. To Riggs's astonishment, Parker demurred.

Riggs explains that after 'congratulating me on my showing ... Parker said I really had Budge going'.

But the crunch came with what Parker said next: he 'insisted Budge was white, actually shaking'.[2]

What Parker was indicating was far more significant than that Budge had found himself pressed. True, playing it close was rare for Champion Budge.

But it was not unique. Indeed on the short wartime pro tour, Riggs had put up a respectable showing against the champion, and snatched the odd win. No, to Parker, Budge had changed, internally and crucially: the titan seemed to have suddenly glimpsed the possibility that he was not invincible. And this *was* unique: Budge was conceding that he might actually lose a series.

In essence, Parker was telling Riggs: *You, Bobby, have found the crack we've all been searching for. For God's sake, don't give up now!*

We will never know whether Parker sensed the importance of what he'd said or where it might lead. He could have been sharing an observation, one pro to another. But at once, Riggs twigged that Parker's insight could change his fate.

As the GIs slowly drifted off through the coconut trees, Riggs remained beside the improvised court on which he had suffered a debilitating defeat. And, stewing in the heat, he weighed Parker's words.

Within a few days, Riggs tells us that he was beginning to see things differently.

The first steps in his progression of thought were logical: Parker's observation allowed Riggs to conclude that the competitive balance between the two antagonists had shifted.

But what happened next was more mysterious, and more wonderful.

Following on from a shift in Budge's way of viewing himself, within Riggs something comparable arose. Like Budge, Riggs felt different; but unlike him, Riggs sensed he had become more, not less, powerful. Riggs lets on that a mere week after the defeat by Budge in Peleliu, he'd come to believe that, finally, he *was* the best. And he was about to prove it.

Such turnabouts of the heart ('suddenly I knew I could do it' or 'then and there, I realised I loved her') remain forever mysterious. But a famous aside from another tennis champion some 30 years later would surely have resonated with Riggs in Peleliu in 1945. Said John McEnroe: 'Tennis is 90% mental, and the other 10% is mental.'

The new Riggs went on to victory in each of the next three wartime matches against Budge, so winning the five-match series 3–2.

The mountain had not come to Mohammed. Against the hideous backdrop of war, an unlikely but brave and far-seeing character had gone to the mountain, and brought it down to size. After the second match against

Budge – as with Tilden after his epiphany at Wimbledon – Bobby Riggs was different, as a player and a person.

But could that transformation in Riggs have occurred without a confluence of other forces in his make-up?

Let's discover how he began.

Origins and apprenticeship

Born on February 25, 1918 in Los Angeles, the youngest of five boys and a girl, Robert Larimore Riggs was to grow up under three transparently formative influences.

The first arose from his family origins.

Bobby's parents had come from the impoverished farmlands of Tennessee. Despite becoming a minister in the fundamentalist Church of Christ, father Gideon possessed the gifts of entrepreneur and showman that became the hallmarks of his youngest child. Gideon had moved to the better prospects of the West, and founded a string of churches across California. Yet the juiceless values of his family – prudence, austerity and God-fearing work – dominated his life.

The second force at work on the youngest son grew from the role his parents assumed.

When Bobby was born, his father was 50 years old, and preoccupied with his godly mission. He left the household in the hands of his wife, the shy and retiring Agnes. As their mother went about the home, endlessly cleaning and cooking, the seven children were left to look after themselves.

Before long, the fervently sporty world of the five elder sons became the core of the life of their favourite kid brother – and the distance from his parents widened. Despite being spoiled rotten, young Bobby was required to be tough – and to perform, indeed to lick any opponent. When they dropped him into any sort of competition his brothers said bluntly, 'Win – and we'll take you to the movies. Lose – and we'll kick your ass.'

Riggs recalled that his first memory was of a contest! Apparently, soon after he had learned to run, he'd been pitted against a neighbouring boy in a foot race. Crucially, his brothers had set up the race: his opponent was older and bigger, and the bets were on. Naturally, so Bobby claims, he won.

Though the church frowned on gambling – as on smoking, dancing and drinking – the Riggs boys bet on anything. From this arose the third influence on the young Bobby: an ineradicable passion to mix betting with competing and winning.

Riggs's biographer, the perceptive Tom LeCompte, points out that the Riggs household came to possess two faces. Their rambling two-story house, slam-bang next to father Gideon's church, oozed puritan piety; but below the surface thrived another order – rambunctious and unholy. That world was about showing off, competing and winning at games – and betting on the outcome.[3]

The youngest boy knew where he belonged; as soon as he could run he was one of the gang.

His brothers immediately saw that although he was small, the kid was a natural at all sports, even boxing. Now this combination of small stature and big talent was not only rare, but also deceiving – and thus temptingly 'backable'. Soon they had him playing everything. Except tennis. Indeed, he was 11 years old before he held a racket in his hand.

The first occasion he did so turned out to be more than usually instructive.

Like the young Don Budge, Bobby's older brother introduced him to tennis. John, seven years Bobby's senior, had been playing tennis for a while. One day he extracted Bobby from the throng, and got the kid to the local public courts. There he showed him how to hold a racket and hit the ball.

As Riggs tells it, while the two lads were engrossed in these preliminaries, to their surprise a young woman came up to them. She was slim, with tight curly hair. Quietly, she introduced herself: 'My name is Esther Bartosh,' she said, 'Doctor Esther Bartosh.'

John already knew the woman: she was a fine player, locally famous in state competition. Apparently she'd been scrutinising John and his new pupil. She told the boys that the kid had talent. Then, in a kindly way, she made them an offer.

'I live nearby,' she continued in her calm tone, 'and I would love to coach the youngster. Do you agree?'

Both boys were thrilled, and said yes.

On the way home John started raving about his kid brother's luck. Dr Bartosh was not just ranked No. 3 amongst the women in California – she was a somebody, established as a teacher at the local medical school!

But there was a problem. Since John needed his own racket, how could Bobby find one for his lessons?

The way he managed this small feat enhances the Riggs mythology.

As Bobby tells it, a few days later he spied an 'old schoolteacher' throwing a racket to his dog to chase and fetch. Spontaneously the tiny but speedy 11-year-old boy dashed off, beat the dog to the racket and took it back to the dog's master. With his ever-characteristic mix of insouciance and cheek, Bobby told the man that he was about to start tennis lessons – but didn't own a racket.

Disarmed, but with a grin and a 'good luck', at once the old fellow handed the implement to the boy.

The racket was ancient and battered, with its throat chewed by the dog. However, it proved serviceable for his first lessons with Bartosh – at least until a few weeks later when Bobby discovered a better one owned by another neighbourhood kid.

He explains that at once he lured the unsuspecting owner into a game of marbles. Of course Bobby was the local marbles champion. It wasn't long before the other kid found himself in a deal. Very soon after that, he was rich in marbles, but devoid of his racket. But this set-up didn't last long either: in a quintessential denouement – recorded in an equally quintessential boast – Riggs claims that by that very afternoon he'd won back his marbles, leaving the poor kid with neither marbles nor racket.

Despite tennis having the reputation of being sissy, Bobby was hooked. He loved the challenge of developing the basic strokes, and the growing sense of control over the ball. Free spirit that he was, Riggs felt that there was something direct and liberating about a game that placed such emphasis on the skill of a single protagonist.

Bartosh turned out to be a perfect foil for little Bobby. A teacher by profession, she was childless, and could focus her spare time on the boy. Immediately, Dr Bartosh saw that despite his size, Bobby owned more than a God-given talent: beneath the sass was a deep reservoir of desire, pugnacious resilience and competitive edge.

Outside her skill as a coach, Bartosh had something unique to offer Bobby. Although he doesn't say so, here was an adult like none other: this one could be attentive and caring without being moralistic.[4]

Esther Bartosh gave Bobby three fundamentals: sound, long, orthodox Eastern strokes; a tennis posture that depended on consistency and defence; and an attitude to the game. Here, while she required that he play his heart out, she insisted that when defeat came, it was to be accepted honourably. Strokes, strategy, attitude – they stayed with Riggs for his lifetime.

To Bartosh, the mental side of the game was crucial. Sitting Bobby at her feet, she'd tell her tousle-headed and pintsized pupil, drinking in her every word, that most rallies end not with great winners, but with errors. 'Listen to me, Bobby,' she would emphasise, 'do you know the simplest way to win tennis matches? It's to make fewer errors than your opponent.'

And for the really smart – so Bartosh believed – every move on court is made with meaning and purpose.

Within that field of tactics and mental attitude - so often treated as mere addons by lesser teachers - Dr Bartosh then turned to the business of the opponent.

In Bartosh's approach – using much of the same deliberate delicacy she applied to her work as an instructor and demonstrator in human anatomy – every opponent was a specimen. She told Bobby: *Take up the opportunity! If you do, soon you will be able to tease your opponents apart ... and not just their game, but their tennis character.*

To this particular lad, the Bartosh gestalt was singularly apposite. Since Bobby was small and slight, he needed to take advantage of his gifts of agility, speed and retrieval. LeCompte points out that, curiously enough, Bartosh's emphasis on the mental aspects of the game complemented a less obvious side of her charge. Bobby was by instinct a gambler: he realised that as such he was required to perfect the skill of balancing his own hand against the opposition's intentions and capabilities.

Any insightful opponent of Bobby's soon came to realise two things. For one, his own defects and strengths had been laid bare; for another, the only way to beat the kid on the other side of the net was by winning points, not waiting for errors.

Years later, when coaching, Riggs used to say that to become a champion you needed to own a unique resource. Holding it didn't guarantee success; without it, give up wanting to reach the top.

In Riggs's thinking, behind every champion, stored like a stash in the bank, was a period when they played tennis 'for ten years, three hundred days per year, six hours per day'. In the six years succeeding his fortuitous meeting with Esther Bartosh as an 11-year-old, day-by-day Bobby Riggs deposited the bulk of this requirement into his bank account.

After the early Bartosh years, the teenage Riggs sought further quality coaching. A second chance meeting warrants special mention.

When Riggs was fifteen, and investing endless hours at the LA Tennis Club, a regular visitor was the then-best tennis player in the world.

He was a tall, whipcord-slim young man, whose sweet smile and amiable disposition hid an explosive game. One day, H. Ellsworth Vines Jr sat down in front of the clubhouse, stretched out his long legs, and took a look at the juniors.

'Who's the little tyke who chases everything?' asked the champ. It was Bobby Riggs.

When top players didn't own the entourage of an Eastern potentate, they would need practice partners. In addition to serious competition, when repairing or grooving a shot they also required someone who could just return the ball. So *Little Bobby* (as he was fast coming to be called) was enlisted for this purpose.

According to Bobby, before long Elly Vines was telling everyone in his charming drawl that in Bobby Riggs he had discovered 'a regular human backboard' who represented 'the best practice in ... California'.[5]

Soon Bobby Riggs found he had been given something more than a chance to walk the same court as the world's best player. For this 15-year-old battler, a product of distant parents and competitive siblings, catching esteem from Ellsworth Vines, world champion and good man, meant much.[6]

Despite minimal support from officialdom, from the time he took up his training with Esther Bartosh, Bobby rose steadily through the Boy, and then the Junior, ranks of tennis.

Next we catch him as teenager becoming man, and learning the ropes of the twin passions of his life.

Life games: tennis and hustling

If the stories in later chapters of this book on Ken Rosewall and Rod Laver seem quintessentially Australian, the tale of Robert Larimore Riggs – gambler, huckster, scrapper, skirtchaser, loudmouth, eventual world champion athlete and, finally, notorious celebrity – is American through and through. Born into American fundamentalism, in boyhood Riggs drifted towards the maverick edge – and never left it.

By the time he was seventeen, Bobby had graduated from high school, and was the top junior in California. Nevertheless, already offside with the rulers of Californian amateur tennis, Bobby had had almost no exposure to tennis beyond the state – indeed only through prodigious personal effort had he got himself to the US National Junior Championships. And won.

Snubbing his nose at the panjandrums, now sure his future was tennis Riggs decided that he had to go East, join the major grass-court circuit, and try himself against the men.

Seen from this distance, the objections made by the authorities against Bobby's attempts to gain a wider experience seem nonsensical. At the same age as Riggs, Rosewall and Laver were entered in the main draw of Wimbledon! It seemed the amateur authorities wanted to punish him. At least so Riggs thought.

The young Riggs's *bête noire* was Perry T. Jones, lord and master of Californian tennis. Notwithstanding Bobby's white Anglo-Saxon Protestant background and acceptable high school record, the autocratic Jones couldn't abide the teenager. The kid got under his skin.

Riggs's biographer, LeCompte, puts it succinctly: to Jones, *Little Bobby* was 'sassy, unkempt, and walked like a duck'. And small. To be in with bachelor Jones, you had to be neat and well behaved, and it helped if you were tall and smacked the ball. And, as Pancho Gonzales was to confirm a decade on, if you weren't one of Jones's boys, you were nowhere.

Jones ruled from the Los Angeles Tennis Club, which he managed. Although Jones was ever present, the club was Bobby's second home. In this big bad city, down a few wide roads from Hollywood, the club was a watering hole for a whole set of characters, many of whom were either actors or hangers-on to the movie set. And if Errol Flynn and Charlie Chaplin were there, playing and watching and barracking, there were plenty who merely wanted to be near them.

However, reflected glory was not the only drawcard: an afternoon at the club also offered a chance to pick up a few badly needed bucks. For many – players and hangerson – gambling of one sort or another was an indispensible part of getting on at the Los Angeles Tennis Club. And this fast set didn't bet for peanuts, nor on cards and big matches: a favourite diversion was putting money on the juniors!

So who rocks along but young Bobby Riggs, who couldn't remember a time when he hadn't been betting on something. The result? Young Riggs was soon spending as much time laying bets, mainly with the adult members, as playing tennis.

One of the most conspicuous of the colourful characters gracing the club at the time was a certain Jack Del Valle. LeCompte captures him beautifully.

No one really knew what he did, but he had 'more money and time than he knew what to do with', and was flashy with it. Del Valle played little tennis himself. (LeCompte described Del Valle's own game as 'wild and unorthodox', and quotes the shrewd Jack Kramer as saying that Del Valle 'probably had another name and just picked that one'.) But this florid character did love tennis – or better, he loved hanging about with tennis stars. And Jack would bet on anything.

Then, up jumped little Bobby Riggs. Birds of a feather, in a flash Jack and Bobby were buddies.

At that time Riggs was pleading for Jones to support him to join the Eastern circuit, while Jones was insisting Riggs stay home. Then Bobby took a big step: he told Jones he was going anyway, if necessary under his own steam. Jones was so incensed that he slammed Riggs to his chums running tennis on the other side of the continent. Without his approval, Jones told the boy, he was finished.

Almost certainly over a bet (for by then there was hardly any other way to interact with him), before long Bobby was telling everyone about his troubles. Soon his new pal Jack Del Valle was hearing that things were so bad Bobby and his mate, doubles partner and fellow gambler Wayne Sabin, were trying to raise their own cash to fund their trip east.

Was Del Valle shocked! And, well ... he couldn't but help his young buddies out, could he? Before long he was offering to sponsor Riggs and Sabin with his own money. Then, in his huge white convertible, he would personally conduct them east himself!

LeCompte tells how Del Valle 'fancied himself ... as a wheeler-dealer' who claimed he had looked after prize-fighters. Soon Del Valle was extending the offer: now he would 'manage' the youngsters.

To the likely lads, here was a package too good to refuse. Quick as you can say 'game-set-and-match', the two kids were piling into the white convertible alongside the glib, over-dressed and shrivelled-up old guy with the phoney name. Then they headed off, all three, into a rising sun ...

The dubious trio, the big white car, the tournaments big and little strung along the highways and byways, the odyssey winding its way across the gigantic continent towards the climactic Nationals in New York – what a road movie! And for this particular saga, there was only one backdrop: mid-twentieth century America. Although this huge country might have been struggling out of the Depression, to the quick and the smart it was, as ever, a land of gold.

Soon the picaresque intensified. Though Jack had promised to bankroll the tour, before long the three had stumbled on a better angle. Why shouldn't they follow the tradition of generations of itinerant rogues, and source the necessary cash directly from the credulous locals? How much more lucrative! How much more fun!

While they widened the range of their private enterprise as the trip went on, their main cons were squeezing tournament officials and betting on their own matches. In the latter activity, Riggs began to perfect what would become his unequalled talent in rising from the dead against lesser players. Indeed, with Sabin and Del Valle working the crowd up to the last minute – and the odds soaring second-by-second against their (increasingly well-backed) man – this skill was becoming a work of art.

Soon Riggs and Sabin had honed a technique additional to – indeed, indivisible from – performing on the tennis court: separating the natives from their cash, and diverting it untrammelled into the pockets of the two players and their impresario/manager. Before a couple of little tourneys had passed, the three gypsies were on the make. As they polished their act – Eureka! Bobby Riggs began to see that in front of him was a concept of tennis – individual, elastic, and creatively entrepreneurial if not shady – that would be the blueprint for his life.

Up to this point, the top amateurs derived their modest income from whatever the tennis associations shelled out to them as expenses for accommodation and travel. This was sometimes supplemented by the sporting goods firms, whose equipment they used and (unobtrusively) advertised, and who might find them a part-time and lowly but legitimate cover job.

Young Bobby Riggs's sources of income were more complicated. While he received monetary allowances from the tennis associations and tournaments approved by the amateur bodies, to extort bigger payments he was soon dealing directly with local officials.

Then he went further. Before long, through direct bets, much of his livelihood was extracted from the public unmediated! This developed into more than a habit: it became a point of honour, and one that lasted to the end of his playing days.[7]

By now it was the mid-thirties and Riggs had yet to work his way up in the amateur tennis world. What did amateur tennis in the US look like at this time, and how did Bobby Riggs fit into it?

Except for teaching professionals and our little band of touring pros – labelled by journalist Bud Collins the 'travelling rug salesmen' and active mainly in the off (winter) season – the tennis world at that time was entirely amateur and, at the grassroots, state or city-based. Over the summer, there were dozens of tournaments, large and small, scattered across the US. Staffed by volunteers and without big pay cheques for the players, they cost little.

As we have seen, the top so-called amateur players were officially allowed to receive 'expenses'. It was through this channel that the system became corrupted.

To build their tourney's gate and status, the associations had begun to vie for the better players. Once the deals were done, they paid the players in cash, under the table and at a rate well above that necessary for their food and accommodation. This fiddle also applied to the major international tournaments. Of course, the bosses of the national Lawn Tennis Associations knew what went on, but the whole edifice depended on this hypocrisy. So they looked the other way.

Even on their first tour, Bobby and Sabin – plus their newfound buddy, Jack Del Valle-of-the-Fancy-Pants – were pushing this shonky system to its limits. By leveraging bigger payments from the tournament organisers, and by betting on themselves and their doubles team, and sometimes on other players and teams, they were multiplying their legitimate expenses. As LeCompte puts it, by then Del Valle was in his element: his role as 'manager' had now 'evolved into bookmaker [who wandered] the courts, promoting "his boys," negotiating the odds'. And collecting the winnings.

When at last they reached the east coast, Bobby Riggs had come to internalise a great truth: America was show business, and the medium the massage. By then, with their own designer uniforms, the flashy car and 'manager' Del Valle, when their show hit town they were an entertainment sensation. When they left, their pockets were full.

It is now clear just how early Bobby Riggs had discovered his life roles.

As a young teenager at the LA Tennis Club, he realised he was going to be a tennis player *and* a gambler. But just after that, on his first tour, he extended the second of these two primal roles. Now he was gambler *and* huckster. This meant that he didn't just bet. Bobby Riggs peddled a line, went into the crowd, worked them up, and convinced them to pass their money over to him. The product that the hustler flogged never really changed: essentially, fun and hope – in the shape of Bobby Riggs.

Despite the off-court hoopla, on this trip Riggs managed to remain deadly serious about tennis. He did well in a number of big grass-court tournaments, and in Chicago won his first significant men's championship, the National Clay Courts.

Eventually, the little band got to the end of their journey, and the National Championships.

Although Bobby had a real chance for a national title, he crashed out in the third round. The circumstances were instructive. Misjudging his opposition, the night before his match he'd gone on an all-night gambling spree. But so much did he learn from this experience that, miraculously, during his career at the top he never again let his gambling seriously affect his play. Further, with the one tragic exception toward the end of his life in the debacle with Billie-Jean King, he never again made the equally catastrophic error of under-estimating an opponent.

Despite this lapse in the Nationals, he finished the year ranked fourth in the country.

In gaudy contrast to the youthful Australians Laver and Rosewall – later to appear on the tennis scene as so earnest, scrubbed and hopeful – here was Bobby Riggs, worldly at just eighteen, and as much professional operator as tennis player. Though acknowledged as a rising tennis champion, his reputation was such that he was commonly known by the nickname *Bad Boy Bobby*.

Yet to those in the know, Bobby Riggs was more than just another tennis rebel. Before them was the legendary travelling showman–salesman, unquenchably loquacious, and a brilliant spruiker. Clearly, besides his tennis, his product was snake oil. And he was a crook. But when he was smiling up at them, many watchers were charmed, and would catch themselves asking: Aren't they strangely lovable, these chatterbox crooks?

For like all the masters of the line, this one possessed a saving grace. To his counterfeit medicine he added a crucial ingredient: a dose of optimism. And, in our often-drab world, who can resist a taste of that? This no doubt explains why so many remained cheerful after being hoodwinked by Bobby Riggs, master tennis player and master trickster – even if they left his show with their pockets a little lighter.

Since the world of the huckster figures strongly in the writings of Mark Twain, I'm drawn to ask: How would Twain see the young Riggs working the crowd?

Let's indulge for a moment:

We catch Twain – white bearded, a large black hat – taking in Bobby as he snatches another impossible victory from the jaws of defeat, and then goes out among the crowd to collect his bets. At the point when the chattering bantam effusively thanks the last bemused spectator – and slips the last banknotes into his carpetbag – Twain bestows on the youngster a spontaneous salute. Right here in front of him is a paid-up member of that line of master conmen whom the worldly writer has celebrated so often, so joyously, and with such delicious irony ...

And how did Bobby see himself in these circumstances?

In fact, Riggs was coy about applying the term 'hustler' to himself. In his second autobiography, he explicitly denies being a hustler, which he defines as someone who 'makes a living by gambling and taking advantage of people through deception'. What he actually is, he tells us, is 'a world champion since the age of twenty-one'. But this autobiography is titled, *Court Hustler*, and its predecessor, *Tennis is My Racket*!

Here we have it. Despite the cultivated persona of wheeler-dealer, in Bobby's own eyes his core identity is that of a sporting champion, and a proud and honourable one at that. Such a contradiction suggests a person wrestling with opposing identities, a conflict that never left him.

As a result of his overt rebelliousness against the authorities and his (slightly) more covert extra-curricular activities, young Riggs soon found himself sailing dangerously close to the edge of the system on which he depended. It was one he despised and whose rulers loathed him.

Yet, though precariously balanced, by his late teens he had managed to get close to the top of the amateurs. At that moment, Bobby decided to re-evaluate his progress and future. After recommitting himself to his goal to become No. 1, the moment seemed ripe to make a detailed plan of how to get there.

Plotting each stage, he concluded that he could do it in four years.

Despite them: rebel and champion manqué

Although from boyhood the feisty Bobby Riggs had chafed against the tottering and corrupt amateur system, by his adulthood overt conflict with his masters had become his way of life. To complete the chart of Riggs's rise to top amateur – and to understand what the pros were up against – here is a battle plan of what I call 'Riggs versus The System'.

At the end of 1937, approaching age 20 and ranked in the world's top five, Riggs made the acquaintance of two wealthy businessmen. Recognising that Bobby was heading for No. 1, they decided to give him a helping hand. So, for token employment, Riggs was provided with steady retainers. His biographer LeCompte explains: 'Between his tournament expenses ... his two "jobs" and his gambling winnings, Bobby was able to support himself quite nicely.'

Everyone knew about the racket whereby 'expenses' were inflated for the top players. However, the whole thing was meant to be discreet and, as the world would discover, discretion was something Bobby Riggs never understood. Before long the USLTA was on to his latest lurk.

When Riggs got wind that he was in more trouble than usual, his response was to try to appear squeaky clean. He'd pay his own way, but arrange for a front man, who also happened to be an LTA official, to pick up his expense cheques from the various tournament officials and put them in Bobby's bank account at home.

But when one day he returned home to check his finances – disaster! The friendly official had vanished, and so had Riggs's money. Then it got worse. On threat of suspension, he was told he was to be hauled before the USLTA. The charge? 'Professionalism'.

When he arrived at the hearing in New York, Riggs recalled the gist of the tough words, if expressed gently, by his first coach. *Little guys in fights*, Esther Bartosh had told him, *need to be smart*. So he didn't own up about his retainers from the businessmen, nor emphasise that it was their own USLTA officials who had agreed to the inflated tournament expenses that they now disputed. What he did tell them was that someone had gathered up his expense moneys, and then fled with them. And this someone was one of their own officials!

The blusterers of the presiding committee knew what they were there for – to preserve the façade of amateurism. The outcome? What they were now hearing from young Riggs seemed so incendiary, they dropped the case on the spot.

Such hypocrisy shocked even the streetwise Riggs. And he'd never been asked about his betting on matches, or his side jobs!

After escaping, just, from losing his amateur status, Riggs realised he was a marked man, and would have to find his own way to the top of the amateurs. In 1938, he forced himself into the Davis Cup team. Budge and Riggs, and with Mako as Budge's doubles partner, won the Cup against the Australians in a close tie. Soon after that Budge departed for the pros and, to the sound of gnashing teeth in the US Lawn Tennis Association in New York, Riggs began to dominate.

In 1939, the last Wimbledon held before the war was a triumph for Riggs: by taking out the rare Triple Crown of the Singles, Doubles and Mixed Championships, he replicated one of Budge's extraordinary feats. Following Wimbledon with victory in the US Championships, he had finally got there – ranked World No. 1 amongst the amateurs.

He was now 21 years of age, and a year ahead of his schedule. After winning his second US Championship in 1941, he decided it was time to head to where he had always wanted to be: with the pros, amongst the fair and square.

Finally Bobby could make a good – and more or less honest – living from the game he loved.

But World War II intervened. By war's end, and with surprising help from the Navy, he was conniving to become top dog amongst the top pack of dogs.

Rolling the Fire Dragon – *Riggs and Budge*

It was the first week of August, 1945. On the island of Tinian in the North Pacific, Don Budge and Bobby Riggs were locked in the climax of their own two-person battle; the deciding match of a five-match series between them.

At that moment, an event occurred that was crucial to the human species. At a top-secret location a few kilometres down the road from the crushed-coral court, scientists, technicians and aircrew were preparing the B-29 bomber, *Enola Gay*, to carry an atomic bomb to Japan. On August 6, it took off bound for Hiroshima.

Within a few days, World War II had finished.

For a weary post-war world, play and games were now possible, and much needed. After a brief reunion with his wife, Kay, and their two young children, ex-Sailor Riggs headed straight to his second home: the Mecca of tennis in the West, the Los Angeles Tennis Club. To his delight, the old pro band had survived – and was raring to go.

During his war service, Bobby tells us: 'I schemed, I planned, and I waited for my chance.' By war's end, Riggs intended to beat Budge and claim the World Title. His plan could now be fine-tuned. First, he had to believe he could win; second, he had to dissect the mind, the body and the game of the incumbent champion; and third, he had to tune his game to exploit his opponent's perceived weaknesses.[8]

How did he do it?

In the midst of his wartime matches, Riggs had suddenly come to believe that he could beat the previously invincible Budge in a series. Then he did so – and after starting from a long way behind. Thus the first requirement was in place.

How did the deceptively studious Riggs evaluate his opponent's strengths and vulnerabilities?

From the beginning, Riggs avoided what the Chinese sage Lao Tsu calls the most serious mistake: underestimating the opposition. Bobby's problem was not to recognise Budge's stature, but to remain undaunted by it. With extraordinary honesty Riggs admits that Budge's strokes were 'always better' than his. However, during the war flaws had appeared in Budge's game.

First, was Budge's physical condition. With his damaged shoulder, the once-fluid Budge serve had developed a little hitch in the wind-up, and lost some bite. His second serve was more affected, and Riggs believed that now he could do more damage with his service return.

The problem with Budge's smash was more telling. Not only did Budge find it harder to kill a smash, the effort drained him.

The final flaw was a technicality: Budge's forehand.

The forehand was never as natural to Budge as the backhand, and in his early maturity, he had needed to rework the shot. Gunslinger style, Riggs quipped that a tennis player had never been born who could laugh at Budge's forehand. Yet even in the wartime contests shortened to best-of-three sets, Riggs had noticed that the shot became vulnerable to pressure. When Budge was tiring, he would try to do too much with it, and the fiercely struck shot would find the net, or miss the lines.

Should one also ask: Was Big Don a bit slow? A footrace in Manhattan helps to answer this question.

Although a power player, and despite his stately, ship-in-full-sail elegance on court – seen in full flight in Figure 2.8 in Chapter 2 – Budge moved deceptively fast. His opponents knew the big man could do the 100-yard dash under eleven seconds, considered at the time to be a measure of a man with real speed.

Yet one day on the wartime tour the other pros started baiting the champion for his apparent slowness. Though at the time the bunch of top players (including Riggs) were walking down New York's Madison Avenue – and Budge's good nature was legendary – this time the champ was riled.

'Slow, hey! Well let's see who can beat me then?' retorted Budge. The bets were on, and Big Don prepared to take on the lot of them in a hundred-yard dash marked out down the sidewalk.

He did so – and came in first, and handily.[9]

So in the same way as the game's most fearsome strikers of the ball – Vines, Hoad, Laver, Connors, Agassi and now Nadal and Djokovich – Budge owed part of his power of shot to his anticipation and speed in getting to the ball, thus enabling him to set up a solid hitting platform on arrival.

In short, Riggs realised he was dead unless he could push Budge so hard that this 'hitting platform' was often teetering at the edge of his balance and fitness. Essentially, Riggs planned to force the Budge serve, forehand and overhead, and such pressure would eventually squeeze an error, or allow him to attack the return. He would wear Budge out.

Riggs's final weapon in beating Budge was his own reconstructed game. As noted, the cunning Riggs had managed to put the war to good use: after inveigling himself onto the staff of a tennis-loving admiral, towards the end of hostilities Riggs was usually found playing tennis exhibitions for the troops or practising at base.

His first task had been to revamp his attacking game. In particular, he had to lift his net game and serve, and turn his solid but relatively docile backhand into a weapon. Thus when he played an exhibition against some hack before 50 gum-chewing GIs, he might play net on everything, or hit almost nothing but topspin backhands, and crunch every one of them.

Sometimes, for a couple of weeks, he would work only on his serve. In the process, when facing the right or forehand court, he might alternate 'spotting' a hard slice with a looping American twist. The slice would hit a few centimetres inside the sideline, a metre in from the service line and break sharply away from the opponent. The twist would be slotted into a few square centimetres of the T of the service box and kick hard in the opposite direction. And after a thousand practices, he could do the trick 19 times out of 20.

And if the indefatigable Riggs found that one opponent was incapable of testing him, he would take on two. Admittedly goaded by the right wager, he would then play his heart out, the whole time working on his game.

As a result, by the time Riggs faced Budge for his pro title, Riggs had surprises for his long-term adversary. It was not just that he had mastered the all court game. At key moments his aggressive new serve, net game and backhand were capable of flummoxing Budge, who'd known Bobby only as the master scrambler with whom he'd grown up.

The whole story is encapsulated in two action shots, pictured in Figures 3.2 and 3.3, taken during two crucial confrontations between them.

Fig. 3.2. Riggs as torturer No. 1. Riggs calmly wrong-foots a desperate Budge in the 1946 US Pro Final.

Fig. 3.3. Riggs as torturer No. 2. Against Budge in the Final of the 1947 US Pro Championship, Riggs has covered the whole court, and then struck a deceptive crosscourt forehand.

In Figure 3.2, Riggs is at net and Budge on the baseline. It is clear what has preceded the instant of the photograph: Riggs has pressed, then wrong-footed Budge. Going the wrong way, Budge leaves a space into which Riggs calmly returns Budge's struggling forehand return with what will be a decisive volley. Now it is the beautifully balanced figure of Riggs that seems impervious, commanding. In contrast, Budge's body language is desperate. Now Budge's countenance is more than 'white-faced' – it is tormented.

Figure 3.3 inverts their court positions: now Budge is at net, Riggs on the run. But again, it's not Budge who's in the box seat. Budge's own placement volley has been good enough to draw his opponent up and wide. Yet Riggs gets to Budge's shot, and retains sufficient control to attempt (off the wrong foot) a masterly counterstroke. He has flicked a top-spun, forehand crosscourt. Struck sharply upward and outside in, the ball will spin up and over the net, swerving away from Budge on an acute and increasing angle.

On this occasion Budge is moving the right way, but his lunge appears too late.

These action shots show that Riggs had become good enough to execute the strategic plan he'd devised. He's so fit, so fast, and his all court game so full of deception and surprise that he has been able to disrupt the magnificent stroking machine opposite. Now it's Budge who's on the hook of fisherman Riggs, and wriggling desperately to get off.

Once the decision had been made that Budge would defend his title against Riggs, in 1946 two warm-up confrontations were set up between the two protagonists. Despite the wartime victory, and although Budge was now thirty and Riggs twenty-seven, few believed that Riggs could possess the wherewithal to topple the reigning champion. Thus Riggs remained underdog, and gambler Riggs could find sweet odds against himself. With newfound confidence, he backed himself to the hilt.[10]

Let's look at the first of these pre-tour confrontations. It took four sets, and hurt Budge badly.

Budge had started brilliantly, and was soon up a set and 3–1 in the second. However, Riggs's lobbing, and his surprise attack on Budge's second serve, had made its mark. Budge began to wilt, and Riggs jumped back in.

By the time Riggs had won 10 of the next 12 games, Budge's shoulder and arm were so sore he was forced to make an extraordinary request. He called for a doctor! The request was granted, a break called, a doctor summoned. But nothing helped.

By then two sets to one up, Bobby ran out the fourth and final set 6–0!

Then a brazen Riggs rubbed salt into the wound. After grabbing his prize money and winning bets, he told the press that though Budge appeared injured, he would have beaten him anyway! Grinning from ear to ear, the ever-modest Bobby finished, 'Shake hands with the new champ, boys!'

The second confrontation, just three weeks later, epitomises the mix of ingredients the crafty Riggs cooked up to throw at poor Budge.

The match was played in LA's Pan-Pacific Auditorium in January 1946, before the biggest crowd that had ever watched a tennis match on the West Coast. The assiduous biographer, LeCompte, discovered a wonderful photo taken of the match. Figure 3.4 shows Riggs about to serve to Budge. Between them, about 35 feet (10 metres) above the net, is a huge clock, fixed to the roof beams.

Fig. 3.4. Little Bobby *the ultimate exploiter. The Pan-Pacific Auditorium, Los Angles, January 1946, Budge about to serve to Riggs. To break Budge, Riggs used the huge clock mid-court as the 'sighter' for his incessant lobbing.*

The clock tells the story.

Riggs had cased the joint and, after hitting dozens of practice shots, had discovered that a perfect lob grazed the clock. If the lob was a fraction high it would hit the clock, and he'd lose the point. A few inches lower, and it would be too easy for Budge to put away. Riggs saw that, fortuitously, he had been given a gift – a sighter for his weapon.

Riggs started lobbing from the first game. He tells us: 'Every time I lobbed I could hear the crowd holding its breath to see where the ball would go ... Only three ... actually hit the clock. I must have lobbed him seventy times in that match.'

Again a magnificent Budge took the first set, and raced to a big lead in the second. But then, after less than two sets, Bobby twigged that once more his opponent was hurt.

So Riggs lifted.

With superlative defensive tennis Riggs ran everything down, and mixing up drop shots with endless lobs, he further broke up the pace by combining slow moon balls with whippy service aces and hard volleys. Thus, from two set points down, and a deficit of 5–2, he squeezed himself back to win the second set from a tiring Budge.

Into the third set, Riggs realised that Budge was in even more trouble. To Bobby, Budge appeared 'deathly ill'. On the third game of that third set, Riggs gave Budge 'seven straight lobs, all of which missed the clock by a hair'.

Budge got every one of them back. Except the last. At that he was finished. Riggs took the last two sets and the match.

Here was a war of attrition, focussed on the weak point of an injured hero. With such a scenario, it was likely that when Don Budge left the scene in distress, many spectators departed feeling the same.

And the departing victor? How he was laughing ... and no doubt kept laughing all the way to the bank! For there was a further bizarre aspect of Bobby's 'clock victory'. In a match crucial to his future and in which he started way behind, Riggs's prodigious pre-match betting *had continued during play!*

When he began falling behind at the start of the match, odds against him would have begun to increase sharply – if there could be someone there to take them. To Bobby, this scenario was irresistible. Improvising brilliantly, honing skills perfected on his teenage tour with Del Valle, he enlisted the help of brother John to work the crowd. Then, whenever he changed sides – buoyed by influential tennis fans Errol Flynn, Clark Gable and Groucho Marx up in the stands – Bobby used hand signals to continue to place bets on himself. By the time he was a set and 5–2 down, he was getting 10–1 odds against himself pulling off the match!

To anyone else, this would have been so distracting as to be unthinkable. But since Bobby Riggs was simultaneously playing his second vocation, gambling, alongside his first, tennis, he wasn't diverted a jot. In fact the opposite was true: the needle of competition, sharpened by the irresistible lure of risk, touched his primal chords. And he was inspired.

Years later, Bobby was to admit simply: 'I like to play all kinds of games ... but I have to make a bet to play my best.'

The resulting victory – his second of the two warm-ups – not only consolidated Riggs's sense of mastery over Budge, it intensified Budge's feeling of vulnerability. After this match, for the first time, those with real knowledge of the game picked up that the turn-around they had witnessed might not be another flash in the pan.

By the time the pro title head-to-head actually began, Bobby Riggs felt pretty certain that he was the one to put an end to Don Budge's triumphant tennis journey. Yet when it got underway, even Bobby was stunned by how his battle plan was working.

It took twelve matches before poor Budge got his first win! Though a desperate Budge fought back, and began closing on Riggs, the challenger's lead was too great. At the end of the tour, by a whisker, Robert Larimore Riggs was the new World Professional Champion.

To most, the last half of the tour suggested that the great Budge was on his way back to his rightful place on top of the mud heap. However, they were to be disappointed. In the next two years following the tour, in the matches that mattered, the new champion consolidated his dominance over Budge. In winning the 1946 and 1947 US Professional Championships – both against Budge – Bobby Riggs unambiguously retained the title he had snatched from the incumbent in their knife-edge head-to-head of 1946.

Four years after Riggs had become Pro Champion, and just after Jack Kramer had superseded Riggs for the title, the old master Bill Tilden noted that during these last few years he had been 'utterly fascinated' by the 'psychological triangle' of Kramer, Riggs and Budge. To Tilden, by a country mile, here were the best three players in the world – and age and skill were a mere part of what explained the pecking order.

In Tilden's eyes, if mental attitude was important in the match-up between Riggs and Kramer, the difference between Budge and Riggs was 'purely psychological'. And tipping the balance between the two was the mind-set of Budge. 'Unwilling to admit he [was] no longer World Champion', says Tilden, 'Budge had to take on the disastrous strategy of attempting to "blow his opponent off the court"'. So the older man was 'jinxed by Riggs, knew it, and was almost helpless in his hands'.[11]

The issue between Budge and Riggs now becomes clearer: if the great Budge, regal and proud, had been able to stand aside and dissect himself and his infuriating little rival (humbly, step by step, à la Riggs), he might have worked out what he needed to do to escape the spider's web.

How right is Tilden! In the end it was feelings, mere feelings, that held the balance ... and decided who would be king. And how sharp is the old master in applying the word 'jinxed' to the fallen king: to those in the know, the usurper, Riggs, was a natural wizard.

Airtight tennis: the style of Bobby Riggs

As a man who never did anything without an eye to the market, Riggs coined a name for his style. 'Airtight tennis', said Riggs, 'is tennis without holes, tennis without errors. It's defensive tennis. It's keeping the ball everlastingly in play. It's letting the opponent make the errors.'

He says that this is what he did – and it *is* what he did. However this description does little justice to the masterful all court game Riggs came to possess at his peak. A richer picture can be found in the words of those masterly contemporaries, Ellsworth Vines and Julius Heldman.

In his *Tennis: Myth and Method*, Vines summarises the Riggs style as follows:

> Absolute master of all aspects of orthodox tennis from serve to lob. Eastern ground strokes with wristless control; forehand strongest shot but backhand also impenetrable. Excellent serve for relatively small man; can hit flat ... twist or slice. Overhead well placed ... Fine touch at net ... Returns serve beautifully. Game characterised by errorless deep shots and ability to vary pace, which allow him to manoeuvre opponent.[12]

Vines, Riggs's one-time teacher, stresses how Riggs's stature in tennis had always been undervalued – here was a 'classic stylist' whose reputation was further damaged by the later 'show business travesty with Billie-Jean King.'[13]

Dr Julius Heldman also believed that Riggs's style was not only deceptive and misunderstood, but also beautiful and captivating. 'The best founded strokes in ... tennis ... belonged to Bobby Riggs ... [and possessed] an accuracy ... fantastic in depth and direction,' writes Heldman in his *Styles of the Great.*[14]

For a relatively small man, Riggs had an excellent – and deceptive – serve, including an outstanding second serve. In fact, he wasn't as small as he was often made out to be – or as he made himself out to be! At just over 5 feet 8 inches or 173 centimetres he was an inch (2.5 centimetres) taller than Rosewall and Segura, and just under an inch shorter than Laver.

Riggs's tricky serve (and brilliant return of serve) provides one of the extraordinary statistics of the whole era. Touring against Kramer, Riggs out-aced the man who to that time probably possessed the best serve ever

Fig. 3.5. More perfect form from Riggs in this flowing backhand. Note the focus, and power generation from legs and core muscles.

in tennis. Later, Riggs would consistently achieve more aces when playing against the supreme server Gonzales.

Though he called his forehand his 'pet', his backhand, beautifully illustrated in Figure 3.5, was also sweet in defence or attack. Thus, from either wing he could attack, defend, change pace or lob with matchless deception and control. Not to forget his superlative drop shot, sometimes struck with such wicked underspin that his opponent would be infuriated to find the ball bouncing back into the net before he'd got to it. At net Riggs was sharp, balanced and completely at home, with the quick, soft hands of the touch volleyer. He backed this up with a deadly overhead.

Confidence, speed and quickness, along with change of pace and control of spin and depth, made Riggs a master of the 'upset' – the capacity to unhinge power players and turn their pace back against them. To Vines' 'constant amazement' when watching Riggs play Budge, such were the smaller man's speed, reflexes and soundness of shot, Riggs could 'borrow' his opponent's speed – so it was not Riggs, but the harder-hitting Budge, who was incessantly unsettled during a baseline exchange.

Then there was the way he put his game together. Here nothing is more apposite than the comments of Pancho Segura and Jack Kramer.

Segura put it this way: 'Of all players, Bobby could make the ball talk.' Said Kramer: 'Every time I go on court against Bobby, I learn something ...' Then Riggs's long-term adversary added, 'Riggs is an awful pain in the neck when he's on the other side of the net, but when he's lecturing on tennis, I'd pay money to listen.' Then he comments wryly, 'For that matter I usually do ... Anybody who plays cards with Riggs will understand.'[15]

How well had little Riggs learnt from his first coach, Esther Bartosh! Unforced errors were surprising, and not only did he never choke, but, like the greatest champions, played better when he was down, or in trouble. (With Riggs the two were not synonymous.)

The usually restrained Vines summarises the issue succinctly: 'There probably has never been a player who could manipulate an opponent better than Riggs.'

As a consequence, in his prime Riggs knew if he was set, at net or in the backcourt, he wouldn't miss, and he believed that he could return the ball to a small handkerchief placed anywhere on the other side of the court.

In short, he considered that he was smarter, more skilled, and fitter than anybody he would come up against.

This description is sharply reminiscent of another of our great pro champions, Ken Rosewall – fleet, resilient, deceptive. Riggs and Rosewall were dark, slight and wiry, with the springy, thickly muscled legs of the tireless and perfectly balanced athlete. Rosewall's beautiful form, mastery of parry and defence, and capacity to turn power back on itself, made him equally the bane of big hitters.[16]

Surprisingly, these striking similarities are rarely noted: Riggs and Rosewall were indelibly moulded into superlative retrievers; both learned to make a virtue of being small; both were superb naturals who developed all court games based on consistency and sound, impenetrable technique. Finally, through Zenlike awareness, they made themselves strategists who covered their own relative weaknesses, while exploiting their opponent's. And both – despite a flagrant contradiction in personality – learnt and loved the game 'from the heart out'.

So how could you beat either of these two dark 'little masters'? The answer is that you couldn't – unless you were able to combine three things. First, you had to be a great and complete tennis champion; second, you had to be a bigger man; and third, you required a fast court.

Such a combination – even in the Pro Era with its tours of dim halls on lightning-fast portable courts – didn't come up often. Unfortunately for Bobby Riggs, champion of the world and loving every minute of it, after only two years of his reign the three strands of this unlikely confluence arrived together.

A great little man versus a great big man: Little Bobby *vs* Big Jack

By the middle of 1947, Bobby Riggs had dumbfounded everyone. He had established his supremacy over Budge, a player acknowledged as one of tennis's supreme champions. The man whom Jack Kramer had labelled a 'little squirt', now wore the crown of World Professional Champion – and was without doubt the world's best tennis player.

However, as ever, the tiny bunch making up the pro circus realised they needed something fresh. Just when a contender to the crown was required, along came John Albert Kramer, a candidate with everything. He was tall, powerful, a war veteran and something of the blue-eyed American boy. And the No. 1 world amateur. Soon the 1947 Wimbledon and US Champion had agreed to join them.

Once Bobby had cemented his position as top pro by beating Budge for the 1947 US Pro Championship, Kramer and Riggs were readied to compete for the crown: this was the high wire, a hundred-match head-to-head. By tradition, the opener was planned for Madison Square Garden, New York, immediately after Christmas, 1947.

Now, as tennis player and gambler, Riggs had depended in good part on his skill in sizing up, then outwitting, his opponent. Thus he had exhaustively prepared for this challenge against Kramer. It wasn't only that he wanted to prove to the legion of doubters that he really was the best in the world, winning was his life-blood.

There was a further crucial motive driving Riggs: he had to win because the pro system was so shaky there was room for only one at the top. Overnight, the vanquished ex-Champion became a has-been. Bobby had seen what had happened to poor Budge, a hanger-on to the tour after Riggs had snatched Budge's title. If this was the ignominious fate of a star as legendary as Budge, what, he asked himself, would happen to him, a battler whose hold on public acclaim was always half-hearted?

The same applied to Riggs's challenger. And this challenger was particularly shrewd. Unlike many a greenhorn from the amateurs, Kramer knew exactly what was in store for him. Paraphrasing Dr Johnston's famous remark on the power of incipient death to 'wonderfully concentrate the mind', the challenger noted: 'There is no greater incentive [to a player] than the threat of extinction'.

Riggs knew Kramer as man and player backwards.

In the long line of Californian champions, they had grown up beside each other at that cradle of tennis in the West, the Los Angeles Tennis Club. Although Riggs was three years older than Kramer, they were close enough to have played together as juniors, and when they had confronted each other as boys, naturally Riggs had dominated his younger rival. Kramer was to remember that at one stage Riggs had reeled off 27 consecutive games against the younger boy. (Riggs had counted them to his opponent!)

Kramer never forgot what Riggs had once said to him as they left the court after one such annihilation. Turning to his vanquished opponent,

Riggs reminded young Jack that one day they would meet again as men. 'Kid,' added Riggs, 'I want you to know who's the boss, for the rest of your life.' Even then, muses Kramer, Riggs was 'ever looking down the road'. And seeking the psychological edge.[17]

But when the time came for them to meet as men, it was ten years and a world war later. Despite Riggs's posturing that he could handle the challenger whenever and wherever – 'I can beat Kramer every day of the week, and twice on Sundays,' he boasted – the champion knew that Kramer was going to be very, very tough. His opponent was not only the possessor of a powerful, aggressive game; it was coupled with an unflappable and merciless character on court. The younger man wouldn't give an inch to the incumbent champion, or be swayed by his experience or reputation – or by his opponent's infamous gamesmanship.

Facing Riggs was neither a legendary hero like Budge – scarred by war, slightly over the hill and fearful of the consequences – nor a fresh young star, plucked from the green and downy amateurs. Here was a 27-year-old war veteran, smart, tough and hungry.

After 100 matches, arduously drawn out over months, a simple question was about to be answered: who would be the first to win 50?

Before the first clash, let's take a look at the match-up.

At the weigh-in, on our left, is the young challenger, tall, lean, calm. His haircut is Navy-minimal. On court he exudes a sort of concentration that is almost frightening, but off-court, he is quietly charming and self-possessed. Any sharp observer would note: this is a serious athlete, with presence, who will go far.

And on our right? The defending champion is short, wiry, self-important. His hair is a mess. Although dwarfed by the quiet man, never does he shut up. The mien is sideshow hustler crossed with terrier. And in there somewhere is the ambivalent dignity of the circus clown.

But spectators, don't be misled! This one must be just about as serious as the calm guy beside him. After all, he's the champ, and has just knocked over the tennis equivalent of Joe Louis! Nonetheless, he's so full of his own hype... Look! Even now he appears to be at work on another half dozen deals – it's hard to believe he is the champion.

The smart money taking all of this in concludes as follows: if Kramer was a class act, then beneath the showbiz so was the reigning champion. To decide which of these two superb athletes – the cool and tall, or the brash and short – would possess the skill, strategy and stamina to end up the one man standing ... well, they'd need to flip a coin!

In terms of tennis, the opening clash between Riggs and Kramer may not have been one of the game's greatest-ever matches, but the whole caboodle making up their first confrontation was a peak of the Pro Era.[18]

The match was scheduled for Boxing Day, 1947, in New York.

As it happened, a few days before December 26, a hush descended on the great city. Then, quietly, it started snowing. And never stopped. By Christmas Day, New York was lying under the heaviest snowfall in 50 years. The subways were closed and transport grounded. To keep basic services operating, emergency crews were working night and day.

It seemed impossible that the capacity crowd would be able to reach the city's famous Madison Square Garden. Promoter Jack Harris was beside himself. No one could turn up, yet he couldn't cancel because thousands of tickets had already been sold. Further, this match – sensationally billed with only a touch of hyperbole as 'The Match of the Decade' – was the opener of the entire series on which the shaky pro edifice depended.

But they were the pros: they played, wherever. With no promotional papers or TV, no transport and few services, the show had to go on.

On the afternoon of the match, a few blocks away from the Garden, four young men looked out from their hotel. What they saw through the window of the Hotel Lexington was a city brought to a halt. Outside was nothing but a hushed whiteness, empty of people and movement.

The quartet consisted of Riggs and Kramer, together with Pancho Segura and the Australian champion Dinny Pails. Riggs and Kramer were the stars, the hire-wire act of the forthcoming show; Segura and Pails the preliminary bout. Turning from the window, the four looked at each other, shrugged and began to laugh. At that, ruefully, they rugged up and, grabbing their rackets and the minimum of gear, went out on foot into the snow.

Clambering over towering snowdrifts, floundering through streets blocked by snow and ice, ploughing past abandoned vehicles, the four star athletes made their way towards the stadium. With everything so humbly reduced by the unequal weight of nature, they were certain that on arrival the auditorium would turn out to be dark, freezing and empty.

But they were astonished. They found that others, like them, had taken to the streets. In their thousands. Some tennis lovers had even donned snow skis and come in from miles away.

Thus, when the evening bill came up to its appointed hour and Jack Harris gazed around the stadium, he was astounded – and beaming.

Filling the space were ten thousand cheering fans, exhilarated with having got there, and feeling like heroes themselves. Furthermore, they were about to witness their own chosen idols in a performance that, by intervention of the gods, could prove to be 'The Match of the Decade'.

This dramatic confrontation went to Bobby Riggs in four sets. After that, the newly super-aggressive Riggs started pulling ahead. The next chapter

Fig. 3.6. Going to plan. In their first match of their head-to-head tour of 1947, Riggs outmanoeuvres Kramer. Displaying a perfect exemplar of his strategy: Riggs at net, Kramer pushed into the backcourt, Riggs aiming at Kramer's backhand.

will reveal in detail that it was exactly then that Kramer began honing a new style. As a result, by a third of the way through the scheduled best-of-100 matches, he'd whittled back the lead, and the two were tied at 14 wins apiece. After that, the younger man began to get even better, and hauled away.

Almost overnight, the challenger had discovered the elusive combination necessary to handle Riggs. Kramer had made himself into a complete champion, he was bigger, and most of the courts on which they played were lightning fast. To the astonishment of most experts, Kramer ground down his previously indefatigable opponent, finishing up by the more than convincing margin of 69–20.

So the pros had a glamorous new king ...

And the old one? He was far from glamorous, but still a great champion, only 29 years of age, and at his peak.

Yet amongst the scratchy pros, he had just been made extinct.

Cast aside and forgotten

Following a war, a strenuous battle to get to the top of the pros and stay there, and a gruelling tour against the younger Kramer, Riggs appeared exhausted. By tour's end, he was an exhausted ex-champion.

At this juncture something more than bone-weariness started taking hold of Bobby Riggs. A studious observer might have picked it up earlier. When the tour reached Los Angeles, Riggs and Kramer were neck and neck – then Kramer broke away. At that point, it seemed Riggs decided the game was over. The position of best, for which he had schemed and laboured for a decade, was no longer his.

Abruptly this great master – still fit, still young – was well on the way to becoming the 'tired and worn fighter' that Tilden was to observe just a little later. Worse, when up against the new top dog, Riggs knew he was fighting above his weight.

And yet, as was commonly the case with the ever-tricky Riggs, things may not have been so simple. Was Bobby foxing?

At least one person, Kramer himself, thought that Bobby's near-collapse in the second half of the Kramer tour was something more than being overwhelmed by a younger opponent. To Kramer, Riggs was, as ever, scheming – trying to lull Kramer, the promoters and the other pros, into believing he was no match for him. Then, with Kramer overconfident, Bobby could make a supreme effort and win the US Pro to be held after the tour had ended – and claim that he was still the best.

If this was Riggs's stratagem, it nearly worked: to entrench himself at the top, Kramer only scraped in to win that trophy from Riggs in June 1948, and consolidate his position at the top.

After the loss of his crown, Riggs struggled on playing for another three years.

In 1949, in Kramer's absence, he won the US Pro for the third time and, also for the third time, worked his hex to beat the unlucky Don Budge in the Final. Then he decided to have a go at promoting, and sponsored the marathon Kramer–Gonzales tour of 1949–50. Soon after that he largely retired from competitive top tennis. Like Vines before him, he had loved being the champion, and never got used to 'hanging around' fighting for the scraps.

Riggs's premature retirement, preceded by this sudden transition to battered fighter, makes sense only if his career is seen in retrospect. LeCompte notes that he may have been addicted to gambling, but what Bobby lived for was competition and winning, or, more precisely, playing while holding the possibility of winning. Against Kramer, on fast courts, no matter what he did the odds remained against him. So it was no longer worth doing. And anyway, though not his first choice, there were other games to play, games with better odds.

He also found what he'd always said he was after: a rich wife. He'd been divorced from his first wife, Kay, for a couple of years when he met Priscilla. She was not only moneyed but also beautiful. After they married, her tycoon father had found Bobby a job as an executive in his family business.

After moving into a palatial estate in Long Island, Riggs began a new life. In essence he became an (under-employed and over-paid) executive by day, and a gambler by night. He also attempted, without much success, to be a father and husband to his growing family. And he discovered another game – golf. It turned out to be more than a challenge: for a gambler, it was a gold mine. For the only time in his life, tennis became peripheral.

It is tempting to leave the present hero at this point. After all, this book is about eight great tennis players and their era. I also agree with the noble Vines that we should remember Riggs as a great champion, not a notorious celebrity.

However, to deny readers even a cursory description of the events following the end of Riggs's retirement from tennis is to do him an injustice. That would be like attempting to build a picture of Tilden without showing him as he lay dying – alone, his borrowed rackets beside him. For some, the ending of a life provides a sense – or a non-sense – of all that came before.

There is a second imperative to follow up the latter part of Bobby's life. At age 55 Bobby managed to influence the course of tennis, and helped push the game from what it was during the Pro Era to what it is today.

So in brief, let's outline the ups and downs of Bobby's never tranquil life after his retirement as champion player.

During the next 15 years, Riggs claimed that he hardly touched a racket. However, he was playing regularly – if with a group of cronies whose focus was more on gambling than tennis. A couple of times a week, they'd bet on their matches and on anything that moved.

Though at this time Bobby tried as hard as he was capable to make a go of business and family life, by then he was dominated by his gambling habit. And he was suffering in another way: as a sporting star he was becoming forgotten. To the man who always saw himself as a champion athlete, this hurt, and pushed him more inescapably into the arms of his gambling buddies.

Biographer LeCompte tells two revealing stories of this time.

One day, just a few years after his period at the top, Bobby entered some watering hole or other. As ever, he bumptiously announced to the gathering: 'Hey guys, I'm Bobby Riggs, the tennis star!'

The crowd responded blankly. Bobby Riggs? Tennis champ? For the first time ever, no one had heard of him. The new *Bobby Who?* admitted he was devastated.

Riggs's son John told the second story to LeCompte.

Riggs had built a tennis court on their Long Island home, and (fairly rarely) played there with his sons. Said the younger Riggs, 'When we played our dad in tennis, the tradition was the first time you won a set you got a hundred dollars. Of course, this never happened against my dad. But I remember one time playing him when I was a teenager and I was "on." I was up 5–2 in the first set and if I won the next game, I'd win the $100. At the changeover, my dad takes out his wallet and pulls out a hundred-dollar bill. He then ... places it in the alley under a rock. Then he says to me, "I want you to think about that." '

At that point Bobby started – hitting 'undercut spin shots' which were 'bouncing all kinds of ways'. Before long the son was so rattled he had tears in his eyes. Crying out to his father that he wasn't used to these spins, he begged him to 'play normal'.

No dice. As John says bluntly, as far as his father was concerned, the fact that this opponent was actually his son 'didn't mean shit'. Bobby Riggs was playing to win, and wasn't winning everything?

Of course John fell apart, and lost the next five games straight ... and his $100.

In defence of behaviour verging on the cruel, when Bobby himself was a kid this was how his brothers treated him. He might have been also trying to pass on some sort of lesson to his son. Yet the story reveals how driven and chained to his childhood world was this father of forty.

But in the late sixties, the mould broke.

In 1968, finally and as if from nowhere, came Open Tennis. Then, arising from it, a Seniors Circuit. So, at fifty, Riggs found that again he could play competitively.

This was more than Bobby Riggs could resist. He would be practising his true vocation, fighting for his pride and some redeeming glory – and for a payout! Since his early teens he had claimed that, for his age, he was the best player in the world. Now he intended to prove it and, in the process, make a decent buck on and off the court.

And so he did. Once on tour again, his love of the game rekindled, and this incurably restless soul found a sort of peace.

Admittedly, he'd joined a mob of older players, and they played more slowly, and got injured more quickly. However, these ex-champions still played well, and people came to see them not only because they'd once been stars. Indeed, to some experts in the gallery, since the subtlety of these master craftsmen was more obvious, it was as enthralling to watch them in their sunset as in their blazing youth.

Riggs proved his boast by winning, in both singles and doubles, just about everything in his age group. Partnered with the legendary master Drobny, this included the Wimbledon Veterans' Doubles.

After such achievement, when the early 1970s began, and with Bobby well into his fifties, his friends and colleagues began to contemplate a weird possibility. Could it be that, even for this life-long *enfant terrible*, a relatively graceful old age was beckoning?

But no! First came a sudden and uncharacteristic depression. His second divorce appeared to be the immediate precipitant. While to Riggs the marriage split seemed to come out of the blue, to anyone who knew his gambling and womanising, it was coming for years.

After that a shocked Riggs moved back west to California. Again, uncharacteristically, he was drinking heavily. By this time Bobby Riggs was more rudderless and alone than he'd ever been.

However, Riggs was nothing if not a fighter. Nor was he about to go out without a bang. Despite Open Tennis and an apparently more level playing field, he found himself getting het up. And since Bobby Riggs was a person whose practice of subtlety was confined to the tennis court or the gambling ring, when he got het up things started happening ...

As usual, this beef had its origins in Bobby's ego, and his wallet. It seemed to him that the senior men playing the circuit might have been nowhere as good as they once were, but sure as hell they played better than those at the top of the women's circuit. And yet the women got paid a load more than the male seniors!

To Bobby, this was wrong. Soon he was starting to boast to anyone who would listen, that he could beat any of the top women hands down. Then the gambler in him surfaced. Not only could he beat them, he'd put up money to prove he could!

LeCompte points out that it was then that the press got hold of it. America was in the throes of the unpopular Vietnam War and plagued by internal dissent, driven by the civil rights and women's movements. So to many, the offer emanating from this loudmouth of a chubby, middle-aged, male ex-sports star seemed curiously appealing. Indeed, the colourful confrontation Riggs was setting up – pitting women against men, youth against age, and perhaps beauty against the beast – became mouth-watering.

The 'Match of the Century' was on its way.

Celebrated at last

The outcome of these shenanigans was two famous challenge matches. In succession, Riggs was to take on the two top women players, Margaret Court and Billie-Jean King.

The first of these, in May 1973, was against the Australian Margaret Court.

Ms Court was a magnificent tennis champion. However – and crucially – this Aussie country girl was of the retiring and religious type, and a fish out of water in the wheeler-dealer stakes where Bobby Riggs excelled.

Court was half-beaten before the match began. For weeks, Riggs had begun his campaign with a barrage of hype that confused her and dented her confidence. Then, on court, he completed the execution. Bamboozling the naturally tall and aggressive Court – she stood over him by nearly three inches (seven centimetres) – with a masterly display of slow-balling, lobs, and vicious spin, Bobby took her apart in straight sets, 6–2, 6–1, in 57 minutes.

Suddenly, Bobby was famous. Gloating at his triumph, flush with his winnings, he was raring to begin on the next one on his list – Billie-Jean King.

The resulting match-up would become in many ways the tennis event of the century.

After an unprecedented media build-up, this horn-rimmed, middle-aged blabbermouth, this self-proclaimed male chauvinist, had emerged to become a national celebrity – and the *bête noir* of the women's movement. The two were booked for a $100,000 winner-take-all challenge in September of 1973. Las Vegas, Nevada, might have been the best place for this much tinsel, but Texas was close enough – so the match was set for Houston, to be beamed to millions.

By now Bobby was a pig in mud. From the age of 17, he had been out on his own. Then, on his first-ever tour through the back blocks of America, he'd discovered the market, and those indispensible ingredients of self-promotion, hype and image. Remember the self-designed clothes, the big white convertible?

This time, unlike the florid Jack Del Valle of his initiation all those years ago, Bobby's manager was no small-town fixer. Nor was Bobby himself the main promoter of this event – as he had once been, flogging the tatterdemalion pro circus on the back streets of America. Pulling the strings this time was one Jerry Perenchio, whose previous effort was running the two-million-dollar heavyweight championship of the world between Joe Frazier and Mohammed Ali.

Now the global TV networks were scrambling over each other for rights. Cooed Bobby: 'This, baby, is the big time.'

They played before the largest audience to watch a tennis match, then or probably ever. Glued to their prime-time TV were 48 million Americans. The match was beamed to dozens of countries overseas. Perhaps another 50 million people, many of whom had never witnessed a tennis match, watched enthralled as Bobby entered the stadium frolicking on a pannier carried by lovely ladies in bathing suits.

At a respectable distance behind was Billie-Jean, towed in by a beefy football team.

For probably only the second time in his career, on this occasion Riggs had become distracted before the match, and had catastrophically misjudged himself and his opposition. Carried away with his own hype and the razzamatazz surrounding the match, he had become mesmerized by his own prowess and the ease with which he had dispatched Court.

The result? Bobby did more than lose. He lost badly, and played terribly. Worse still, in a killer move, gritty little feminist King, another tough product of the LA Tennis Club, point-blank refused a re-match – and the chance for new bets.

Two contrasting explanations have been given why Riggs buckled in the so-called 'Match of the Century'.

The first, and the one emphasised above, was that Riggs was unprepared and overconfident. Against Court he'd trained hard, and worked a strict, smart strategy. Against King he had fallen under the influence of a Hollywood health quack, and neglected his fitness as well as his match tactics.

The second explanation, articulated most clearly by none other than the old veteran and Riggs watcher Gene Mako, was that after major (secret) bets on King, Bobby had thrown the match. On balance however, Mako's account seems unlikely: all the evidence suggests Riggs was backing himself wildly up to the start of the match.

Is it possible to understand the strange events of the Houston Astrodome, when one of the smartest and toughest players in history – and one most immune to 'nerves' – crumpled so badly that some of his many double faults hit the bottom of the net? If the first explanation given above – that Bobby was drastically unprepared – seems the most likely, the multiple medications he was using might also have undermined his fitness. In particular, it appears that for at least a few weeks before the match Bobby was regularly taking amphetamines – a relative of today's speed, but then known as 'diet pills'. Medical opinion indicates that regular use by susceptible individuals can damage focus, judgement and sleep patterns. This could help in explaining Bobby's erratic preparation for the match, and why he appeared so 'out of it' on court.

The veteran tennis champion Gardner Mulloy had known Bobby since Bobby was 17 years old. LeCompte tells us that just before the King match, Mulloy called in to check on Bobby and his preparation for the match. Mulloy was shocked. He caught his old friend in a room clouded with smoke and surrounded cosily by his cheer squad, a bevy of bosomy young women. For Mulloy's benefit, Bobby then sketched out his future. Cigar in one hand, drink in the other, Bobby explained that it was all as certain as night follows day: his coming victory would usher in fame and fortune in abundance previously undreamt of ...

As Mulloy left, his last despairing and prescient words were: 'You've first got to win, Bobby.'

A few hours after the debacle, Mulloy returned. Before him was a situation unique in Mulloy's 40 years of knowing Riggs. Bobby was alone. Sitting on a couch in an empty hotel room, he stared into space. 'Gar, I've blown it,' was all Riggs could say to his friend.

And he had.

The next weeks were hell for Bobby Riggs. Then one day he woke to the phone ringing. After a few minutes of conversation he realised that all was not lost. Despite the catastrophe, somehow or other it appeared that he not only remained a celebrity, but one in demand. He was still needed!

So began his final fling, and which lasted until close to his death at seventy-seven in 1995.

In a slightly new form, for most of the rest of his life he got to practise his twin passions – and in public, for money. For a price, he played tennis, and he bet on the result. Then, as a part of the package, he also opened things (events, competitions, public wagers, anything going), took on sponsorship and endorsements and was featured in advertisements in newspapers and TV, where he became particularly identified with the *Sugar Daddy* lollipop.

Further, this now-notorious celebrity did challenges. Of course, in public and in private, he wagered on them. And if he won most of the challenges, it seems likely he won nearly all the bets. In a TV show at the time, Bobby said, 'If I can't play for big money, I play for a little money. And if I can't play for a little money, I stay in bed'. Since on most days he played tennis, and on every day he made a bet, by then there was little need for him to stay in bed.

Most of these showbiz contests were related to tennis.

As shown in Figure 3.7a, he took on bets where he was handicapped simply by carrying an umbrella, even when serving, or by being incrementally clothed and booted and carrying an increasingly weighted suitcase. Or he inverted the burden by performing a version of striptease, whereby with each game lost he added to his handicap by shedding one garment of his apparel. Needless to say, the fastest talker in the West would soon be down to his underpants and horn-rims. Only then, and against apparently impossible odds, would come the resurrection – eventually leading to a miraculous (and fully-clothed) victory.

Then there were his infamous contests, so distressing to his family, in which he was handicapped by being chained to various animals. (Donkeys were the worst, he admitted. They 'just wouldn't move'.)

The occasional challenge didn't involve tennis at all, as with his bets against the motorbike daredevil Eivel Kneibel. Whatever, Bobby – by now with a public image deliciously described by his biographer LeCompte as 'well-meaning wise guy, and ageless pixie' – loved keeping the persona going. Why not? He was in the limelight and at play – for stakes.

There was another reason why Bobby felt satisfied. Though he lost the 'match of all time' to King, this weird and singular event had become a watershed. Such was the interest and notoriety it generated, tennis was in the news. Here was a game where both sexes could play (separately and together), get quick exercise and keep at it for life. Tennis boomed.

Clearly, there were other factors working to widen the popularity of the game. These included another tennis event, as different as could be imagined from the Riggs–King brouhaha.

Held a few months earlier, but also in Texas, this match had made an equally precocious foray into the crucial TV market. Chapter 6 details the famous battle for the 1972 World Championship of Tennis between the two masters, Ken Rosewall and Rod Laver. This luminous contest between

Fig. 3.7a and Fig. 3.7b. Ever the antic clown: Riggs, playing for money against a handicap.

these two fair-dinkum Aussies – so pure, so laconic – was to lift the standing of tennis all over the world.

If the tennis explosion of the seventies, beginning in the US and expanding world wide, owed much to the two events in Texas of 1972–73, it was undoubtedly the impure and prolix Bobby Riggs who had conjured up the Riggs–King component and helped push tennis into a million homes around the world. Certainly Bobby believed the match changed things, and he relished his part in widening the popularity of the game.

So the older Riggs didn't care a damn whether his newfound fame grew from being admired or mocked; for an unexpected second time he was doing what he loved – playing, winning and hustling. 'Snake oil, yes,' we can hear him saying, 'but don't the fans just love it.' Once he was asked what he wanted for his epitaph. 'I put women on the map', replied the modest-as-ever, self-confessed and unrepentant male chauvinist.

Before long, the game that he had loved and championed to people of all classes and nations was also the occupation of a group of new professionals, the best of whom were famous, sleek and cosseted beyond the wildest dreams of their predecessors in the roughandready pro circus of yesteryear.

And a fast-talking, short and almost paunchy man, in his fifties, and with a whiney voice, an awful set of glasses and execrable taste, had given the game one hell of a push along that road.

Postscript: the fool and the king

While there was always something kingly about Jack Kramer, the man who supplanted Bobby Riggs as pro champion, Bobby appeared more like the King's Fool. And, like the best clowns, there was a touch of sadness about him.

The Canadian humourist Stephen Leacock loved to tell a relevant story, which I paraphrase here:

A patient visits a doctor.

'I am sad, I have no longer any joy,' he cries. 'Doctor please help me.'

The doctor replies, 'At once you must go to see *The Great Reynaldo!* The great clown's right here, in town. His antics, his asides, his acrobatics – irresistibly, they will reawaken your joy.'

'Doctor,' replies the patient, 'I am Reynaldo.'

Behind the face of Bobby the frenetic imp dwelled a quirky melancholy, but unlike the fictional clown, this one rarely owned up to it. From childhood had arisen an unbearable restlessness: this drove him to the top of his sport and into a life of uneasy contradictions.

Resolutely obnoxious, he craved adulation; in his own eyes a pure sporting champion, he often came across as a cheap hustler, betting on himself when roped to animals, the more exotic the better. And here was an insatiably gregarious man who couldn't bear an hour of his own company.

Yet at every step, from little kid through to amateur champion and top pro, he'd been out on his own, struggling against the limitations of his size and style and the opposition of those running the show. In a way Bobby Riggs forever remained the little boy, insatiably needing someone – a buddy, a gang of cronies, a crowd or the public – to fuss over him. One of his sayings rings with this need: 'The best thing in life is to win. The second best is to lose. At least you have competed.'

Embedded in the instruction chapter of his second autobiography is another revelation.

After emphasising that it doesn't matter a jot what you look like and that what counts is whether you win, musingly he adds an afterthought. He says that looking bad could be of real assistance to a certain kind of competitor, for 'if you can both win and look bad, you can [really] make some money'. So appearances can be deceiving, and useful.[19]

It might be best to conclude this account of Riggs with Kramer's vehement words in his own autobiography, *The Game*:

> Riggs looked like he came in out of the rain, but … I guarantee you he is the most underrated champion in the history of tennis. After all the hustler stuff … I want to emphasise it all the more: if you remember one thing from this whole book, remember that Bobby Riggs was a great champion.[20]

So, with Kramer's help, we can put aside the bells and whistles, the motley, the gibes and the carpetbag, and return to the court. There we find a little man of outrageous courage. Bobby revered tennis, and in order to confront and vanquish the Goliaths, he devised his own delicate dance, and became a champion.

Or no! Perhaps the clown is Riggs's true identity and source of his triumph.

For when he was on court, playing the game he loved 'from the heart out', his demons and his masks were all there for him to draw on, making the act of *The Great Roberto* more various, more mischievous, and more masterly.

Notes

1 Tom LeCompte, *The Last Sure Thing: The Life & Times of Bobby Riggs*, Black Squirrel, Easthampton, 2003. Tom LeCompte's fine biography is a main source for this chapter, complemented by Riggs's own autobiographies, written 24 years apart: *Tennis is My Racket* (1949) and *Court Hustler* (1973), written with George McGann.

2 Bobby Riggs, *Tennis is My Racket*, Stanley Paul, London, 1949.

3 LeCompte, *The Last Sure Thing.*

4 Apparently Bobby's mother saw him play only once. According to Riggs, after the match she came out with the inimitable line: 'Bobby, you didn't play properly – you didn't hit the ball back to your opponent.'

5 Riggs, *Tennis is My Racket.*

6 Riggs explains that Vines also directly helped his game, in particular working up his serve, and showing him how to follow it to net. To the apparent 'back-board', these tips turned out to be vital.

7 For contrast, see the Australian larrikin Ken Fletcher's attempt to scratch a living as a 'creative' amateur in the sixties: Hugh Lunn, *The Great Fletch*, ABC Books, Sydney, 2008, and referred to in more detail in Chapter 7.

8 Bobby Riggs with George McGann, *Court Hustler*, Lippincott, New York, 1973.

9 Budge, *Don Budge: A Tennis Memoir.*

10 LeCompte, *The Last Sure Thing.*

11 Tilden, *Tennis A–Z.*

12 Vines and Vier, *Tennis: Myth and Method.*

13 Vines and Vier, *Tennis: Myth and Method.* Vines' observation is spot on. What with Riggs's short career at the top of the amateurs (mainly in the US, never in Australia), a world war, then another short burst at the top of the fugitive pros, even to knowledgeable tennis buffs Riggs had become a largely forgotten figure after his retirement in the fifties. Then the infamous 'Battles of the Sexes' – and notoriety.

14 Heldman, 'Styles of the Great' in *Tennis: Its History, People and Events.*

15 Kramer, *The Game.*

16 One of the goliaths was Tony Trabert, a magnificent player of the fifties and sixties with an allround power game strikingly similar to Budge's. However, he was bulky, and the very best could exploit his lack of mobility. Taking a leaf from Riggs playing Budge, Rosewall explains in his autobiography that the only way to beat Trabert was to unbalance him with speed, quickness, depth and deception.

17 Kramer, *The Game.*

18 Here we have drawn on LeCompte's lovely description in *The Last Sure Thing* – supplemented by Kramer (*The Game*) and Riggs (*Court Hustler*).

19 LeCompte, *The Last Sure Thing.* LeCompte quotes baseballer Buddy Blattner, who spent two years of World War II with Riggs: 'If you were to line up a hundred people, just ordinary rank-and-file, [and put Bobby Riggs in the line] and say one of these is the number one tennis player in the world, I guarantee you [Bobby] would be the ninety-eight pick.'

20 Kramer, *The Game.*

Fig. 4.0. A regal Kramer completes his forehand masterstroke. The racket has closed over the ball, suggesting the drive was struck with topspin and crosscourt. This shot took years to perfect.

4

KING KRAMER

The new pros learned the hard way that a professional's a player who makes almost all of the easy ones and steals some of the tough ones.

Jack Kramer
Foreword in *The Art of Tennis*

CHRISTENED John Albert, in boyhood he became Jake, then Jack. Later, when he had turned himself from champion player into a businessman so commanding he could frighten tennis federations around the world, he was often called *Big Jack*, or even *King Kramer*. In honoured old age, Jack Kramer was to retain an imperial dignity.

Despite world fame, Kramer was American through and through: a hard-nosed, quietly spoken tough guy who came out of a working class boyhood in Las Vegas and then Los Angeles, two cities as brashly American as you could find. And although he never gambled seriously, here was a man from Vegas who based the whole of his long life on odds and numbers.

Jack Kramer's influence on the game of tennis has been unique – as player, impresario, teacher, mentor, entrepreneur and reformer. As player, his reign as Pro Champion falls right in the middle of the forty-odd years of the Pro Era. As a result, he knew each of our other seven pro champions intimately, drawing from his predecessors and mentoring his successors. Early in his playing days as pro, he began to develop his second pivotal role as the power broker of international tennis; for two decades he maintained this role, which lasted into the Open Era.

Kramer, with help from the admirable Frank Deford, the biographer of Tilden, wrote a wonderful account of his life in *The Game: My Forty Years in Tennis.* [1] We begin with two vignettes, derived from this book and seminal to Kramer's evolution as player and person.

Finding the flow: Zen in unlikely places

In the chapter on Ellsworth Vines, we glimpsed the first of the two vignettes: a boy named Kramer spied two tall men playing a tennis match on a racetrack – and had a vision.

What happened?

It was one day in 1935, and Jack was 13 years old. Coincidently, the pros were performing not too far away his home. The venue for the bunch of pariahs making up the pro circus was fitting: the Pomona Country Fair, set up on the outskirts of Los Angeles.

Jack's father, David, loved all sports, so he decided on an adventure. To catch the touring pros, he would take his son on a journey west from their desert hometown in Nevada through the mountains to California. This was Jack's first big tennis event.

When they arrived, father and son climbed up into the little grandstand above the single court and, with growing excitement, awaited the start of the show.

Two figures in white emerged. When they reached the court the lad's breath was taken away. There is still awe in the words of the older man, telling us about that experience 50 years before: 'If you never saw tennis players in their long white flannels,' he says, 'I cannot begin to explain to you how majestic they appeared ... Then tennis clothes were a rare elegance that could transform a man.'

What followed may have appeared majestic, but 'makeshift' best describes the stage on which this majesty was evoked.

The itinerants, managed by impresario *Big Bill* Tilden, had improvised a clay court from the Pomona racetrack, and the spectators filled the little grandstand beside it. Thus, high above the patch of red dirt, the lad began drinking in the action, spellbound by the men-made-heroes down below. Flashing about in white, to him they moved like gods.

At this point we could imagine father David turning to his young son sitting beside him, and whispering: 'The taller thinner one – that's Vines, Ellsworth Vines. He's the new Pro Champion ... that's the Professional Tennis Champion of the World.'

The boy took in this figure.

It seemed luminous in contradiction: though Vines was whip-chord lean, and his movement about the court sweet, almost light, when he struck the ball, the power was crushing.

In sum, the boy thought to himself that in this wondrous and contrary mix he'd 'never conceived of anything so glamorous'.

'There I was at Pomona that day in 1935: thirteen years old, a poor kid from the desert,' says Kramer in his autobiography. 'And here is Ellsworth Vines, six feet two and a half inches tall, 155 pounds, dressed like Fred Astaire and hitting shots like Babe Ruth. From that moment on I never considered ... any sport but tennis.'

Two years after this trip over the mountains, lo and behold, Jack had become a boy tennis champion! One day, out of the blue, the lad was informed of something unbelievable. He was to get a new teacher. And who was it but the being who had inhabited his imagination since Pomona: glimpsed but once, a star was descending to earth, and to him.

Young Jack Kramer was to be taught by Ellsworth Vines, Champion of the World.

Years later, Kramer describes it more prosaically: 'My big break came in the fall of 1937, when I got to work out with Vines. For about four months we played two long sessions a week at the Beverly Hills Tennis Club ... '

Before long the smitten lad had copied everything he could from his hero-turned-coach, right down to his shuffling walk and slight bum-waggle before crouching down to take serve. In technique, he tried to develop his serve with Vines' slow, sinuous wind-up, culminating in the stock-whip crack of the wrist. As for his forehand, we have Kramer's own words: 'every forehand I ever hit was modelled on Elly's.'

A month after his first lesson came the epiphany.

It happened in a second: he saw the flow of his teacher as if for the first time. The same components of his first vision remained, but now they seem assembled for a different reason. At that moment Kramer grasped that the movement of the master – that surge, light and sweet that had caught his imagination – was not a thing of detached beauty, not just a dance. It was gloriously functional, focussed, purposeful.

'It was at the Beverly Hills Tennis Club one day when it all came together,' says Kramer. 'I remember it perfectly – I was playing with Vines one October afternoon, 1937. I suddenly saw how to be a forehand player. What I saw was how Elly used weight transfer.' Other than admitting that this experience 'speeded up my development by several years', that's all he says about the matter.

While the pupil does not elaborate, the teacher does. Clearly, Kramer is talking about what Vines himself tried to analyse when he was ferreting out the secret of the phenomenal Segura forehand.

Explains Vines: 'On every shot there is a transition point where the weight shifts from the rear to the front foot.' But what Vines calls so elegantly the 'summing up of forces' actually takes place *before* the forward weight shift. The outcome, in terms of maximisation of power, depends precisely on the prior coordination and organisation of 'all aspects of [the athlete's] body'.[2]

Some Eastern martial arts traditions describe the transition Vines speaks of in this way: the first phase involves 'integration and loading'; the second, 'expression' or 'weight shift and action'. While Segura could 'sum up his forces' in every shot, Vines says 'his two-hand forehand was the nonpareil – with every sinew of his body being utilised.' Vines concludes that it was this summing up – or the 'loading' and 'expression' – that 'so dumbfounded players a half-foot taller [than Segura] when they found themselves being out-powered'.

In his brilliant little book entitled *Zen in the Martial Arts,* Joe Hyams explores the process.

Hyams once saw a brave (and foolish) visiting friend question the power of his teacher, the famous martial artist Bruce Lee. Since Lee was slight and small – just about the same size as Segura – the well-built visitor decided to 'put Bruce to the test' and pressed Lee into a demonstration of his strength.

Hyams tells it this way.

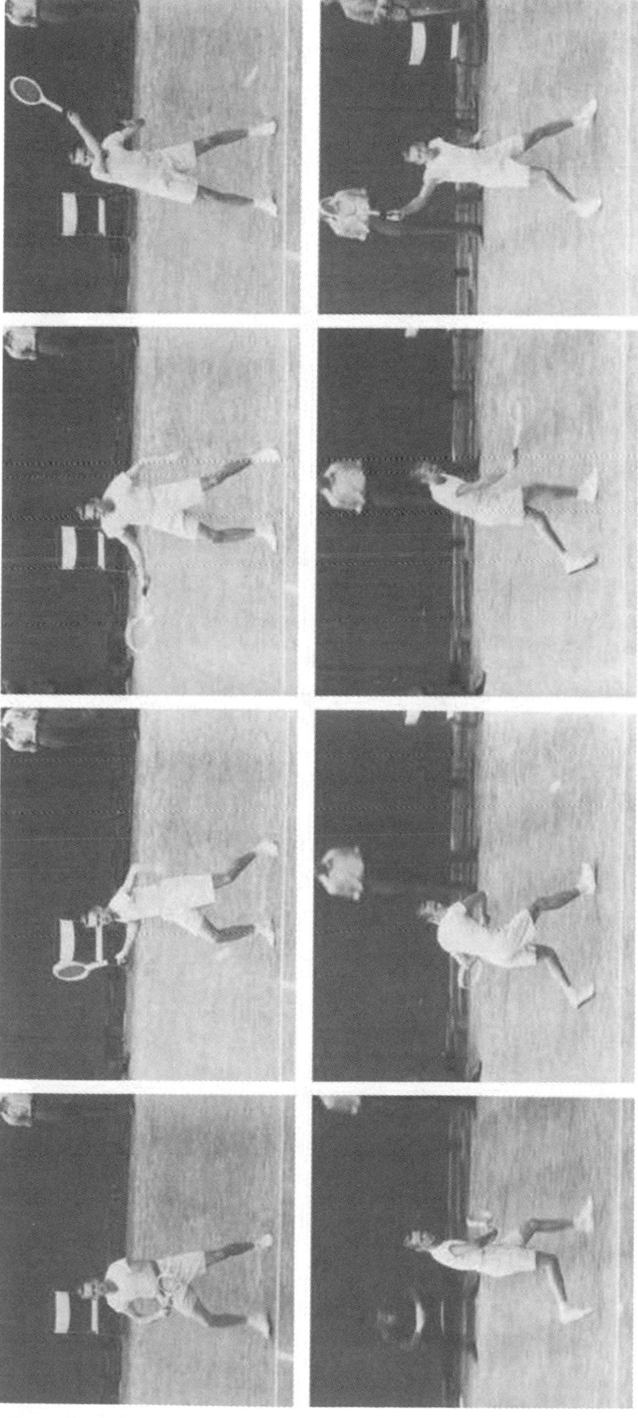

Fig. 4.1. Awesome: the Kramer groundstrokes as amateur. Despite the Big Game, serve/volley tag, Kramer's groundshots were always solid. Note the power-generating shoulder turn on the backhand, and the strength of the follow through on both wings.

> 'Brace yourself,' said Bruce, as he placed his hand, fingers outstretched, on my friend's brawny chest. 'I am only going to close my hand into a fist and I will knock you over.' 'No way,' said my friend, who nevertheless braced himself. Bruce suddenly closed his fingers into a fist — a movement of perhaps one-quarter of an inch — and my friend flew backward into the pool. [3]

This was Lee's famous 'one-inch punch'. According to Eastern teachers, it arises from a concentration of energy, integrating the individual's mental *and* physical resources. It is believed that this power is harnessed from the energy that informs the whole universe, and requires years of discipleship and training to distil. This quintessence is what young Jack stumbled upon that October afternoon.

In addition, and in his own way, the lad in the stands had grasped another aspect of the Eastern way of understanding: such power is believed to arise from an essential polarity between a state of calm and a state of force, the generative move from relaxation to tension. From the age of 13 onwards, Jack Kramer cosseted an image of the explosive Vines, but recognised the calm underlying it. It was Vines' loose-limbed, almost languid figure that harboured his thunderbolts: Kramer's 'Fred Astaire' against his 'Babe Ruth'. While never appearing as loose as Vines, Kramer was to perfect the art of calm, concentration and focus, composing an inner platform from which he could unleash his stroke-play.

Usually smaller men seem better at integrating their energy with maximum efficiency, but Figure 4.1 shows tall man Kramer exemplifying Vines' summation of forces. Figure 2.1 in Chapter 2 pictures another of the few tall ones who perfected the process: Master Vines himself. And Figures 4.2 and 4.3 show two of the greatest of the little masters, Pancho Segura and Ken Rosewall, just when the camera flash captures 'every sinew' being charged with potential energy.[4]

Now we come to the second vignette and turning point.

It is a decade later. Towards the end of World War II, Kramer was in the Pacific, serving as a junior officer in a small landing-ship. By the time they reached the fighting it so happened that he'd become about the most popular officer aboard. It seems this arose from a particular personal preference: only he wanted the so-called mid-watch, from 12 midnight to 4am.

Why?

Fig. 4.2. 'The summing up of forces' No 1. Though run wide, Little Pancho *Segura concentrates every sinew into this backhand.*

Fig. 4.3. 'The summing up of forces' No. 2. A coiled spring, Rosewall readies to return one of tennis's most difficult shots – a wide, high backhand from deep in court.

Kramer explains that it was then, in the dark of night in a vast sea, that he'd begun discovering himself. In a reverberating solitude made more wondrous by being unexpected and unwanted, here was the first chance in his previously hectic life – *to try to work it out.*

It is possible to imagine him, high on the bridge of the little ship, a tall man with the lean, balanced body of the athlete, but a mere 24 years old. The dim light beside the wheel catches the strong lines of his face, his deep-set eyes. Alone and awash, he tells us that it was there that he had begun asking those questions we all need to ask ourselves, and often avoid.

He summarises: '... being cooped up on a boat in the middle of the ocean in the midst of a war ... I had a lot of time to think ... ' With the clarity arising from the knowledge that his short life could easily be over at the next landing, he began by surveying his achievements.

From that pinpoint, he found them wanting.

True, he realised, before the war he had been a very good tennis player. After it, the way he was going, he might end up close to the top. But though he'd worked hard, he saw that he was too soft: 'I had gotten used to enjoying good times, making a few bucks, playing a game that came naturally ... ' But where was he heading? Answering himself, he realised that without money or education, if he didn't get right to the top of tennis, he could easily 'end up pumping gas somewhere ... '

At this point he came to a decision. Tennis would no longer be a pastime: it would be his life.

'Yes,' he concludes matter-of-factly, 'I matured a lot out there.'

Then he admits to a related insight: he realised that you 'have to care to carry yourself past a certain level'. When he saw that he did care, he became focussed as he'd never been: he intended to climb the pinnacle of tennis. And stay there.

Again, the Eastern tradition can add something relevant.

After years of training and discipline, the student who develops control of his craft and of himself may come to possess two hallmarks of the master.

The first comes into being once technique, action and response are freed of the thinking, judging mind – and begin to flow unconsciously. In modern terms, the responses are 'hard-wired'. Japanese Zen masters use the word *mushin* – literally 'no-mind' – to describe the state when mind and action become one.

Then welling up alongside arises a second quality, one the Chinese call *sai*. This captures the master's kind of quiet confidence, a resonant but unobtrusive presence, a gravitas. *Sai* is a sense of power so imbued, so opposite to showy, it may not require exhibition.[5]

Two contemporaries, Adrian Quist and Ken Rosewall, provide a relevant slant on the Kramer character.

Quist put it this way: '[Although] there was nothing personal about it ... Kramer had an air about him, a type of aggression that is hard to define ... he played every point as if it was life and death.'[6]

Ken Rosewall saw Kramer play only when Jack was past his peak, but in his memoirs Rosewall tells us that he retained two lasting impressions of Kramer the player: first, his extraordinary concentration; second, his capacity to know exactly what shot to play next.

Such focus, instinctive timing and anticipation grow out of the cultivation of *mushin*, and lead to the presence of *sai*.

When Kramer re-joined the amateur circuit at war's end, he seemed to fit the image of a crew-cut ex-navy officer on his way to a rags-to-riches American story of fame and success. Further, he doesn't speak of the martial arts in his books on tennis. Yet Jack Kramer had begun to blend instinct, awareness and action with a purity that would have satisfied the most exacting Eastern master – and in the years of difficulties on his way to the top, these reserves were tested again and again.

Bearing in mind these pictures of Kramer at two crucial points in his development, let's turn to his origins.

Depression child

Jack Kramer was born on August 5, 1921, in Las Vegas, the town the gentlemanly Vines describes as that 'garish monument to American greed'. However, prior to the early thirties when gambling was legalised in Nevada, Vegas was far from the symbol of empty glitz it has become. In fact, the place of Kramer's birth was an isolated frontier town, in the midst of a hellishly hot desert. And, says Vines of the town, it was 'a damned poor one'.

Kramer's early childhood was spent in Vegas, and then came the Depression. During his later life Kramer was sometimes accused of being ruthless and money hungry. Perceptively, Vines elucidates: 'Las Vegas explains a lot about Kramer. As a boy, Jack had to endure both Las Vegas and the Depression.'[7]

Kramer tells us that as a grown man, and a rich one, he always carried a stack of cash with him. Foolish he admits, but having 'a couple thousand bucks' in his pocket was security, a throwback to a childhood where he scratched out jobs after school, and the household took in boarders. In Aussie street-talk, the Kramers were battlers, making do with three-fifths of five-eighths of bugger-all.[8]

Jack was the child of David and Daisy Kramer. David was a railwayman who, starting with nothing, had taken a job with the Union Pacific Railroad at age 11, and never left it. Eventually he worked his way up to being a locomotive engineer. Although he took a pay cut, he kept his job during the Depression.

Wife Daisy was a big help. In Jack's words she 'made the dough go a long way ... [and] was the one who kept the family together, always organising get-togethers and outings'. These two built a secure and loving family around their son. Though Jack turned out to be an only child, from early childhood Jack's aunt came to stay. She was only a little older, and became 'just like a sister' to him.

As a poor kid, father David had never had much chance for fun. Now ... Wow! Was he going to make up for it with his own boy! In fact, the father's tough schedule on the trains – shifts of three days on, three days off – worked a treat. During the off days, the lad had a frisky father almost to himself.

And how they played! 'We'd play ping-pong on the dining room table,' Jack tells us. 'He helped me build a pole-vault pit in the yard. I ran races. I was a basketball nut.' While the two tried out most games, and the kid was good at them all, his favourites were baseball, basketball and football.

Though David might have been generous with whatever he had, indulgent he was not. The father required strict standards in the household, and he modelled them.

One story described in Kramer's autobiography is exemplary. It dates from Jack's early days playing Boy's tournaments.

'The minute I started to show any kind of big head,' says Jack, 'Dad would call me "cocky" and stick me right back in my place. One time when I was just starting to win, I began to think I was a big shot, and I carried on a running argument with the umpire. When he called me for a foot fault, I ... threw my racket over the fence. I looked up and saw my father approaching the umpire's chair. I felt like a million dollars: my old man was going to show this guy that his boy couldn't be pushed around. Yes sir!'

But after conferring with Jack's dad, the umpire suddenly stood up and announced the match was over. It had been awarded, by default, to Jack's opponent.

Subsequently, the discussion between father and son was 'very brief'.

' "Cocky," said his father, "you ever do that again, and you'll never go back on a tennis court as long as you live in my house." '

Jack tells us that from then on he never lost his temper on the court in a similar way. Tell this to the 'ugly parents' of the win-at-all-costs brats plaguing today's arenas!

With touching honesty, Jack explains: 'if you want to know anything about Jack Kramer, you must start with my father, because he's the guy who made me. In a nutshell, what is good about me is a gift from my father, and what is bad is my own doing. It is a great comfort in life to grow up secure in the knowledge that your father is the finest man in the world.'

As a part of this priceless gift, father David not only played games with his son – they went places. And as they talked – or maybe just sat watching a game, a train, or the world go by – the son drew on the father's calm well of confidence. With a mother whom our tough guy tenderly describes as 'such a comforting person', this son knew that his family was exceptional. With poignancy, he explains that his greatest regret was that he hadn't bestowed on his own sons the time and attention that his father had given him.

One morning when the lad was 11 years old, father David made an announcement. He'd found a couple of tennis rackets and discovered a court they could use. That afternoon they'd try out a new game!

The court itself stood on the site of what is now one of the world's biggest casinos, fronting the street known today as 'Glitter Gulch'. Then it was the grimy Union Pacific depot, at the back of the main train station. Run down, the court was used mainly for basketball, but David ('who was game for anything', says his adoring son), had noted that tennis lines had been painted over it, and an old tennis net was stuffed away. The pair dragged it out and strung it up.

Thus it was in these less than salubrious circumstances – and via his father – that young Jack received the rudiments of the game.

A nice-mannered boy and a very good student

At first, tennis didn't mean much more to the boy than another way of spending time with his dad. But then David got the chance for a year's advance railroad training in San Bernardino, east of LA.

When the family moved from Las Vegas, the lad got to play more. It was equally important, he tells us, that San Bernardino was where he actually *saw* his first good player. Although unremembered in the annals of tennis, Robin Hippenstiel must have been an eye-catching player, for the young Jack felt irresistibly drawn to the public courts just to watch the older boy play.

'Soon,' Jack tells us, 'I was getting up at six to play with Robin's younger brother Glenn.'

Though he was starting to improve fast, Kramer says he still didn't know a thing about tennis. 'I used one grip for all shots ... swatted the ball and ran all day.'

Nevertheless, eventually this energetic improvisation was good enough to get the lad into his high school team. Before long the team was entered into its first-ever tournament. So at thirteen and a half Jack found himself on the way to a boys' tennis event in Santa Monica.

When he arrived carrying his racket (an old model Tilden Topflight) and wearing a brown mohair sweater, the 'poor kid from the desert' was shocked. In shining white, shorts and shirts pressed, with their hand-knitted V-neck sweaters showing more of the Tilden influence, the other boys had stepped from a clothing catalogue. And each carried two or three gleaming rackets!

'It was quite a gathering,' reminisces Jack. 'Little Bobby Riggs was there, little Joe Hunt [Hunt was to play Davis Cup with Kramer, but perish in the war], little Ted Schroeder. Throw in the unknown Jack Kramer and there were present in one junior tournament four boys who would win six US National titles [and three Wimbledons] within the next dozen years.'

Our hero and rumpled country cousin soon discovered that the splendour of the other young stars, already well coached and being fed into the Californian tennis machine, was not just show. He lost in the first round – and not even to one of the top youngsters.

Eventually, Bobby Riggs won the tournament. And if young Jack had judged that the scruffy terrier from down the road in LA appeared immaculate, how intimidated must Jack have felt!

At this point (Jack's fourteenth year) three crucial developments came together.

First, the lad's visit to Pomona to see the pros not only won the boy over to tennis, it changed the father. With his serene gaze and generous imagination, David Kramer recognised that his child's inner world had been altered by what they had witnessed. When the lad began to prove that the fervour was coupled to talent, David took careful note. With characteristic honesty, the son tells what happened next, the second crucial element in the confluence.

At the end of his year in San Bernardino, David decided he would risk taking a lesser position in LA and move the family there. In LA his son could develop his tennis.

But loyal Jack is anxious for us to get the picture right: 'Now understand,' he says, 'Dad wasn't taking out any tennis annuity on me that he figured to cash in ... later.' At that time, Jack explains, there was little money in tennis, and little evidence that the son was going to have success at the game. Of the move from Vegas to LA he simply says: 'No, Dad just decided it would be best for all of us because I loved tennis and because he loved me.' He adds, tellingly, 'and because Mom wanted to get us into a different world from Vegas'.

Vines is succinct: 'Finally the Kramers made it to a town on the east side of Los Angeles called Montebello – not much of an improvement but at least he was out of the desert.'

Yes, this lad knew caring. A decade later – alone on the bridge of a ship on the ocean in the midst of war – Jack Kramer found the meaning of the term in relation to himself. We can now see that this was a rediscovery – a recapturing of the lambent gift that his parents had once bestowed on him.

After the Pomona Fair and the move to the big smoke came the third part of the confluence: Jack got into the tennis system of Perry Jones.

We have seen how Perry T. Jones ran the amateur tennis world of Southern California, and how the ruler fell out badly with young Bobby Riggs (and would later do the same with little Richard Gonzales). But this new boy Kramer was no pint-sized kid-hustler, cheeky and untidy like Bobby. Nor was he a Chicano skiver like Pancho. Conscientious in everything, young Jack was also tall, and whacked the ball.

Jones's response? At once he made the boy an honorary member of the illustrious Los Angeles Tennis Club. Then, says Jack, 'he kept his eye on me ... He didn't go overboard until I came through some, but Mister Jones wanted a nice-mannered boy.'

Before a couple of years were out – and after the lad had well and truly 'come through some' – Elly Vines re-entered the picture. It was Jones who arranged for the world's best player to provide the youngster with teaching sessions.

As well as Vines, Jack's father David had found young Jack a fine new coach in Dick Skeen. Skeen rebuilt, then vigorously emphasised, the lad's previously inadequate ground strokes, as well as facilitating a skill he would soon perfect – the art of 'concentration'. The teenaged Kramer was further blessed by contact with another of our pro champions, *Big Bill* Tilden himself.

Tilden had by then moved west, and this increasingly lonely figure had made that Mecca of tennis in the west, the LA Tennis Club, his second (or in many ways his first) home. The juniors saw him there most days; soon Kramer had managed to secure sessions with him.

So opportunely were these various combinations coming together, that at 15 years – and un-seeded – Jack was good enough to win the US National Boys' Singles. To those aficionados who, like Vines, kept an eye on the rising talent, the lad was developing so fast that he could turn out to be a 'world beater'.

To these various surges up the ladder, a crucial influence must be added. It appeared in the shape of a fascinating man: Cliff Roche.

Roche had been a successful automotive engineer in Detroit, where apparently he had made his money (of which he had loads) by inventing the automatic transmission. How apt, then, that a man of his background should spend the last part of his life on a mission: to make tennis imitate a seamless and automatic engineering process.

'Until you've gone broke twice, you never really get smart,' Roche, from the balcony overlooking the courts of the Los Angeles Tennis Club, would inform the spell-bound young tyros at his feet. Then having captured for himself the charisma of success and invention, the man the youngsters nicknamed with a touch of irony 'Coach', would be ready, diagrams and blackboard at hand, to expound his (less than charismatic) breakdown of the game.

Roche had never been more than a good club player. But he considered this an advantage, not a handicap. Coolly, the objective scientist – not the sweaty jock – dissected the game of tennis as if it were an assembly line: a set of repetitive actions, a technical process, a combination of forces, spaces and angles. While the end-point was not an object like a car, this tennis sequence did lead progressively to a tangible outcome – a point won or lost.

With a little licence we can imagine him reaching the climax of his spiel: 'And this outcome, the point won or lost, is decided so simply! Yes, boys,' and dropping his voice for their attention, 'you win or you lose the point *in only one way* ... You win or you lose just because one of the two players on that court is unable to return the ball! One guy can't get the ball back into the 27 feet by 39 feet – the one thousand and fifty-three square feet of the opposite court!'

Then he would have added: 'Now I'm going to tell you how to be ... *the other guy*.'

In essence, Roche saw tennis as repetitive actions within a specific and confined space: each action increased the probability of winning or losing, first a point, and then – cumulatively – a game, a set or a match. After elaborate study, he claimed that he'd worked out what a player, faced with such geometry, needed to do to increase his winning probability.

In essence, he argued: first, put yourself in the right spot at the right time; second, choose shots and construct points that hold the maximum chance of hindering your opponents from reaching *their* right spot and hitting *their* best shot.

After some time, this analysis came to be called 'percentage tennis'. Vines in his *Myth and Method* warns that though Roche's distillation may sound 'obvious and simplistic', if thought out in Roche's way, the ramifications are complex and heady.

Central to Roche's argument was the value of the net position. Since it is easier from the forecourt to hit the ball in *and* to achieve better angles, there was usually an incremental value in being closer to the net.

Like most inventions, Roche's had its predecessors. In particular, it drew on the 'zoning' theory of Vines' coach Mercer Beasley who, by extending the Tilden approach, inspired many young stars including Vines and Budge.

Beazley divided the court into three zones after the red, yellow and green traffic signals, and corresponding to the back-, mid- and forecourts. Each offers different risks, and likely outcomes and necessitates different responses.

In the red zone behind the baseline, the likelihood of an outright winner is low, and the smart response is defensive or temporising. The yellow zone from baseline to service line, allows for more aggressive hitting, depending on the score, your opponent's skill and your court position. The green zone approaching the net, where the angles of placement are wider and your opponent has less time to get set, offers the greatest opportunity for all-out attack.

But Roche took the 'zoning' theory further.

First, he emphasised that the objective was the green zone: *the goal was the net*. He urged upon his acolytes that victory favours the brave, that attack is easier from close in, and that they should be perpetually making plays – the right plays – to allow them to head net-wards.[9]

Roche argued that the odds could be shaded further by bearing in mind several other variables. These included whether the player was receiving or serving, and the state of the score.

'You can never lose a tennis match if you never lose your serve', argued Roche, and of course in the days of five-set matches without tie breakers, this was indisputable. So he taught that one's energy should be directed at winning serve, then conserving oneself to tighten, but carefully and judiciously tightening, the screws on the opponent's serve ... until it cracks. Kramer was to become a peerless master of this component of 'Rochism'.

To Roche's calculating mind, the state of the score was also crucial. Jack was taught that in any one game, 15–30, 30–All or 30–40 were *the* crucial points where risks must be reduced, odds enhanced.

On these points, if serving Jack learned to 'work the percentages' by getting in a good, but not hugely ambitious, first serve, usually to his opponent's weaker backhand wing, and playing the point as if everything depended on it. But if the score was 30–Love, he would loosen up a little. Giving himself a longer lever by sliding his hand a little down the handle so the butt sat more in the palm, he could risk the big ace – perhaps his vicious wide slice, or, his favourite, the cannonball down the middle.

However, a key to the 'percentage game' was recognising the right ploys to reach the key 'green' zone of the net. Apart from the serve, the overwhelming favourite was the heavy forehand down the line, and landing the ball every time in the 2-foot-by-3-foot rectangle in the backhand corner.

Despite preaching a barrage of attack, Roche acknowledged that, sometimes, the forward surge needed to be postponed. Then, if Roche's player had been forced back into a baseline exchange from the backhand side, unless he had the chance of a certain winner down the line he was urged to return with a deep crosscourt.

To 'Coach' Roche, tennis tactics were so damned simple. We can imagine him exhorting his pupils: 'Boys, if crosscourt backhands earn more points than backhands down the line, and down the line forehand approach shots earn more than crosscourt forehands – and see here from these figures just how they do! – never use the backhand down the line, and never come in behind a forehand crosscourt!'

So, underlying the Roche approach were 'sequence routines', plays that followed one another and ratcheted up the odds. What Roche aimed for was that his players would become – like his preferred motor car gear change – 'automatic'. They would limit their choices to a few shots and plays, each grooved and indestructible. They would choose attack, but would base this attack on focussed patterns that, by building pressure, favoured them in the long haul.

To label this analysis simplistic is to do Cliff Roche a disservice, for there were three subtle but crucial aspects of the method overlooked by most tennis followers.

The first was that the emphasis on attack was designed for fast courts (in those days cement and grass, plus indoor wood for the pros). On slower courts, the odds were the other way – with the baseliner. Kramer himself admits that he only learned how to 'play dirt', that is slow clay, when he was a mature pro facing that clay court master, Bobby Riggs.

The second qualifier to the apparent attack-at-all-costs method of Roche, was the matter of the relative skills of the opponent. Roche's unalloyed, net-driven percentage game presupposes that his follower's serve and volley can outshine or at least stand up to the opponent's ground game.

Here Kramer himself again reveals his grasp of his teacher's method: he admits there were some opponents – in his case, less than a handful – so supreme in their return of serve that it was disastrous to follow in every serve against them. In fact, instead of contradicting Roche's theory, this tactic extends it: against these maestros, there was no percentage in going in on every serve.

The third and final qualifier was that the 'advanced' Roche method demanded an unusually smart head to drive it! Indeed, according to Vines, Roche's theory would work only if the player had a measure of serve, strokes *and concentration* of a Kramer to carry it out. 'Kramer,' said Vines, 'had one of those computer-like minds which allowed him to mix up the sequences and still keep everything in order.'

Above all, Kramer owned one extraordinary weapon: his serve. What Roche's strategy seemed to do more than anything else was allow Kramer to hone this weapon. If there is one thing that opponents and close observers of Kramer speak about with awe it is his serve, and above all his second serve.

Listen to Ellsworth Vines, a man who knew serves, in *Myth and Method.* The master tells us ringingly:

> Kramer's first serve had a perfect relaxed motion, precision and penetrating power, but his second serve was unequalled. His ability to 'spot it' wherever he wanted it with no apparent effort was astounding ... Kramer had total command [of all variations of serve] ... He was as likely to ace you on a second as on a first, then trip you up by using the kicker as his first delivery on the next point.

The subtleties of the Kramer style become even clearer when we hear what he himself has to say about his serve, return of serve and forehand.

He tells us that the most important single shot in tennis is the second serve: it must make a dependable platform from which to attack, and restrict your opponent's chances of doing so. Then Kramer adds that 'at the other end of the court' an attack by the receiver on the opponent's second serve is also an essential 'percentage' ploy. Why so, when this appears to hold no percentage? Kramer's answer: because it shifts the confidence from the server, who should have it.[10]

If you use Roche's system in these ways – so Kramer is arguing – at most times against most players you can build a kind of attack that will not only work, but also strengthen your own confidence and weaken your opponent's. However, as Vines emphasises, to do this consistently against decent opposition, you need to possess a sound game, a back-up of solid ground strokes, a hell of a serve and volley, and a smart head.

Germane to this discussion is Kramer's use of his forehand drive.

In making an approach to the net, on the backhand the forward attack comes naturally: the well-produced stroke unwinds from closed to open stance, swinging the player into a fluid movement that surges to the net.

But the usually more powerful forehand starts with the body opened up, and sometimes with the player squared to the net, before the strike is made by closing the arm into the body. (This point is made of the time before the recent fashion for square-chested, hugely top-spun forehands, in which the player remains exaggeratedly square to the net throughout.) Nevertheless, both the sideways, open-to-closed stance and the modern 'stay-open' stance, make it much harder to convert the forehand stroke into a forward movement.

Yet here, as on serve, Kramer was exceptional: having internalised the Vines' coiled spring, even when pressed and on the baseline, he had cultivated something more than the ability to maintain his forehand's power and depth. He found that 'naturally' his version of the Vines 'summing up of forces' was balanced enough to set up a platform from which he could surge forward, with a thrust that resembled one of his father's freight trains. This uncanny facility opened up endless opportunities for attack.

Serve and forehand: these were the two components of his game that, in his prescient words, 'set me apart [and] couldn't be taught'. Then in a few words in his autobiography, Kramer himself gets to the essence within the essence: 'Very few experts figured out what I was doing and how unusual it was ... [and so] I busted up all the percentages.'

In short, the making of the Kramer game seemed to be a rigorous application of Roche's method based on a systematic exploitation of winning odds. But something lifted it beyond that. This pupil – that conduit of Master Vines' divine flux of energy – was quite capable of breaking the rules he seemed to abide by so meticulously. On serve and forehand, he could take risks with such confidence and with such skill that the points swung his way. Indeed, to his opponents, they swung with the lugubrious regularity of a tolling bell.

Bobby Riggs says everything when he describes precisely what enabled Kramer to beat him: he couldn't 'get set' on Kramer's serve, more his second than his first. By Kramer's maturity, nor could anyone else. But this 'unsettling' of his opponents was not confined to Jack's serve: as noted, there were plenty of other permutations Kramer's 'computer mind' could string together to unbalance the fellow on the other side of the net, together making it just about impossible for his opponent to amass sufficient points to take a five-set tennis match off the master.

Though Roche's expositions from the balcony may have been dazzling, at first few took any notice. Indeed, according to the wonderful Julius Heldman, it took years before Roche found his 'first disciples' – none other than Jack and his buddy and doubles partner, Ted Schroeder. But as time went on, more would-be champions and their coaches started taking in Roche's ideas, and the so called 'Big Game' was on its way.[11]

Inadvertently, from the first, we can see how Roche had also touched a stream from Kramer's boyhood back in Vegas. There, though father David had sworn off betting from his son's birth – and son Jack played cards only for fun – the family knew gambling, and had taken in dealers as boarders.

We can visualise them on a stifling Las Vegas summer evening, spilling out onto the front veranda of the Kramer house:

Tough, quiet, single men on the edge of things, they gather around the card table. Intently, fluidly, they shuffle the cards. All the while, just outside the circle, a young boy, Jack – or Jake as the dealers dubbed him after their own preferred term of 'jakes' for jacks in cards – follows their every move with matching intent.

To a lad who'd absorbed an understanding of risk and odds with his mother's apple pie, Roche was seminal. Eventually, the appeal to the rational meshed with his vision of tennis as a concentrated flow of energy. With this marriage of head and heart, he could weigh the odds, sharpen the point of attack – and then, concentrating the gods' sweet flow, bust the odds and crack the game apart.

Yes, few understood what he was doing. Nor did he say much to enlighten them. But after such a felicitous confluence, Jack Kramer was away.

Dark clouds with silver linings

By the middle of 1939, world war – at least in Europe – seemed inevitable. By August, when young Jack turned eighteen, it had begun.

As it happened, just before this birthday and the opening of hostilities in Europe and Asia, John Albert Kramer made his entry on the world tennis stage. He was picked in the team to represent his country and defend the Davis Cup.

The confrontation with the challengers from Australia proved so dramatic – and so inspiring to our young hero – that a brief description is irresistible.

On the first day of the tie, the Cup looked to be securely American: Bobby Riggs and Frank Parker won their singles to put the US 2–0 up. Since there was no dominant doubles combination in the US team, in an all-or-nothing move the selectors picked a pair of brilliant teenagers – Jack Kramer and Joe Hunt. They were to be thrown into the key rubber against the great Australian team of Adrian Quist and John Bromwich. At the age of 17 years and 11 months, Kramer became (at that time) the youngest player to play Davis Cup.

Despite youth and the occasion, in their Cup debut against the world's best doubles team, Kramer and Hunt never cracked. After being up a set and with a break in the second, they were worn down by the uncanny strategic sense of the pair opposite them, particularly wizard playmaker Bromwich.

Figure 4.4 is a set of stills taken from a movie made of the match. It shows exactly what the young Americans were up against – like a chess master, *Brom* manipulates the other three players as if they were pieces on a board. Though the two lads lost, it took four tough sets, and the newcomers had earned themselves the greatest respect.

After clawing back the doubles rubber to make it 2–1 to the US, the Aussies were still in it. The final day was to provide one of tennis's great climaxes. Taking it all in from the stands, enthralled by every ball of the day, was teenager Kramer.

Australia's No. 2 was Adrian Quist. A brilliant doubles player, Quist was outside the very top in singles. Here he was facing Bobby Riggs, the amateur world No. 1. But Quist took in the circumstances: a looming war, his battling little country, and against him the Wimbledon and US Champion. And was inspired. Taking great risks, and playing the game of his life, Quist upset Riggs.

The two countries were now locked at two matches all.

The decider was up to Parker and the eccentric Australian master John Bromwich. (Bromwich keeps bobbing up in this story, rather like a brilliant bit-part actor who makes repeated cameo entrances, and steals scenes.)

The Aussies called him *Old Brom*, which catches something of his saurian mien. This time, as Bromwich shuffled out on the court carrying his half-dozen rackets with their pencil-thin handles and fishnet-loose stringing, so dire was the occasion that his legendary dourness seemed impenetrable.

Dourness also characterised his opponent, Frank Parker. Don Budge explains that once he and Groucho Marx were watching a match of Parker's. 'Inevitably,' says Budge, 'Parker came across as utterly cold and unemotional. The match was half over before Frankie showed ... any expression at all. He pursed his lips.'

Tennis lover Groucho whispered to Budge, 'There's that Parker, hysterical again.'

This time, tennis writer Allison Danzig was in the gallery to witness the two 'hysterics' play the climactic Davis Cup match.

In the first rally between these two human backboards, Danzig said he counted an almost unbelievable 90 *shots* before poker face No. 2, Parker,

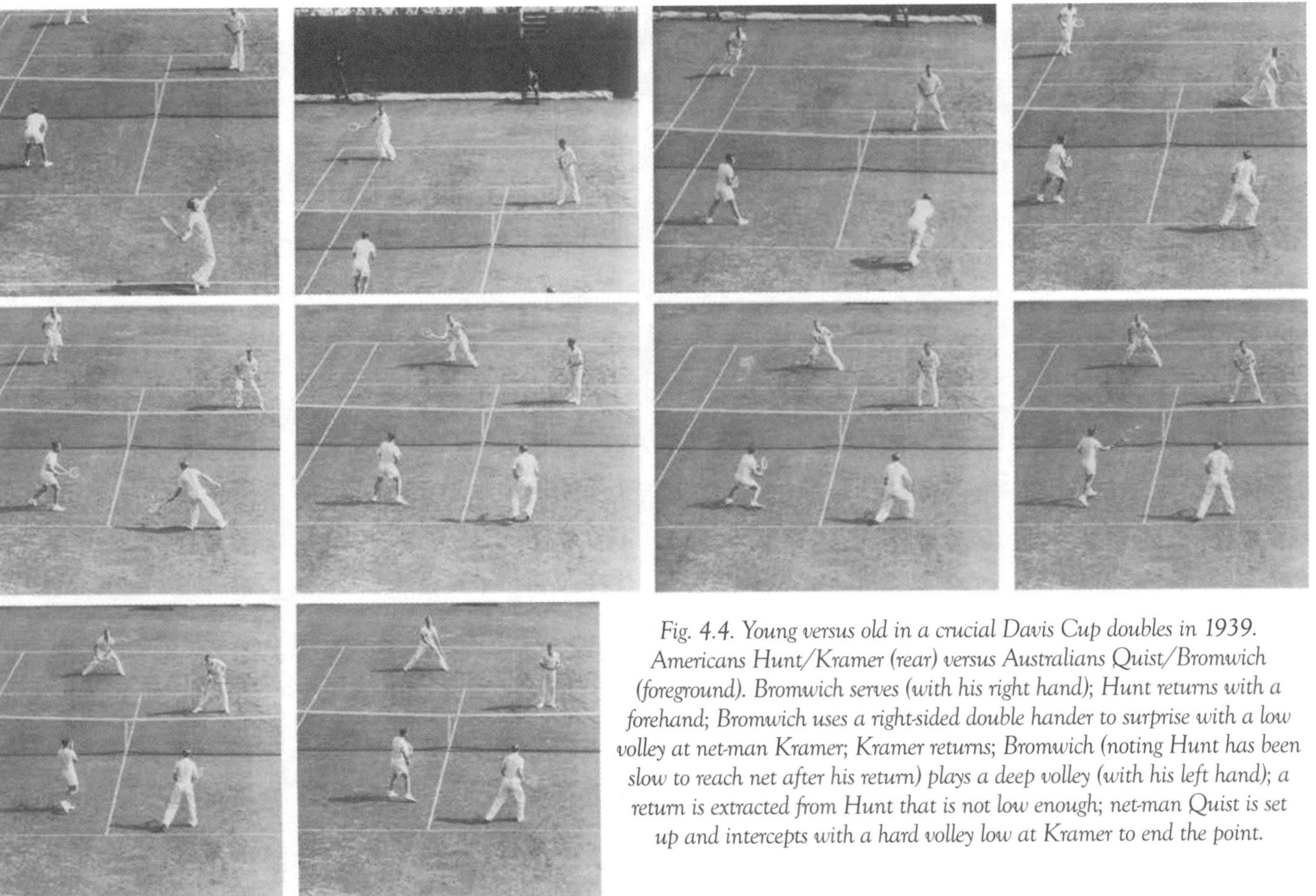

Fig. 4.4. Young versus old in a crucial Davis Cup doubles in 1939. Americans Hunt/Kramer (rear) versus Australians Quist/Bromwich (foreground). Bromwich serves (with his right hand); Hunt returns with a forehand; Bromwich uses a right-sided double hander to surprise with a low volley at net-man Kramer; Kramer returns; Bromwich (noting Hunt has been slow to reach net after his return) plays a deep volley (with his left hand); a return is extracted from Hunt that is not low enough; net-man Quist is set up and intercepts with a hard volley low at Kramer to end the point.

netted the ball. (Quist said 90 might have been an exaggeration, but in his count the rally lasted for at least 40.) In any case, from that excruciating point on, it was all Bromwich – and, three matches to two, a stunning victory to Australia.

With the match ended and the Cup awarded, the young Kramer watched the victorious Aussies make a hasty exit for an even greater contest: war service. Proud and moved, he knew he'd taken in the world stage and seen what it demands of character.

After this sensational entry at the top of the tennis world, the 18-year-old Jack Kramer was tennis's hottest property, and a dazzling future seemed around the corner. In Figure 4.5 Jack and buddy Ted Schroeder, still teenagers, are snapped having have just lifted the US Doubles.

Fig. 4.5. Victory as teenager. After winning the US National Doubles of 1940, teenagers Kramer (right) and buddy Ted Schroeder look unbelievably young.

Yet, during the next crucial six years of his early manhood, in a period further dislocated by war, Jack suffered a series of setbacks that might have permanently damaged someone of lesser resources.

In 1939, in his first attempt at the US Nationals, he lost in the early rounds. Then the lads Kramer and Hunter bowed out in the key Davis Cup Doubles just described. The next year he was out of the US in the semi-finals, and the year after that in the quarters.

After the wartime break, and despite the deepening maturity and renewed commitment discovered during his years in service, the disheartening run continued. Though top seed at his first Wimbledon in 1946, he didn't even get to the finals. Stopping him was the wily lefty Jaroslav Drobny, later to be the young Rosewall's nemesis in a Wimbledon Final.

By then people were beginning to ask: was this obviously strong man flawed? And when David Kramer's son refused to make excuses for his defeats, the doubts increased. But in hindsight, there were reasons behind these apparent failures.

In essence, he was dogged by bad luck.

In two of his defeats in the US Nationals he had to play with gastroenteritis, one from a dish of clams. Then there was the match against the brilliant but flawed Frank Kovacs, on one of his days so made in Heaven that – as Don Budge said pungently – 'you might as well stay home'. And during one (wartime) US Championship, appendicitis had forced Kramer's withdrawal. For most of this time he was also troubled with blisters on his racket hand. Against Drobny at Wimbledon, they were so disabling that even picking up the racket before the match was painful.

Then things came together. Blisters gone, and a diet devoid of seafood, he became more lean and hungry; within, the masterful qualities of *sai* and *mushin* had been incubating.

The change began to show in 1946 when he led the US team down-under to retrieve the Davis Cup, stolen from the Americans prior to the outbreak of war. Triumphantly, the Americans brought it home, with Jack winning both singles and doubles with buddy Schroeder.

The next year they swept through the Australians to retain it.

But this was not Kramer's only triumph in 1947. At Wimbledon he made it to the final without losing a set, then annihilated his opponent in a record 47 minutes.

After his Wimbledon win and a second US Championship, Jack Kramer was untouchable. Although he did not try to emulate Budge and win the Grand Slam, by then he was not just the World No. 1 – there wasn't a single amateur who could give him a decent game, at least not on the fast courts on which all the big tournaments except the French were played at the time.

If the overdue triumphs proved his resilience, Kramer later believed that his delay in reaching the top of the amateurs had been a boon. If he'd got there earlier, he reasoned, it was likely that the pros would have lured him with an offer too good to refuse. If thrown into the pro cauldron at that stage he felt that he couldn't have handled a just-over-the-hill Don Budge, let alone Champion Riggs, at the hill's summit. And, in the scratchy little world of the pros, he would have ended up another also-ran.

So at the end of 1947 when he did turn pro, Kramer was still learning; but twenty-six and battle-hardened. Facing him for the pro title was Bobby Riggs, the man who'd once been the victor in Jack's first-ever tournament, a tournament where the 13-year-old Jack hadn't got past the first round. They were now mature men, war veterans who, first-hand, had known victory and defeat in its most extreme form: life and death.

The sporting stakes were high. First prize was the crown of the tennis world, and a lot of money spread over at least the next couple of years. Second prize was quite a lot of money, followed by virtual ignominy.

At this point the challenger realised that here was the test he'd once glimpsed, alone at war, lost in a sea of midnight reflection. Here was another ordeal: against one of the toughest and smartest racket wielders ever, Kramer was to face one hundred matches, night after night, in a three-month tour played over several countries. Here was his chance to answer those questions of meaning and worth that, with death at his right hand, he had once asked himself.

A calm internal voice reminded him: *Win or lose, I am about to learn how much I care.*

Kill or be killed – Riggs versus Kramer

I have explained how, up to this point, the new pro Kramer had evolved a style that was more attacking than that of most of his predecessors. But it was the Riggs tour that made Kramer fine-tune his game into an even more aggressive form, and one that would become the springboard for the influential 'big game'.

What happened?

Riggs, confident and ruthless, had decided precisely what he intended to do to expose Kramer's game: paradoxically, and from the first match, the master defender intended to attack at every opportunity. By doing so, he would seize the net and, with his focus on his opponent's relatively weaker backhand wing, dominate from there.

At first Riggs's strategy ran like clockwork. The opener was the famous match described earlier as the 'Match of the Decade', and played in a New York paralysed by the worst winter storm in 50 years. After winning this match, and as the train pulled out of freezing New York, an ebullient Riggs summoned Kramer and promoter Jack Harris.

'Sit down boys,' Riggs told them, 'and hear why things have just changed.'

Then he told them that he wasn't the underdog any longer, and just proved it. So he wanted his contract re-written. Reluctantly, the furious promoter and shell-shocked challenger bowed – and the cock-a-hoop Bobby had squeezed another two and a half percent of the winnings!

For challenger Kramer, his first two days as a pro could hardly have been more demanding: playing in an ice storm, enduring a bad loss, and being forced into a cut-price contract.

What was the challenger's assessment of the evolving situation?

After providing a glowing account of the completeness of Riggs's tennis, in *The Game* Kramer has this to say about what then eventuated.

> [Riggs's] strategy was to smother me. That sounds ridiculous, given my … size and power, but Bobby had the confidence, the speed and the agility. When we first started touring he came at me on his first serve, on his second serve, and on my second serve. He could come to net on his second serve by lofting a high-bouncer into the far corner of my backhand service box. I couldn't generate any real power, and with the high bounce, he [could take] the net.

At the beginning of the tour, Kramer had not perfected the kicker serve, and was not regularly following in his second serve. So he was finding out that Riggs, not he, was usually first to net. And this was occurring not only when Riggs was serving, but also when Jack had the apparent server's advantage! Worse, and as neatly illustrated in Figure 3.6 in Chapter 3, Kramer was often facing Riggs sitting on net, having been opened up by a deep knife into his backhand.

For the first time in his tennis life Kramer, the disciple of *Win-Your-Serve-At-All-Costs* Roche, was finding himself in a 'crazy situation'. Unless he was getting in an unusually high percentage of great first serves, he was the one more vulnerable to service breaks.

So, after the first dozen matches, what did Kramer do? On the road in his first pro tour, getting behind against an increasingly confident and aggressive champion, he decided on two things, and fast.

First, he made technical improvements.

He built up his American twist or kicker, so giving his whole serve more variation and bite, and a better platform for the net. Before too long Kramer's twist serve became one of the best.

He also developed his backhand return of service. While he couldn't ever jump it with topspin *à la* Budge, he taught himself to hit earlier, and harder. Immediately this helped him get on more even terms with the server. Before long, despite – or, in this case, because of – constant pressure, his whole backhand stroke started to improve.

Second, strategically, Kramer decided that in this do-or-die situation, it was he who was the bigger and stronger. It was he who needed to 'think attack constantly'. He found he had to 'rush in and try to pound [Riggs's] weakest point – his backhand which had control, but not much speed – pound it, pick on it, smash it till it broke down'.

Kramer summarises: 'For the first time it was kill or be killed. So the style I became famous for was not consciously planned; it was created out of the necessity of dealing with Bobby Riggs.'

He tells us: 'I was beginning to get comfortable with this new style [all-out attack] by the time we hit Los Angeles.' At that stage Kramer had fought back to twelve matches apiece.

He expands:

> After we split there, we went up to San Francisco: I won there and a couple other places. Then we flew to Denver, and Bobby got something started with the stewardess, and that gave me Denver ... Then to Salt Lake City, where we played on a tremendously fast wood surface ... and all of a sudden, from dead

> even I was up six or seven matches. That was it. In one week the whole tour had come apart.

Riggs, in *Tennis is My Racket*, put it his own way.

> My arm was growing weary ... my serve was slowing down a trifle ... Jack leaped to take advantage of it ... [and soon] he was murdering my serve ... his [formerly mediocre] backhand blossomed ... I began to get discouraged ... [so] naturally he ... [felt more] confident ... his serve [got] faster than ever ... he went for the kill every time ... [leaving me] hanging on the ropes ...

With grim finality Riggs adds, 'From that point on, Jack had the tour wrapped up in cellophane ... he always won the close ones ... I was exhausting myself in a losing struggle ... One night I stood him off until the sixth match point ... But Jack got the last one. He invariably got the last one.' [12]

The upshot? After leaving California ahead of the champion by a mere 16 to 15, the challenger won 53 of the next 58 matches, winning the tour 69–20.

Yet to settle the succession Kramer still had to win the US Pro, scheduled just after the tour ended.

If, by some generous fate, I could revisit one of the many great contests of the Pro Era, this event would be my first choice. It held – on a knife-edge – the future of not one, but three, of the game's greatest players.

First, the great and unlucky Don Budge was there for his final fling at the top spot, cruelly snatched from him. Second, gambler Riggs was plotting to sneak back to the top by stealing the tournament, so proving that the tour against Kramer was an aberration. Finally, new boy Kramer was trying to show he was the goods.

Both Budge's last-ditch comeback and Riggs's steal nearly worked. And Kramer himself needed every shred of technique and guts to even reach the semi-final against Budge. He'd been nearly knocked out in the quarters. Welby Van Horn, playing the game of his life, finally succumbed to Kramer 3–6, 16–14, 4–6, 8–6, 6–4.

Although forgotten by history, Kramer's semi-final against Budge must be one of tennis's most poignant matches.

After nearly three hours of superlative tennis from both players, a fired-up Budge was two sets to one up and holding two service breaks in the fourth. Then came disaster for the part-time veteran: with Budge crumbling with cramps, Kramer managed to climb back and take that fourth set. With the match tied at two sets apiece, ruthless-eyed, the younger man then saw it all: Budge was shattered.

In the final set a pitiless Kramer found the resources needed; poor Budge had used up his. The set went to Kramer 6–0 – and so the match.

As the umpire announced game, set and match to Mr Kramer, what must Budge have been feeling? He was not, simply, spent. Gone was his last hope of a comeback. Gutted, appearing to Kramer as 'grey and swaying with exhaustion', Budge could hardly walk from the court.

After that it was the Final, against a Riggs whose path had been easy, and who was now on *his* last make-or-break.

A grim first set went on and on before Kramer could break Riggs's serve and take the set at 14–12. In the second, Kramer got ahead early, and soon Riggs was two sets to Love down. But coming back was the Bobby of old: fighting like the terrier he was, Riggs took a masterly third set, and the match was far from over.

Kramer tells us that he realised that this was his point of no return. He'd tracked a debilitating road to the Final, Bobby was fresh and on a roll. If the match got into a fifth set, he felt that it was Bobby who must be favoured. And he who lost this match, lost everything.

The focus then narrowed further. As Roche's man Kramer saw it: the one who first gave up a service break in this fourth set was likely to lose the set – and the championship and all that went with it.

This was how it turned out. All that was needed was a single break. And it was Riggs's serve that cracked. Kramer, as intense as ever, held his own serve to close out the match in four sets.

Now, one way or another, without a bleat from Bobby Riggs or anyone else, Jack Kramer was the World Professional Champion.

This was the beginning of a long reign for *King* Kramer. It was fully five years before a succession was decided. And, for the only time in the Pro Era, the imperious champion determined his successor.

Re-stylising Tennis – 'The Big Game'

After the Riggs tour, and then convincing head-to-head victories over Gonzales and Segura, Kramer's game had peaked. To add to his frighteningly efficient attacking game, he now possessed a magnificent set of ground strokes, which he could use masterfully in defence as well as attack. In some concession, master lobber Riggs ruefully admits that by the end of their tour Jack would sometimes humiliate him with a darned smart lob.

When Kramer was at his peak in the early 1950s, what did his game look like?

Kramer's service motion was so deliberate that Heldman described it as 'almost a stylised version of a serve'. In particular, the deep-sweeping, rocking motion that moved his weight backwards and then forwards into the forward surge has rarely been equalled in power and balance. Gonzales and Newcombe, and later McEnroe and Sampras, most resemble Kramer in the confidence they held in their marvellous and deceptive deliveries, and in the relentless pressure they could generate as a result.

In practice, Kramer followed the common custom of using small ball boxes placed on the service court as targets, but in an individual exercise he also placed small round rings a few inches above the net from one side to the other. He would then pick a ring and attempt to serve through it.

On one occasion, he was demonstrating this technique to a documentary film crew. To their astonishment, when he marked a ring, took the ball and served, in his first four attempts, one after another, Kramer hit through the ring he had picked out!

The net game that backed the Kramer serve was lethal. Riggs claims that they might play a dozen matches before Kramer missed a smash. And a Kramer smash, even to a retriever *par excellence* like Riggs, usually meant end of point. As to the volley, according to Vines, 'There may have been better volleyers than Kramer, but you can count them on the fingers [of one hand].'

As shown in Figures 4.0 and 4.1, the Kramer forehand, despite its peculiar 'rocker-arm' motion, relatively open stance and late strike, was one of tennis's great shots. When he struck his forehand with a Vines-type flat force and sidespin into the far backhand corner, and charged in behind it, you needed to be Budge or Rosewall to keep making a pressing reply.

We saw how, early in his career, he'd perfected this down-the-line forehand as both passing and approach shot. However, by the years of his maturity he had found another way to 'bust up the percentages': by hitting a forehand crosscourt with topspin any time he wanted. Even as an amateur, Kramer realised how much he needed this shot.

Immediately after winning Wimbledon in 1947, Kramer was asked by journalist C. M. Jones what he intended doing next. To Jones's astonishment, Kramer replied that he was flying to Chicago to meet coach Bob Harman for a week's intensive work on his crosscourt forehand. This followed a Wimbledon victory in which he'd not lost a set.

Though the Kramer backhand was also a little unorthodox, it was basically sound and won him many points. Often employing a shortened backswing, he struck the ball semi-flat, or with some underspin. Nevertheless, Vines notes that the shot was strengthened by his secure Eastern grip, precise timing and a fine follow-through. While he greatly improved this stroke as pro, the glorious action sequence shown in Figure 4.1 is from his late amateur days, and reveals just how solid the shot had already become.

Like his forehand, Kramer's backhand could disguise direction; a boon for a 'taught' player such as he. According to Riggs, Kramer was an example of a 'late-hitter', and this helped him hold back the shot's direction. Kramer also went for a lot of winners off his backhand, particularly on his excellent return of serve, and he frequently brought them off. The observant Vines notes that: 'As with everything Kramer did, this ... was well thought out; if he tried to return service safely he was just as likely to make an error as if he hit hard.'

Although knowing precisely 'what was going on' in the match – the score, the previous sequences, his form and his opponent's – *Big Jack* owned the extraordinary gift of playing one point at a time; this was of special help when he'd lost a point from error, or received a bad call. Like so much of the Kramer tennis gestalt, he seemed to have pared down action and movement to the essentials.

It was as much as anything this peculiar mental force that explains Kramer's dominance of both amateurs and pros in the period 1946 to 1954. In response to the unwavering focus he brought to each shot or point or game, in some strange way almost all his opponents – even, of all people, Bobby Riggs! – seemed drawn into trying to beat him at his own game. And if you did end up serve-and-volleying with Jack Kramer, you weren't likely to win.

It's true that Kramer often appeared machine-like on court, more so on faster surfaces. Even his admirer Vines admits that Kramer was sometimes dull to watch, and never approached the fluidity of form and beauty of movement of a Gonzales or a Rosewall (or a Federer). But even the bitter Gonzales, after stressing that Kramer was not a 'natural player' or particularly fast, reluctantly admitted his nemesis did possess 'the knack of winning.'[13] Some understatement, Pancho!

What came to be called the 'big game', turned out to be the legacy of the Kramer style. Though the big game was, simply, Roche minus his qualifications, it was claimed as a new invention, and dominated modern tennis for the next 20 years. In essence, the assumption was that the serve and volley relentlessly applied would inevitably overcome the ground stroker.

Such claims were dubious. Indeed, to many judges including Vines, Tilden and eventually Kramer himself, the big game was a myth, and one that came to hurt tennis. It took until the mid-sixties, and the emergence of Ken Rosewall and Rod Laver, two glorious little masters as accomplished off the ground as at net and as equal in defence as in attack, to restore balance. At the height of the new fashion, the idea that the bedrock of a solid tennis game was strong ground strokes, arduously constructed over years, seemed ludicrously fuddy-duddy.

At this point it is instructive to contrast the style of Kramer with his contemporary and friend, Ted Schroeder.

At his peak as a pro in the early fifties, Kramer says that there were only three players against whom he was forced to stay back on serve consistently: Budge, Kovacs and Bromwich. Budge and Kovacs drove the return so well, and the master returner Bromwich dropped the ball so accurately – just past, or into the feet of, the server – that the server lost the advantage.

Kovacs was a player with sublime strokes, but limited strategic sense and motivation, and whose eccentric character inspired many stories, one being relevant here.[13]

Ted Schroeder played the simplified 'big game' and went in on everything. Tom LeCompte (Bobby Riggs's biographer) tells how, in one big match, Schroeder was facing an in-form Kovacs, nicknamed the *Clown Prince of*

Tennis. Though Kovacs was murdering his serve, Schroeder, knowing no better, kept following it in. After having seen his serve drilled past him once more, Schroeder served again, and once more headed netwards. Nonchalantly, the ever-loose Frankie dropped his racket and, to Schroeder's rage, caught the ball in his hand.

'Ted,' cried out Kovacs, 'you must be joking!'[14]

In short, 'big-gamer' Schroeder had neither the nous nor the rock-like strokes of his friend Kramer: he couldn't do anything but go in.

Vines seems right: though the Kramer mystique had kicked off the new fashion, it arose from the misreading of one unique player's subtle application of theory. Clearly, Jack Kramer did not *invent* either the serve-and-volley style or the 'big game' version of it. But by emphasising attack, and because he was so dominating a champion, Kramer did – in the prescient words of Bill Talbert – 're-stylise' the game.[15]

As a consequence, Kramer was more than a great player: he changed the way the game was played.

King of the Pros

What happened in the nearly six years of Kramer's reign as king pro?

To retain his title, Kramer played three more head-to-head tours.

The first and longest was against the young Pancho Gonzales. Then he made a shorter tour against the 'Little Pancho', Francisco Segura, who had by then emerged from relative obscurity to become a master, and probably the second-best player in the world at the time. Finally, in his last tour as champion, and by then significantly handicapped, he faced the Australian Frank Sedgman, who came from the amateurs as World No. 1. While Sedgman pushed him, Kramer won each of his four tours convincingly.

In the key pro tournaments, such was his dominance that the imperious champion chose when he would play, and when he did do so he usually won. It is this selectivity that has given his detractors grounds to baulk at the Kramer legend.

Even his proud master Vines noted that as the champion amateur, Kramer wasn't a 'particularly active' competitor. Kramer avoided the few competitions that were held on slow courts; he never, for instance, played the French on their notoriously sluggish *en-tout-cas*. In his autobiography he admits this, explaining that a 'surprise' loss in the French would have cost him more than an exhausting victory. Again we see his mastery of what to do – and even more of what *not* to do – as he went about building his aura of invincibility.

Towards the end of the Kramer ascendency, Gonzales had so reconstructed his game that, if given the chance, he would probably have snatched a head-to-head from the ailing champion. Nevertheless, from the 1947–48 tour with Riggs to when he retired in 1954, Kramer was more than the acknowledged 'King of the Pros'. To any observer with a thorough understanding of the game, he was the best tennis player in the world. And once we know the physical handicaps that Kramer had to endure during the last half of his reign at the top of the pros, his stature as player rises further.

It was soon after the marathon Gonzales tour of 1949–50 that Kramer found himself suffering from debilitating pain and stiffness in his neck. This spread to his shoulder and back, and began to affect his mobility and serve. Without the timely intervention of the 'wonder drug' cortisone, Kramer's career as a pro would then almost certainly have been peremptorily and prematurely scuttled. For the remainder of his playing career, Kramer kept himself going with strategic courses of the drug, administered by his physician in tapered bursts.[16]

So it was that from fairly early in his pro career – and like his fellow legend Lew Hoad, whose fate is recounted in the next chapter – Kramer played with pain. Though he kept going, and remained at the top, by the last third of his career as Pro Champion a measure of his speed and power had gone and an extended playing career stymied.

With these considerations in mind, let's take a quick look at Kramer's last tour against the brilliant Australian Frank Sedgman in 1953.

When he took on Sedgman, Kramer was 32 years of age and, dogged by his arthritis, had begun to protect his champion status with a limited playing schedule. In contrast, Sedgman was 24 years old and fresh from dominating wins at Wimbledon, the US Championships and the Davis Cup finals. Here was one of the fastest and fittest athletes who ever picked up a racket.

Sedgman volleyed as well as anyone. Kramer says simply that no one he'd ever seen played so few second volleys as Frank Sedgman. (This was before John McEnroe came on the scene.) What Kramer means is that if Sedgman

Fig. 4.6. One of tennis's great shots, the Frank Sedgman forehand volley. Lightning fast, he dupes his opponent by feinting slightly left, makes space, then pounces.

got his racket on a volley, no matter where he was in the court, so rapier-like was the stroke that it usually meant end of point.

In Figure 4.6, Sedgman is at work doing what Australians of that time – nearly all master volleyers – called 'hunting' a volley; that is setting up – sometimes by dissembling – a space for the killing punch. If the forehand volley Sedgman is shown delivering here was one of tennis's great shots, his backhand volley was even better!

While Sedgman owned a superb net game with a glorious smash, he was also one of tennis's masters of the mid-court, and backed this up with good if not great ground strokes, and a fine serve. When Sedgman won the bulk of the first few matches of his tour against Champion Kramer, it looked like there might be a replacement at the top.

How might Kramer have reviewed the situation facing him?

Kramer concluded that while Sedgman was fitter, faster and possessed a deadlier volley, there his advantages stopped. First of all, since Sedgman was a self-confessed exponent of the unalloyed 'big game', Kramer asked himself whether the younger man owned those attributes essential to back up an unrelenting attack: a great second serve, a balanced all court game and a very smart head. Compared to the admittedly beautiful 'natural' athlete he faced, even the ailing Kramer thought that he owned better serves and ground strokes, including return of serve.

And Kramer also knew that in big match tactics and pro savvy, he was ahead of the dashing challenger. Sedgman, fresh from the pampered amateurs, was now on the road every day, playing the equivalent of a Wimbledon Final every night of the week.

So Kramer returned to his tennis fundamentals. Perhaps with a passing memory of those hot nights in Vegas with the card dealers in his boyhood home, he recalled his mentor Cliff Roche and the secret of winning a tennis match.

All you had to do was hold your serve, and once in a while break your opponent's. Jack figured he needed to do this in only 51% of the matches making up the whole tour or, after having given up an early lead, say, 55% of those remaining.

Counting the numbers, calculating the odds, he called up his physician for more cortisone, and got fitter. Slowly he began clawing back the lead. By a third of the way through the tour, *Big Jake* had got back to 18 matches all. Then, helped by a few wins on slow clay ('I'd learnt to play dirt by then'), the Champion jumped in front.

All of a sudden his beloved 'house odds' had begun to swing behind him. This *was* all he needed. Even though the pair actually split the last third of the tour, Kramer worked the numbers, and kept in front. Eventually he got his 51% of the whole tour, with a nice little buffer of 6%.

At 54 matches to 41, it was all over.

The killer – 'in the clinches', says Jack – had been his second serve. Focussed on what he calls Sedgman's 'little slice backhand', this still-fabulous serve gave him enough of those 'hard' points – at 15–30, 30–All, and 30–40. As Kramer explains in this chapter's epigraph, these a true pro is required to steal ... and the rest followed.

Describing this last tour in his autobiography, Kramer concludes with a telling point. Almost harshly, Kramer confides that he couldn't quite count Sedgman as a 'great player'. As Kramer sees it, a true great would have found the resources to beat a man who was marginally, but significantly, 'over the hill', just as Kramer had needed to do against Budge. If an over-the-hill Jack Kramer had defeated the brilliant Sedgman, how we must salute his stature as a player when, a couple of years earlier, he'd sat on top of it.

It was after this tour of 1953 that Jack decided it was time to call it a day as player; as manager and entrepreneur he would have plenty to do.

The account of the champion's 'retirement' presents the only anomaly in the Kramer story as told in the wonderful Kramer–Deford autobiography.

Kramer explains that as the pros' promoter, he threw the field open to an extraordinary quartet of pros: Gonzales, Sedgman, Segura and Budge – the best of the pros, and surely the best in the world. Impresario Kramer tells us he set up this formidable battery of challengers to 'fight it out for my crown'.

But later in Kramer's book, along comes a second version of this changing of the guard. Seeming to forget having said that he willingly left 'his title' for the challengers to scramble over, he indicates he'd never really abdicated. Now he says that for some two years after the Gonzales succession, since no one had taken his crown directly off him he still looked upon himself as the true king. As late as 1956, he admits he was contemplating a tour of himself against Tony Trabert – to decide who was the *real* Professional Champion!

However, this confrontation never came about. Tough guy Jack admits that it was a tearful phone call from *Big Pancho*'s wife that finally persuaded him to give Gonzales the chance to defend his crown against Trabert.

Despite his views on who was the rightful Champion, in effect Kramer's days as a top player were over following his 'retirement' in 1954. Yet from time to time in the following five years he would appear on court: one of those returns to centre stage forms a jewel in the pros' story – and the Kramer swansong.

Return to centre stage, or What a champion is made of

In 1957 the pros were in the doldrums. In response, a desperate Kramer had set up legendary Aussie Lew Hoad, brilliant, popular and fresh, to supplant Champion Gonzales, intractable and over-exposed. However, to get the challenger up to Gonzales' pace, Kramer had to teach the new boy the ropes.

The time was during Hoad's six-month tutelage; the place, the Empire Stadium, Wembley, and the 1957 British Professional Championship.

This particular event held pride-of-place as one of pro tennis's few big tournaments, and on this occasion the importance was accentuated by the timing. After decisively winning his second Wimbledon, in July of that year Hoad had turned pro. Under mastermind Kramer – by this time manager and virtual owner of the pro circus for a decade – Hoad had spent the next months on an intense post-graduate course, served up by an extraordinary battery of Professors Gonzales, Sedgman, Trabert, Segura and Rosewall.

By the end of September when the British Championships were held, impresario, financier, bit-player and guru Kramer had room for optimism. Though the tough veterans couldn't teach the happy-go-lucky Hoad how to play real smart, mostly he avoided playing real dumb.

The event was a sell-out. The British tennis aficionados had seen Hoad dominate the Wimbledon just past, and they knew he was going for Champion Gonzales.

Further, on the heels of that pair, in the draw was their much-loved Rosewall, and he was backed up by the fantastic and popular master Segura. And that wasn't all. Kramer believed that the financial future of the pros depended on Hoad. And the only way he could properly supervise his investment in the stunning new boy was on court – so that the lucky Brits had yet another all-time great in the field – Jack Kramer!

Following back-to-back Wimbledons and an improving few weeks on tour, the British organisers had, rather optimistically, seeded Hoad No. 2. In the second round, to everyone's delight, the second seed came face to face with none other than the former king of the high wire and current ringmaster, Kramer.

Some aficionados decided that the boss was in an impossible position, and it was not only because he was 37 years of age, semi-retired and ailing. The journalist and tennis historian, Joe McCauley, described it as the 'invidious situation of hoping to win on the one hand, and not wanting to beat his prize draw card on the other.' British professional Peter Cawthorn informed the press bluntly: 'How can [Kramer] knock out Hoad? He wants to build him up.'

Equally bluntly, Kramer retorted: 'I have never laid down in my life. If Lew wants to win, he will have to play pretty well.'[17]

Whatever the side-bets, Kramer came out of his corner in typical style – composed, focussed and ruthless.

The famous indoor Wembley court was fast boards, and the early rounds were the best of three sets. Kramer attacked on his every serve, and crushed anything from Hoad that was vaguely short. The blonde Australian ace owned every shot in the book and had power to burn, yet when he had time to catch his breath, he discovered he was down a set and with only one game to his name!

Right then, Hoad must have reminded himself: *I'm Lew Hoad, the reigning double-Wimbledon champion. And who am I playing? Apparently an injured has-been, dragged from retirement.*

Two decades later, in his autobiography Kramer describes the match from *his* point of view: he asks the reader to imagine how *he* might have been feeling at this same point in the match.

He says, 'As player, by instinct, I hated to lose ... and had got myself high for this match.' But as promoter, in both the short and crucial long term, a Hoad victory was vital.

He then lets us in on a little secret: after blitzing the first set, he admits 'the businessman in me took over'. As the second set began, Kramer began easing up. Trying to allow Hoad a chance to get back in the game, Kramer took his foot off the accelerator, and started staying back on serve.

Then came two surprises.

First, Kramer's more defensive game was still so sound, his serve so good, that he was unable to lose his first two service games! With Hoad then holding serve, soon the second set was even stevens at 2–2.

But in the next, the crucial fifth game of the set, Kramer suddenly broke Hoad! Again, try as he might to ease off, the newly timid Kramer still managed to hold serve, and found himself sitting on a break and 4–2.

The second surprise, like the first, was unseen by crowd or critics.

Suddenly old hawk-eye Kramer formed the impression that Hoad was favouring a leg. In fact, to the ever-observant Kramer, this made sense. One reason he was still ahead was that Hoad wasn't moving freely, and the slower but extended tempo of the exchanges was stretching his opponent as much as his earlier rapid-fire onslaught.

Yes, years later, Jack Kramer admits to his readers that for once he had been prepared to 'jump in the tank'. After a terrific show, by force of exceptional circumstance, he'd been ready to lose (gracefully, surreptitiously) to the pros' potential saviour.

However, Kramer now saw that 'the kid wasn't right'. And things were different. Sure as hell, the old master wasn't going to cop out to any kid who wasn't OK himself!

So the Kramer psyche of old clicked back in: as ever, he was playing for his life.

At this same point in the second set, Hoad was also thinking hard. He realised that sore leg or not, there was only one way for him to come back. He had to overpower the older man, and not concede a single easy point in the process.

At 2–4 Hoad held serve. Then, displaying his legendary capacity to take the ball on the rise, he broke Kramer's serve to 4–4. Trading service games, Hoad then led on service to 8–7.

What a show!

Even so, within the cheering crowd, the doubters remained: Was this the time for the old champion to hold back a little and, respectfully, take his bow?

But Jack Kramer couldn't do it. His fires were burning: *he was the real champion*, the one whom no one had ever unseated.

So Kramer won his next serve, and with the help of a couple of errors from his opponent, broke Hoad's. Now attacking on every opportunity, with errorless tennis Jack held his serve to take the match 6–1, 10–8.

The watching crowd was thrilled, yet stunned and awed.

Jack's friend, the British tennis writer C. M. Jones, followed him to the dressing room. There Jones found Kramer 'literally speechless with rage'. It took half an hour, Jones confides, before he simmered down.

Then Kramer told Jones, 'There is only one way I know how to play and that is to win. How much tonight may cost me never came into the reckoning.'[18]

Now, years later, it is clear that the outcome of the match *had* entered 'the reckoning', if only for a few minutes. Nevertheless, *Big Jack*'s admission sings such an honest song it makes our apparently flawless champion seem more human. And what a tale it tells of the stuff that makes a champion!

Kramer didn't win this tournament, but he survived long enough to play off for the championship's third place. By then he was still so fired up that – from a set down and to the fury of his opponent – he beat an underdone Gonzales! He completed a magnificent tourney by making the doubles final. Though Kramer and partner Segura (how the two loved playing with each other!) ended up losing that match, their opponents were Hoad and Rosewall, and that superlative team needed five brilliant sets to beat them.

As it turned out, Kramer failed to replace Gonzales with Hoad – or turn the long-term fortunes of the languishing pros. In the shorter term, despite Kramer's fears, his triumphs over those two legendary champions in London were no setback for the box office. This tournament and the tour that followed were sell-outs.

Perhaps the crowds came partly because many tennis lovers still believed in the greatness of the veteran and former champion. Indeed, to them, alongside the marvellous efforts of the pros at Wembley in 1957, the Kramer victories were hardly upsets at all.

Somehow they had come to share Kramer's view of himself: they expected that when *King* Kramer walked out on the court, he would rule.

Ringmaster, circus owner and kingmaker

For most of the decade from the early fifties, by virtue of his capacity to contract the top professionals and lure the top amateurs Kramer became the most dominating single person in world tennis. Yet during this period the fortunes of the pros, never consistently bright, deteriorated further. Though increasingly well organised under the tough and efficient businessman that was Jack Kramer, he called this time the 'Dark Decade'. In recognition of Kramer's key role, here is a brief account of that period's highs and lows.

It takes until halfway through his autobiography before Kramer begins to reveal the strength of his feelings about the world of amateur tennis. In Kramer's eyes – and he was a careful man not given to hyperbole – the amateur system was 'evil'. Hiding behind pompous autocrats spouting sporting values, dependent on a raft of under-the-table payments to survive, the amateur system was fundamentally dishonest.

To Kramer, it was not just this hypocrisy that made the amateur game 'rotten to the core', or that the best players in the world, his pros, were banished and ridiculed. The worst was what it did to the players on whom the game was built. The domination of world tennis by the Pooh-Bahs of the Lawn Tennis Associations meant the marginalisation – even the destruction – of many worthy players. Except for the tiny elite cosseted by the amateur system – and the few with assets sufficient to remain independent – players could aspire only to the status of poor, and usually temporary, servants of the great house.

Complementing Kramer's necessarily American version of the 'shamateur' world, the wonderful Italian tennis historian Gianni Clerici explains that the Europeans had their own name for the system: *l'amateurisme marron*, indicating a kind of shameful amateur status. He then puts the position in a nutshell. 'Poor people', he says, 'had begun to arrive in the tennis world, and when a poor person played better than a rich one, there was always a sponsor, glaring paternalism, and bombastic national anthems somewhere near.'[19]

Kramer says that as soon as he came to understand the way the system worked, his aim was simple. He wanted to make tennis, like golf, a game where the best played each other, gave their all to a public who enjoyed the display, and were rewarded fairly for doing so. From his first venture as a promoter he pursued this aim doggedly throughout the next 14 years.

Until Kramer took up the reins, the promotion of the pros had been a mixed bag.

After a flourish following the war, the increasingly troubled Tilden had given up as promoter, and a brief interim had followed when businessmen, not players or ex-players, ran the show.

Then the entrepreneurial Bobby Riggs tried his hand. Kramer learnt the ropes of running a tennis circus from Riggs, when they worked hand in hand to promote Kramer's second head-to-head tour against Gonzales in 1949. After the Kramer–Gonzales tour ended in 1950, Kramer took over and, working from a tiny office in his own home, began to contract the top professionals and manage and control their program before the public.

At first, while cautiously experimenting with different ways of packaging his performers, he consolidated the format of the circus as it had evolved in the thirties.

Following the illustrious line from Tilden through Vines, Perry, Budge and Riggs, Kramer brought onto the high wire in the big top the best amateur he could lay his hands on. After Gonzales, he lured a string of amateur champions, starting with Sedgman, then Trabert, Rosewall, Hoad, Cooper, and Olmedo. Backing the top bill was the supporting core of seasoned pros, who from time to time came together in small tournaments such as the British Championship at Wembley just described.

In its way this system worked. But how it cost! While sometimes the whole troupe made good money, often it was only the pair at the top who got a decent reward, and only then in their few hours of glory on the head-to-head tour. Moreover, for good or little money, the pro circus remained gruelling and lonely work – and not quite kosher, even a little dodgy.

During Kramer's first years at the helm nothing changed for the better. Then, despite his unceasing efforts, things got worse.

A perennial problem facing the pros was the perception among many that their matches were at best 'exhibitions'. At worst the matches were seen as 'fixed'. As any detailed investigation of the subject will reveal, almost all of the time the pro competition was not only fair but also fierce, and the exceptions confirm, rather than negate such a view.

An interview with a former West Australian Lawn Tennis Association official, Mr Vic Anderson, provided a fascinating slant on the Kramer pros on tour and on the nature of the competition between them.

Although a top umpire in the Australian amateur world, Anderson had bravely defied the local LTA by agreeing to officiate for the Kramer pros when they were barnstorming Australia in 1958. From the top bill of Hoad versus Gonzales down, what most astonished Anderson was the intensity of the competition between all the players. He was further shocked when he discovered that their fire was stoked by the participants themselves, for they were riding some heavy side betting on the outcomes.[20]

On much of the tour, as in this case on a two-night stand in far-distant Perth, Western Australia, prestige and glamour were hardly abundant. These pros were playing for just two things: money and pride. Nevertheless, the old tennis lover explained, they were 'all at each other's throats'. Then, aghast, he added, 'Gonzales and Hoad seemed actually to hate each other!' And Mr Anderson had umpired for years at the top level of the amateur game!

Indeed, if it was simply money and pride that spurred them on, often the spoils were so meagre that they played for pride alone – as shown in the following story Kramer tells in his autobiography.

In 1956, the little band of Gonzales, Sedgman, Trabert and Kramer were finishing up a tour of South America. Very often the venues outside the US provided better conditions than many of the dim and truncated arenas of the North American backblocks. But this time, their last two venues, played back-to-back, were a dance hall in Montevideo and an entertainment park in Buenos Aires, and these were as testing as any.

Although in two different countries, Uruguay and Argentina, Kramer explains that the two capitals, on either side of the River Plate, were close enough that they would 'play the dance hall, then cross to BA in a boat, sharing a cabin, getting no sleep whatsoever'. On the other side, the arena in the amusement park in BA was a shocker, not only freezing and windy, but with a court that was 'too fast' and with lights 'too dim'.

Kramer recalls that on this 'memorable night', he and Trabert had got so despondently cold that they had found a trash can and some fuel. Dragging it right beside the court, they had made a bonfire in it.

To make this particular evening even more miserable, the group of spectators braving the icy winds to watch them was not only sparse, but surly. Kramer explains this as a consequence of a previous pro tour when the twin clowns, Perry and Kovacs, had hammed it up. This little crowd was frozen stiff and many of them convinced that the pro games were neither serious nor straight.

Worse, on this occasion all the players had ended up entirely dependent on guarantees for playing, and these were fixed on spectator receipts, not individual wins. It was 35% for Trabert, 25% for Kramer and 20% each for Sedgman and Gonzales.

On the previous night of the two-night stand in the arctic entertainment park, Sedgman and Gonzales had beaten the first two, so now they were playing each other in the 'finals'. This explains why Kramer and Trabert had ended up watching the match 'sitting around a blazing fire [they had] lit in the trash can at courtside'.

Says Kramer:

> Damn, but were they mad — Gonzales particularly. There was 60% sitting around the fire, laughing and warming our hands. Trabert [who loathed Gonzales] could whistle at the good shots too, and he could whistle like a train coming through a tunnel. The 40% had to stay out on the court and play like madmen in the cold and the dark. [21]

But did they give up? No. Finally, 'Pancho beat Sedg', Kramer concludes – but it didn't happen until they'd gone to 12–10 in the fifth set!

However, the pride shown here by Gonzales and Sedgman shouldn't be seen as only a personal thing. It was bound to the preservation of the fiercely contested pecking order, and this governed a player's future chance of playing and winning.

Yes, by the time they had fought their way to the top of the pro world, the best pros enjoyed, often contrarily, the quality of pride-of-performance in bucketfuls. Can't we just hear the thoughts of the top dog in Buenos Aires, the glowering, suspicious Gonzales! *That bastard Sedgman, he's so bloody good, and so close, if I let him win, even once in this dump-to-end-all-dumps, he might just get the idea he's better than me ...*

Eventually, as they battled their way through such times as these, Kramer began to believe that there was only one way forward for the tiny band – to expand the troupe.

Before long he was luring not just the top, but also some of the lesser amateurs. In addition, this time Kramer didn't look to the leading two countries, the US and Australia: Kramer began poaching from Britain, Europe and South America as well. Since these countries' reserves were weaker, their national teams began to get badly hurt, and resentment rose.

Tennis historian, Will Grimsley, put it this way in his fine book, *Tennis: Its History, People and Events*: '[Kramer] had become the game's most prosperous and controversial promoter ... for close to a decade they called tennis "the big green world of Jack Kramer." '[22]

As Kramer's 'Dark Decade' unfolded and the pros expanded, the amateur rump became so emasculated that attendance at the big amateur tournaments started to fall. Nevertheless, the pros themselves, despite having more of the best players, seemed to be gaining little from the amateur malaise. So much were they struggling that for the first time, promoter Kramer started losing money.

By the end of the fifties, a newspaper cutting and a photograph tell the whole sad story.

In *The Game*, Kramer explains that he was employed to cover the Wimbledon of 1958 as a journalist. Immediately on his arrival, he was shown a story in the *Daily Sketch* 'complete with a screaming six-column headline that read: "Keep away from our kids, Kramer. We didn't groom them for you." '

The article continued:

> Wimbledon starts today. Sitting in the stands will be immaculately dressed, suave, plausible Jack Kramer — Public Enemy No. 1 to amateur tennis.
> In ten years his Hollywood smile and million-dollar cheque-book has skimmed the cream off the amateur game.
> Now the man who was born in money-mad Las Vegas again brings Wall Street to Wimbledon.
> We can't keep him out. It wouldn't make much difference if we could, for money talks and Jack's a whale of a talker.
> He has weakened the American and Australian game and now he is after new blood! For his circus must have a yearly transfusion. BUT KEEP OFF OUR KIDS, KRAMER!

And the photograph?

Figure 4.7 finds Kramer in Australia in 1955. He tells us that though he might have pinched quite a few of Australia's champions, somehow or other he'd managed to receive fairly decent treatment from a nation that prided itself on a fair go. Now the Aussies began to turn against him.

Kramer is seen facing the Australian press. At that time he had already stolen Sedgman and McGregor, and the media knew that he was after their

Fig. 4.7. The King embattled. The strain shows as Kramer faces a hostile Australian press. The pros' boss wanted to steal their heroes, Hoad and Rosewall – and everyone knew it.

heroes Hoad and Rosewall. To them he seemed more than anything a hit-and-run bandit, and – a double offence to national pride – American as well.

This tough child of Depression Las Vegas admits that their attitude hurt. In the photograph his eyes reveal what the long struggle was costing him.

As a consequence, by the beginning of the sixties Kramer was beginning to feel the stabs of that terrible duo, hurt and impotence – and he was going broke as well. Then and there he decided that it would be better for the whole game if he left off running the pros. With the boogieman gone, the game might clean itself up.

However, the decision was unexpectedly difficult. When he began phoning his closest comrades-in-arms to tell them of his decision, several indicated that a future without Kramer might be bleaker than one with him. Indeed, the most generous of all, the indefatigable and loyal Pancho Segura, struck the cruellest blow.

'Pancho came at me,' Kramer says. Segura told him bitterly, 'You're running out on us, Jack.'

Kramer's response to *Little Pancho* is worth hearing in full.

He writes in *The Game*: '"No I'm not [running out on you] kid,"' I replied wearily. I didn't want to argue any more. The fight had gone out ... Look ... I had tried everything: star tours, round-robins, traditional tournaments, different rules, different scoring, different serves. "There's nothing more I can do. I've got to get out or we'll never see an open game."'

Thus, under the aegis of the professional organisation he had founded, in 1962 Kramer left the show to the players to run themselves, and took a back seat.

Nevertheless, when open tennis actually arrived six years later, Jack Kramer was right in there ...

'Shamateur tennis was finished one afternoon during the Wimbledon of 1966,' he states boldly. And the place of its demise, appropriate for the coincident demise of the pro circus, was a tent.

How did it happen? Kramer was in the BBC's marquee as part of their broadcasting team. A few days into the tournament, he received a surprise visit.

It was the influential British official Herman David, accompanied by members of the Wimbledon committee and a couple of BBC executives.

After polite chitchat, the visitors came clean. While attendance at Wimbledon was just holding up, TV ratings were down, and everywhere else the amateur game was in a mess. Soon David told Kramer and the BBC executives that, in essence, they were 'tired of putting on second-class tennis as "The Championships".'

Then came the bottom-line question to Kramer: Would the fans support open tennis?

Kramer's reply to the little group was an emphatic yes.

After this, Wimbledon and the BBC agreed to work with Kramer. Together they decided to support an eight-man trial pro tournament the following year at Wimbledon.

It turned out to be a smash hit. Open Tennis was on its way.

And the man who got the brokers and performers together, then made the deals between them, was the boogieman himself.

After that, except for a few inevitable hiccups, Jack Kramer's life work in tennis was pretty well done.

Leader of men – the Kramer legacy

From the time he reached the top, through most of the next 20 years *King* Kramer seemed to rule the game. Although his enemies were entrenched within the national Lawn Tennis Associations, by his last years in the sport most of those involved in tennis had come to respect him as no other.

In all of this, the tall and imperious Kramer seems the opposite of the man he supplanted as Pro Champion, the little brawler with the squeaky voice and bad haircut named Bobby Riggs. Yet in addition to superb athletic skills, these two had one thing in common. Undoubtedly born with outstanding gifts, both had to work unceasingly at surmounting their own considerable limitations, and against longstanding opposition.

Pancho Gonzales' extraordinary comment on Kramer – 'Jack is not a natural player' – must be taken with the understanding that Pancho saw Kramer as his enemy, and was himself a one-in-a-million 'natural'. Yet the insightful Julius Heldman and Kramer's master Ellsworth Vines are in some agreement with the jealous and incendiary Pancho.

As they saw it, Kramer was above all a man who shows what discipline, hard work and perseverance can do. Kramer *was* probably slightly less gifted in speed, balance and coordination than any of the seven other super-athletes who make up our pantheon of pro champions.

Reaching the top entailed conscious, studied learning and practice before Kramer's tennis flow could be internalised and naturalised. With the help of master teachers, he programmed himself to become as close to a machine as possible for an athlete. In Zen-like manner he gained a thorough knowledge of himself, his strengths and weaknesses, mental and physical. He learnt how to work with them. By the time Kramer had reached maturity amongst the pros, he had connected head to heart and made himself a master of all aspects of the game, honing his technical mastery with a mental force that reduced and intimidated his opponents.

Once at the top, Kramer drew upon his honesty and passionate spirit to foster the game he revered. Jack loved his pro circus, and served it devotedly. When Open Tennis became a possibility, this change was not to his personal advantage, yet he became a mid-wife to its birth and gave the infant the benefit of his wisdom and support.

To any who know the game in its long history, Kramer was a towering figure, and a uniquely worthy one. He was a mighty champion. And, more than anyone, he came to be seen as 'the man who made tennis honest' – so ran the headline of the *Los Angeles Times* obituary.

As a young man in the midst of a war, in a vast ocean and facing death, he asked himself the great questions of meaning and worth. Except perhaps to those who believe in a personal God dispensing rules in a way we humans can comprehend, no mortal soul can answer these questions with certainty. But most who knew him, along with a subsequent legion of tennis players and tennis followers, would agree that Jack Kramer left the world a better place.

This king died in 2009 at the age of 88 years. Jack himself said that he made a thing of playing 'with the house', that is, with the odds on his side. But with the benefit of history, the two great battles of his life – to become a champion and to make the game honest – were long struggles against the odds.

As a consequence we can more fully savour and respect his hero's journey.

Notes

1 Kramer, *The Game*. All quotations in this chapter that lack specific attribution are from *The Game*. The chapter draws extensively on this excellent book, and on a book of instruction by Kramer that is full of revealing insights: Jack Kramer with Larry Sheehan, *How to Play Your Best Tennis All the Time*, Atheneium/SMI, New York, 1977. Four other sources, cited previously, have been useful here: the autobiographies of Budge and Riggs, Vines' *Tennis: Myth and Method*, and Heldman's *Styles of the Great*, in Will Grimsley's *Tennis: Its History, People and Events*. The epigraph to the chapter is taken from Kramer's Foreword in *The Art of Tennis*, ed. Alan Trengove, Hodder and Stoughton, London, 1964.

2 Vines and Vier, *Tennis: Myth and Method*.

3 Joe Hyams, *Zen in the Martial Arts*. Though Hyams collaborated with Gonzales on an instruction book, he seems not to have elaborated on the connections between tennis and Zen.

4 The wonderful Federer exquisitely illustrates this seeming paradox. On his backhand wing in particular, a slow motion replay makes it appear that just before the moment of impact his whole body – head, trunk and legs – have been curiously stilled, an elastic launching pad, taut with potential energy.

5 Joe Hyams gives a Chinese take on apparent strength. He retells the famous Chinese story of Po Kung-I, reputed to be the strongest man in the kingdom. When the king eventually met Po, he was dismayed at how weak he looked. Questioned by the king, Po replied mildly that he was so strong he could 'break the legs of a grasshopper'. The king, aghast, thundered that he was so strong he could 'drag nine buffaloes by the tail, yet I am still shamed by my weakness.' So how could Po be so famous? Replied Po quietly, 'My teacher was Tzu Shang-chi'ui, whose strength was without peer in the world, but even his relatives never knew it because he never used it.' Hyams, *Zen in the Martial Arts*.

6 Adrian Quist, *Tennis: the Greats 1920–1960*, ABC Books, Sydney, 1984.

7 Vines and Vier, *Tennis: Myth and Method*.

8 Kramer, *The Game*.

9 Of the later players, John Newcombe, John McEnroe and Pete Sampras were right out of the Roche mould. McEnroe in particular backed a lethal serve with an equally lethal volley and, beneath his explosive temper, a smart head. The outcome? On anything but the slowest courts, Mac's opponents would find themselves becoming spectators – watching the master, at net, peculiarly poised, almost contemptuously putting away volley after volley. Arthur Ashe once described McEnroe's backcourt game as 'only adequate', but in a sense that Roche would love, it was *truly* adequate to set up the forecourt platform required for ruthless victory. Mac knew how to make the ploys to put himself in Roche's 'right spot'.

10 Kramer, *How to Play Your Best Tennis All the Time*.

11 Apparently Roche did not leave any writings on tennis, but the reader can get a feel of his method from two excellent books by Bill Talbert and Bruce Old. They do not cite Roche as a mentor, but their unique compilation of the statistics of winning plays in championship tennis reflects Roche's method and forms the basis of their strategy for singles and doubles. William F Talbert and Bruce S Old, *The Game of Singles in Tennis*,

Revised Edition, J B Lippincott and Co, New York, 1977, and *The Game of Doubles in Tennis*, 3rd Ed, Lippincott, New York, 1969.

12 Riggs, *Tennis is My Racket*.
13 Dave Anderson, 'His Greatest Rival', *The Fireside Book of Tennis*, ed. Alison Danzig.
14 LeCompte, *The Last Sure Thing*.
15 Bill Talbert, quoted in Grimsley, *Tennis: Its History, People and Events*.
16 This drug would now be classified as a 'steroid', and thus illegal in sport!
17 McCauley, *History of Professional Tennis*.
18 Owen Davidson and C M Jones, *Lawn Tennis: The Great Ones*, Pelham Books, London, 1970.
19 Clerici, *Tennis*.
20 Mr Vic Anderson was interviewed in 2005 by Roger Underwood, who generously assisted me with research for this book.
21 This and much of the rest of the chapter draw on Kramer, *The Game*.
22 Will Grimsley, *Tennis: Its People, History and Events*.

Fig. 5.0. Taut as a bow, Gonzales serves at Forest Hills.

5

NATURAL COLOSSUS - GONZALES

Pancho's no saint.

Pancho Segura on Gonzales.

IN his marvellous little book, *Zen in the Martial Arts*, Joe Hyams alludes to a famous fable:

> A Zen master, out for a walk with one of his students, pointed out a fox chasing a rabbit. 'According to the ancient fable, the rabbit will get away from the fox,' the master said. 'Not so,' replied the student, 'The fox is faster.' 'No, the rabbit will elude him,' insisted the master. 'Why are you so sure?' asked the student. 'Because the fox is running for his dinner, the rabbit for his life,' answered the master.[1]

In this chapter we will discover how Pancho Gonzales played tennis as if he were both rabbit and fox in the fable. He was rabbit in that he played every game as if for his life; he was fox in that every opponent was his potential dinner. His incentive appeared to switch back and forth between the fight for survival and a feast of power.

Such a ferocious drive fuelled a triumphant career. However, we begin with a vignette of one of the few instances when the famous Gonzales anger misfired.

Losing it Pancho style

The scene is the Olympic Auditorium, Los Angeles, on an evening in late March 1954. From high up, the stadium is so large that the tiny stage, a single tennis court, is like a sink plug in a vast and smoky bowl. The big crowd is noisy and expectant. Then comes a roar: two figures in white emerge from the concrete stairwell opening just above the court. They are to play the opener of a pro tournament.

Immediately, one of the pair catches the attention of the crowd.

He is swarthy and, though tall, moves with a lithe grace. To many, he might be one of the big cats, a leopard perhaps. As the two stride across to the umpire's chair, the dark man, carrying a half-dozen rackets in covers under his arm, suddenly pauses in mid-court. At centre stage, he looks up and around. Then, raising his arms like a prize-fighter, he gives the cheering fans a huge and infectious grin.

The man so generously acknowledging the tribute of his fans was born Ricardo Alonzo Gonzalez. However he was officially known – and so doubly misnamed – as *Richard Gonzales* (with an 's'). But to his adoring fans, in deference to his ancestry and gunslinger style, he was simply, Pancho. To his less adoring fellow pros, however, he was usually *Gorgo* – in part after the mythical creature from ancient Greece that could turn anyone to stone with her stare.[2]

However, on that particular evening in LA, the joyful gesture to his fans arose not in response to the judgement of friend or foe, but from deep within. In this great, dingy space the man smiled for one simple reason: he was feeling good about who he was and where he was.

During the previous 26 years of this Mexican-American's life, such *joie-de-vivre* was rare. Indeed, to find a time in the years of his manhood when he might have felt so happy we would have to put back the clock five years to when, as an amateur, he had held aloft his second US Championship trophy.

But here in LA, *Big Pancho* had good reason to feel that he was well and truly back. Very soon, he believed, he would be sitting on top of the pile – acclaimed as Richard Gonzales, the Professional Tennis Champion of the World.

Getting to this point had been hard. From the time Gonzales, a raw 21-year-old, had turned pro after back-to-back victories in the US Championships of 1948 and '49, things had gone sour.

First up, he had been pitched straight into a tour with the reigning pro champ, Jack Kramer, and a never-to-be-forgotten thrashing.

Worse was to follow. After the beating by Kramer – fatally coupled with, so he felt, his own business innocence – he had been cast aside. Unwanted by the pro tour, he felt forgotten, angry. And he was just about broke.

Forbidden by his professional status from playing in the great championships around the world, for almost two years he had been stringing rackets and giving lessons in a run-down public park in LA. As Pancho later bluntly recalled in his autobiography, after the Kramer shellacking 'I was left a bum'.

But now he was out of the shop, back in the game, and before the fans. And there was more to his joy than a professional performer's need to ply his trade, to smell the crowd, to hear the turnstiles click; even to compete for a world title. This unquiet man knew in his bones that, finally, as a craftsman he had matured. His vocation was to be a champion athlete. Now he was one. And peerless. He could run with the wind.

The world crown was vacant. In the previous chapter we saw how Gonzales' nemesis, the mighty Jack Kramer, was on the wane. Two months earlier, his back ailing, *King* Kramer had announced his retirement. Gonzales had been summoned from the obscure reaches of his pro shop in Los Angeles. A tour was put together. Over three months, four protagonists were to fight each other. Eventually, one would claim the crown.

This was why, on that evening in March 1954, that a former battler made over as Pancho or *Gorgo* Gonzales and now a master of his craft, strode out onto the stage of the huge amphitheatre in LA and, pausing before the multitudes, embraced them. Surely he could hear the cry: '*The King is dead, long live the King.*'

And with a little license, we imagine the ever-present rebel in him thinking: *And yes, if the bastards who own the show can be stunned a bit longer it's finally me, an immigrant kid from the back streets, who'll be the reigning big shot,* Numero Uno. *And ready to crush any challenger.*

Next he reaches the umpire's chair, unzips his racket, and notes the twang of the strings as he slaps them with his hand.

With another glance at the crowd, our would-be hero couldn't but remind himself: *And this is my hometown! Listen to the roars! I'm their prodigal son, from oblivion returned.*

But there was to be no more joy for *Big Pancho* in the match that followed, or in its aftermath.

What happened?

To find the new champion, the four contenders had started on the other side of the continent two months earlier. Now, near the end of the tour, the pros were making a stop in the biggest metropolis on the West Coast. The four – Frank Sedgman, Don Budge, *Little Pancho* Segura and *Big Pancho* himself – were there in LA to play a 'round robin' tournament. The prize money would be allocated on points based on the performance of each against the others. But even more crucial than the money was the final pecking order: this would determine the new champion.

For the Los Angeles tournament, *Gorgo* had been picked to play Budge in the opening match.

The popular J. Donald Budge – former World Pro Champion, one and only winner of the Grand Slam – was a legend. But Budge was 38 years old, and a good few years and lots of tennis matches had passed since the legend had been created.

On this tour, the old hero was struggling. The *Los Angeles Times* had been unflattering to the former master in its pre-tourney wrap-up, describing him as 'aging and faded'. Indeed, when *Big Pancho*'s fellow Latinos in the crowd observed the somewhat ample Budge squaring up on the other side of the court to that lean figure, so swift and agile, they might well have recalled the image of the bull and the matador.

Despite the early drubbings, the enforced layoffs and the bitterness, the aspiring champion had eventually put the last dismal years to good use. As the contender to the throne and the once-and-former king began to hit up, Gonzales knew that every part of his body and tennis game had been scrutinised, tested, and then fitted into a machine that was close to perfect.

From Kramer – and even more from the master tactician Segura – he had learnt not only the necessity of an unshakable technical control, but the strategic means to execute it. And from the toughest teacher of all – indifferent experience – he had also built a discipline that had not come naturally to him. Now he studied his opponents, ate carefully, trained hard, played dead smart, and never gave up.

The result was a tennis game that backed the fearsome power of his serve and net play with a magnificent and deceptive set of ground strokes. These were now coupled with the nous to tune, juggle and blend the parts as needed, and a physical and mental toughness that would allow him – after a gruelling match and to the chagrin of his opponents – to end the match with a blistering service ace, a habit he relished showing off and displayed often.

This all-round game had pushed Gonzales steadily ahead of the other three contenders on the 1954 tour, and he looked set to take Kramer's crown at a canter.

On this particular night in Los Angeles, there was a further boost to his confidence: so far on tour his opponent, Budge, had not taken a single match from him. Now we can begin to understand why *Big Pancho* was feeling – in the simplest terms – so darned full of himself.

But oh, hubris! What happened next gives an insight into the grim world of pro tennis, and the personalities of no less than three of the key players of the era.

There are two eyewitness accounts of the match that followed. The first is from tour promoter Kramer, watching courtside; the second from protagonist Budge. Both are drawn upon in the story that follows.

In *The Game,* Kramer precedes the account of the match with some prescient remarks on the character of Pancho's opponent.

According to *Big Jake*, who spent years on tour with him, Don Budge was a uniquely decent man. In the chapter devoted to Budge, we took note of a crucial Kramer insight. Despite the greatness of Budge's sporting achievements, Kramer saw him as suffering from a lack of one of the most necessary gifts of the gods – luck. A luckless good person is a particularly beautiful creature. And so gentlemanly was Budge that Kramer reflects, 'In all the years I was with him, I only once saw him lose his temper'.

And when was that? In the 1954 Los Angeles match against Pancho Gonzales. 'Typically,' says Kramer, '[it all] came about because Don was trying to be helpful.'[3]

●●●

Offering no hint of what was to follow, the start of the match was tame, and predictable. The two men finished their warm-up. Gonzales won the toss. Serving first, he took out his serve easily. They changed ends.

Budge strode to the baseline, took the balls, and prepared to serve.

Like so many of the venues the pros had to put up with, the old Olympic Auditorium was poorly lit. Budge himself tells us that when he looked up to serve, and managed ('in the gloaming', as he puts it poetically) to outline his opponent on the other side of the net, he noticed something unexpected. He could make out, perched in the shadows, courtside, 'a scramble of photographers ... down by Pancho, hoping desperately to find enough light to catch a quick shot ... [of their hometown boy] ... for the morning editions.'

Good-natured Don couldn't but help them.

'You guys want a shot of Pancho hitting one back?' Budge hollered down.

Sure they did!

Genially, Budge takes a few steps into the court and, genially, pats a baby serve towards Gonzales. And, anything but genially, the matador on the other side of the net leaps on it, and creams it back. The cameras pop. The photographers have their action shot. They scurry off.

But when Budge returned to begin his serve, and looked up a second time, he found Gonzales had moved over to the ad court. *Gorgo*, cock-a-hoop, was acting as if the stunt for the photographers was for real – as if it was the first point of the game. And he had won it!

At first Budge thought that Gonzales must have misunderstood, or was kidding.

So, helpfully, he tried to straighten him out.

'Hey Pancho, listen!' cried Budge plaintively. 'That was just for the photographers. Come on.'

But Gonzales didn't move, and Budge saw his opponent was serious. Dumbfounded, the old champion shook his head in disbelief.

Then he turned to the referee.

But Kramer considered 'the ref must have been asleep during the whole business'. The referee told Budge 'to shut up and serve at Love–15'.

'But,' responded the exasperated Budge, 'I made my serve a yard inside the baseline! At least declare a foot-fault on the first serve – and give me a chance on a second.'

But this is the good old days. 'We aren't calling foot-faults tonight Mr Budge. Love–15,' replied the referee.

'The umpire wasn't buying,' says Kramer, 'and Gonzales was screaming, "C'mon Budge, quit stallin' and serve!" '

The incredulous Budge shook his head again, paused, then gazed over the net at his opponent.

Into the dark reaches of the hushed auditorium he threw out one last cry: 'All right, Pancho, if you're that desperate! And for one lousy point!'

Slowly, he returned to the baseline to serve.

In his own account of the match, Budge, the man who never lost his temper, admits he was 'seeing red'. Yet he tells us he stilled himself. Deliberately, he took the balls. He became icy, focussed.

A point down – and cheated – he began his serve.

And he won his service game.[4]

Down in the dim pit, the two were at each other's throats.

One was a proud young genius with a grudge against the world, ruthlessly on his way to the top. The other was a gentle man, prematurely old, and fast on the way down. But something had happened. The two men had been exposed, their competitive souls bared. Neither was the fox of the fable: both were playing for their lives ...

Grimly, the two exchanged serve to 4–All. With Gonzales serving, Budge edged to 30–40 and break point.

As Gonzales took the balls to serve, he must have reflected on how much had happened since he had paused mid-stage, and waved so joyously. Now the would-be king was no longer soaring. Abruptly, his wings seemed pregnable; by the minute, it was getting hotter.

Pancho went for everything on his first serve.

Budge explains: 'He smashed one of those 118 mph [190 kph] jobs at me – but I managed to get my backhand in front of it.'

The legendary Budge backhand was still alive. The return 'passed [the server] cold'.

It was Budge at 5–4, his serve.

Grim, desperate, chasing everything, Budge managed to hold – and took the set.

The next set followed an identical pattern – the pair traded serves to 4–4. Ellsworth Vines, that most insightful student, believed that, technically, Budge was always a better player than Gonzales. He wrote later that even at this stage of his career, Budge could often win the first set – or even sometimes the first two sets of a five-setter – but would still usually lose to the younger man.

So Budge knew that here, in his own gloaming, this second set was his last chance. He must break the fearful Gonzales serve, and hold his own.

He broke.

Though Budge does not explicitly tell us so, we sense that, as they changed ends at 5–4, our unlucky good man must have then taken a moment to look back. Both his past achievements and his thwarted dreams floated before his eyes. He must have thought: *If I am the person I think I am, I cannot waver.*

Budge edged to match point.

With a backhand Gonzales couldn't return, Budge held his serve.

There was a silence. Then someone clapped. Slowly, the crowd began to cheer.

In this best of-three-sets-match, *Old Porky* had beaten the best player in the world. And in straight sets 6–4, 6–4 – in a game the young champion was desperate to win.

Before the match Pancho had seen himself as at his peak against a has-been. Yet, here in his hometown, before parents, friends and family, he'd lost his cool and the match.

Now he really goes crazy.

Gorgo storms off, then goes berserk down in the locker room and smashes up his rackets. Next – and this makes him even madder – he grabs an expensive suitcase he has just bought and tramples it to bits.

●●●

After this additional performance, there were two surprise visitors to the locker room and its carnage.

First, a 'Mr Gonzalez' asked to see Budge.

It was Pancho's father. Judged at once 'a gentleman' by Budge, the visitor immediately explained his embarrassment over his son's behaviour.

Budge doesn't say what other words passed between himself and Manuel Gonzalez. But if forgiveness was involved, then the second gentleman present, Don Budge, is sure to have given it.

The second caller was Jack Kramer.

The wily promoter was ecstatic over the sensational contest just ended. So much so that Kramer, ever the businessman, had had an inspiration! Not quite tongue in cheek, Kramer told Budge that the just-completed match had shown the world that a fired-up Budge could yet turn the whole tour around. And win back his title! ... to say nothing of packing Kramer's venues – and his pockets.

Despite one battle lost, it was the insolent matador who won the war. Eventually, the kid from the wrong end of town did become *Richard Gonzales, World Professional Champion.*

His rule would be long but, as expected, not benevolent.[5]

Getting there – the road to the top

Among the flat and crumbling suburbs of outer Los Angeles, the child destined to become one of the greatest players in the history of tennis was born on May 9, 1928.

Ricardo was the oldest of the seven children of Manuel and Carmen Gonzalez, who a few years earlier had fled their origins in Chihuahua in Mexico. The colourful tennis historian, Gianni Clerici, tells us that Chihuahua was a small town celebrated only for 'its dogs and its poverty'.

His early experience as a struggling Chicano born in the Depression scarred Ricardo's psyche as permanently as a childhood accident marked his face. Though many thought – and Pancho, the man, would sometimes appear to agree – that the long scar on his left cheek resulted from a knife fight, there's a more likely explanation, only slightly less florid.

His autobiography, *Man with a Racket*, tells how one day the little Ricardo – even then infatuated with speed and machines, and equally unhappy with restrictions – was out riding his toy scooter. A good way from home, he was hit by a car, which cut his face badly and left the permanent scar. For certain, an unruly boy was to grow into a brooding loner.

The epigraph to this chapter, by fellow pro the marvellous *Little Pancho* Segura, is to the point. After reminding us that Gonzales was no saint, in his Foreword to Pancho's biography Segura added: 'Pancho is very even-tempered – he's always mad.'[6]

Though the Gonzalez family struggled, they were never really poor. Despite the Depression, father Manuel kept a job as a house painter, while mother Carmen found extra work to make ends meet.

In his autobiography, Gonzales' first wife, Henrietta, is quoted as saying: 'He is ... wild ... almost like an animal, always running somewhere after something.' This book also contains an 'appendage' mentioning his 1958 divorce from Henrietta. Gonzales' very last words in the book read as follows: 'Something inside me makes me want to run, run, run – in all directions – and none of them lead toward my home.'

Here again the Zen master's anecdote comes to mind – and the distinction between running for one's supper and running for one's life. With further haunting echoes of this story, Gonzales himself says his family was ceaselessly on the move, for 'the slums were always just behind us'. Without question, an innate disposition joined forces with this unsettled boyhood to form an inescapable feature of Ricardo's character: a deep-seated restlessness, sometimes as unbearable to him as to those around him.

Young Ricardo forever roamed the wide streets and, as boy became teenager, found some haunts in which to hang out. One was a sports store not far down the road. It was run by one Arzy Kunz, who was to become protector and friend of boy and man.

It was in Arzy's store that Gonzales spied his first tennis racket. By 11 years of age, he'd managed to get himself one. And the way he got it is instructive: his mother, desperate to get him off the streets, bought the racket as a bribe. It was an el-cheapo, by mail order.

'At first, I wasn't interested,' he tells us. But this didn't last long.

His gang of kids used to hang out at a nearby public park. Exposition Park lay in the shadow of the LA Coliseum, and was to play a central part in Gonzales' life. It's not hard to picture the little band of kids – mainly blacks and Chicanos in t-shirts and jeans; restless, smoking. The park had eight cement tennis courts, and sometimes the gang would extract themselves from scratch games of basketball, lounging or fighting, and take in the tennis.

One day, one of the group began to take a greater interest in what was happening on the tennis courts. The swarthy youth, his face showing a long scar on the left cheek, soon found himself pressed against the wire, absorbed in the play.

Here in front of me, he must have thought in a flash, *is something worth chasing.*

Running home, he got out his mother's present. From that moment on, tennis was his life.

He learnt the game by hitting any old balls against the wall of his house, and by watching and then playing at Exposition Park, but the process by which the young Ricardo mastered the fundamentals of stroke production remains controversial. Gonzales claimed he never received a tennis lesson in his life. Certainly, his style to the end remained more fluid, his stroke production more extempore, than those of any of the other great masters. Fastidious Ken Rosewall goes so far as to describe the Gonzales grips, the bedrock of his strokes, as 'all of his own invention'.

Without doubt Gonzales was by far the most self-taught of all the pro heroes. At every stage of his career Gonzales' primary method of learning was direct and unmediated: he watched, and then he copied. However, although this served him brilliantly, it appears that he received rather more direct guidance than he admitted. A haphazard training in the basics of stroke production did take place, and with crucial consequences.

At this very beginning of his learning the game, two persons were central.

Chuck Pate, who was a few years older than Ricardo, hung out at Exposition Park, attended Ricardo's high school, and played a beautiful game of tennis. It is likely that Pate had provided the 11-year-old Gonzales, peering through the wire, with his early epiphany.

Pate was tall, and possessed a powerful serve that was also extraordinarily simple and elegant. The wind-up was almost truncated, so that the racket head never dropped. Instead, it moved out in a wide arc, coordinated beautifully with the left hand; the weight then flowed into the toss just as it reached its maximum. All was economy, yet the action one fluid motion, free enough for the wrist to be adjusted at the last instant before the explosive strike.

To this Pancho added only his own idiosyncratic prelude. As beautifully described by journalist Rex Bellamy, Gonzales began with 'a few fidgety mannerisms (flicking beads of sweat from his brow, hitching a sodden shirt from his shoulders)'. Only then came the delivery, 'classically fluent and unfussy'. [7]

That excellent critic, Ellsworth Vines, wrote that years after the lad had discovered his model at Exposition Park, you 'couldn't tell the difference' between Chuck Pate's serve and Gonzales'. *Gorgo* himself says that on the rare occasions when his serve was off, he had a simple remedy: return and watch Chuck Pate – then back it would come.

Way before the appearance of books like *Zen and the Inner Game of Tennis*, Gonzales knew the power of the image. Throughout his life, he held in his head a slow-motion picture of his own service action. Every time he prepared to serve (as he fidgeted and hitched up his shirt), Gonzales was re-playing that image. Luminously, it was to sustain him, player and person, for the rest of his life.

The second crucial figure in Gonzales' early education was Frank Poulain.

In his autobiography – co-written, and with obvious colour, by Cy Rice – we are told that Poulain ran the far-from-swanky pro shop at Exposition Park. Poulain soon saw that within this truculent youth was a God-given talent. Before long he had befriended the young Chicano.

What happened then – the next episode in our hero's never-tranquil life – was crucial to Gonzales' tennis education, and to his character.

We have already seen that any young person from Southern California who wanted to get on in the game came under the sway of the 'czar': Perry T. Jones. So one day Poulain took this Chicano kid, rough and with 'attitude', but possessing a fabulous serve and moves, across town. They were to call on 'The Boss', Jones, ensconced in the swanky Los Angeles Tennis Club. If Jones would take him on, the kid would be on his way.

What followed is disturbing.

Jones did take a look at the kid. Although he didn't much like what he saw ('too lackadaisical', said Jones), he recognised a talent. But, after the cursory inspection, at a stroke Jones banned him from playing in his junior system – indefinitely.

Jones may well have been a tyrant, but it couldn't be said that he lacked dedication. Before Poulain and the gawky kid had arrived in his office, Jones had done his homework: he'd got hold of the boy's school records. They showed that Ricardo Gonzalez spent more time out of school than in it.

Jones had an inviolable rule for all his young charges: *first attend school.* So, aged 14 years, and fast becoming one of the best juniors in California, Jones' last words to the lad and his minder were: 'And kid, without a decent school record ... don't come back.'

According to Gonzales and co-writer Rice, here is what happened as the two were driving back from the Los Angeles Tennis Club to the Gonzalez home:

Poulain: 'Made up your mind about school?'

Ricardo: 'I'm finished with school. All I want to do is play tennis ... '

Poulain: 'Well if that's the way you want it ... '

Ricardo: 'That's the way I want it.'

Nearly 20 years later Gonzales adds: 'And that's the way it was.'

One can only register awe at the young teenager's self-belief and resilience – at a point when the establishment had peremptorily turfed him out. Or, we can't help asking, was this more Gonzales bravado?

As it tuned out, three years had to pass before the young firebrand got to play in another tournament – and, by then, escape the czar's jurisdiction.

With hindsight, we know that a few years under the control of Jones, with quality coaching from local pros such as Vines or Tilden, would probably have made Gonzales' game more stable and more orthodox. Certainly, Pancho's immediate predecessor, a more pliable lad named Jack Kramer, was one of many to take full advantage of the Jones system. If young Gonzales had been able to join in, he may also have become more of a team player, with a smaller log on his shoulder.

Whatever the outcome, being banned at a key stage of his junior career was a significant factor in the making of his character. If the youngster didn't know it already, he now believed that he owned only one resource: himself.

To link the angry loner of Pancho's adulthood with this seminal experience as a boy, here is more from the interview with Jones, and then a flash-forward to the veteran champion, as pictured by his fellow pros.

In his autobiography Gonzales claims that Poulain broached the interview by introducing his charge to Jones as 'a future champion of the US'. Jones was unimpressed: how many future world-beaters would have been brought before him? He'd seen 'hundreds of promising boys', he told Poulain, but most of them couldn't 'pass the test'.

Poulain exclaimed, 'You have a test? Test my boy!'

Jones replied that only one would work: 'Take a dozen boys up a steep slanting roof,' he said. 'Give them a push. Out of a dozen, maybe two would figure [how not to be] killed. From these two, one would make the grade.'

Pancho says he then spoke for the first time. 'Mr Jones, take me to the roof.'

Certainly, from then on young Ricardo Gonzalez treated the world as if it were the 'Perry Jones Roof Test', and this extreme of self-preservation never endeared him to his fellows. As Rod Laver admits years later in his memoir, *The Education of a Tennis Player*, the other pros so loathed *Gorgo* that they would barrack, if surreptitiously, for his opponent. But they had to be careful, for they knew that if they got him upset, there would be trouble. Worse, the demon would play better! [8]

Gonzales' team skills reached their nadir in the mid-sixties when he bitchily sued fellow pros Rosewall and Laver for 'restriction of business'. And their apparent crime? They'd tried to get Pancho to stick within the rules they'd all devised in order to help their tottering circus survive. [9]

But putting the clock back and returning to the mid-forties and Pancho's banishment by Jones, we arrive at a second interruption to the young man's career.

At 17 years of age, towards the end of the war, Gonzales joined the US Navy, and stayed there into the first months of peacetime for a total period of 18 months. This long gap could easily have badly hurt Pancho's tennis career, but in the end it didn't; when he finally returned, Gonzales went straight back into tennis, and was by then old enough, and good enough, to drop directly into the tournament circuit.

Now he was unstoppable. By 1948, he'd got to the big tournaments, and was electrifying the crowds with his looks, presence and sensational game.

So began a meteoric rise. From a No. 17 national ranking, and un-seeded, that year he took out the big one: the US National Championship. The following year, after 12 months of ups and downs, he not only successfully defended his crown at Forest Hills, but also came back from two sets down in the final to beat his then-nemesis, Ted Schroeder.

Although in that year he had crashed out of his only (amateur) Wimbledon, he actually managed, with Frank Parker, to take a 1949 Wimbledon title by winning the doubles. (The self-centred *Gorgo* never really cared for doubles, but he must have been pretty good at it!)

Further, he had played beautifully in his only Davis Cup tie, winning both singles. As it happened one of these was a victory against another upcoming young star of the same age, the marvellous Australian Frank Sedgman, later to become one of his toughest opponents as pro.

Then came a turning point.

Though relatively inexperienced, after back-to-back US Championships and his Davis Cup triumphs, the young *Gorgo* was beginning to feel ready for anyone. But unlike the man he'd just vanquished in the Davis Cup – Frank Sedgman, now tucked under the wing of Mother Hopman in Australia – *Big Pancho* had no trusted mentor. Here he was, out on his own, and full of himself into the bargain.

So in 1949, Pancho, all of 21 years and with the hungry eyes of the poor boy from the other side of the tracks, turned his gaze towards the pros. And what could he see? Money, big money.

The boss of the pros, Kramer, was interested: for sure, the kid could play, looked gorgeous, and the crowds loved him. So Kramer made the young man an offer.

Echoing the words of a recent US President who also laid claim to the gunslinger style, Gonzales responded: 'Bring 'em on!'

Before too long, the outcome was there for all to see.

While Sedgman, only a couple of months older than Pancho, was collaring half a dozen Grand Slam titles in the world's capitals – and becoming a national hero by securing the Davis Cup for his country – night by night the new pro Gonzales was being carved up by the mature master Kramer. Moreover, he might find himself tasting the bitter ashes of defeat at midnight in a dance hall in Grand Rapids, or a tent in Memphis.

Watching all this, and travelling with them, was one old master – the irrepressible, wily and genial Pancho Segura. Years later, reminiscing in a television retrospective, Segura admits how sorry he felt for the young challenger. Apparently Pancho would psyche himself up against Kramer to such superhuman levels that he would finally manage to snatch a match from the master. Then, one after another, he'd lose the next four, or six – or on one occasion twelve, in a row! [10]

Writing in *The Game*, Kramer confirms that the new boy was in 'way over his head'. With little idea of diet and training, he further damaged his cause by 'swigging Cokes' throughout a match.

'Polite gentleman that I am,' says Kramer, 'I made sure there was a cold and unopened bottle waiting for him at the cross-over.' He adds, 'I never said a word about the Coke until long after we finished touring – after I was through as a serious competitor ... Then ... at some tournament [in Africa] ... Pancho started swilling another Coke [and] I just stood there and said: "You know *Gorgo*, you got to be crazy to drink that stuff during a match." He didn't say a word back – only stared right through me with those dark eyes. I think it had finally dawned on him.' [11]

Yes, we see that the pros weren't real big on helping each other. Even the younger Gonzales does not readily excite pity, yet when observing the Kramer–Gonzales tour we're drawn to respond like Segura: 'Poor Pancho...'

Still, for the most part Gonzales learned fast. Years later, as a veteran of forty and still good enough to test the elite, he was so ruthlessly conditioned and disciplined that he would say bluntly: 'If I am even two or three pounds overweight, I'm certain to lose.' In the years between acolyte pro and veteran, the word 'pitiless' had come to characterise player and man.

The Kramer–Gonzales tour of 1949–50 had been a marathon humiliation. A 'death march' was the expression Kramer himself used to describe the final stages of the head-to-head of 126 matches, the longest of the pro era. But worse was to follow.

At tour's end Pancho found himself back where he'd started, hanging about in Exposition Park, Los Angeles. Returned was the ghost of the once-reluctant student, the same who had been forced to sleep on Frank Poulain's couch when hiding from the truant officer. After touring the world with the stars, he'd reached the level of racket stringer. Here was

Pancho Gonzales, a mere 22 years old, and already a Davis Cup victor and holder of two Grand Slam trophies, eking out life like an ex-tennis player.

Before long he was also an ex-champion estranged from his wife and young family, and nearly broke from a serious poker habit.

But even down there in what he himself called 'dead-end street', *Gorgo* never gave up. Somewhere inside him he preserved an image of himself as pure and powerful, and he waited for it to re-emerge.

And it did. He never tells us why, but one day, cold turkey, he stopped gambling. Next, he started on his fitness and a renewed study of his craft. Soon, ruthless-eyed, he began to believe that if he ever got another chance at the big time, he was ready.

Though the bitterness swelling in his mouth never left him, eventually the moment came. When *Big Jack* Kramer stood aside, *Gorgo* sprang.

This time there would be no going back.

Staying there: the stuff of a champion

So far this chapter has provided an outline of Pancho's origins and his early development as a player. We saw how, despite a messy studentship and a short and erratic amateur career, he managed to rise to the top of the amateur tree. Then came his early pro years, at first unpropitious, then bleak, until his irruption onto the pro scene as Pro Champion after the round robin tour of 1954.

We left him at the end of this tour, having survived an inconvenient, but temporary meltdown in his hometown. He was then aged 26, the legitimate successor to *King* Kramer, and on top of the world. However, as every champion (and every artist or businessman or general) tells us, getting there is one thing, staying there is another.

It is time for another snapshot. Fast-tracking four years, the incumbent champion is caught battling his all to remain on top. If his quarrel with Budge in his smoky hometown was a nadir in Gonzales' career, we now glimpse him at an apogee, definitively displaying the qualities that fashioned his greatness as a player.

In the four years since he took over *King* Kramer's crown in 1954, *Big Pancho* had done what he believed he could always do. He'd got on top, and he'd stayed on top.

First were the tournaments and mini-tours. He won most of them, and in doing so established superiority over the two other leading pros, the brilliant masters Segura and Sedgman. Then, a relatively easier task, he had faced head-to-head tours against the champions of the amateur world that the pros had lured into their ranks.

His first tour as champion began with Tony Trabert in 1955–56. Bluntly, in *Man with a Racket*, Gonzales shares his feelings about this tour against Trabert: 'If I lost to Trabert, I was a bum again – unemployed, unwanted. If I beat him, he was a bum. [One of us had to be] a bum – I didn't want

Fig. 5.1a. Tough for the new boys. At Kooyong, Australia, 1957, under lights, the pros are having a rare outing on grass. Fig. 5.1b. Gonzales pours the power into his service, with the artillery aimed at first-up pro Kenny Rosewall.

it to be me.' After the tour, the nastiest of the era, a shell-shocked Trabert said: 'The way [he plays] I think his real name is Pancho Villa [the Mexican bandit], not Pancho Gonzales.'

Next came Ken Rosewall a year later. Although both Trabert and Rosewall were thrown straight in at the deep end of the pro world, and both, especially Rosewall, did well, *Gorgo* stared down the usurpers. He defeated Trabert 74–27 and Rosewall 50–26.

Now Richard Pancho Gonzales was not just the undisputed Professional Champion of the World. To anyone who knew anything about tennis (the exceptions being those like Harry Hopman who were in the pay of the opposition), the 30-year-old was the best tennis player in the world, and by a country mile.

It was at this point that Gonzales found himself facing his greatest test. The next contender lured from the amateur ranks was to prove the most formidable he ever faced.

After trying for a couple of years, Kramer finally snared the amateur champion he wanted: Lew Hoad. After Hoad's second Wimbledon victory, Kramer had managed to contract the second (and the more popular and flamboyant) of the brilliant Aussie 'tennis twins', Rosewall and Hoad. For the title of Professional Champion of the World, over four months in a best-of-100 head-to-head, Kramer was going to pitch the blonde prince of the amateur world against the black king of the pros.

Two pieces of information are crucial to understanding what happened next.

First was the role of Kramer. The shrewd Californian ran the show and contracted the players. And he'd got *Big Pancho* in a deal that forever soured the relationship between the two men.

In essence, following new boy Pancho's whipping by Kramer in their tour of 1949–50, Kramer felt the newcomer was dead at the box office. Or perhaps, more fairly, the pro troupe was so small and so dependent on the regular infusion of head-to-head battles between the pro and amateur champions, little space was left for the (drastically) defeated contender. The upshot: Pancho's banishment to the public park.

But when the wily promoter found he could use him again, he was able to negotiate a contract with the desperate Gonzales that fixed his pay, and bound him for seven years. This became intolerable to Gonzales, especially by the time he'd got back and entrenched himself at the top of the slippery pole.

The second crucial feature of the current context was the immense disparity between the pro and amateur game.

To begin with, there was the difference in quality. Before his death in 1953, in an attempt to summarise what he had learnt in his lifetime of tennis, Tilden wrote his *Tennis A–Z*. There he tells how he used to watch the aging pro Don Budge practise with amateur champion Ted Schroeder. Day in, day out, *Schroeds* was carved up so badly he could hardly win a game, let alone a set, against the old master. And Tilden knew that Budge was playing little competitive tennis, and his game was well below the level of the three top pros, Gonzales, Segura and Sedgman.[12]

Likewise, a little later the amateur star Vic Seixas used to lure Segura on to the practice court for regular sessions – and Seixas would suffer the same annihilation as Schroeder. At the time, Schroeder and Seixas were Wimbledon champions at the top of the enfeebled amateur tree.

That the pros were far and away the best is further supported in a revealing anecdote from Gonzales himself.

The (ever-modest!) Gonzales tells us with relish that some time in the mid-fifties, two leading Italians, both clay court champions on the amateur circuit, came to him for a few tips. After a quick look, the champ decided to have some fun. Pancho would give them a contest – but play from the baseline, and soften up his serve. As well as showing them their place, it would give him a chance to work on his ground play.

The amateur stars were lucky to win one game each in the four consecutive sets that the champion deigned to bestow on each of them.

My own view of a vast disparity between pro and amateur was reinforced during a telephone conversation with Ken Rosewall. Talking about his early days with the pros, with a laugh he told me simply: 'Yes, when we first turned pro, each of us got a bit of a thrashing.'

The delightful South African Ray Moore had his own take on Rosewall's observation. Once, when asked how he was getting on in the pros, Moore replied: 'Since turning pro I've become much more consistent. Now I lose all the time.'

That disparity in quality – as well as the character of our particular hero – was once driven home to me directly.

It was about 1959, and the USA was playing an Interzone Davis Cup match at King's Park in Perth, Western Australia. To assist the young US team, Gonzales had been roped in. He must have been at a temporary loose end, and well paid: he hated coaching, and the national interest rarely coincided with his own.

This time *Gorgo* was working on his charges' serves. Then he swapped, and they had to return his serve. It was a hot day, and the world champion was bored. Even to the half dozen idolising schoolboys watching this lion from behind the wire, it was clear he saw the whole business as beneath him, and his opponents as inconsequential.

He began to send us a few asides to this effect, and then decided to have a little fun at the expense of his pupils.

The earnest American boys seemed to be doing OK; Pancho was serving, giving them a series of returns, backhands for a while, then forehands, so they could find a groove.

'But watch this,' whispered Pancho to his enthralled audience behind the wire. 'If I do this,' and he made a fist behind his back so we could see but his pupil-opponent couldn't, 'you'll see something.'

He went on serving, but from time to time, he threw us the signal.

Now the beautiful spring uncoiled a fraction more purposefully; at the top of the swing, almost imperceptibly, the wrist turned minutely.

And the hapless young representative of the great nation was aced so comprehensively that he had hardly moved before the ball had struck the backstop.

Gonzales could ace them at will. And he wanted to show us he could.

The image remains with me. It showed his superiority as a player, and the savage grace of his movement and presence. But it also reveals a man with the need to impress a few schoolboys he'd never seen before. Beneath *Gorgo*'s mask of implacable warrior was a real insecurity.

Such sheer technical ability was only part of the difference between the top pros and the top amateurs.

The amateurs played only by day on manicured courts, and got an easy run through the early rounds of their well-spaced tournaments. We've noted the terrible conditions the pros had to put up with, night-by-night, and that every game was like a final against another champion. Before long, to the new pro, the amateur world was some sort of distantly remembered pastoral.

Bud Collins tells a relevant story.

Neophyte pro Earl 'Butch' Buchholz was to face Tony Trabert, a multiple Grand Slam winner, somewhere in the sticks. The change room was a soap-box.

'Where in hell do I hang my clothes?' cried the new boy in despair, hardly able to turn around.

Street-wise Trabert responded by pulling out a hammer and nail and whacking the nail in the wall.

'Here!' Trabert replied with glee.[13]

One more trap for the new boys was the pros' stage.

As shown in Figures 1.7 in Chapter 1, and Figure 3.6 in Chapter 3, the physical 'turf' on which the pros of the era usually played indoors in the US, and onto which the new recruits were thrown, was a portable canvas sheet, tensioned by guy ropes.

Basically it played fast but true, but depending on the tension and on what lay beneath, the canvas could also sometimes shift alarmingly underfoot. Apparently the same (and hardly tended) court lasted for years, because Kramer tells of a short bit of worn seam deep in the first service box, just inside the centre line. Find it, and a decent serve became unplayable. 'We all knew about it,' says Kramer, 'but it was just right for my best serve – the cannonball down the centre.'

All of this was not a bit like Wimbledon, and 'stiff bickies' for the new boys!

However, it might seem that if anyone could adapt quickly to the rigours of life with the pros, it was surely Gonzales' challenger of 1958, Lew Hoad.

At this stage, Hoad was not just a sublimely gifted tennis player. Physically, he appeared to be at his peak and as strong as a bullock. And by then Gonzales was 30 years old. Yet when Hoad turned pro and set out to play *Gorgo* for the pro title, the smart money remained on Pancho. Long-time tennis watchers were only too well aware of the toughness of the conditions, and the toughness of the champion.

More than anyone, the ringmaster of the circus knew all this. *Big Jack* Kramer was fiercely proud of his pros. And all of them – with the possible exception of *Big Pancho* – found the boss to be as straight as his incomparable down-the-line forehand.

But by now Kramer had had enough of Pancho.

It wasn't only that the champion was an angry loner with a huge chip on his shoulder, and that the chip was held especially against the boss. Outside playing tennis, *Gorgo* would never lift a finger for the struggling circus of which he was a vital part. Whenever the other players were working together on their crucial publicity and community relations, or doing their best to build solidarity and hold the band together, the incendiary outsider was somewhere else.

The journalist and historian of the pros, Joe McCauley, relates a contemporary interchange between ringmaster Kramer and his star performer of the fifties.

'How are you getting on with the champ?' a mischievous reporter, clearly in full knowledge of the strained relations between the two men, asked Kramer.

'Pretty good,' acknowledged *Big Jack*, replying in kind, 'Why, he even said hullo to me the other day.'[14]

In short, because the box office needed a new star at the top, and because of *Gorgo*'s recalcitrance, Kramer had made up his mind – a succession was overdue.

But there was one further complication, which makes what happened next even more significant, and more poignant. Kramer felt that, at that very moment, the prize for which the pros had been fighting during a period of 40 years was nearly theirs: a truly open sport where pros and amateurs could compete freely against each other.

In the chapter devoted to Kramer we saw how, at that time, the weakened amateurs were losing their top players and their followers. In addition to Gonzales and Segura, Kramer held Sedgman, Trabert and Rosewall. These last three were former amateur truly-greats who held a dozen Grand Slam titles, and were national heroes and Davis Cup legends. And all five were close to the height of their powers! And now *Big Jack* had finally managed to snatch the glamorous Hoad, straight from winning back-to-back Wimbledons and coming within an ace of the Grand Slam.

In his autobiography, Kramer asked rhetorically at the time. 'Who would you rather see play? Cooper versus Anderson [two good but second-ranking

Aussie amateurs] for the championship of Australia, or Hoad versus Gonzales for the championship of the world?' The shrewd Kramer reasoned that if Hoad beat Gonzales, he would not only hold a new champion who was 'handsome ... popular ... cooperative,' but also one who 'could bring amateur tennis to its senses and force open tennis'.

Now we can now see that the Gonzales–Hoad tour was momentous – and for several reasons.

Apart from a world championship, here was a divided land, an empire waiting, an arrogant king and, in the wings, a comely prince of the royal line. And from Kramer's viewpoint, the sweet-natured young pretender could tip the scales for Open tennis – yet was likely to remain amenable to the man who, from behind the throne, was pulling the strings!

The tour lived up to all these expectations. It proved to be the most sensational of the dozen major head-to-heads of the pro era.

To deliver his coup and get his man the crown, there were three things that Kramer had to do. First he had to size up the incumbent, *Gorgo*. This could be counted as done. Then he had to assess his own man, Hoad, and his weapons. Finally, he had to work the contender up. But at every step he had to be very, very careful.

After the boss's first hard look at his new boy, the old pro was appalled. Even though the youth was so prodigiously gifted that the miracles he could conjure with a tennis racket often had the other pros turning away in despair, Kramer realised that seizing back power from the grizzly one was going to be far harder than he'd imagined.

There was profound shock in Kramer's initial assessment. When Hoad joined the tour, 'it was sickening, he had no defence at all'. As Kramer saw it, the first thing Hoad needed to learn was what Gonzales had taken four agonising years to discover. At this exalted level of skill, the greatest error you could make was to think you could survive if you relied solely on attack. Hoad's teachers Kramer and Segura may not have carried the *Tao Te Ching* with them on tour, but well they knew the gist of its message concerning confrontation: Says Lao Tsu in this ancient Chinese book of wisdom: 'When great forces meet, victory goes to the one who knows how to yield.'

Kramer describes how the pros' guru Segura would be almost reduced to tears trying to get the young warrior Hoad to lob. And he describes how Hoad was the only person he ever saw who, when forced wide and six yards behind the baseline, would try to 'make the return with a hard snapped topspin crosscourt'. Though the Adonis with a wrist of steel could sometimes bring off such shots, the percentages weren't there. In Segura's witty words, unlike the amateurs the pros had to pay tax. If you didn't, you couldn't live with Rosewall, Segura, Sedgman and Trabert. And you'd be mincemeat if thrown to the champion.

So what did Kramer do? Said *Big Jake*: 'I took him out.'

Unlike Trabert and Rosewall – and unlike Pancho himself when he was thrown at Champion Kramer – the contender was given six months to bring himself up to par. Only after this would Hoad be thrown at the Pro Champion Gonzales.

'Gonzales knew exactly what I was doing,' says Kramer, 'and he was furious.'

As we saw in the chapter on Kramer, when Hoad wasn't firing he was so off the pace that even Jack himself, significantly injured and way out of competition, could still give him a 'bit of a thrashing'; Ken Rosewall's words for the usual fate of the new boy on the pro block. But bit by bit, and with many ups and downs, to almost everyone's surprise and delight by the time the six months came to a close Kramer's plot seemed to hold a chance of success.

While Hoad never became a masterful defender, he did learn how to control his attack, reduce his errors to a minimum and stay in a point or game by keeping the ball in play. And sometimes, extracting a wry smile from the burnished Inca face of Segura up in the stands, Hoad would change pace with a chip or a dink, toss up a surprise lob to back his opponent off the net or, when way out of position, temporise with a high defensive one.

Gonzales watched, and saw everything. He knew this was going to be his toughest opponent. On the first occasion they faced each other – in the tour opener in Australia in Brisbane in January 1958 – Hoad proved that he had graduated from his master's course, with honours.

How then were these two superb athletes matched?

Hoad possessed *Gorgo*'s power, and his serve and overhead were equally severe. If he moved almost as well as the gorgeously fleet and balanced Pancho, he volleyed even better. (Gonzales 'chipped' his volleys, said Quist, whereas Hoad punched them). Further, Hoad's ground strokes, and particularly his glorious backhand – often struck on the rise and over-spun – were almost as deceptive as the wristy creations of the champion, but more impenetrable.

Then, sometimes, when the moon was in the right quarter, Hoad could take his game to another plane. Then he would create shots that weren't in the book, certainly not in Gonzales' book, and not – at least until Rod Laver came on the scene some years later – in anyone else's.

Sparing in his praise of opponents, Gonzales admitted (of course much later!) that even he could feel disheartened when Lew was 'on' and would start 'volleying away my smashes.' Just before Gonzales died, he made what was for him a stupendous admission. In Jenny Hoad's touching memoir, *My Life with Lew*, Pancho concedes that of all the opponents he ever met, Lew was – when both were playing at their respective best – the only one he felt he couldn't beat. [15]

Thus it appeared that Hoad was as strong as the champion, possessed a more complete game, and had learned to temper his own aggression and happy-go-lucky nature. So on paper, the young lion of a contender was ahead, if just ahead, of the incumbent.

But a tennis match is not played on paper: it is not machines, but two fraught human beings that are pitted against each other. Beyond technique, the old champion was harder, and craftier.

The balance was square.

At first, the technical side of the analysis looked on track.

The first 13 matches were to be played in Australia and New Zealand. From the start, the challenger began winning matches, especially on the few top, fast, grass courts the pros had been able to snare. By the time they left Australia for New Zealand, Hoad was just 4–5 behind. But by the end of January 1958 – with the 'Down Under' leg behind them, and the pair headed for the US – wonder of wonders, the amiable blonde was leading the disagreeable swarthy, eight matches to five!

There are some insightful contemporary accounts of this crucial stage of the battle.

Gloria Kramer, Jack's wife, was travelling with the troupe. Just as the first leg of the tour was finishing, she wrote a letter to the tennis journalist, Jeane Hoffman, and it appears in *Man with a Racket*.

After raving about the sensational match-up between Lew and Pancho, and the spectacular public interest and takings, she continues: 'No doubt you are surprised Lew is leading. So is everybody ... I keep saying to Jack, "Why ... ?"... Jack ... had said Lew was a great kid [but] he didn't think he'd ever win! Obviously, the little "warm-up" trip did a lot of good ... It's sort of cute how Jack watches over Lew like a mother hen ... Lew is very co-operative ... is built like an ox ... appears the stronger ... and is hitting with tremendous confidence.'

Clearly astonished at the way the tour is unfolding, she then breaks from writing to ask 'the boys' whether there could be 'anything wrong' with Pancho. The other pros reply that the champion seems fine. Pancho himself comments later that though he was in fact fit, in all other respects Gloria Kramer's analysis of Hoad's relative strength was on the button.

But remember the irrepressible 14-year-old Gonzales in the car with Poulain after being thrown out by the establishment? Well, he's still there. And what Gonzales goes on to say in his autobiography shows just how irrepressible he remained.

Right at this point Pancho asks himself a question: *OK, the kid's ahead, but what's in store for this would-be usurper?*

'No,' answers Gonzales, 'there was nothing basically wrong with me that a tour grind wouldn't fix up. Hoad is very strong and he is built like an ox and if I wanted to make a bad joke I'd say that I love to eat oxtail soup. And speaking of soup ... Lew wasn't going to get any more of a native Australian specialty which was kangaroo tail soup. He was about to embark on a foreign diet. I knew what my stomach was made from – cast iron. Lew's stomach was going to get severely tested from restaurant to restaurant, night after night, and the strain on his eyes – whether he's driving or a passenger – watching that concrete ribbon of roadway could exact its toll. '

The ruthless old lion with the cast-iron stomach may well have been more jungle-wise than the challenger, but at this point in the tour he was in even deeper trouble than he admitted. It was precisely at this point in the tour that two imponderables began to emerge. Unknown at first, they would tip the balance – and seal the fate of both men, one of them forever.

The first was that Hoad had well and truly drawn on his newfound knowledge of his craft: he had discovered the champion's Achilles' heel.

In short, Hoad realised that under extreme pressure the Gonzales backhand was not only suspect, but also predictable. Self-taught Pancho used an idiosyncratic 'hammer' grip, with fingers bunched, for both forehand and backhand. The result? If forced on the backhand wing, especially by Hoad's powerful first volley or heavy approach shot, without the full support of his wrist he could only return with underspin, and down the line ... straight into the omnivorous Hoad forehand volley. Bang! Point over.

In fact, Hoad's discovery was nothing new. A decade earlier, a major reason Kramer had annihilated *Gorgo* was because Kramer had the power on serve, and the penetration on approach, to press the Gonzales backhand.

Fig. 5.2. Gonzales in his untutored youth. Long before his time as pro, Pancho's bunched grip is too much on top of the racket. The pro battleground forced him to restructure the shot.

Then it would 'push up' to yield Kramer the killing volley. Even though, in the meantime, Gonzales had greatly improved his ground shots – his forehand, said Hoad simply, was 'tremendous' – a flaw persisted. The problem with his backhand might now be harder to pick – and tougher to expose – but an elite could do so.

Hoad was proving the ancient tennis adage: *all other things being more or less equal, the player with the better strokes wins.* Though Gonzales never admitted it, Hoad had found him out. When he needed it, the champion couldn't find a winning cross-court backhand drive.

On such apparently trivial matters swung a crucial point and consequently a match ... a series ... and a world title. And both players knew it.

What then did Gonzales do?

In Hoad's own words, he 'changed his grip'. Well into a grinding tour, on the road, falling behind and hanging on for dear life against the most formidable opponent of his mature years, the old champion realised something crucial: a technique that had been good enough was no longer so.

So came the unthinkable. On the backhand, Pancho spread his fingers, and moved his hand around a quarter turn behind the handle. Suddenly, to Hoad's utter amazement, Pancho started hitting hard crosscourt winners off his backhand. Later Hoad, writing an instruction chapter entitled *The Backhand Myth*, said, 'Only a colossal natural ... could have done it.'[16]

Just a week off the plane from Australia, with the first part of the tour finished and Hoad forging ahead, Kramer came across the Champion in an unguarded moment, and their eyes met. Kramer recalled: 'They were the eyes of a beaten man.'

But only a few weeks on and fully into the US part of the tour, the tide was beginning to turn. *Gorgo* admitted he felt different: he was beginning to flow. In his toughest moment, the proud old champion had found a response, and proved to himself that he remained a master. True masters may get beaten, but they are never shown up. [17]

It was around this time that the second imponderable came into play.

In two words, it was Hoad's back. As it turned out, the frame of the young man built like a truck driver was as flawed as Gonzales' technique.

Hoad's back problem was not new. He had suffered from it for most of his adult life, and (to our modern horror) on one occasion during his

Fig. 5.3. New tricks from an old dog. With his rebuilt backhand, the mature pro Gonzales demonstrates beautiful Eastern form in this running topspin backhand.

amateur career had been placed in a plaster cast for months. Now he was in a murderous tour lasting five months. Night after night he played, often in best-of-five-set matches without tie breaks. And day after day, from venue to venue, he spent hours in cramped cars on the road. The strain was killing him.

Only from his wife Jenny's recent memoir can we learn the degree of escalating hurt and disability her poor Lew had to endure. She tells us his back was so bad that for much of the US leg, Lew was in constant pain and couldn't even bend to tie his shoelaces. One day, at the end of a long cold car journey, Hoad was in such frozen agony that the others had to unstick him and carry him from the car. That night (or the next night, or both) he had to face a ravenous Pancho Gonzales baying for blood in a match usually played on un-giving hard courts.

As anyone in modern sports knows, the only solution was a decent break, with time for rest, therapy and recuperation. Hoad and Kramer considered this, but the schedule had been pre-arranged to the last detail, and the struggling show had to go on. And on, and on ...

However, it took a while for these two unknowns to work their way through.

As noted, Hoad had started off well: with a dozen matches completed as they departed Australia and New Zealand at the end of January, he was in front, and then he kept going at the beginning of the US leg. During the first weeks of February, of the next 13 matches played, Lew took 10 of them.

Precisely then came the turning point.

The progress of the tour is shown graphically in Figure 5.4. It highlights when, seven weeks into the tour, the champion began clawing back Hoad's lead.

For Hoad the month of March, two months after the tour had started, spelt disaster. From a lead of 18–9, he lost all but three of the next 15 matches. The two men were locked on 21 matches apiece, with still another 40 or 50 to go.

By now *Gorgo* had begun to get his new backhand together, and was playing beautifully; in contrast, Hoad was often partially crippled, and rarely able to move freely, or hit an overhead or serve at anything like full pace.

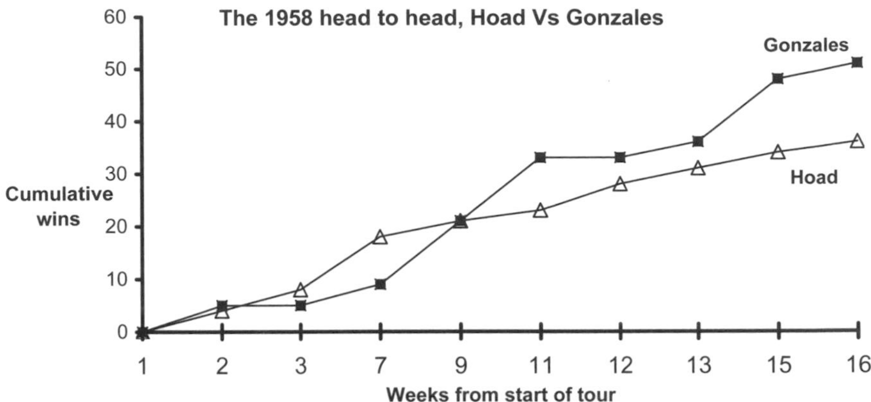

Fig. 5.4. The 1958 World Pro head-to-head, Gonzales versus Hoad, match by match. Hoad's early lead is whittled down, then, nine weeks into the tour, as the challenger's fitness cracks, it's wrenched away.

Then in April things got worse for the challenger. The Champion took all but two of the following 14 matches. He was breathing easier.

In his autobiography Pancho recalled this moment: 'With a 10-point bulge, 33 to 23 ... I felt certain Lew would begin to crack, and I would win in a breeze.'

In his autobiography Pancho recalled this moment: 'With a 10-point bulge, 33 to 23 ... I felt certain Lew would begin to crack, and I would win in a breeze.'

But the incumbent was overconfident. Hoad had a brief respite from his pain, hung in 'like a bulldog' and 'won the next four straight'. And then took four of the next seven.

After 67 matches, Gonzales held the slenderest lead, 36 to 31.

For poor Hoad, those last four wins were Pyrrhic victories. It had been too much: his run was finished. In the next 15 matches, he could grab only three. The champion was ahead 48 to 34, and needed only three more wins to reach the best of 100 and clinch victory.

Hoad fought it out, but the proud incumbent got the required three from the last five matches. By 51 to 36, the reigning champion had kept his crown.

At the end of the head-to-head battle, Pancho admitted that the Hoad tour was 'the worst strain I ever went through'. Yet as it happened, the master had ended up more than winning, he'd found a new backhand and a renewed respect for the depth of his own resources.

And what about the challenger?

After this head-to-head, Lew Hoad was never the same player. He never regained the fitness that allowed him to play consistently at the superlative level of skill and stamina that he showed in the first third of the Gonzales tour, and from time to time during the latter part of it.

For several years after this tour Hoad remained close to the top of the pros, and on occasion he could still call up bursts of tennis made in heaven: yet by then these were the sweet but sudden stuff of dreams. The Hoad genius, glimpsed in full flower at the beginning of the Gonzales tour, did survive, but the frame necessary to sustain it did not. The strongest and most gifted player of the modern era had been fatally wounded.

The final image on page 366 of this book pictures Lew Hoad in the dressing room just before his last amateur Wimbledon Championship. In his *At Home in Australia*, Peter Conrad provides a moving two-paragraph commentary on David Moore's photograph.

For Conrad the picture captures the would-be victor's vulnerability: here is a man caught between 'the camouflage of the street – discarded on those [clothes] hooks – and the costume required by the stage ... the court'. And, like 'all Australians', Hoad is 'worrying about his inadequacy'. On this occasion, the light streaming from the open window 'awards him an aureole'.[18]

A few moments after the photograph was taken, out he strode, and triumphed.

With the uncanny capacity of art to mimic – and to prophesy – life, photographer Moore has discovered the fragile in the conquering hero, even when it was most hidden and fleeting. However, by mid-way in the Gonzales tour, this hero's vulnerability had become obvious, and permanent. And there were no further shafts of redeeming light.

In situations as dramatic and tragic as this, the *what if* questions are irresistible. What if Hoad's body had been able to take the strain? Or what if this tour had taken place with modern opportunities for therapy and rest? In either case, would the result have been different?

While no one will ever know the answers, it's clear that when Hoad was at his peak, fully focussed and fully fit, he was by a fraction the better player of the two, and had climbed ahead on tour. Even when we recognise that Pancho was the more seasoned campaigner, improvising brilliantly, it seems likely that a fit Hoad would have been able to keep his nose in front – and become the next champion. Yet in the end it was just as the scabrous *Gorgo* had foretold: the last man standing was the harder of the two, the old warrior with the 'cast-iron' stomach.

Thus Kramer's coup failed, and doubly. The sweet young contender did not conquer the throne, nor did the pros gain what they craved and most needed: a new order that would have been irresistible to the paying public and to the mossbacks that held the power.

Another decade of doldrums would have to go by before the game was made Open.

The style of Gonzales

Although most tennis followers paid tribute to the power and beauty of Gonzales' serve and net attack, and some also acknowledged the quality of the fluid game that backed them up, the core of his game was rarely grasped by most contemporary analysts.

This was because the Gonzales style was so gloriously individual, and so nuanced, that few could see it for what it was. Beyond the awesome serve, the crashing overhead and the pinpoint volley, the mature Pancho had developed a way of playing tennis that was a far cry from the relentless serve and net attack associated with Kramer, Hoad and Sedgman, and with which he is usually linked. The acute Bobby Riggs even went so far as to characterise Pancho as 'essentially a defensive' player!

To understand Riggs's point we need to hear what Gonzales himself says about what he called the 'hardest lessons' he had to learn on the way up. Early on, Gonzales had learnt how to direct his strongest weapons against his opponent's relative weaknesses. But experience taught him that even his own greatest strength, his usually lethal serve, could at times be turned against him. Even on fast wood, when facing supreme masters of the return of serve, he saw the futility of following every serve into net. Against the superlative Segura or Kramer forehands, or against both wings of even the aging Budge, it was useless to go in after anything but one of his best serves. Better to swallow pride, hold back the prized weapon, and sometimes keep to the baseline. Better for the server not to suffer the humiliation of being 'aced' by the returner ricocheting his thunderbolt past him.

Like the best generals, Pancho had discovered that defence was crucial. If he was being pushed down and back, he now knew how to invert the aggressive tactics of his earlier days, and scramble and dissemble, graft and lob. This enabled him to stay alive – and then, maybe, find a way to get back.

Vines expands this description of the reigning champion as follows.

'Gonzales' style was misunderstood,' says Vines. Although 'he had big shots,' these were 'almost incidental to ... his game.' Yes, Pancho 'never choked and was a superb competitor and a clever tactician'. Vines points to what really set him apart: his reach and his moves. Undoubtedly Gonzales could 'windmill' the net – and with his reach, agility, and reflexes he could set up the clinching smash or volley – but the secret of his craft was the surreptitious way he got to that point.[19]

According to Vines, Pancho was an individualist with a unique 'freedom of movement' on all of his shots, and this allowed him to improvise a variety of hard deep drives, or soft chips and 'deep junk' (slow high balls)

Fig. 5.5. The Gonzales reach. Playing with Rosewall, veteran Gonzales dumbfounds opponents Okker and Reissen by covering almost the whole court for an interception. This one won't come back.

through which he could jerk an opponent all over the court. Only then came the clincher: a huge, whipped forehand or, having climbed what Rosewall beautifully described as the Gonzales 'invisible ladder', the buried smash. Sometimes he would even holster that canon and let escape the audacious 'drop smash', merely tickling an angled overhead over the net while his opponent was flinching metres behind the baseline. Always, if ambivalently, in love with his bad-boy image, on an occasion like this he would further humiliate his hapless opponent by flashing his I've-sacked-the-joint, Mexican-bandit grin.

Gonzales' main criticism of the acolyte pro Hoad was that he tried 'to finish off a point too soon'. The older Pancho remembered only too well his crushing defeats at the hands of Jack Kramer. Though he went hard for the jugular, as a mature champion Kramer knew exactly how to set up a point that would end with a put-away, and how to defend with the best of them.

But the mature Gonzales went further than Kramer: he loved to rally. As Vines observed, this gave him a chance to 'saunter', until he could force the net and break open the point.

We can isolate this 'saunter' by turning our attention away from Pancho's opponent and the ball, and focus on Gonzales. Cropping up continuously as part of a series of thrilling exchanges – and so easily missed – once recognised and observed this was a gorgeous thing.

According to Vines, the Gonzales saunter was 'a weaving motion in which he swayed on his toes from side to side while gradually moving ... to the net.' This shifting flow allowed him to exploit his balance and mobility. Coupled to his superb half-volleying, it maximised his exemplary facility to move sideways or to reverse.

Alongside a tiny group of champions including Cochet, Perry, Sedgman and Rosewall, Gonzales was a master of the mid-court, a normally taboo area Paradoxically, it was often from there that he would set up – perhaps two or three shots away – the exact moment to pull out a big gun, and shoot to kill.

Pancho was tall, but he resembled a 'stalking tiger' (Vines' words). This particular tiger gave the daunting impression it was 'never really extending itself' – and behind the seeming ludic saunter were the teeth. No wonder

Fig. 5.6. Speed, reach, and movement. His lunge brushing back his hair, Gonzales is perfectly balanced in mid-court, strangely enough an area he seemed to relish.

Hoad admitted that when he first played Gonzales he felt that he had been caught in the 'jaws of a vice'.

Gorgo himself says it all. In his autobiography he explains that what had won for him, in the end, was not his power, but 'my legs, retrieving, lobs, and ... change of pace.' Only then he added, almost as an afterthought: 'And my serve.'

Once, when asked about his love of hot-rod racing, Gonzales added a relevant throwaway line: 'But a man can make his own thunder.' And playwright Jean Cocteau described the artist as 'a sort of prison from which works of art escape'.

By the time of his maturity, Gonzales was a performer so dazzling that he could provide his own thunder; and so creative that he could escape from the prison of his angry self to make art.

A sort of retirement

Space does not permit a full account of the later achievements of Gonzales. Gloriously, they continued until he was well over forty. Before he entered his first 'retirement' in 1960 and Rosewall took over as Pro Champion, Gonzales had gone from defeating Trabert, Rosewall and Hoad to conclusive victories over amateur champions Olmedo, Buchholz, McKay, Anderson and Cooper.

However, after apparently retiring in 1960, he came back – and kept coming back.

In 1961, he beat Sedgman for his eighth US Pro Championship. In 1964, then 36 years old, he won the US Pro Indoors, defeating Laver, Hoad, and Rosewall on successive days! Three years later, perhaps sensing the Open Era to come – and having played very little tennis for two years – he entered and won several tournaments. During these he inflicted several defeats on Laver at his peak.

Like his ability, his attitude seemed little softened by time.

On one occasion, straight from another 'retirement', he was signed for a mini-tour in which he had to play the amateur champion and rookie pro Fred Stolle. Gonzales took Stolle apart, night after night. After watching one match, a dumb-founded Lew Hoad commented, 'He still plays for his life!' At the same time Gonzales himself was reported as saying: 'Fred [Stolle] has a lot to learn ... but I'm not going to teach him.'

In 1971 Gonzales, now forty-three, defeated the up-and-coming Jimmy Connors, aged 19, for the Pacific Southwest Championship. This was a tourney Pancho had first won 23 years earlier (in 1948), when he was the same age as his opponent.[20]

While Pancho continued to play and win after the 1969 Open Wimbledon, his performance in that tournament could be considered his true swan song. With his coal-black hair touched with grey, by then he was leaner and more lupine than ever – and to any opponent, even more intimidating. When he returned to play in only his third Wimbledon, even the unconvinced posh of the All England Club recognised the aura of the man. In one of the very greatest matches ever seen there, at the age of 41, he faced 25-year-old Charlie Pasarell in a seesaw battle that lasted over 5 hours.

Because this extraordinary contest concentrates so much of the Gonzales style and character, it is worth examining to finish this account of his tennis life.

Gonzales lost the first set. But, in the era before the tie break, it was by 22 games to 24. And in that set, Gonzales had saved 11 set points!

Then dark and drizzle descended.

When the umpire, then the tournament referee, refused to call the match off, Gonzales reacted with petulance, which turned into anger, which turned into fury. After that it was obvious that, mentally as well as physically, the veteran felt he'd had enough.

Fuming, Pancho threw the next set 6–1.

Fig. 5.7. The veteran reveals control at full stretch – but the strain shows.

At this the crowd also got angry. When eventually bad light did stop play, the usually politeness-itself Wimbledon crowd had become incensed by Gonzales' unsporting behaviour on their sacrosanct turf. Probably for the first time in the tournament's history, they booed him from the court.

The next afternoon, the pair was back to finish their match.

But lo and behold! *Gorgo* had had a change of heart! Now he was trying so hard he took the next two sets 16–14 and 6–3.

His new feeling was again infectious. Now *the crowd* was experiencing a change of heart! We can imagine the Brits saying to each other with astonished wonder, 'Marvellous, marvellous, this chap is marvellous!'

But feelings are not enough. By the opening of the fifth set, the older man looked exhausted. Further, his young opponent – four years old when Gonzales had first played Wimbledon, and won the Doubles title – was in no mood to let sentiment get in the way of winning.

Pasarell edged ahead, and reached match point.

By then, the crowd had come to admire the young hero and forgive the old one. In front of them was a veteran who might never have reached the final rounds of the Wimbledon singles tournament yet, beyond doubt, had today proved his greatness. And opposing him was a gutsy and brilliant youngster with his future before him.

At this point, most watchers were ready to concede a great match to Pancho's brave young opponent.

But out on court, Gonzales felt differently: he had not given up. *Forget the past!* he must have told himself, *I'm in a tennis match, playing for my life.*

One by one, Pasarell got to another six match points, but Gonzales didn't flinch. He won every one of them.

Nevertheless, Pasarell kept ahead until he reached 9 games to 8.

What happened next suggests a *third* 'change of heart' in our hero. As with the first, when Gonzales had nearly thrown the match, he must have decided that he'd 'had enough'. But this time he was finished with losing.

We can almost hear the thoughts of the veteran, near exhaustion: *This kid is good, but he's not Jack Kramer. Not Lew Hoad. And I am Gonzales. All I need is this: two of my service games, and one of his.*

He flicked at his shirt. He looked inside. There, waiting, was the magical spring of his serve.

Then, reeling off ten straight points, he ran to 10–9, 40–15. And match point.

Again he paused. He hitched. He looked. He found.

And served. An unplayable ace.

It was his set, 11–9.

So, after a record 112 games, his match.

As he left the court, those who had earlier broken convention and booed him, now gave him one of the greatest standing ovations offered to a player in the tournament's history.

●●●

From the beginning, this great contest on Centre Court seemed to hold a sharpened sense of theatre.

At first, it was youth versus age. As the match progressed, it became beauty versus the beast. But from the turning point when the match resumed after rain, the two protagonists appeared to take on qualities more various and more human. As a result, when the players left the court at the end of the match, to the spectators they were heroes. As the crowd filed home, they must have been filled with wonder at the possibilities of being human. How resilient, how brave, how enduring are we!

Indeed, there were many things at work in this fabulous confrontation. For a start, this match had been calling up tennis ghosts aplenty. Where — so the crowd must have been asking themselves — had this triumphant hero and his fellow prodigals from the old pros *been* for the last 20 years? And why, for Heaven's sake, was this old master playing in only his *third* Wimbledon?

I suspect that, beyond tennis history, the match's rich resonances were compounded by contemporary events.

The larger society, not just the tennis world, was in a period of rapid change. Pancho Gonzales could be seen as one of a group of mould-breakers who had arisen right at the midway point of the twentieth century and touched such deep chords that they had changed the way society saw itself. Like the actors, Marlon Brando and James Dean, or the musician Miles Davis, *Gorgo* had made a thing of being a rebel, or a rebel-without-a-cause, brooding and inarticulate. Yes, these might have been brave men, but they

Fig. 5.8. The matador with an endless stream of admirers. In a rare drop into gossip, Rod Laver noted: 'Pancho was hell with the sheilas,' (sheila, Aussie slang for woman).

Fig. 5.9. Working the crowd. As usual, Pancho is engaging with the spectators, and/or intimidating, and/or charming the linesman. Rosewall noted there was 'an incident' every time they played.

also managed to sow a sense of restless alienation, a bitter essence of the later twentieth century.

As with these three contemporaries, Gonzales also possessed what the Spanish call *duende,* the capacity to summon emotion from the audience. It is a quality distilled by great matadors or flamenco dancers.

With striking relevance, Miles Davis's biographer John Szwed examines this quality and those contrary personalities that it inhabits. He notes that '*duende*, like the blues, was personified as a demonic spirit capable of troublemaking and bringing with it irrationality, earthiness, a strong sense of death'.[21]

As with Davis, such hauntings were never far from the figure of Pancho Gonzales.

Beyond the poignancy of witnessing the final act of a great master – one just home from exile – these were some of the great gongs that resounded during that incomparable Wimbledon contest of 1969. Striking the gongs, letting loose the music, our darkly troubled protagonist battled his way to victory.

But we realise that his heroism, forged throughout a lifetime of struggle, was the modern kind. This man would die for victory. Yet he is one of those outsiders who, walking out alone into the rain, in the final reckoning judge victory and its spoils as nothing. They are anti-heroes, owned by different, darker gods than those of the mere accountant player who tallies victory, or defeat.

When he finally retired from the circuit in his late forties, the old warrior's demons began to let him more alone, and he softened a little. But the man his fellow pros called *Gorgo* never lost his rage. Aware that it could erupt at any time, all who knew him and shared time with him – even those sometime-larrikins like the Australian champion John Newcombe – treated him carefully. As the usually restrained Ken Rosewall says in his memoirs, there always hung about him 'an ineradicable aura of violence'.

The source of this anger cannot be entirely explained by his background, and family of origin. The Gonzalez family were tough and pretty poor, but they provided a supportive home. And though a Chicano from the wrong side of the tracks, on his own admission, he never faced significant racial prejudice until adulthood.

Gonzales might also never have found a true mentor, but there were many like Chuck Pate and Frank Poulain who put themselves out on his behalf, and did their best to guide him through a turbulent youth and early adulthood. Even more, as he reached maturity as a player, an abundance of magnificent role models were available. Amongst his competitor contemporaries, Don Budge, Jack Kramer, Pancho Segura, Frank Sedgman, Tony Trabert and Ken Rosewall retained the values of true sportsmen.

No, born with what some cultures call 'an old soul', Pancho had started off angry. And here's the rub. Like a number of great artists, very early he knew the price of getting to the top. His anger would stoke his desire to be the best. As for 'happiness', it remained forever a trap, a diversion from the main game.

In his autobiography, written at only 30 years of age, he said that one day, when he turned 70, he might stop chasing and 'slow down'. Pancho never reached 70, but died in 1995, aged 67. True to himself, before that he had never really slowed down.

The tennis journalist Richard Evans visited him in his quasi-retirement, and found the old wolf almost as minatory as ever. And as singular. Evans caught him striking golf balls from his back porch into the sunset of a vast Nevada desert.

Then Evans watched as *Gorgo*, alone, went to scratch them out from the sand.[22]

●●●

I have heard of a belief that there is a section of Heaven to which great performers, in sport as well as the arts, are granted special entry. By their sublime display they add to the heavenly bliss of the residents. Given the temperament of many artists, that access may be temporary, but an entry nonetheless.

If such celestial entertainers exist, among them is certain to be found a less-than-friendly figure, darkly handsome and scarred of face. But when a tennis racket is placed in his hand, this man raises his arms, flashes a hugely infectious grin and – crying 'bring 'em on!' – leads his fellows out to play.

Soon the watching saints and gods are unable to resist. 'Go on, Pancho,' one of them calls out. 'Show us how to saunter!'

At this point, a fellow player – a good-natured redhead hailing from California, and one of the few artists and sportsmen in permanent residence – is happy to help out.

'You guys need a good take of the Pancho saunter?' he hollers genially, and taps a few pat-balls back for his opponent to attack.

Then, because this is Heaven, the recently reconstituted Ricardo Alonzo Gonzalez at once begins to show them how it's done – and just how easy it all is.

Soon every one of them on those heavenly fields is laughing.

And in a flash, gods, saints and sinners are beside him, and at play together.

Notes

1 Quoted by Joe Hyams in *Zen in the Martial Arts*. My main source for this chapter is Pancho Gonzales, *Man with a Racket: The Autobiography of Pancho Gonzales*, as told to Cy Rice, Thomas Yoseloff, London, 1959. Gonzales also wrote a useful instruction book: Pancho Gonzales with Dick Hawk, *How to Play and Win at Tennis,* Souvenir, London, 1962. All Gonzales quotations and references in this chapter are from *Man with a Racket*. Other sources drawn upon are the fine autobiographies of Kramer and Budge; Laver's memoir, *The Education of a Tennis Player*; and Hoad's autobiography, Lew Hoad with Jack Pollard, *My Game*, Hodder and Stoughton, London, 1958.

2 'Pancho' was used on all but the most official occasions, and I use it here in the same spirit, not as a nickname. 'Gorgo' had its origins in 'gorgonzola'. As a rising amateur, Gonzales lost some big matches he should have won. Thus judged soft, he came to be called the 'Cheese Champion.' So from 'gorgonzola' to the alliterative *gorgonzales*, and the nickname. But later, it stuck with the pros and seems to have retained the whisper of the derisory, with resonances as mythical as mundane. However, relying on the listener's ignorance of Spanish, overweening Pancho could claim *Gorgo* was *gorilla* in Spanish! (It isn't). The spelling question also has a story behind it. Kramer believes that a social climber amongst *Gorgo*'s many wives (*Big Jake* says Gonzales was married 'about six times', including twice to the same person) discovered that Gonzalez with a 'z' was the spelling used by the aristocracy. Consequently, she began pushing the original spelling. But it didn't stick, and though some modern tennis writers have preferred the correct spelling, here I keep the name used when he was Pro Champion. 'Now I have to sign my cheques with an "*s*",' said *Gorgo*. That seems good enough for us.

3 Kramer, *The Game*. In his own autobiography, Gonzales also recollects the match with Budge. After mentioning the newspaper's slighting description of his opponent, he admits that this loss before his hometown was a low point of his career. He does not give details, yet how the defeat must have scarred! Pancho recollects the score as 6–2, 6–2, much worse than it was!

4 Budge, *Don Budge: A Tennis Memoir*.

5 A fascinating summary of the 1954 'World Championship Series' appears in McCauley's *History of Professional Tennis*. Gonzales won with an overall record of 30–21 against Segura, and the exact same against Sedgman; Segura just edged Sedgman (by a match!) into second place, 23–22. Budge won only a few matches, but one of them, against the champion-to-be, became the stuff of legends.

6 Gonzales had asked the popular Segura, his only friend among the pros, to contribute an introduction to his autobiography.

7 Rex Bellamy, *Love Thirty: Three Decades of Champions*, Simon and Schuster, London, 1990.

8 This rare quality of playing better when angry is not the only one Gonzales shares with his successor in notoriety, John McEnroe. Both understood that their anger could upset their opponent. However, John Newcombe, who knew both, claims that compared with *Gorgo* McEnroe was a wimp! John Newcombe, *Newk: Life on and off the court*, Pan Macmillan, Sydney, 2002.

9 Laver, the unsophisticated boy from the bush, had long been intimidated by Gonzales,

who never ceased acting like top dog even when Laver was on top of the world and *Gorgo* a part-time veteran. There was also something in *Gorgo*'s game that the usually unflappable Laver found unsettling: the crafty Pancho could serve to Laver – or rather *at* him – in a way few could emulate. With this set of tricks, Gonzales knew how to rock the apparently unsinkable Laver boat.

10 Pancho Segura, in video documentary *Kings of the Court.*

11 All Kramer quotations and references here are from *The Game.*

12 Tilden, *Tennis A–Z.*

13 Collins in McCauley, *History of Professional Tennis.* Tony Trabert himself had found the transition from amateur champion to pro journeyman particularly rough. When the genial and blue-eyed All-American boy asked Gonzales for some practice at the start of their bad-tempered tour, Pancho declined point blank. Why give the would-be usurper any help?

14 McCauley, *History of Professional Tennis.*

15 Jenny Hoad and Jack Pollard, *My Life with Lew*, HarperSports, Sydney, 2002.

16 Lew Hoad, 'The Backhand Myth', *Lawn Tennis the Australian Way,* Jack Pollard, ed, Lansdown Press, Melbourne, 1971.

17 I can find nothing on how Gonzales, while on the road and facing Hoad night after night, undertook the change in his grip. Even we hackers know that any change in technique requires practice outside match play and usually results in an immediate drop in performance. If there were 87 matches played over about 20 weeks, the pair must have played on average just under 5 matches per week, leaving precious little time for rest, let alone practice. So *Gorgo* must have practised the change in the limited time available between matches and travel, and even during match play itself. Wherever possible, *Gorgo* preferred practising with Segura, and Segura joined the whole tour. Perhaps the little master could enlighten us? The astute Vines in *Myth and Method* noted a fascinating detail: *Gorgo* kept his old hammer grip for his backhand return of serve, switching to the new Eastern for baseline exchanges. *Gorgo*, says Vines, knew it was too late in his career to change grips 'unconsciously' on the quick return of serve, but a baseline duel allowed a fraction more time. *Gorgo*'s technical feat, says the amazed Vines, is 'unheard of'. See also Hoad's autobiography, *My Game*, and his chapter in *Lawn Tennis the Australian Way*, cited above.

18 Peter Conrad, *At Home in Australia*, Thames and Hudson, London, 2003.

19 Vines and Vier, *Tennis: Myth and Method*. All the Vines quotations in this chapter are from this source.

20 As Vines sees it – and so do I – Gonzales was one of only three players who at forty was close to the world's very best. The other two were Tilden and Rosewall. (The unheralded Pancho Segura, his tennis confined almost entirely to the poor pros, might have been the fourth.) Although Vines says that when all three were 40 years old, *Big Pancho* was the best of the lot, on anything but fast grass, I would by a gut-string favour Rosewall. His record as a 40-year-old is unique.

21 John Szwed, *So What: The Life of Miles Davis*, William Heinemann, London, 2002.

22 Richard Evans, *Open Tennis: the First Twenty Years*, Bloomsbury, London, 1988.

Fig. 6.0. Ecstasy! Or is it relief? Rosewall at the instant of winning the 1972 World Championship of Tennis. By then almost forty, having been banned from the major championships for over ten years, for once Mr Unflappable reveals all.

6

MAGUS – ROSEWALL

In tennis ... Rosewall is Bach.
Jeff Borowiak

AS this chapter unfolds, I hope that readers will discover for themselves how apt is Jeff Borowiak's epigraph comparing Rosewall to J. S. Bach. Both Bach and Rosewall began as prodigies, and became giants. Yet for only one of them do we know the first occasion when these *wunderkinder* dazzled the public.

It was Rosewall, and he was twelve.[1]

Prelude

The date was Saturday December 20, 1946, and the place Sydney, Australia's largest city. As usual in mid-summer Sydney, the morning began hot and sultry. The *Sydney Morning Herald* forecast a temperature of 90 degrees Fahrenheit – 32 degrees Celsius in today's measurements – with the threat of rain.

Some of the city's devoted band of tennis enthusiasts must have scrutinised this forecast more carefully than usual. They planned to attend an unusual event, and it would be too cruel if the skies were to open with one of Sydney's downpours. Although scheduled at an unremarkable suburban tennis club, the day's contest – so they felt in their bones – promised the stuff that gave birth to legends. And they wanted to be a part of the legend's making.

Seven years earlier, in one of the most dramatic of Davis Cup ties, underdog Australia had won the 1939 Davis Cup; in Chapter 4, we saw how World War II was declared during the event. There were no Davis Cup matches during the war, but as soon as it was over, the competition reopened. Within 18 months of the war's end, the resurgent Americans, led by the world's No. 1 amateur, Jack Kramer, had journeyed to Australia and retaken the trophy with a resounding victory over the depleted custodians.

The tie had been played at the Kooyong Club in Melbourne. In order to appease the avid Sydney fans starved of tennis during the war years, an enterprising Lawn Tennis Association had brought the new Cup holders up to Sydney, and arranged an exhibition by the Americans at a tennis club in Rockdale, a local suburb.

If these fans found it tempting to scrutinise the famous conquerors at first hand, what made it irresistible – especially to the local players – was the event's extra attraction. In a brainwave by the organisers, the matches involving the Americans were to be preceded by a 'Special Event'. This bonus was a contest between two youngsters who had been creating a sensation in district competition – and who were as much a part of Sydney as the Harbour Bridge.

So the event had the lot. Here were big international stars and little local heroes, maturity in full flower and youth green in promise. And, perhaps, the beginning of an epoch.

The name of the first contender was Lewis Alan Hoad; that of the second, Kenneth Robert Rosewall. Both had just turned twelve.

Although their precocious talents had already been much celebrated within the little world of Sydney suburban tennis, the two were facing each other for the first time. It is said that the gods play games incessantly, and a favourite sport is to play with the fate of we mortals down below. If so, it seems that these gods must have been gleefully at it on that particular day: only they knew that these two lads – born just three weeks and nine miles apart – were about to take the first step in the creation of a saga. In the years ahead, in contests scattered across the globe, and to the delight of hundreds of thousands of spectators, the pair were to face each other a thousand times.

The crowd thronging the courts of the tiny suburban club in Rockdale was brimming with excitement. Yet, when they saw the two boys step onto the court, they must have sensed something – for a strange hush descended. Perhaps the courtiers of France felt the same way in 1764 when they saw Leopold Mozart carefully perch his eight-year-old son, Wolfgang Amadeus,

Fig. 6.1a, 6.1b and 6.1c. Ken and Lew starting the game. Top left, the dark Ken's racket seems huge, while top right, the blonde Lew is beautifully poised. Below, by eleven years, as neat as ever, Ken is accumulating trophies.

onto his specially made piano stool and indicate, with a bow and a flourish, that the lad would commence with one of his own compositions.

History tells that at least one spectator marked the event as both extraordinary and prophetic.

The star of the show was Jack Kramer, a man with the tennis world at his feet. In his autobiography, Kramer tells us that when the two lads walked onto the dusty off-yellow court he was in Rockdale's little clubhouse getting changed for his match, scheduled to follow the boys' preliminary. Through the change room window, he caught a glimpse of two youngsters out on court. He had never seen them before. They were playing their hearts out, and they were brilliant. Kramer was enthralled.

Fig. 6.2. Rosewall's shadow. By eleven years of age, the Hoad style is inimitable and dazzling.

Soon it appeared that they were about to end their single scheduled set. Kramer thought to himself: for these two fantastic kids, a world champion can wait. At once, Kramer sent out word to the organisers. 'Hey, can't these little marvels be asked to play a second set?' he enquired.[2]

One of the protagonists also knew that there was something in the air. Years later Ken Rosewall was to write about the encounter: 'Even then as I chased against the raking shots of the young giant across the net – for so he appeared to another 12-year-old – I recognised in Lew a touch of greatness.'

Lew Hoad's account of the match is equally brushed with prophecy, and also furnished with a wealth of human detail, illumining the occasion and the times from the vantage of a boy, young and poor, gingerly taking his first steps on that fabled road to fame and fortune.

In his autobiography, Hoad begins by telling us that by the time he was twelve he had won all the events open to him in his district of Balmain. 'Up in the Illawarra district of Sydney,' says Hoad, 'another boy of my age had won everything too and people were saying what a terrific little player he was.' Everyone wanted to see how the two prodigies would go against each other.[3]

When the match approached, Lew claims that everyone in his boisterous working-class home in Glebe in inner Sydney was 'as excited as a trunk full of galahs'. For days his mother Bonnie fed him raw carrots to improve his eyesight. And when the big day dawned, while a couple of the family were polishing his wooden racket, she was ironing his shoelaces!

At the ground hundreds were being turned away, leaving two thousand packed into the club courts. Lew's father, delighted that his young son's name graced the official program, was astonished that it cost seven shillings and sixpence (about $25 in today's terms). This was a lot for those days, and especially for Alan Hoad who worked on the Sydney trams. But he bought one.

What happened next needs Lew's own words.

> About one in the afternoon, I went out into the sun on to the off-yellow hard court in my freshly laundered clothes, carrying the racket we'd polished. My opponent's family were all there, too, in the seats that rimmed the court. I had never seen him before, and when I looked at him and shook hands, I saw he was dark and that the racket seemed too big for him, and that we were a … tiny

> pair, smaller than the ball boys. I brushed my blonde hair back and the umpire introduced us, and when the clapping stopped I looked up over the net at him. His name was Ken Rosewall.'

In appearance, they were strikingly different.

One was dark-haired, small, slim, almost fragile, the other snowy-haired and sturdy-framed. In the match that followed, this contrast was heightened by their opposing styles. Hoad was ever the attacker, and tried to hit every shot for a winner. 'But,' said Hoad later, 'though I hit a lot harder ... his racket attracted the ball like a magnet ... and his placements were remarkably accurate.'

Though their rallying was marvellous, to the astonishment of the crowd it was the delicate-looking counter-puncher who won most of the points. Eventually it was little Ken who ran out the winner at 6–0, 6–0!

Years later, their accounts of the match vividly reveal their personalities. The shy victor, Rosewall, doesn't mention the score; the flamboyant loser, Hoad, highlights it.

On Lew, on Rod and on a hardly heralded champion

Much of what follows in the rest of this chapter – the tale of the smaller boy – is prefigured in this jewel of an encounter. A whole book is required to explore in detail the subsequent trajectory of Hoad and Rosewall, yet their relationship remains so intriguing that I'm unable to resist a further brief reflection on it.

Both boys were to end up supreme stylists and exponents of their craft. However, although born so close together, and later apprenticed to the same tough school under the same master, for the next 20 years they remained more striking in their differences than in their similarities. In a sense, each became the other's shadow. As with many of the greatest artists, they discovered their own beat early, but even when sharing the same stage they danced to a different music.

Yet with lovely irony, it came to pass that the smaller and less obviously gifted of the pair lasted longer, and in a way triumphed over his apparently stronger twin. This was not least through his superior capacity to learn, to struggle, to withstand and to adapt.

The source of Rosewall's enduring success was the stratagem he so enticingly revealed in their very first encounter. By drawing on the power of his bigger and stronger opponent, he multiplied his own. Of the many adversaries Rosewall was to face in his long career, Lew Hoad was the first and the archetype. In their own words, from first sight of each other on the 'off-yellow' Rockdale court, Rosewall would forever perceive Hoad as the 'the giant', while to Hoad, Rosewall was 'the magnet'.

They were so close that after the marvellous US Final of 1956, in which Rosewall had ruined Hoad's chance of a Grand Slam, Rosewall shed tears for his friend. Lew touches us when he writes later that Ken's 'grief for me was very solemn and genuine'. But so tight was their competition, the then boss of the pros, Jack Kramer, would drop anything to watch the two play each other. 'It was always a grudge match,' says *Big Jack* in his autobiography, adding with emphasis, 'even when the boys were practising.'[4]

With poignant relevance, after Hoad's premature retirement, Rosewall found himself a second 'twin'. If Hoad served as Rosewall's alter ego as he came up, then Rod *The Rocket* Laver served the same purpose as Rosewall approached the end of his career.

I am convinced that a major reason for Rosewall's extraordinary longevity was the challenge that arose from his confrontation with this second extravagant tennis genius. This match-up kept going into the 1980s – into their days as Grand Masters. 'They just bring out the best in each other,' said one fellow pro to journalist John Sharnik, who covered a Grand Masters tour and became obsessed with their rivalry.[5]

Whether boys of twelve or veterans past forty, when Rosewall walked out to play Hoad or Laver, something was in the air, everyone came out to watch, and they were stilled.

And how long the smallest of these three great champions lasted as a player!

Rosewall's achievements in his late 30s and early 40s are unparalleled. No player – not Tilden and not Gonzales, who were among the world's best when they were 40 years of age – won majors 20 years apart. Rex Bellamy, in his *Love Thirty: Three Decades of Champions*, imagines a young person reading the records of Rosewall's major tournament victories spanning the years 1953 to 1973. The youngster wonders: 'Were all these guys the same Ken Rosewall?'[6]

As an amateur, Rosewall won all the major championships except Wimbledon, was a triumphant Davis Cupper, and gained all the major doubles crowns into the bargain. As a pro, he edged out Gonzales. Then, before eventually surrendering to Laver, he reigned as the World Pro Champion for five years.

But this was not the end. He came back, returning to the Open Era to repeat his wins in every major except Wimbledon. And, finally, he surpassed the waning Laver in securing, two years in a row, the title then fairly named the World Championship.

Yet as suggested in the Preface, there is no tennis player – and apparently few sportsmen of any code – whose reputation stands at odds with such achievement.

'The teenage Lewis Hoad in the fifth set of the decider of the 1953 Davis Cup,' was the choice as one of the nation's great sporting moments in an Australian Bicentennial publication.[7] Extolling the famous match by the teenage Hoad in the 1953 Davis Cup is understandable. However, though this contest was indubitably a mother lode of heroic myths, it was not the 'Cup decider' as the piece claims.

With the score standing at two rubbers all, the decider was the next and final match: the fate of the Cup rested with none other than Hoad's diminutive twin, Ken Rosewall. In a match delayed by rain – so increasing the tension – the unsung Rosewall faced the tough American veteran Seixas. And with superlative skill and courage, it was the 19-year-old Kenny who brought the Cup home.

Rosewall's biographer, Peter Rowley, has taken the matter of Rosewall's neglect to heart. Indeed, his fine book, *Twenty Years at the Top*, occasionally loses conviction through a desire to bring him to that place in the sun that Rowley believes he so richly deserves.

While I count myself among Rosewall's most fervent admirers, I cannot agree with Rowley's strenuous assertion that Rosewall was 'the greatest player ever', nor his startling claim that our hero's second serve was better than Gonzales'! Rowley notes that at one point in Rosewall's seemingly endless career, some reporters – reflecting the otherworldly beauty of the little master's game – began tagging him 'Saint' Rosewall. Rowley's obvious approval of the tag nudges his book from biography towards hagiography.

While the hyperbole associated with the writing of saints' lives could hinder our recognition of Rosewall's real achievements, even those who might be expected to be least moved towards excess – Rosewall's fellow pros – would usually shake their heads and give up when trying to describe the ageless master.

Not one to be lost for words, the marvellous Arthur Ashe couldn't resist the temptation for the celestial, putting it bluntly: 'Rosewall is like God, motherhood and apple pie. You can't argue with that.' And the touring pro Jeff Borowiak needed to call on our greatest musical genius, Johann Sebastian Bach, for his comparison.[8]

Nonetheless, despite the unique triumph of becoming one of the very best tennis players in the world for 20 years, of toppling dozens of opponents bigger, stronger and younger, and of doing so with a style unmatched in grace, the achievements of the *Little Master* have often been undervalued or ignored, and his game misunderstood and even disparaged. In consequence, my aim here is to explain not just how his play evolved and his achievements multiplied, but why it has been so hard for so many who follow the game to measure his stature.

But first, what of the development of the young player?

Boyhood and the making of a champion

'KR. Rosewall': so stands his name on the honour boards of the great clubs holding the major tournaments of the world. He was born under the sign of Pluto, on November 2, 1934. His place of birth was Sydney, where he was to grow up and where he still lives.

The astrologer may conclude that the cool, dark powers of Pluto were responsible for the development of a style often described by both opponents and the public as composed, careful and intense, and even sometimes magical and mysterious. But, as with many prodigies, the origin of Rosewall's brilliance may lie closer to hand. A more immediate, if more prosaic, influence was his father – a grocer, and a keen club player.

Rosewall himself states with unusual emphasis: 'In all my tennis life, my father has been my only teacher.' The statement is striking in that his first coach, father Robert, had been fairly quickly supplanted – and by none other than the famous Harry 'The Fox' Hopman. The long-standing Australian

Fig. 6.3. On a leash. The 'tennis twins', Hoad and Rosewall, might be tourists, yet can't escape the watchful eye of Harry Hopman, coach, minder and king-maker.

Davis Cup Captain then supervised Rosewall throughout his amateur career. In what follows, the reason for Rosewall's adamant insistence on this distinction will become clearer.

Although the Rosewall family was not wealthy, this was a land-rich era for many Australians. As a consequence, for a time the Rosewalls owned their own tennis court. Here, and on the local club courts, the boy started learning the fundamentals of the game from his father. We have already visited the club at the beginning of this chapter, but well before his famous match-up against Hoad it was on the Rockdale courts that young Ken began his tennis life.

By about the age of six, the lad had picked up a racket and started hitting balls. Right then something happened that was to have lasting consequences for Rosewall's game – and was to spawn a myth.

Though Rosewall was a right-handed tennis player, he was a natural left-hander. Even at forty, despite a much more heavily muscled right arm as a result of years of tennis, he could still throw a ball twice as far with his left arm. Right- or left-handedness tends to run in families, and both his sons are left-handed.

So, how did he come to play right-handed?

A partial explanation comes from Rosewall himself. It seems that when he first wielded a racket as a very small boy, he started with his father's. Since it was heavy for the little fellow to hold, he used two hands and began 'hitting the ball from the backhand side' (or more precisely, and as befits a natural leftie, the left side). But, says Rosewall, 'when my father decided I should try to play with one hand using a lighter racket, I settled for the right [hand].'

And what myth was spawned?

I grew up in Australia a decade later than Rosewall. Like thousands in tennis-mad Australia, as a boy I followed his progress avidly. Worshiping from afar, we rejoiced in his victories and despaired in his defeats. However, it was recognised amongst tennis aficionados of the time that our hero was a natural left-hander – and a tale went around that explained why he had not become a left-handed tennis player. *He had not been allowed to do so.* We were told (and believed) that his father was something of a tyrant. Robert Rosewall, so the story went, had strapped the youngster's right hand to his racket to force him to become a right-handed player. It was said in explanation that Robert did not like left-handers and used to point out that of the many good left-handers only one could be called a world champion, and that was Norman Brookes half a century before.

This story did not emerge in print, and Rosewall himself did not repeat it. Yet while it cannot be taken literally, like most myths it may hold a kernel of truth.

Certainly, the elder Rosewall was a tough and deeply ambitious teacher for his son. We can gather this from Rosewall's own two phrases to his biographer: ' ... my father decided I should try to play with one hand ... ' and '[m]y father ... follows everything I do, but he can be overly critical.' These hint at something more than the eternal ambivalence of the student towards the once-omniscient master who taught him everything – here compounded by the eternal ambivalence of the son towards the father.

There remains a compelling sense of 'What if?' – a sense that with a mentor other than the rigid if devoted Robert, and one more sympathetic to the inherent attributes and capacities of his pupil, Kenny would have ended up a left-hander. And an utterly different tennis player. Then we would be telling another story.[9]

However intriguing the legend, the nexus between ambitious father and earnest pupil cast the mould; here was built the rock-like foundation of Rosewall's strokes.

In this first tutelage we have already noted a lovely resemblance to another of our youngsters, the equally dark and slight Bobby Riggs. Like Riggs's coach, Esther Bartosh, Robert Rosewall built a basically defensive posture into his son's style, and one that depended on the accuracy, consistency and primacy of his ground strokes. His natural agility and speed complemented such an approach. Likewise his slight frame made control, rather than power, the appropriate focus.

Ken's father had studied tennis. An admirer of our mighty American hero, *Big Bill* Tilden, Robert also revered the long flowing drives of the Australian champion of the 1930s, Jack Crawford. In the rigorous early-morning sessions that soon developed between father and son, this aspect of the game was emphasised. The serve was just a way of starting the point, the volley a less-than-crucial refinement.

Paradoxically, the young Ken's natural left-handedness fitted well into this developing pattern. As a right-hander, his serve, with its throwing action, was always going to be unassuming, while his in-built preference for the left side must have assisted in the cultivation of his backhand drive, soon to become one of tennis's jewels.

While laying down the basic strokes, and then mobilising them into the beginnings of a strategy of match play, Robert Rosewall instilled another lesson in his son: an iron discipline. More than any other, this feature marked the boy out, carried the youth to the top, and kept the man there for 20 years.

Any reader of his accounts of those days must be struck by the rigour and dedication of both teacher and student. Here again is an apprenticeship reminiscent of the traditions of the Eastern martial arts, or of Western classical music. This immersion and dedication seems more intense than that expected from the easy-going, rough-and-ready world of lower-middle class, post-war Australia.

Later, the man tells how the boy studiously laid out his clothes and equipment every night before bedtime, ready for their daily hour-long practice sessions starting at five the next morning. Very soon, other activities, other sports, then other ways of making a living, were shorn away. From the first, the destiny of Kenneth Robert Rosewall was to be a master — a master tennis player.

Success came early. He started winning junior tournaments at the age of nine. At 12 years, on that court in Rockdale in 1946, young Ken was already sufficiently magisterial to do more than captivate the hearts of two thousand enthusiasts: unknown to the boy, Jack Kramer — the world's best amateur player — had been studying him, and had discovered genius.

Two years later, such was his ability that he was often upgraded to play with the men. Then came a crucial turning point: he was invited to play doubles with the legendary and unorthodox champion, John Bromwich.

In 1948, when the 14-year-old Rosewall first made a team with Bromwich, *Old Brom* (as he was called Down Under), may have been past his peak as a singles player. However, he was currently only two-thirds of the way through his run of eight consecutive Australian Doubles titles, and still the best doubles player in the world.

The pair played a tournament in Orange, 200 miles (300 km) from Sydney. Ken says that if necessary, he would have walked there, a statement that recalls the image of Bach's hundred-mile walk to hear his hero Buxtehude play the organ.

Though they didn't win in Orange, man and boy made it to the final of the doubles.

When asked who was the best doubles team he ever saw, Rosewall usually answered, 'Bromwich and anyone!' As his comment suggests, *Brom* was a supreme master of every aspect of the two-handed game. This included the return of serve, often taken early and spun softly at the server's feet, but also the full-blooded drive and the (disguised) lob. It is said that he once missed only two returns in a whole five-set Wimbledon final round match. But the return of service was merely the first step in a set of manoeuvres designed to manipulate and unbalance the opposition. To do that young Ken saw that *Brom* needed complete control of the ball: he would place the ball exactly where he wanted it, preferably after disguising its destination.

There is a legend told about *Brom's* control — apocryphal, but beautiful.

Such was his command of his loosely strung racket, so it went, that in mid-stroke Brom could glance up, check the wind on the flagpole and make the appropriate adjustments. Without further interruption he would complete his stroke.

Rosewall has admitted that although he learnt much from the master, he never 'modelled his game' on his ex-partner's. It could well have been *Brom's* unorthodoxy that kept the older man from reaching the exalted status of 'model' for his more conservatively minded pupil. *Brom* hit a double-hander on the right side and a (left-handed) one-hander on his left, but gripped his loosely strung racket by a shaved-down, pencil-thin handle to serve and smash with his right hand! For an idea of right-court doubles Bromwich-style, the modern aficionado might recall the more recent exploits of the superlative double-handed Frenchman Fabrice Santoro, whose magic can be seen on YouTube™.

A year after the tournament in Orange, we find Rosewall, then just five feet tall (152 centimetres) in his tennis shoes, partnering Australian champion Ken McGregor, who stood at six feet two and a half inches (189 centimetres). *Macca*, a huge-serving tennis champion as well as an Aussie Rules football star, would soon be the other half of the all-conquering Sedgman–McGregor doubles team. The contrasting duo was matched against Frank Sedgman himself and George Worthington, both nearly six feet tall (183 centimetres) and world-class doubles players.

Only a little later, at 16 years and playing the major Australian State Championships, Rosewall again paired with Bromwich – and ended up winning the Tasmanian State Championships. With typical understatement, he tells us: 'I learnt a lot from Bromwich.' Indeed!

Young Ken was then the best junior in the land, and a force to be reckoned with in the seniors. By the time he was 19 years old, he had won two majors: the Australian and French Championships. Then, with Hoad, he snatched the Davis Cup from the experienced Americans Trabert (then World Amateur No. 1) and Seixas (a Wimbledon title holder).

Three years later, when the 22-year-old had turned pro, he had added another Australian and the US title, and triumphantly retained the Cup. In addition, and with several partners, but especially Hoad, he won all the major doubles titles, most of them more than once.

How strange it was then, that despite these triumphs, the Australian and international public placed the young champion just outside the limelight. Indeed, most tennis lovers seemed, more than anything, surprised when

Fig. 6.4. Hoad in full flight. In this continuous sequence of serve, volley, and smash, one can easily understand why opponents could be overawed by Hoad's power and magnetism.

he won a major tournament. In the panoply of sporting heroes, somehow Rosewall forever remained the best man, not the bridegroom.

What was going on?

I believe Rosewall's neglect can be attributed to three factors, each compounded by the years in the pro wilderness that followed.

The first was his so-called 'twin', Lew Hoad. It was not enough that Hoad was one of the most gifted players ever to pick up a racket. By the time he had reached senior ranks his game had become one of the most arresting. There was nothing he couldn't do. Built like a truck, Hoad had a wrist of steel and an arm like a tree trunk. Yet he was fast, and, as suggested by Figure 6.4, moved beautifully.

Hoad played the aggressive serve and volley game in the manner of Jack Kramer and Frank Sedgman, but he added a touch of genius. With his magnificent serve, and glorious overhead and volley, most times he would crush his opponent by straightforward attack. But when the fleet powerhouse was 'on,' he could turn the screw with inventions not of this world. Then, besides being crushed, the opponent would feel demoralised. Even the unflappable Rosewall admits that, when facing this young lion on one of his days, it was 'actually frightening' to be on the other side of the net from him.

Moreover, Hoad was outgoing and fun-loving. And blonde.

How tough was all of this for Hoad's so-called 'twin'! Kenny was a shy, darkly dapper little fellow, who in those days – to use Rosewall's own wonderfully unassuming words – 'popped a serve in ... and retreated to the baseline'.

He was also the one who – in typical Aussie parlance – had collared his historic nickname, *Muscles* ... because he hadn't any.

The second factor was Hopman. As teenagers Rosewall and Hoad had been blooded early into the nation's Davis Cup team, and Harry 'The Fox' Hopman ran the team with a rod of iron. From there he exerted a vast influence on Australian tennis and on the world amateur game. Yet Hopman consistently undervalued Rosewall. More to the point, he misunderstood him.

In one of the most extraordinary misjudgements in Davis Cup history, during the famous 1953 Davis Cup, at the very last moment the selection panel dumped Rosewall from the key doubles rubber. Against the seasoned veterans Trabert and Seixas, they pronounced in favour of Rex Hartwig to partner Hoad, who was always Hopman's favourite.

Understandably the little-tried pair then lost – to leave the teenagers on the last day attempting to salvage the last two rubbers and the Cup. At that time Rosewall was just behind Hoad as a singles player, and far and away the next best amateur singles player in Australia. Moreover, the Hoad–Rosewall pair formed the preferred, and almost certainly the best, doubles team. To be dropped so precipitously, while still a teenager and in his first Davis Cup, must have been a savage blow to Rosewall's confidence, wavering after his first-up singles loss on Day 1 and under the spotlight of the nation.

Despite this bungle, as we have seen, the two youngsters triumphed, and the Cup was Australia's. [10]

Although Hopman trumpeted his role in discovering the famous 'twins', in fact he appeared to do little to build up the weaker aspects, or to capitalise on the strengths of Rosewall's game. Following on from father Robert, Hopman believed that Rosewall could only play a defensive, counter-punching game, and insisted that he play from the backcourt. This is astonishing when we consider that Rosewall, superlative at doubles, must already have been a very good, and potentially masterful, net player.

In fact Rosewall is convincing when he says he would have won his 1954 Wimbledon Final against Drobny if he had known enough to attack the net against Drobny's weaker backhand. It seems that Hopman, at that time always in Rosewall's corner, suffered from a set of fixed assumptions about his protégé – and to Rosewall's detriment, the old martinet never challenged them.

These prejudices emerge clearly in Hopman's book, *Aces and Places*. Nowhere are his views so revealing or – as proven later – so wrong as in the account of his response when Rosewall eventually sought his views on turning pro. 'I don't think he is suited to professional tennis,' said Hopman at the time.

Hopman seemed to perceive Ken as over-protected and passive. In *Aces and Places* he says that Rosewall needed 'ideal conditions' to play well, and he adds, 'I don't know how he will get on ... night after night in what are, after all ... exhibitions.' This demonstrates not only Hopman's bias against the pros (to him they were the opposition, and threatened his power), but an astonishing lack of understanding of what was perhaps Rosewall's outstanding attribute – his depth of character.

In a most revealing statement to his biographer, Rosewall asserted that he found the pressure on him as a pro far less than as an amateur. With the pros, he was his own man, and he relished it. He comes as close to bitterness as he is capable, when he describes Hopman's attitude to his former charges once they had left him for the pros. Says Ken: 'It was as if we all had never existed.'

In *A Serve to Authority*, a history of the Kooyong Tennis Club, author Richard Yallop helps us to understand more about Hopman. He draws a picture of an isolated and childless man who lived for his protégés and tennis, but who demanded complete control.[11] But fairness requires that we give Hopman some due: clearly, he helped foster Rosewall's exemplary court behaviour, which shames so many of his successors.

The third factor that contributed to the meagre acknowledgement of Rosewall's stature, was his failure to win Wimbledon.

According to the players, this tournament was no harder to win than the US Championships and not as tough as the French – and Rosewall won both several times. However, to this day the tournament the British immodestly call 'The Championships' remains the unofficial world title. As an amateur Rosewall reached two finals, losing narrowly to Drobny, and then to Hoad. In the Open Era he got to two more, against Newcombe and Connors, the last when he was aged almost forty. But he never could take the title.

To those many who place Wimbledon on a pedestal, whatever else Rosewall did would never make up for this blemish. 'What about Dick Savitt, or Budge Patty,' I hear the Rosewall supporter cry, 'or Vic Seixas, or – for heaven's sakes! – Bob Falkenberg or Yvon Petra?' (These were all Wimbledon winners and good players, but inarguably Rosewall's inferiors.) Alas, no convincing answer is forthcoming. Many of these apparent nonpareils would be unknown to Rosewall's detractors – and to the tennis public.

But it was enough: Rosewall hadn't won Wimbledon; ergo he couldn't be one of the greats. In a recent television documentary, Rosewall himself, smiling, provided the real answer: 'When I first played Wimbledon, I was too young. When eventually I got to the finals again ... too old.'

And what of the years between?

After our hero's stellar apprenticeship and his rise to a relatively unacclaimed amateur supremacy, he turned pro. With a stack of Grand Slam titles and Davis Cup triumphs behind him, he was still very young.

How then, did this mollycoddle, as Hopman saw him, take the challenge of the pro tour? What happened in those years following Rosewall's early entry into the pro ranks – a time when he was neither too young nor too old?

Apogee at last: the pro years 1957 to 1968

It was to controversial publicity that, at the end of 1956, a 22-year-old Rosewall forsook the amateurs for the pros. The reason for the reaction was obvious: he was deserting the amateur ranks with his best years to come. Further, Rosewall was not then the number one amateur. This honour had gone to none other than Rosewall's 'twin'. After being behind as a junior, Lew Hoad had eventually caught up with, and then in early manhood gone ahead of, his long-term stable-mate.

But Hoad was only just ahead, and could never be sure of victory against him. With the triple crowns of the 1956 Australian, French and Wimbledon championships already behind Hoad, Rosewall was the clear underdog when the pair squared off in that year's US Final. In a marvellous match, a brilliant Rosewall snatched Hoad's chance of a Grand Slam.

Rosewall did it by unexpectedly throwing away a little of his characteristic caution – and attacking the net. The result? The smaller man surprised, and then flummoxed his more powerful rival. Disturbed by the wind and a bad court, and thrown by his opponent's clever tactics, Hoad was unable to respond in kind. Despite the conditions, and his opponent's unexpected attack, the bigger man just kept blasting away – and the match slipped from his hands.

Watching in the stands was another of our heroes, the wily Ellsworth Vines. Though himself famed for his explosive play, the old champion was perplexed by Hoad's strategy. Vines was heard expostulating: Why doesn't Hoad mix it up a little? Why not throw up a few lobs against his short friend?

In this their swansong as amateurs, Rosewall had stumbled upon a new style: his defensive resilience was locked into an attacking *all court* brilliance. Though no one observing this apparent upset could have known it at the time, here was the first rendition of the triumphant Rosewall signature tune. When Hoad joined the pro ranks a year later, Rosewall had so perfected his act that Hoad was never able to re-establish the authority he had built over Rosewall in the final years of their amateur careers.

However, the start to Rosewall's life on the road as a pro could not have been tougher. On January 14, 1957, in his hometown of Sydney, he walked onto the court to face one Richard *Big Pancho* Gonzales.

Gonzales seemed to be at his absolute best. Then aged 28 years, to retain his pro crown he had just decisively beaten the previous challenger, the American Tony Trabert, who had entered the pros as undisputed world amateur champion. And *Gorgo* also had to face an even tougher job – keeping ahead of his fellow pros. These included two superlative players: the maestros *Little Pancho* Segura and Frank Sedgman. While Sedgman in particular always remained a problem for Gonzales, Pancho had managed to keep his place at the top of a very greasy pole.

When little Kenny joined the pros, Pancho – who, at 6 feet 3 inches (190 centimetres) towered over Rosewall's 5 feet 6 inches (173 centimetres) – was not only the swiftest big man in tennis history, but also one of the smartest. We have already discovered that though Gonzales' serve and overhead were lethal, he had also learned to graft and scramble as well as the best defenders. As a reminder of what exactly young Ken was up against, here is an account of one contemporary response to Gonzales' dominance.

In the mid-fifties, Boss Kramer had trialled the 'three bounce rule' – the ball had to bounce three times before either player could play a volley. Apparently the idea was to prolong the rallies and make the game more interesting. However, the immediate aim was to hobble Gonzales and his majestic serve and net game. Alas, to Kramer's disappointment, *Big Pancho*'s defensive game had by then become so good that, even when he had to let the ball bounce a bit more, he still kept beating everyone. And this often included Pancho Segura, an all-time master of defence and the backcourt![12]

But perhaps more than anything else, the tough veteran facing Rosewall knew the exacting pro conditions backwards and, like the street fighter he was, relished them.

Fig. 6.5. David and Goliath. As he towers over Rosewall, Big Pancho *Gonzales, having just won the opener of their head-to-head tour in 1957, allows himself a rare grin. If he lost, he wasn't so happy.*

The head-to-head was planned to be the best of 100 matches, with at least half of them played on 'Gonzales' street'. This was the canvas court the pros carried with them – stretched over whatever surface they could find and tightened with guy ropes. It has been noted earlier that the court played lightning fast, and sometimes moved disconcertingly as a player propped during a tight rally, and in the tin-pot arenas such as the local basketball or dance halls in which they were forced to play, the lighting was frequently terrible, often an even greater problem for the smaller man: the lights and roof were so low that Rosewall couldn't lob the giant panther swooping in to net.

For the novice pro there was also the matter of his own capability. As shown in Figure 6.5, the neat little grocer's son from Australian suburbia was dwarfed by the physically intimidating Mexican-American from the back streets of Los Angeles – but Rosewall's biggest problem was that his game relied mainly on parry and defence.

Although Rosewall was very quick, his excellent (and very beautiful) ground shots required an extended back swing and long follow-through, and needed time to set up. His serve, a little stilted by being right-handed, was reliable, but at this level, small and friendly. His net game was solid, but undeveloped and underused. In short, *Muscles-because-he-hadn't-any* possessed great speed, good armour, but few penetrating weapons. He was also very young and, as Hopman pointed out, had previously always been under someone's wing. Now he was right out there on his own – on the pro road, without coach, trainer, practice partner, or racket stringer.

And at first it seemed like no contest.

Though the first match went to Gonzales 9–7 in the fifth set, and Rosewall won the third, Gonzales began to dominate the tour early. Rosewall himself admitted (if later) that he felt he had been 'thrown to the wolves'. So he had. It appears that before they walked onto the court for the first match, Rosewall had been given no opportunity whatever to check out Gonzales' tennis style. In fact, he had never met Gonzales! Moreover, he had almost no experience playing indoors or under lights. Tell this to the modern pro preparing for a big match with the help of coach, detailed statistics, video footage and so on ... !

What Rosewall learnt in the next six months – the most brutal tennis lesson of his life – was what turned him from fine player to great one. Within two years after the end of the Gonzales tour, Rosewall was close to top pro; by 1960 he was there – acknowledged as Pro Champion and, among the players at least, as the best tennis player in the world. He remained so for five years, and close to the best or second-best for another five years.

Astonishing to the modern eye, on his first tour as pro young Rosewall not only figured out what he had to do to reach the top, but he did it by himself, and in the heat of battle.

In broad terms, his discoveries were both tactical, and technical.

First, he matured strategically. To become world champion he had to win in all conditions against the best pros. Since all were brilliant net players, and much of the tour was played on fast wood and canvas-covered courts, a crucial priority for him was to master the net.

Soon Rosewall saw that, despite his modest serve, he could take net and employ his supreme anticipation and agility together with what was becoming a great volley and overhead. Before long he was completely at home in the forecourt and on the fastest indoor courts. This allowed him to do more than just 'mix it up'. A fine net game could help to wrest the initiative from an opponent, expose his weaknesses, and clinch a point.

In an almost chilling phrase in his memoirs, Rosewall once supplied the following description of himself: 'I make the other players surrender.' That brilliant strategist and Rosewall look-alike, Bobby Riggs, defined his own strategy as 'attack within a defensive posture'. This was the core of Rosewall's all court game.

Second, he developed his technique.

As well as building up his serve and net game, he worked at making his already superb ground shots more compact, and harder to read. On the lightning-fast canvas, with Gonzales firing thunderbolts at him, there wasn't time for a long flowing swing *à la* Tilden.

So he shortened the backswing on his drives, concentrating on hitting the ball in front with his weight going forward. This was crucial to the forehand, which he had a tendency to hit a little late. Here he also found he needed to reconstruct his acutely angled crosscourt. This was perhaps the shot he found most difficult of all, and an absolute necessity against Gonzales' marvellous wide slice to the first court. Without it, he was feeding cream to the cat – the towering but gorgeously balanced figure of Gonzales, swooping in behind his serve and tending to his left.

Figure 6.6 snaps the mature Rosewall displaying what he has learnt. He has been pulled out of court on the forehand return of serve, but despite extreme pressure and at the end of his reach, he remains balanced, and the compact reply looks convincing.

As the nightly odyssey wended its way from town to town – and as the mighty Gonzales edged inexorably ahead – the young Rosewall made his third discovery.

Probably the most important, it is the hardest to define. Perhaps it might be called *the power of knowledge* – of others and himself. Crammed with the other pros in one of boss Kramer's station wagons, by day they drove the concrete highways, by night stopping for a match and then a sleep, alone in some shabby motel. Yet this shy young man found time to think it out: ceaselessly, meticulously, he studied his opponent, himself, and the interactions between the two.[13]

Fig. 6.6. Rosewall stretches for the return of serve. Gonzales, not given to praising opponents, admitted Rosewall's return of serve was peerless.

In doing so he developed an unsurpassed understanding of his own game, and the ability to tune it against his opponent's. Equally crucially, he consolidated a different kind of knowledge: an indestructible sense of himself as an individual. It seems that Rosewall came to believe that, while as a player he might have been crushed this time on the court, as a person he had not.

At this stage we can almost overhear his thoughts after each painful defeat: *next time, tomorrow night, I will still possess the will ... and so I may win.*

This inner confidence was paradoxical: with good competition from Vines and Laver, Rosewall remains the most modest of our great champions. Yet his touching awareness of his own vulnerability was to become a strength and hallmark of the man. Writing years later in his memoirs, the veteran says simply: 'No matter what's happened in the past, I always think I've got a chance.'

The game that Rosewall fashioned was a connoisseur's – unobtrusive, subtle, wickedly employing all the adornments. Here was the drive that, at the last split second, became a lob. Here was the feathery drop shot. Using all the width and length of the court, he would sometimes construct angles so tight along the net that his opponent – if he could reach it – could only return the ball back at virtual right angles to the court's long axis. In addition to the manoeuvre of hitting the lines over and over again, inch-perfect, he constructed a matchless deception about his movements and the direction of his shots.

However, the whole was more than these parts. What the mature master built up was a highly developed capacity to refine and sharpen this array in response to the play of the opponent. After a short while into this first tour, Rosewall came to see exactly what he had to do to realise his boyhood dream. Years earlier, laying out his clothes on his little bed before the dawn practice with his father, he had hoped to become the best tennis player in the world. While he did not have the physique to play in the way of his tennis twin, Lew Hoad, he came to believe that he could become better than that strapping blond god. To be the very best, he would need to garner up his opponent's power, then focus it back – on where it would most wound.

Thus, pitted against the towering Gonzales, this little David had made a set of leaps. Yet we can see that this was part of an evolution that had begun with a confrontation with his first giant, far back in the suburban reaches of New South Wales. Rosewall's trajectory was to reach its zenith among the pros after the end of the Gonzales tour. From then on, he found more Goliaths to be confronted – and vanquished.

But for the time being, the first pro giant he faced was too strong; on the tour against Gonzales, Rosewall won only about once every three times they played, losing the tour against Gonzales 52 matches to 27. Yet considering the handicaps with which he started the tour, this was a phenomenal effort. The bald statistics also hide two other factors of significance.

One was that despite exhausting defeats and an opponent who got even tougher as the tour progressed, Rosewall improved along the way, holding or lifting his winning ratio towards the tour's end.

The other is raised by Jack Kramer. After the tour, Kramer, who watched most of these matches, and whose understanding of the game was second to none, made an extraordinary observation: 'Kenny would have won the tour, if he could have chosen a single point to win [that he lost] in ten of his close matches with Pancho.'[14]

Ten points in 79 matches! It was that close.

After this beating, the little man of the paradoxical modesty had no intention of giving up: he knew what he wanted – to reach the top of the tree. And to do this, he had to find a way around not only Gonzales, but the other top pros as well.

These included one in particular who was barely known to him – or, it seemed, to anyone else.

To his astonishment, in his first year as a pro Rosewall found himself getting mauled by a bandy-legged little bloke approaching forty, and one who had never won a major amateur championship – indeed had never reached the final rounds of one.

His tormentor? The incredible *Little Pancho* Segura.

Confronting the new boy was another 'little master' – fleet, resilient, and a superlative strategist. The other pros called him *Segoo*, a perfect name for the droll magician he was. At that time Segura could defend as well as Rosewall, but in addition possessed one superlative weapon, his double-handed forehand. This veteran had mastered a skill the younger man was only beginning to learn: how to finish off an opponent. Later Rosewall explained, 'Pancho [Segura] just hit too hard.'

The result was that Rosewall took his master classes as much from the genial *Little Pancho* as from the incendiary *Big Pancho*. But how the youngster was learning!

Though Gonzales never acknowledged Rosewall as Pro Champion, the king went into a sort of retirement at the end of the 1950s, and by 1960 Rosewall was recognised by everyone else as the pros' No. 1. Until the mid-sixties when Laver edged him out, Rosewall showed his superiority over all the other pros, whether the marvellous trio of Segura, Sedgman and Trabert, or the string of champions lured from among the amateurs into the pro ranks. And among the latter were two of tennis's greatest: Hoad and Laver.

This period coincided with a low point of the Pro Era. Public and media support was weak and, until Joe McCauley wrote his history of the pros, records were hard to find. But in the three major pro tournaments Rosewall won the French Professional Championship *each year* from 1958 to 1966, the British Professional Championship in 1957 and then each year from 1960 to 1963, and the US Professional Championship in 1963 and 1965. He was top dog.

It is not easy for a writer to do justice to the marvellous level that Rosewall's game had now attained, but for those lucky enough to have seen the little master at his superlative best, the most luminous memory is of his movement. On the court he was everywhere – and he danced.

A perceptive writer for *The New Yorker*, Herbert Warren Wind, had discovered something surprising. By watching the top players, not the ball, and by counting their steps, Wind found that on average Rosewall ended up with double the steps of his opponent. With these tiny skips, coupled with his anticipation, speed and strategic sense, he was not only wonderfully balanced, but positioned earlier. As a consequence, even when appearing in trouble, he could often turn the point around and hurt his opponent.

Here is an example.

Forcing an opponent to half-volley usually sets up an advantage, but this was not necessarily so with Rosewall. In a throw-away during one TV commentary, the shrewd John Alexander noted that what got him most of all about playing against both Hoad and Rosewall was their extraordinary half-volleys. 'If you thought you were lucky enough to make them half-volley,' said Alexander, 'they would throw you out with as good a return as someone else's better volleys.' Kramer said Rosewall's half-volley was, with that of Gonzales, 'the best', and so a fertile backstop to his net game and serve.

Worse for the opposition, Rosewall's lovely on-court flow was strangely hard to read. It might suddenly veer, so that the little man was not where his opponent expected him to be.

According to Rowley, Arthur Ashe, a brilliant human being and an Open Era Wimbledon and US champion, was once asked how to play Rosewall. He replied bluntly: 'Don't ask me, he beats the shit out of me.' Apparently a major reason was one of Rosewall's most uncanny and disconcerting habits. In a TV interview, Ashe explained that: 'During a baseline exchange, you suddenly look up, and the little bastard is at the net, quietly volleying away your drive! And you've no idea how he got there!'

Rowley notes that another top player, Marty Riessen, made a similar – if more poetic – observation on Rosewall's courtcraft: 'You do not hear him coming, and you do not see him coming.'

There was a further deceptive feature of Rosewall's court behaviour, especially for new and unsuspecting opponents. This was his typically flat mien. Indeed it could be said that looking tired and sometimes dejected became something of a Rosewall trademark.

However, those who knew him saw it differently. Commented Tony Trabert: '*Muscles* starts moping around and all the ladies want to mother him. Meanwhile he's cutting you to ribbons.' Once, a reporter was sitting next to Hoad as they watched Rosewall in a big match. The reporter concluded that Kenny was struggling, and commented to Hoad, 'Gee! Kenny's looking so tired.' 'Tired?' retorted Hoad, 'He looks exactly the same as when I first played him when we were twelve!'

Again, we can detect the Bromwich influence in this Rosewallian trait. An anecdote tells of a reporter covering the early rounds of Wimbledon. He found Bromwich, up against a lesser player, but 'dejectedly moping around'. Suspecting an upset, he asked a spectator the score. 'Brom is up 6–1, 6–0, 5–1,' came the reply, 'but he just missed a return of serve.'

Rowley's biography of Rosewall, *Twenty Years at the Top,* includes some remarks of Fred Stolle that illuminate the supreme *mental* challenge of playing Rosewall.

Stolle says that the pressure is always on you because Rosewall is never 'off,' and if you hit one bad shot, the point's gone. Stolle knew Rosewall's game backwards: 'He's got you crazy because his return is so good ... If you miss your first serve, forget it, he'll murder your second ... So you press so hard you usually miss the first ... then you're at his mercy.' Stolle concludes, 'I'd rather play Laver any day.' Apropos, one pro told tennis journalist John Sharnik: 'Laver mauls you; Rosewall breaks your heart.'[15] On another occasion, in a TV interview Stolle, himself a two-time Wimbledon finalist, remarked in passing: 'Some say his forehand's weak, but I'd have it for any shot of mine.'

Gonzales made a fascinating and relevant aside to the master coach Vic Braden.[16] Pancho confessed that in long matches against Rosewall he found that, as the match progressed, Rosewall's forehand would get better and better – so much so that Pancho would be forced to switch the attack away from his opponent's so-called weaker side and towards his killer backhand! This calls to mind Elly Vines' dilemma in deciding which side to serve to Don Budge.

Braden also offers a further droll insight into why Rosewall's fellow pros loved watching the master, but hated playing him.

The English pro Mike Davies told Braden that, when playing Rosewall, he would find himself lured into watching ... not the ball, but his opponent! Before long Davies would find that he was taking note of his opponent's pure form and seamless movement; then he would discover that he was singing praises to his opponent, saying to himself, 'God, look at him staying over the ball ...' and other paeans of this sort. Thus mesmerised and distracted, more spectator than player, Davies would find that his own game had fallen apart.

Richard Evans cites a lovely story told by Bud Collins that illustrates several of these points.

In the early seventies, Sherwood Stewart – an excellent doubles player, but a journeyman singles player – was facing Rosewall for the first time. On one point, there arose a 'furious duel of cross-court backhands, each hit faster and lower than the one before. These skimmers continued for a while ... Then whack, with that undetectable ... change ... Kenny drove down the line, tangle-footing Stewart who collapsed in a wild giggle.'

At that Stewart cried out, 'I don't believe it, but I've seen it now!' He then yelled out to Rosewall, 'How much do you charge for lessons?' [17]

And yet it is all too easy to forget that most of these observations, including those of Arthur Ashe, were made about a player nearly a decade past his absolute best!

Like Roger Federer in later times, Rosewall never seemed to hurry. As if there was some invisible buoyancy, a resilient moving stream that carried him along, he appeared to float on the court. But as we have noted, abruptly the stream could change course.

On careful study, the uncanny turn-around arose only in part from his superlative balance and speed: it could also be traced to Rosewall's 'vision'. This was that heightened capacity of great athletes to observe and register their opponent's movements and balance. The champion then used this knowledge, garnered and processed in split seconds, to surprise and upset the opponent.

In the best of them, this processing became an unconscious habit, and was displayed most dramatically when both players were engaged in a strenuous rally. Figure 6.7 is a series of stills illustrating Rosewall's play during a rally against fellow pro Andres Gimeno. It provides at least two instances of these lightning ripostes.

Another example appears in a segment recently re-shown on YouTube™ where Rosewall confounds Arthur Ashe with one of his favourite tricks. At mid-point in a rally, just when Ashe arrives at net and is about to volley, Rosewall darts in – and volleys away Ashe's volley.

By the early sixties, Rosewall's game was near complete. He backed up his superlative backcourt game with a skill at net as good as anyone's and a deadly overhead angled to either corner.

Even before the match began, his peerless return of serve presented a discomforting problem for his fellow pros. On winning the toss, would they prefer to face his serve or opt for their own and risk his return? By then, his own serve was so reliable, well-placed and deep – and his ball toss and small stature kept the ball so low – that he made it surprisingly tough for the returner, especially on grass.

Though Hoad never got over thinking that he was a better player than his famous 'twin', when he turned pro a year after Rosewall, Hoad couldn't believe the trouble he was having with Rosewall's 'little' serve. And he was astonished at the brilliant net game the former baseliner had developed to back it up.

And just when Rosewall had nicely entrenched himself at the top of the pros, time marched on, and along came Laver.

Decline, comeback and swansong: the Open Era 1968 to 1975

The focus of this book is the pros and their era. However, to do justice to both the general story and the particular trajectory of our present champion – and of Laver, his successor – it is necessary to look a little into the era that followed.

By the end of 1967, the world had just about had enough of the silliness of 'shamateur' tennis. All of a sudden, the bastion, Wimbledon's All England Club, broke ranks: they invited the pros to enter their sacred precincts for a pro tourney. From a small field of the best pros, Laver and Rosewall surged to the top – and Laver ended up beating Rosewall in a brilliant final. The crowds loved it – but so did the new power brokers, the television producers.

The Open Era was on its way.

In early 1968 came the first major tournament open to all comers, then the first Grand Slam Title (the French). Rosewall beat Laver to win both. The first Open Wimbledon followed immediately after the French.

At the dawn of this new era, Ken Rosewall must have felt both satisfied and anxious. He was satisfied because he knew that he and a very select few had carried on in the pro wilderness, and had made it through. For over half a century the pros had devoutly wished, and toiled, for an open field in tennis. Here was the consummation.

But was it too late for Rosewall? By then he was 33 years old, and Rodney George Laver had succeeded the older man as World Pro Champion.

The man nicknamed *The Rocket* was then at the height of his powers. As would be expected of one who has made such a rich thing of modesty, Rosewall distrusted superlatives and comparisons, and used words almost as carefully as he hit a drop shot. Yet by now, the former champion had come to the conclusion that the Laver powers were, simply, unmatched. While it had taken almost three years for Laver to climb to the top of the pros, once he had added consistency to his incomparable originality and brilliance, he had got there, and stayed.

These two old friends – one the former champion and now contender, the other the former contender and now champion – knew that, more than any others, it was they who had kept the creaky pro boat afloat. Yet Rosewall fretted: Could he continue to play sufficiently well to satisfy his pride and ambition? Despite age and Laver, these drives were as strong as ever.

History showed he could compete, and gloriously. Space does not allow us to detail his splendid swansong, but here is something of his final achievement.

After a whirlwind start in winning the first two Open tournaments, for almost two years Rosewall won no majors. By then, most observers thought that his career would soon be over. But somehow he found a new wind. By the early seventies, alongside Laver and John Newcombe, Rosewall was still the one to beat. By then approaching forty, he had added a second French Open to his 1968 crown and again won the US and Australian titles, the last twice. And he reached, but sadly lost, the finals of two more

1
2
3
4
5
6
7
8
9
10
11
12
13
14
15
16
17
18
19
20

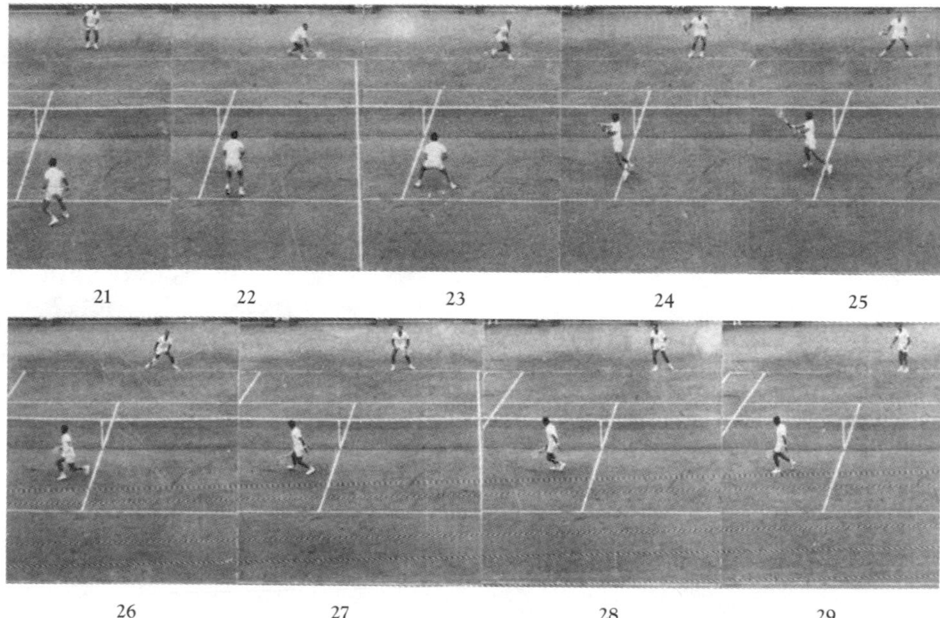

Fig. 6.7. Rosewall's moves flummox Gimeno. In this sequence from the early '60s, from his first stroke Rosewall repeatedly steals the initiative from his opponent. Note his sudden dart net-wards in frames 13–16.

Wimbledons. It is unlikely that Rosewall's achievement – winning three national championships that he'd won 20 years earlier – will be repeated.

In many ways Rosewall's game against Laver in the Final of the World Championship of Tennis (WCT) on May 10, 1972, exemplifies Rosewall as player and man. Yet it represents a pinnacle not because the two combatants were at their best as players – for Rosewall this had been a full decade earlier – but because of how it was played, and how it was won. And though just outside our major focus, the style and significance of the contest made it a denouement to the Pro Era, and so it would be cruel to deny it a place in our story.

Several millions watched this drama live – and still they watched as the match continued into its third and then fourth hours. So compulsive was its hold that the American TV producers kept it going on air, cancelling the scheduled programs! In Chapter 3, on Bobby Riggs, we saw how this one match has been credited with making a significant contribution to the tennis boom in the USA that followed.

Fig. 6.8a. and 6.8b. Two Rosewall volleys: left, a searching forehand, and right, what might become one of Rosewall's most subtle masterstrokes – the last-second backhand lob-volley.

The classic confrontation not only prefigured an international and electronic era: it was the stuff of almost-forgotten dreams. For here, from the 'Old Days', were the two aging diggers, *Rocket* and *Muscles.* It was they who had again pushed to the top of a majestic field, and were now to walk out, alone, into the footlights. These gnarled veterans, survivors of the tatty pro circus's nearly 50 years of struggle, were to make the bridge into a new era, into the modern and the glossy. And they rose to it: in the match that followed they were to pull out all the stops.

It is fitting that the gallery contained a cluster of tennis kings. With the exception of Tilden, gone for 20 years, in 1972 all our former pro champions – Elly Vines, Don Budge, Bobby Riggs, Jack Kramer and Pancho Gonzales – watched this match. And loved it. And must have felt vindicated by it.

But first, what was happening in the lead-up to this great contest?

By 1971, three years into the Open Era, conflict between the leading pro players and the national Lawn Tennis Associations had still not been fully resolved. So much so that Lamar Hunt, a Texas oil millionaire, had contracted most of the best players, including Rosewall and Laver, and set up a separate tour entitled The World Championship of Tennis.

This tour culminated in a set of finals for its eight leaders. To decide the champion, a grand-final showdown was planned between the two top players, scheduled for Dallas, Texas. Laver and Rosewall got through to the Final. There, in a marvellous and dramatic match – in which Rosewall was nearly put out of the event when struck in the eye by a ball – Rosewall trumped expectations and won.

The following year it was the same format – and the same pair of Australians went for it, and got through to the Final. At 37 and 33 years of age, by far the oldest of the finalists, here they were, facing each other for the hundredth time. And this match was one that, for different reasons, both saw as perhaps the most important of their long careers.

Although still recognised as King, Rod Laver knew he was slipping. While his career achievements were unsurpassed, this WCT Championship was one title he'd never won, and he wanted it badly. Moreover, the previous year, the old contender Rosewall had edged him out. It was truly Laver's turn.

For his part Rosewall knew this might be *his* last chance at something like a true world championship. Further, as befitted the new era, through global television this one was to be played to the world. Even more, he had astonished most – if not himself – by winning the previous year. At long last, recognition of his stature as one of the true greats was beginning to flow. Modest to a fault, he still wanted to prove he was up there with the very best who had ever played the game. Even for his sternest critics, back-to-back victories over the player considered by most tennis followers as the best ever would be hard to overlook.

When, pre-match, the media questioned Rosewall on how he felt facing Laver, they reminded him that his opponent held a considerable advantage over him in their recent personal duels. Rosewall replied tersely, 'Each match is a fresh start.'

His comments after his win a year before in the first WCT Final are also relevant. He said at the time, 'I played well tonight – but I've played better against Rod, and lost.'

We are lucky to have extant tapes of the 1972 match, and can also draw on Rosewall's own commentary in his *Play Tennis with Rosewall.*

●●●

The match began 'in a flurry of Laver brilliance,' said Rosewall, 'and in no time at all, I was four [games] down, though I did not feel I was playing badly.'

Admitting to feeling 'desperate', he found a rare service ace, and won his first game.

But then, after reaching 5–1, Laver went slightly off the boil, and Rosewall somehow climbed back into the set. He got to 4–5, and had a number of points for 5–5 on Laver's serve. But one shortish lob, and *The Rocket* was airborne. When the huge Laver smash erupted from behind his right (off) ear, it was curtains for Ken in the first set.

Rosewall's thoughts? Simply: 'I knew I had a battle on my hands.'

He might have been struggling, yet the irrepressible tactician was at work: how might he turn the match around?

Courtside at the changeover, Rosewall computed that although Laver had already struck three winning smashes in the just-completed first set, he had made one error. This was against his own three winning smashes, with no errors. Overhead the lights were blazing and it was getting very hot on the court, so Rosewall decided that his marvel of an opponent would soon find himself a lot nearer to those little furnaces: he would be jumping into them every time he chased lobs, and would become very tired doing so.

What was more, his arch foe would face mental, as well as physical, torture. Laver, charging towards his 'favourite launching pad in the forecourt', would find himself agonising: Was he about to be forced to turn around? Was he going to have to chase down one more gently arching ball, conjured from nowhere into air, thin air?

Seated between the sets, Rosewall dried his face ... and weighed up his options. We can almost hear him concluding: *lob him, yes, but if I get a look at a smash, I will need to treat it emphatically, without any room for error.* [18]

The next set began with a desperate struggle. But, after starting the game with a double fault, it was Rosewall who eventually took the first game – with an angled backhand volley so mysteriously simple, a finger snap, that the assembled crowd was stilled. Then they released their collective breath – and began to clap.

In the stands, many of the pros were awed by what they were seeing. After one such Rosewall volley, a reporter overheard Cliff Drysdale saying to fellow-pro Marty Riessen, 'Look at that volley! We couldn't do that unless we miss-hit the ball!'

Then came the unexpected.

With the sort of tennis he had played a decade earlier, coolly and precisely Rosewall took the next six games, and the set – *to Love*! At this point, like Rosewall at the beginning of the match when *he* was losing, Laver wasn't playing badly. He just wasn't over-the-top brilliant. Meanwhile his opponent's tennis was hard, polished and flawless as a diamond.

By now, Rosewall was using a technique he had perfected against Laver in the 1971 final. Inverting the established maxim, he was not punching his volleys deep, but finessing many of them short, angled, and low, so making Laver move forwards and down. This reduced the room for the phenomenal running angled topspin drives that Laver loved to create from the baseline.

Fifty years earlier, the equally dark and studious French star René Lacoste held a secret notebook filled with details on each of his major opponents. There he noted that the only way to overcome Tilden was to give him no room at the baseline to make his running drives. Half a century later, Rosewall had reached the same conclusion: the free-swingers had to be cramped, or they would fillet you.

Rosewall recalls that at the end of the set he found himself trying to dredge up from his memory the last occasion he'd stolen a 6–0 off the champion: he couldn't remember *one*. And he'd just lost the previous set – and the all-important first. He admitted that he felt 'amazed'.

By the crucial third set, the TV commentators were already saying that Rosewall was looking tired.[19] Yet he tells us that in the very first point of the set he delighted himself in succeeding with something he'd been attempting all night – the sharp, wide serve to the first court.

A risky move against the magisterial Laver backhand! Taking a huge sweep, *The Rocket* drilled Rosewall's best serve of the match for a clean winner down the line!

But Rosewall somehow held on. Games went with serve to 2–all.

After a glorious passage of play, in Laver's next service game Rosewall gained the breakpoint, then the game. With both grimly holding serve, eventually this one break gave Rosewall the set.

Between sets, tirelessly, Rosewall was observing and dissecting.

He recalled that Laver's serve had lost a little of its edge, and, from the corner of his eye, he noted that his opponent, perhaps fretting a little, was now changing his racket. But he also recognised that his own returns had been good – so good that they'd not given the Laver serve much help at all.

The little general was at work: he was tightening the screws.

In the fourth set, he gave them another turn. It was one all, on Laver's serve, with Rosewall at break point. As Laver surged in behind a huge

Fig. 6.9. Laver versus Rosewall, Dallas 1972, the World Championship of Tennis Final. Not only one of tennis's greatest matches, this one changed tennis history.

forehand, Rosewall (oh, those tiny steps!) ran it down – and conjured an early-struck crosscourt backhand made in heaven.

Two sets to one up. And a break.

At this moment, Rosewall tells us he knew two things. First, if he could hold serve, the championship was his. Second, at these times, 'Rod is at his most dangerous.' The wily John Newcombe once said – and not entirely tongue-in-cheek – that against Laver he never knew when he was in more trouble, being up two sets to Love, or being two down! Time and again such a dire situation would be the spur to Laver's brilliant best.

Rosewall knew this, but reassured himself that 'it would not happen this time'.

It did.

Hitting his way out of trouble with unreturnable shots from every part of the court, Laver broke back. But Rosewall somehow managed to keep his serve, and they advanced on serve to 6–all and the tie break. Despite a good start by Rosewall, back surged *the Rocket*. With six straight points, most on winners, Laver took the tie break.

Thus the fourth set was Laver's. Of the set's 68 points, Laver had won 36 to Rosewall's 32. The four-point margin was the exact difference of the tie break, 7–3.

Now Rosewall admitted that he not only looked, but was, exhausted: the pair had been playing for nearly three hours, and the television lights were baking. At that point, Rosewall, the irrepressible monitor, made a surprise discovery: 'My legs felt like they had been filled with lead, but, oddly, the pain was bearable between rallies.'

Yet despite the ballast, the final fifth set began with some of the most marvellous tennis of the match. So good were both players' fitness, control and depth of shot, in several long rallies they found themselves pinned to the baseline. Around the world, hundreds of thousands of spectators were equally pinned – to their screens, and being shown something of the all court art of an earlier era.

Yet, somehow or other, the key points were swinging to the older and smaller of the two: it was Rosewall who was beginning to edge ahead.

In the second game, Rosewall broke serve, and held to 3–0. With another lob, this one so perfect that it caught the baseline, he reached breakpoint on Laver's serve, and the chance of a 4–0 lead.

But on Laver's crucial next serve, Rosewall had a rare lapse: his return was, in his own words, 'the wildest forehand of 1972'. Still, as only the great can do, he centred himself, and persevered. And managed to create another four chances to break. He lost every one of them. Three–one to Rosewall.

Again Ken caught himself wondering: Can I hang on, or will Rod find the unplayable shots?

Ken did hang on – to 4–2, his serve. But once more *The Rocket* took off: he broke back, and held serve. It was four games all. Rosewall held serve to make it 5–4. To stay in the match, Laver had to win his serve.

We know that Rosewall had studied the artful way the aging Gonzales returned the Laver serve – softly, with underspin, and at his feet. Perhaps, too, Rosewall recalled another relevant image, this time from much earlier:

his former doubles partner, that seemingly awkward bird, *Old Brom* – predatory, voracious, dancing netwards to pick up the serve on the rise and finesse it back.

So time and again, Rosewall had been scooping up a serve a few inches above the turf, and feathering a return an inch above the net – straight into the path of the hapless Laver racing in. Repeatedly, Laver had been forced to bend and put the pace on his volleys as Rosewall's returns slid, infuriatingly, into his toes.

Now let's take a seat courtside and watch what followed.

●●●

Match point to Rosewall, Laver serving, second court.

They both take a deep breath. With a serve Rosewall hasn't expected, Laver is fearless as ever. He aces his opponent down the centre.

Deuce. Laver steadies, takes out the game. Five games all.

Now, after three and a half hours of seesaw drama, the score stands at 6–all.

Hollow-eyed, the two exhausted men stare at each other. To decide the match, they face another tie break.

In the tie break on which the championship hangs, Laver starts strongly. He gets ahead. Then stays ahead. He leads 5–4. The redhead, the only winner of two Grand Slams, has two serves to take the championship.

But then: the epiphany.

To Rosewall, staring at defeat, it is now or never. From the depths of his exhausted mind he concludes: *I must do something different.*

To know and to act are one and the same, runs the Samurai maxim.

Laver is now serving to the second or ad court. He serves powerfully, his lefthander's serve searing wide to the Rosewall backhand.

But Rosewall knows. He has anticipated it. He acts.

Now there are no more soft-spinning sliders *à la Old Brom*. Stepping in, he takes the ball early and spears a crosscourt bullet.

As it flashes across him, the charging Laver just gets to it. Rosewall, waiting, watches Laver's groping half-volley 'balloon over the baseline'.

Five points all. Laver is wondering. Rosewall is wondering. He thinks that now Laver 'must try his favourite serve, down the centre'.

Laver does. It's a beauty, again swinging to Rosewall's backhand.

For a second time the older master swoops – the poise, the arc, the strike.

This time Laver can't put a touch on a clean winner down the line.

Six–five. Rosewall is serving now. His second match point. He tells himself, 'go for depth.' And does – but the serve is a let.

Fig. 6.10. The dancing master. The ageless veteran gets up on his toes for a backhand drive. Poised, he could strike either way, and with his characteristic balletic scissors movement, was ready to move anywhere.

The next serve is again deep, jamming Laver's backhand.

Laver's return strikes the net, just below the tape.

It bounces back towards him.

There is a hush.

Rosewall has 'made his opponent surrender'.

This match tells us much about Rosewall's often little-understood style. He won because he was able to harness all that he had learnt in a lifetime in tennis. Here was the all court mastery, the errorless consistency and brilliance of stroke play. Here was the extraordinary backhand, unsheathed in at least three crucial moments.

Though arresting and beautiful, these are manifestations, not the essence. We have seen how Rosewall studied his opponent and, with a peculiarly deep concentration, found – even lured – a chink. Then, drawing on the power of his 'complement' – the opponent – he struck. Indeed, such was the magnetism of the older master's spirit, many of the spectators must have felt a sense of the uncanny: it was as if Rosewall *made* Laver offer him the two serves he needed to turn the match.

Of all the great champions described in this book, the most modest is the most inspiring. Straight-jacketed as an amateur by the self-interested and unperceptive Harry Hopman, and then ignored during the pro years when he reached his superlative best, Rosewall not only survived, but triumphed gloriously.

More than the achievement itself, what touches us is the way he did it. When asked late in his career what kept him going, Rosewall answered: 'I've [always] been ... a little guy trying to beat the big guys.'

As the little man taking on the world, Rosewall is the most human of all the great pro heroes. For, to the gigantic cosmos, we are all little men and women. The small and the modest remind us that any power we hold is not just evanescent – it is borrowed. A little is lent, for a little while. Then passed on.

'No matter what has happened,' says the gutsy player born of dark and magical Pluto but with the calm practicality of the grocer's son, 'you've always got a chance.'

But a chance for what? To survive with dignity? That's no mean feat.

However, if we are lucky and brave, we can do a little more, and use a little of that power lent to us — to create beauty.

For his demonstration of this, we thank Ken Rosewall from the bottom of our hearts.

Notes

1 This chapter has drawn mainly on two sources: Ken Rosewall with John Barrett, *Play Tennis with Rosewall*, Queen Anne Press, London, 1975; and Peter Rowley with Ken Rosewall, *Twenty Years at the Top*, G P Putnam's Sons, New York, 1976.

2 Kramer, *The Game*.

3 Lew Hoad with Jack Pollard, *My Game*, Hodder and Stoughton, London, 1958.

4 Kramer, *The Game*. I am strangely reminded of the mysterious throwaway comment of Winnicot, the British child psychiatrist, to the effect that twins usually love, but often do not like, each other. Of interest is Rosewall's only recorded instance of exaggeration: he once claimed to his biographer that from the time Lew turned pro, he 'owned' the big blond. If, as the months and years passed, it was usually Rosewall who was on top of his old rival and twin, I doubt if any tennis player could claim to own Lew Hoad.

5 John Sharnik, *Remembrance of Games Past: On Tour with the Tennis Grand Masters*, Macmillan, New York, 1986.

6 Bellamy, *Love Thirty*.

7 Alan Gilbert, 'Playing Games in the "Banana Republic"', in *Australia: 200 Years and Beyond*, Fairfax and Sons, Sydney, 1987.

8 Cited in Rowley, *Twenty Years at the Top*. Richard Evans, a fine tennis writer, misquotes tennis pro and Rosewall contemporary, Jeff Borowiak, in his *Open Tennis: The First Twenty Years*. Evans says that Borowiak, a good touring player who knew music, likened Rosewall to *Brahms*. In fact, biographer Rowley later confirms that Borowiak's comparison was to the more cerebral Bach, which is better.

9 Peter FitzSimons, *Great Australian Sports Champions*, HarperSports, Sydney, 2006. FitzSimons interviewed the aging Robert and got another twist on young Ken's handedness, and on Robert's teaching style. Father Robert explained: 'When Ken was little he liked to do a double-handed backhand, which I didn't like, and so I cut off the end of his racket – meaning there was only space for ... one hand. That was the end of the problem.' Vic Braden adds an extraordinary comment: he claims that Ken once told him that if he had his time over, he would serve left-handed and play right-handed! Vic Braden and Robert Wood, *Vic Braden's Mental Tennis: How to Psych yourself to a Winning Game*, Little, Brown and Company, Boston, 1993.

10 Harry Hopman, *Aces and Places*, Cassell, London, 1957. Hopman says he was surprised by the last-minute decision of the selection panel. He does not convince: in the warm-up to the Cup, Hopman himself broke up the Hoad–Rosewall partnership and substituted Hartwig for Rosewall.

11 Richard Yallop, *A Serve to Authority: Kooyong: a Hundred Years of Heroes and Headlines*, MappCorp, Melbourne, 1992.

12 Kramer, *The Game*.

13 Understanding of Rosewall's achievement is incomplete without taking into account his marriage to Wilma McIver. They married just before he turned pro, and became devoted partners; it is said he wrote to her every day on the Gonzales tour. It seems Wilma's faith and understanding made a major contribution to her singular Kenny's climb against the odds.

14 Kramer, *The Game*.
15 Sharnik, *Remembrance of Games Past*.
16 Braden and Wood, *Vic Braden's Mental Tennis*.
17 Evans, *Open Tennis*.
18 The match statistics on smashes indicate the success of Rosewall's strategy. Laver hit 21 concluding overheads, of which 15 were winners and 6 were errors. But of the 18 struck by Rosewall, all but one were winners. This recalls Paul Metzler's lovely re-telling of an interchange between the legendary Frenchman Henri Cochet, and the young Australian champion Adrian Quist. (Cochet, like Rosewall, was a small man who commanded the paradox of a relatively inoffensive serve and a devastating overhead.) 'Quist: "M'sieu Cochet, I've never seen you hit a smash hard." Cochet: "But mon Adrian, have you ever seen me miss one?"' Paul Metzler, *Tennis Styles and Stylists*, Angus and Robertson, Sydney, 1969.
19 What happened *after* this match shows how exhausted Rosewall was. The players and spectators had long gone when officials discovered that Rosewall, a person famously 'careful with money', had left his winner's cheque behind on the court!

Fig. 7.0. A running Laver forehand on clay. Hair brushed by his speed of foot, Laver has struck a fierce drive down the line, the racket closing over the ball to impart huge topspin.

7

THE MAGICIAN WHO BROUGHT DOWN THE CURTAIN – LAVER

The only trouble with this guy is that he doesn't understand that what he is doing is impossible.

Cliff Drysdale

THE words of Laver's fellow pro Cliff Drysdale in the epigraph to this chapter were spoken in South Africa in 1967. They followed a tournament that Rod Laver had just won without losing a set. [1]

Just two years later the 'impossible' was exactly what Laver was planning to do. He had told no one about it, but he intended to win the Grand Slam – for the second time. By the middle of 1969, at the end of the Wimbledon fortnight, he was on track. He had already won the Australian and the French, the first two legs of the four great championships making up the Slam. Now he was into the third and greatest, Wimbledon, and had reached the Final.

Facing Laver was fellow Australian John Newcombe. Though Laver loved Wimbledon, and was the reigning champion and top seed, Newcombe also felt at home on the famed Centre Court. As well as two

Wimbledon doubles titles, Newcombe had slipped a singles under his belt: the 1967 Championship, the last Wimbledon before tennis became open. He relished the fast true grass, and at 25 years he was approaching the peak of his powerful and intelligent game.

In contrast, Laver was thirty-one and had been playing continually since the Australian Championships in January. Newcombe's confidence had been reinforced by the performance of his Aussie mate, Tony Roche. Although Roche could not win the major tournaments from Laver, during the course of the year he had notched up more matches against him than he'd lost. Newcombe believed that he was just ahead of Roche – and he scented blood.

He told his intimates that he had a better-than-even chance of winning his first, and the second-ever Open Wimbledon.

Newk (as he was universally known) had thought hard about his strategy against Laver. After joining the pros he had spent hours sitting in the stands studying the old masters Laver and Rosewall. Aware that Laver liked pace, *Newk* decided he wasn't going to offer him any.

'Good thinking,' observed Laver in his autobiography. 'He wanted to jerk me around ... he chipped his returns ... when I came to net he lobbed me ... '[2]

What happened next sums up the Rod Laver genius.

The wizard takes off

The first set was tough, but Laver held up to take it. Nevertheless, *Newk*'s 'defensive' strategy had started to work: already, many times Laver had been forced to jump for lobs, and the older man was beginning to show it. Laver began missing a few smashes, and more than a few first serves. The challenger was playing very smart and very well, and his great serve was on.

Newcombe took the second set 7–5 to make it one set All.

In the third set, Newcombe made a crucial service break, and he was up 3–1. Holding serve, it was 4–1. At this point, to most observers the young gun was playing the game of his life: if he won this set, as he looked almost certain to do, he would be well placed for the championship.

In *The Education of a Tennis Player*, his excellent autobiography written with Bud Collins, Laver explains that it was then that something happened within him.

The crowd was getting excited. Here was an old champion in trouble and facing a challenger who was young, brave, handsome and on song. Laver sensed that the spectators were hoping 'things would get even tougher for me'. But he was far from being put out by this. To him, their sentiments were 'all right'.

Then he admits to something even more astonishing: in the space of a few seconds, 'all the anxiety and fear' that he had faced in reaching this point of crisis dissolved.

'I was on my stage,' the old pro tells us, 'one that I knew and loved, and it was up to me to strut like a proud player and do my act'.

At 1–4, and 30–All, Laver was serving in a game he had to win. Newcombe threw up one more lob. It was pretty good – but not good enough. Once more skyward goes *The Rocket*, and buries a glorious smash for 40–30.

Next, 'I stepped to the line and cracked an ace'. It 'felt fantastic'.

What then arose within the old champion was something more than the proverbial flood of confidence. With serve and overhead firing, suddenly he believed: *I can do anything.*

It was now 4–2, with Newcombe still a service break ahead and serving. After Laver won the first point of the game for 0–15, a rally developed on the second.

'Newcombe,' says Laver, 'belted a forehand crosscourt wide to my right. As I lunged for it he pressed tight to the net ready to cut off anything [I could return]. He edged a bit to his left, figuring logically that if I got to the ball all I could do was try and slap it down the line. A down-the-line backhand is my favourite in that situation.'

But this performer had just slipped on the player's mask with its mysterious power, and stepped up to his role on the great stage. Although 'everybody' knew that his favourite shot was the down-the-line backhand, usually struck hard with topspin, he made up his mind 'to go the other way'.

We catch him at this instant – behind, on a dead run, at the end of his reach, and at a key point in the Final of a great championship. Then and there, the wizard unwraps his wand. He invents a stroke resembling a karate-chop and slices a low, softish crosscourt skimmer.

The ball, invested with a life of its own and running almost parallel to the net, keeps 'fluttering along'.

As if held on a string to the puppet-master's hand, and eluding the frantic efforts of Newcombe at the net, the mesmerising thing eventually drops – poof! – an inch within the sideline.

Laver tells us he himself couldn't believe the angle. Neither could Newcombe. Clearly, his opponent was 'shocked'. And because of that one action, the match was more or less over. From then on, Laver was playing out of his mind. He won the third set easily – and then the fourth for the championships.

As with most great artists or craftsmen at the height of their creative fever, the shot seemed to come from somewhere else. 'You don't plan a shot like that,' he says. 'I had a general direction in mind and the rest just happened.'

As Laver reflects back on his performance, he then puts aside the player's mask and magician's cloak.

Before us is the ordinary man. This one is small, red-haired, with bandy legs and a hundred freckles scattered over a serious, almost sad face. From the distance of the years, this reconstituted observer sums up with anti-climactic modesty: yes, he says, for the audience at the time, his little play must have been 'nice to watch'.

John Newcombe was a champion: resolute and shrewd, with a commanding all court game. Like every true champion he also had a habit of finding great responses in a crisis. But never in his sporting life would he make a shot like the demonic floater with which, at the perfect moment, Laver transfixed him in that Wimbledon Final.

For a shot like that you need more than loyal service to honourable gods: you require some acquaintance with the devil and his magic.

How do you become a wicked wizard?

Bush childhood

It started in Queensland, the state Aussies sometimes call – with a mixture of respect and derision – the 'Deep North'. On August 9, 1938, in the northern coastal town of Rockhampton (population 33,500), Roy and Melba Laver greeted the arrival of their third child. He was a healthy boy.

Named Rodney George, he was to become Rockhampton's most famous son.

Only a month after the birth, an event occurred on the other side of the world. Apparently unrelated, it was to have far-reaching consequences for the new baby: another redhead, the American Don Budge, completed the first-ever Grand Slam. It would become young Rod's dream to repeat Budge's odyssey coincident with his birth.

The Lavers were a rural clan of bushmen and sportsmen. (These descriptors are not gender-specific: only days before she died at ninety, Rod's grandmother was still riding a horse.) Father Roy ran cattle stations ('ranches' to Americans), and at times worked as a butcher. Mother Melba was named after the famous Australian opera singer Dame Nellie Melba, the same who had idolised *Big Bill* Tilden in the twenties and the aunt of the man that Tilden vanquished for his first major title.

The baby was taken back to Langdale, a smallish cattle run Roy managed, just out from Rockhampton. When Rod was eight years old, the family moved to another station 30 miles (50 km) from Marlborough, and over 70 miles (100 km) inland from Rockhampton. Marlborough, a hot little cattle town, contained a primary school for Rod, as well as a local butcher's shop that his father ran along with the station. But within a year, Roy and Melba decided they wanted a better education for their children, and moved the family back to Rockhampton.

Thus Rod Laver's early boyhood was shaped by two major influences: the spirit and genes of the Laver tribe, and the Queensland bush. In Aussie lingo, he was a 'bananabender from beyond the Black Stump'.

By the time the Lavers had filtered up to Queensland at the turn of the century, they were a large clan – proud and tough. And passionate about sport. Father Roy was one of 11 boys, and the Laver lads made up a whole cricket team widely celebrated in the backblocks. Moreover, they possessed talent to match their passion: Uncle Frank Laver had played cricket for Australia.

In the nuclear family, it was tennis that held pride of place.

In both Langdale and Marlborough the passion was such that the Lavers built their own tennis courts. The means of construction was uniquely indigenous. Excavating the giant anthills ubiquitous in the dry north, they crushed the red dirt, laid it down, then levelled and rolled it. Eventually they

Fig. 7.1. The outback kid. Rod is barefoot, and both kid and horse are happy. The place is probably Langdale, the family's cattle station where Rod spent his early boyhood.

had an excellent 'hard' court; cooler and softer than bitumen or concrete, it played like fastish clay.

On weekends, competitive and social tennis was at the centre of their little community. The bush families would gather at one or another of their neighbours' homes, a visit sometimes requiring a return journey of over 100 miles (160 km).

When Rod was nine and back in the town of his birth, the first thing they did was build another anthill court. To clear the space they faced scrub and trees thick enough to hide a venomous six-foot (two-metre) brown snake. Someone managed to dispatch the intruder – appropriately enough, with a tennis racket.

This court was not only wired in behind chicken netting, it was also lit, if somewhat dimly, to enable play in the cooler evenings. Four great hanging 1500-watt globes were strung down the long axis of the court.

We now zoom in on Rockhampton and one night in 1948. The improvised Laver court was ablaze under the lights. The tennis was on.

And as it happened, just a few yards away, a young boy had been put to bed – but was unable to sleep.

The lad was just 10 years old and the youngest of the boys of the family. Stealing from his bed, he crept down to the scene of family activity. Pyjama-clad, the little red-haired kid reached the court and, enthralled by the goings-on under the lights, gripped the chicken-wire fence with his hands.

Seeing the delight of his older brothers, he could not help asking himself: Why was it that everyone else was having all the fun? But the lad was so shy, he decided that if kept out of the way no one would notice him, and continue worshipping these dashing figures in white.

But someone did notice him. The Lavers had invited a visitor to play with them. He was a tall man, and elegant. Suddenly he spied the little monkey hanging on the wire.

In one encompassing glance, the die was cast.

The student finds the master

There is a saying in the East that when the student is ready, the master is found. One sweaty night in Rockhampton, the meeting of master and student seemed peculiarly destined.

The tall visitor was Charles (known as Charlie) Hollis, and he was a pro. His job was teaching tennis. The shy boy was to become his most famous pupil.

Who was he?

At that time Charlie was about 40 years old, and a bachelor. In *The Education of a Tennis Player*, Rod lets the reader know in passing that the residence of this particular bachelor was one of the town's hotels. This explains much about Charlie.

Half a century ago, country towns in Australia tended to be more isolated and self-sufficient. This appealed to those who felt at home in a small close-knit community, far from the bustle and anonymity of the big smoke.

In those days every dusty township seemed to harbour one or two men or women with a stamp so individual as to make them renowned (for good or ill) in the community: they were the local 'characters'. Some never gave up the gypsy inside them. Soon after arriving, they were ready to 'clear out', and before long were on their way to another outback township. But there were others who, having dropped in years earlier, became a fixture.

Some of these wanderers derived further distinction from remaining disentangled from the conventional appurtenances of house and family. With a qualified concession to their once-nomadic status, they would 'camp' on a mate's veranda, sometimes for a decade. Those with a more reliable income would make their residence the local hotel or boarding house.

Like Charlie, for many the scars of war contributed to their choice to live outside the nuclear family: they joined a group that provided for them. Further, as if to relish – and publicise – their status of permanent guest, some would cultivate a certain sense of style. These individuals wished to be seen in the town as a person of some class, a *gentleman* or, as the case may be, a *lady*.

Mr Hollis, as the local children called him, was one such character. Figure 7.2 catches him in his soldier's uniform at the war's end. His arm bears the distinction of the sergeant's stripes, and with open bushland as his backdrop, he confronts the camera boldly. After the uniform had gone, to the Laver tribe he still cut his jib distinctively and smartly, even in his tennis clothes. And he struck them as not just a fastidious dresser. This tall and suave man took pride in his manners and social grace.

In short, Charlie Hollis was set apart by his style, his itinerant past and his lack of a conventional occupation or the trappings of domesticity. To the bush communities, here was the real thing – a true pro, with the cachet.

And tennis was his life. Charlie was never a top player, but he had been a good one, and his vocation was teaching the game he loved. For years he had floated around northern NSW, and then North Queensland, before ending up in Rockhampton. There he instructed the locals, and visited the little towns and schools in the hinterland.

It was the Lavers who had lured Charlie to Rockhampton to set up his coaching school. As soon as their anthill court was ready, even without other guests Charlie could always find sufficient numbers for a decent game among hosts Roy and Melba and Rod's older brothers, Trevor and Bob. The older boys were becoming good. Ambitious for his sons, Roy was

Fig. 7.2. The master coach. Charlie Hollis, about 1945, just back from the war.

forever pressing the local pro to scrutinise them with a view to improving their tennis.

On that particular night in 1948, Charlie was as usual displaying the ample riches of his game. Watching him cracking his long Eastern ground strokes from both wings, and acing the opposition with an easy swinging serve, the older Laver boys were captivated. As for the kid brother in his pyjamas, he believed he'd never see anyone play so beautifully.

It was between sets, over a tot of rum, that Charlie spied the child hiding behind the chicken-wire fence. Speculating that it must be the youngest

Laver, the elegant visitor abruptly turned to Roy. 'Now then, Roy,' he asked, 'who's that kid hanging on the wire?'

Roy Laver, surprised at finding his youngest still up, told Charlie who he was.

'He's keen,' said Charlie Hollis imperiously. 'Let the little bugger have a hit.'

In keeping with all the best legends, this pupil was shy, astonished, eager and unknown, and his first step towards fame and fortune was made barefoot. In nothing but his pyjamas, the tiny youngster was brought in and handed his mother's racket.

Before half a minute had passed, he was tearing all over the court trying to return the ball to the hawk-eyed visitor.

Master and student had found each other.

Mollydookers and the early apprenticeship

At once, Hollis recognised the boy's exceptional ball sense. 'He's got an eye like a hawk,' Charlie informed Roy and Melba. Despite this, at first Charlie considered that the kid might be too small to get anywhere – but before long, he changed his mind and took him on.

He had soon honed in on a further three attributes evident in his new charge. First, Rod was left-handed. Second, he was inexhaustible. Third, he was innately calm. Hollis understood that each held a well of potential, but required exceptional care.

The kid's left-handedness was the first excruciating challenge to the coach.

Writer Hal Porter, referring to what Australians judged to be marginalising traits, once famously compressed these into a string of adjectives: 'mollyduked, atheist, over-educated, young, leftist, Queensland-nurtured'. Such prejudice against the left-hander (called a 'mollydooker' or 'mollyduker') is of special relevance to tennis.

Like Ken Rosewall's father, Robert, Charlie had studied the line of great champions. Conequently he knew that the game of every left-handed champion of the past was, at the highest level, flawed. Yes, their penchant for spin and swerve, along with their relative rarity, gave them advantages over most opponents. But their apparently immutable preference for the left side invariably produced a distortion. They may well have loved crunching a swinging forehand wide and easy from their natural left, but when they were pressed on the right, the backhand that escaped was usually little more than a cramped and defensive slice. Thus a class player could find them out, and prise them apart.

Despite realising all this – and unlike Robert Rosewall – Charlie Hollis decided his new pupil was going to remain a left-hander. But in a heroic first, he would possess a real backhand. And the education of this tennis player would begin by confronting the left-hander's hoodoo – the backhand.

Charlie himself possessed a freewheeling attacking backhand. This was the boy's model.

Then and there young Rod was taught that the movement of a proper backhand stroke was a liberated arc. From a side-on position, with shoulder fully turned, the arm would then be freed, straightening as the body unwound through the stroke. While the ball would be struck hard and largely flat, with the racket head moving through the ball in Tilden's prescribed 'level of the ball', the path was low enough at the beginning and high enough at the end to produce some controlling topspin – and to finish with a full and triumphant follow-through.

Hollis's repeated cry of 'Hit through the ball!' became the mantra of his most famous pupil. On pain of the coach's severe displeasure, Rod's original backhand, the left-hander's pokey jab with elbow up and pointed, was banned from the first moment.

Figure 7.3 shows the mature Laver backhand. The stroke is so sweet that I am reminded of how Michelangelo sensed that his David was hiding in the block of marble. Likewise, all Master Hollis needed to do was chip off the clutter.

The wider setting helped. Rod's first year in school coincided with a change in Australian education: children who preferred to write with their left hand were allowed to do so. By the time the future champion was joining the crowd, the conflation of left-handed with clumsy and marginalised was giving way. Indeed, with Charlie behind him, it might be a stroke of luck. [3]

Two of our present heroes can help explain more about left-handedness in general – and about Rod Laver's in particular.

Fig. 7.3. Laver unleashes his magisterial backhand. The fifth sequence clearly shows his last split-second wrist flick.

It can be seen that though Ken Rosewall's left-handedness was suppressed, the imprint of his dominant left side remained in the shape of his masterly backhand, and in his relatively modest serve.

Don Budge's miraculous backhand is also relevant: Laver's left-handedness resembles Budge's right-handedness in that the preference is partial or balanced. Like Budge, Laver is right-handed in games requiring two hands, such as golf, or in the batting parts of cricket or baseball. However, when kicking a football, both prefer their left foot. [4]

It appears that the young Laver seemed to hold two natural advantages: besides the left-hander's potential strengths, with assistance from Charlie he held enough inherent balance to offset the lefties' weaknesses.

After examining the physical attributes of his new charge, Hollis began sizing up the mental capacity hiding behind the meek exterior of his latest charge. After plenty of ruckuses and even near punch-ups – these Lavers were passionate people – the flamboyant coach was soon announcing his conclusion: it was Rodney, not Trevor or Bob, who would end up at Wimbledon.

'He's got his mother's manner,' said the coach to Roy, 'easy going – not quick-tempered like the boys or us.' And tractable and tireless he proved to be.

Rod's two memoirs, *How to Play Winning Tennis* and the later *Education of a Tennis Player,* provide an entrancing picture of his next steps on his road to mastery.

To get in some practice before their morning lesson starting at 6.30, the boys would get up at 5.00 am, then ride their bikes the five miles to the town courts where Charlie held his lessons. These were near the hotel in which the coach lived. Being the smallest, Rod was the one dispatched to fetch the balls, securely stashed under Charlie's bed in his hotel room. In the dark Rod would creep in and, stealing under the bed of the sleeping coach, try to collect the balls without waking him.

In this way – at first by themselves, then joined by Charlie after he rose from his bed and took his breakfast in the hotel dining room – the eager students filled in the hours of each day before school.

Hollis's method was based on drills, which began without the ball and were repeated until ingrained. Thus the boys would have to simulate, then hit, 100 backhands. Then, after modelling 50 serves, it would be time to crunch another 50, rapid-fire for 10 minutes, into the wire around the court. By the time they left for school their arms felt ready to drop off.

At the end of the day, when they finally fell into an exhausted sleep, their ears would still be ringing with Hollis's catchphrases, many of which they would shout as they drilled: 'Up, change, punch', for instance, was the verbal cue to model the volley. Laver tells us that throughout his playing life he would call up this phrase, then, mouthing it, replay it over and over. When he was a 31-year-old world champion at a key point in his quest for the Grand Slam, Laver's volley began to wobble. It was by reiterating these words that he was able to reset the required pattern of hand, eye and brain.

To keep the interest of his pupils, the coach would also draw them in for talks about the game. Here they learned its rules, as well as the lore of the great players and the famous arenas on which they performed.

With a little elaboration of the story as told by Collins and Laver, we might join Charlie as he abruptly calls a spot quiz, which the students were required to pass on pain of punishment:

'Now you,' says the tall inquisitor to one of the little group seated around him, 'who was *Gentleman Jack*?'

'Gentleman Jack was Jack Crawford, Mr Hollis,' replies the questioned.

'Correct, Trevor. And, Rodney, why was he given the moniker *Gentleman Jack*?'

'Because he was a fine sportsman, and he was always well groomed, on and off the court,' pipes back the studious tyro.

'Correct again. Now go and hit a hundred serves into the wire – and bend your scrawny little legs and smack that ball until you break the fence down,' orders the coach.[5]

As implied, tennis was not all that Hollis taught. Though he might choose to live alone in a none-too-swanky country boozer, Charlie Hollis liked it known that he had moved amongst the better classes.

On one occasion when Charlie came to dine with the Lavers, he observed that the lad was wolfing down his food. Turning to the boy who had become his pupil, Hollis observed sharply: 'That, Rodney, is not the way to hold a fork. If you are to play at Wimbledon, you must learn to eat properly, not like a savage.' With élan, he would then demonstrate what was acceptable in the way of table manners.

Another time Hollis was expounding his requirements of a champion – technique, the work ethic, mental and physical fitness ... Turning to young Rod, he suddenly asked, 'Well Rodney, on that score, how do you think you shape up?'

In local slang, the kid replied modestly, 'Pretty crook!'

'As well as how to hit the ball, it looks like I have to teach you how to speak!' retorted the offended coach.[6]

There were social activities apart from tennis. The boys swam, went bush and even hunted kangaroos. They were keen on fishing too, and took out a small boat in search of the sea life that abounds in the tropical ocean off the coast at Rockhampton.

As a family friend, sometimes Charlie came along. Though he enjoyed the occasions, it seemed this singular man could never be free from his obsession with the game he loved. Laver and co-writer Collins tell that one day when young Rod excitedly showed the coach a beauty he had just reeled in from the sea, Charlie – his eyes far away – only remarked, 'You know, that Fred Perry sure had one marvellous forehand ... '

On the way back, Charlie might feel inclined to talk more about his greatest heroes, all of whom have graced the pages of this book: Ellsworth Vines with his grenade-like serve, *Big Bill* Tilden and the majesty of his forehand, or Henri Cochet and the dazzling improbability of his angled, backhand smash.

The master might be so moved with wonder that it would not be too fanciful to see him stand up and, grabbing a boat hook, demonstrate to his enthralled audience the compact beauty of the incomparable Budge backhand.

These stories were revered and internalised by the eager pupil – so much so that when Laver was introduced to Ellsworth Vines, to the older man's bafflement he blurted out, 'But I know you already'.

And when Laver eventually observed Don Budge hit a backhand, the stroke appeared entirely familiar – at his master's knee, he'd already seen it.

Hence the boy knew a great lineage. Soon, his only desire was to join it.

Making wizardry – the wrist and the sleight of hand

A gifted boy had fallen under the sway of a great teacher. Hollis' 10-year-old pupil was to be a balanced and attacking left-hander.

However, it was not long before the old coach began to conceive more extravagant ambitions for his young charge. As Charlie Hollis lay awake in his bed he must have ruminated on the complex link between achievement and style – or, in modern parlance, between outcome and process.

As he candidly informed those closest to him, Charlie thought that his own game had been close to the top. But Hollis had never made it past the last 16 of any of the bigger tournaments. From his experience, he realised that the highest achievement requires the combination of superlative and reliable technique with equally superlative and reliable fitness, both physical and mental. Doubtless, he wanted such achievement for his young charge. Yet the teacher must have required something from his pupil that was greater than results: he wanted to foster a technique that was groundbreaking. Emerging in front of him was virtuosity so arcane as to be almost an end in itself. Yes, there were grave dangers in such a development, but Charlie must have concluded that here was a God-given opportunity to expand the possibilities of the game he loved.

What happened next in the subsequent evolution of Rod Laver might be best analysed by isolating two aspects of the lad's developing game: spin and personality.

Hollis loved topspin: this aficionado of Tilden's Eastern style saw topspin as a natural outcome of the proper path of the racket head through the ball. As they went through their unending drills, he commanded: 'Foot across; racket in line with the ball; come forward from slightly below; hit through it; *make it spin.*'

But as Charlie studied the young lad, small but surprisingly long-armed and free-wristed, it dawned that spin could be more than he'd ever envisaged. And this is where the matter of grips again enters the picture.

Since Hollis had started young Rodney with the backhand, he'd insisted on the proper grip as the basis of the stroke. To support the stroke, the wrist needed to be behind the racket handle. The hand had to be placed so that the V of the thumb and forefinger lay along the top rear edge of the racket. This resembles the Eastern backhand grip, but it is also close to the Continental, used by its proponents for all other shots, the forehand included.

After laying down the rudiments of a free-swinging backhand, the pair progressed to the southpaw's 'natural' (left) side, and the forehand.

To what must have been Hollis's surprise – perhaps his displeasure – when the youngster began hitting forehands, he began to resist his coach's preferred grip. Of course this was the Eastern forehand grip, with the racket for a left-hander turned a quarter turn anti-clockwise from the backhand, so bringing the palm nicely behind the handle in the shake-hands grip. But no! The boy was beginning to hit a forehand with just about the same grip he used for his backhand: the Continental, with the palm more on top of the handle. Yet the result seemed lovely, with the reach, quickness and 'wristiness' characteristic of the Continental style. We are reminded of the way the aging Tilden stumbled on the delights of the Continental, and astonished Fred Perry.

Hollis deliberated. After a while, he concluded that the whole caboodle looked so sweet that changing it would be a crime.

So, early on, the youngster got to keep his one-shot Continental grip. Yet the master teacher knew that though the Continental might throw up gains, it held flaws. Thus Charlie set himself the daunting task of retaining the style's flexibility and brilliance, but incorporating the inherent power and reliability of the Eastern.

At first, Charlie's emphasis on spin was merely an extension of the orthodox idea of spin as control. Charlie would tell the boy bluntly that he was a runt, and the only way a runt could belt the ball was by hitting it with a lot of topspin – otherwise it would always go out.

All of this seemed natural to young Rod – from the first he loved to 'make it spin'. Soon he realised how right Charlie was: even if he gave the ball that glorious smack he loved from the time he picked up a racket, with oodles of topspin it could pass comfortably over the net and, dipping, stay in court.

This ability to blend control with topspin never left him. On one occasion, as a rising player on the amateur circuit, his form deserted him. In desperation he returned to Queensland and Hollis. After only a few moments Charlie told him the trouble: he had forsaken his creed – he was hitting his strokes largely flat. At once, Laver went back to his basics. And before long, he was creaming his ground strokes with blistering topspin.

Returning to the learner stage, the coach has left an account of a key moment in this development.

Hollis tells of an instance when he was playing the 14-year-old Rod in a practice match. From nowhere, the youngster cracked a dipping forehand past him, whipped with an extreme last-second flick of the wrist.

Charlie was appalled. 'That shot's no good – cut it out!' yelled the master.

A minute later, Hollis tells us that the kid 'bloody well did it again!' And this time the usually meek youngster couldn't disown his own artistry. Immediately the boy retorted to Hollis, stranded at the net, 'It seems to be okay to me.' [7]

This time the wise coach saw, heard, considered and said nothing. In front of him was something original, an innovation so effective that Hollis admitted: 'it was the first time he had been able to [pass the older man cleanly] when we were playing fair dinkum.' We catch Charlie reflecting: *It might be different ... but ... Crikey Moses! ... how it works!*

Now the challenge was not to ban the tehnique, but to consolidate it.

Laver came to develop all his ground shots with the strike preceded by a sudden snapping of the laid-back wrist. These 'Ping-Pong' strokes allowed Laver to change direction, or drive or lob at the last instant. And, for Laver,

Fig. 7.4. Laver returns serve on the forehand. Pressed into an open stance, he still generates formidable topspin, power and control.

the last instant could begin *even after the stroke had begun,* and allow him to slice under, or topspin over, the ball. The apotheosis of this process came when the wizard bamboozled the hapless Newcombe in that moment in a Wimbledon Final.

In anyone else, such a departure from the tried and true Tilden method – racket through the ball with wrist locked – would have spelled instability, if not disaster. This didn't happen to Laver for two reasons.

First, he made his wrist the size of most people's forearm, and his forearm the size of their leg. At maturity, Laver's arm dangled from a slight frame standing at just over 5 feet 8 inches (174 centimetres) and weighing 147 pounds (67 kilograms). But his massive forearm measured 12 inches (30.5 centimetres), the same size as the forearm of the champion boxer at the time, the powerful middleweight Rocky Marciano. Laver's wrist, at seven inches (18 centimetres), was an inch larger than that of the world heavyweight champion, Floyd Patterson.

The second buffer against instability in his strokes was his temperament: this allowed him to practise so hard and long that the complex pattern became grooved in his nervous system – soon it flowed like clockwork.

If technique in the form of outrageous spin became the first of the two aspects making up the exotic Laver style, the second was personality.

Although this earnest lad was blessed with a temperament so equable as to appear almost drab, how he enjoyed being naughty! While he loved nothing more than the sound of the smack of racket on ball – 'Yes, I love to give the ball a nudge', admitted the understating Laver – there was something beyond power that turned him on. It could be designated *the fiendish.* Wicked spins, uncanny angles, and shots conjured from nowhere, these were what made the game such an entrancing and endless celebration. And these paid for the physical strain, the lonely toil and the endless practice that made up his life as a touring athlete.

It seems ironic that, from his earliest days, this self-effacing man's greatest joy was to astonish his opponent by a shot appearing to defy the laws of physics. Laver tells us that as a top junior, he would go on tour playing exhibitions in country towns with his friend Frank Gorman. They would both spend hours secretly working up surprise shots. When they could successfully unsheathe them at a key moment of a game – stone the crows, their day was made!

Such magic never lost its capacity to enchant him – nor to disarm his opponent.

As the complex Laver style evolved, Hollis became even more acutely aware of the dangers inherent in it. 'You must master the spin, not [let] the spin master you,' he exhorted. Further, he realised the strokes they were forging demanded exceptional fitness and strength.

As a result, Hollis steadily intensified his programme of physical conditioning. Besides running and exercises to build up stamina and speed, they worked on strength, particularly in chest and arm. And to build up the wrist, he urged the kid to squeeze a squash ball in his spare time.

The result was that the once-scrawny youngster was to become one of the most feared fifth-set opponents in the history of the game.

'It's his speed that kills you,' said Arthur Ashe after losing a big one to Laver at Wimbledon. On watching Laver pick up a ball an inch off the turf after running the width of the court, Fred Stolle commented: 'He gets to balls like this because even in practice, he never lets the ball bounce twice.' And American Gene Scott, a top player and tennis writer, epitomised Laver as: 'Laver's a little guy, but that left forearm and wrist – this is what he beats you with.[8]

But Scott then added a telling three words: 'And his pride.' From the beginning, Hollis had been on the money. It was Laver's character as much as anything else that kept him winning. By the time he had mastered his beloved spin so he could hit out and flick the ball where he wanted, he had also become as tough as his dad's fencing wire. Even in the elite company of other top sportsmen this fusion of the physical and mental set him apart.

As noted, the raw material for his legendary physical attributes of speed, power and stamina was unpromising. Not only was the 10-year-old small for his age, but he had a 'sunken chest' and was not naturally fast. Even at 15 years, the teenager was still physically unimpressive – and this was celebrated famously in the story of Laver's first meeting with kingmaker Harry Hopman.

Laver explains that Hollis had taken him down to Brisbane to be 'once-overed' by Hopman, then the nation's leading coach. Rod says that even before he'd hit a ball he had to hang about listening to Charlie's bragging. While Charlie was telling the sceptical old hand about the soon-to-be world-beating prowess of his young pupil from the bush, young Rod, covered with embarrassment and shyness, was leaning awkwardly on a rail a few yards away, hoping the earth would swallow him up.

When Hopman could get away from Charlie's effusions, he caught his first proper glimpse of the budding hero – a tiny, scrubby, freckle-faced redhead, his long skinny limbs entwined monkey-like in the rail.

Clearly nonplussed, he turned back to Hollis and cried: 'Gee he's so small!'

'But Hop, wait till you see his strokes!' responded the proud coach.

Hopman gathered up some balls and walked over to the youngster.

'Come on *Rocket*,' Hopman called out ironically to the gawky little kid on the rail, 'Let's see you serve a couple.'[9]

Just as young Rosewall had been called *Muscles* because he didn't have any, in true Aussie-drongo style Rod received his famous nickname because he appeared at first to be anything but rocket-like.

Gordon Forbes, in his delightful memoir, *A Handful of Summers*, throws more light on what allowed Laver to earn his sobriquet – without irony.

Forbes was a good touring player who once found himself stranded for over a week with Laver, then the world's No. 1 amateur. Forbes was astonished by the champion's discipline.

They began every day with a ritual: the strict application of a famous Hopman exercise.

For an hour and a half, Laver and Forbes – starting slowly and building up the pace – would hit ten minutes each of cross-court forehands, down-the-line forehands, cross-court backhands and down-the-line backhands, followed by forehand and backhand volleys. Then they would move to serves, and end with smashes and lobs. Only then would they start practising match play.

After a week of this, Forbes tells us he was playing the best tennis of his life.[10]

Laver's penchant for practice applied even if he was about to play the Final of Wimbledon and even if, on the previous day, he had played an arduous match. Such preparation meant that he felt grooved, ready. This faith helped to make him such a dangerous opponent when appearing beaten. The naughty kid hiding behind the sad face relished the challenge of appearing trapped: he trusted that his flow and invention were never far away.

And before long, Rod *The Rocket* was further comforted by a deliciously complementary belief: if he *was* going to lose, Charlie Hollis's boy would go out in style.

Apprentice to Grand Slammer

By the time the boy from Rockhampton had reached his high teens, the kid from the bush was becoming a very good junior player. Yet he was never as precociously brilliant as the famous Aussie twins Rosewall and Hoad, who had come before him by just a few years. This was not because of lack of opportunity or dedication. Even by the age of 15, Laver had come to realise that tennis was his livelihood, and would remain so for the foreseeable future.

A year before that he had been hit by a bout of hepatitis so serious that he missed most of a year of high school. When he recovered, he was required to repeat his year. After talking it over, Charlie suggested it might be best for the boy to give school a miss, and to find a job that would give him time for tennis.

Eventually the sporting goods maker, Dunlop, where the former great player and wise man Adrian Quist held a senior position, came to the party.

Soon the lad had left 'Rocky', as the locals called Rockhampton, and was down in Brisbane working as a storeman for Dunlop. And playing almost as much tennis as he wanted. In return, Laver used the Dunlop rackets and their products, and undertook country tours for the company, giving exhibitions while their goods were spruiked in the local store.

Though at first desperately homesick, the shy country boy was getting top coaching in Brisbane, and his tennis was improving steadily. After a while he made some good friends, and as their families welcomed him into their homes he stopped pining for his family.

Rod sometimes also travelled interstate, and one family in Sydney was to influence his whole life. They were the rough-and-tumble Hoads.

Laver had long worshipped the young lion Lewis Hoad, four years his senior. When the chance arose for him to stay with the family, Rod jumped at it. At first downcast on discovering that Lew was away at the time, Rod was inspired just by being in Lew's home and experiencing the warm and exuberant atmosphere. When he was told that Lew was at that time playing Wimbledon, more fire was added to the youngster's ambitions.

Rod also gained some practical help. Swinging one of Hoad's rackets, his mind leaping away to a future of heroic victories, he found that though Lew was strong, he used what was then considered a relatively light racket, with the weight more in the throat, further lightening the head. The result? A perfectly manoeuvrable weapon, dead right for spins and flicks. Rod had his racket made up identically – a Dunlop Maxply, head-light at 14.5 ounces (400 grams).

Later, when he began to study Hoad on the court, his admiration grew. 'Lew was my idol,' said Laver simply. Though the strapping Hoad was physically gifted in a way Rod could never match, the iron-wristed Hoad was another exponent of the one-grip Continental style. The way Lew smacked the ball on the rise, with wondrous lashings of power and spin, deliciously widened the possibilities of Rod's play.

At this point a businessman approached Hopman. If Hopman could find a couple of promising juniors, the man would support their development. To almost everyone's surprise, one of the pair Hopman selected was the 17-year-old Rod Laver.

So in 1956, under the tutelage of Hopman, Laver made his first overseas tour.

Although Rod won some big tournaments in the junior grades, to most observers he remained a long shot; the red-headed left-hander appeared promising, but unstable. Years later Boris Becker would win his first Wimbledon at 17 years; at the same age Laver lost in the first round in straight sets.

Despite this relatively slow progress, Hopman and Quist (Laver's boss and mentor), at once realised that if Laver never scaled the heights, it wouldn't be from lack of effort. It appeared that such was the Laver capacity for work, it could become counter-productive. Thus the youngster eventually admitted he had been playing for weeks handicapped by pain in his back. An X-ray revealed a chipped bone. Quist explained the youngster's stoicism as the result of his bush toughness, and counselled him on the necessary balance between bravery and the protection of his athlete's body.

All the same, it seemed to take forever to get his complex game together.

Fig. 7.5. Laver's model and hero. Included in Laver's first autobiography and not attributed to any source, the sketches clearly show Lew Hoad modelling a topspin backhand.

At long last, at a ripe 21 years of age, he got through to the final rounds of a major – the 1959 Wimbledon. In the Final, he found himself confronting the Peruvian-American Alex Olmedo. Olmedo was strong, possessed a fine serve and volley, but was neither very quick nor very strong off the ground, particularly on the backhand. Laver possessed an all court game, and understood exactly what to do to exploit his opponent's weaknesses. But he lost in straight sets.

Back home, Charlie was furious. He knew that the young Trojan had not only got through the draw to reach the Final of the Men's Singles, but he'd managed the same in both the Men's and the Mixed Doubles! Officials informed Rod that he had engaged in over 600 games, many in the five days before the Singles Final. It might have been a Wimbledon record, but it had taken the edge off his game.

If this had taught Rod the necessity of focus, at first the results didn't show it. When the young man returned home in 1959, he contested another four significant singles finals, and lost the lot. To most observers, the flashy left-hander was beginning to look like the perennial bridesmaid.

Despite this, the next year started so well that it seemed the doubters were wrong. To win his first major, the Australian Championships, Laver finally got past another left-hander in Neale Fraser. But he only just made it. To defeat the man, who up to then had often been his nemesis, required Laver's Houdini act: surviving the loss of the first two sets and a match point against him.

But after this victory, the bridesmaid returned. In the 1960 Wimbledon Final, it was Fraser again. This time the Victorian won through in four tough sets. Then the same Fraser repeated the dose in the Final of the US Championships. Fraser had a vicious serve, a great looping forehand, tricky volleys and a pokey little backhand – the epitome of left-handers who had served as a reverse model to Hollis and to Ken Rosewall's father. An elite player would have exploited the flaws in Fraser's game; Laver had not yet arrived among that elite. [11]

Nor was Laver setting the world alight when he squeezed his way into the Davis Cup team. In 1959 he had played his first Challenge Round matches against the US – and lost both singles.

Despite appearances, over these two years Laver was steadily learning to harness his power and spin sufficiently to reduce the lapses that damaged his game. Further, this diffident product of the 'Deep North' had come to recognise another of his crucial deficiencies: the lack of killer instinct. He realised that true champions, once they've found a weakness in their opponents, get them down, and keep them down.

Off the court he was also maturing. His fellow, fun-loving Aussies found that their shy mate was becoming more outgoing, both within their group and in public. This confidence was immediately apparent when the Wimbledon of 1961 came along. Rod played superbly throughout, and ended up with his first Wimbledon, and his second major title. While he didn't add any other big trophies that year, he forgave himself because he knew that he'd been held back by a series of minor but debilitating injuries.

Finally, by the beginning of 1962, he felt ready.

Laver has admitted that as soon as he climbed near the top of the amateur tree he began to form a secret ambition: to win the famous Grand Slam. What was the Slam, and why did it have such status?

The term was popularised by the only winner, Budge himself. In his book, *Don Budge: A Tennis Memoir,* he dedicates a whole chapter entitled, *The Grand Slam – My Favourite Invention*. There he explains why he made the Slam his final goal in amateur tennis.[12]

It was not called 'The Grand Slam' when Budge started after it in 1938. In the absence of an eponym, Budge's object was simply to win the four major championships of Australia, France, Great Britain and the US in the one calendar year. He chose these countries because they were the only nations that, by 1938, had won the Davis Cup.

Apparently the term had been coined some years earlier by a *New York Times* writer, John Kieran.[13] When Kieran brought it up, the great Australian Jack Crawford had managed to win three of the four major national championships. Purloining the term from the card game of bridge, Kieran applied it to the four championships, so raising the stakes for someone to pip Crawford and sweep them all. The term had been more or less forgotten – and Budge had tried to keep quiet about his quest – but towards the middle of 1938, with Budge on his way, the term was rediscovered. And stuck.

After Budge took the Slam he turned pro, and was of course banned from the great national championships. Almost 20 years later, another great Australian, Lew Hoad, had emulated Crawford, and in 1956 got to within a match of winning the Slam – there to be thwarted by an inspired Rosewall.

Let's take a brief look at Laver's attempt in 1962 to emulate Budge's unique triumph a quarter of a century earlier.

The first leg was the Australian Championship in January. Except for Roy Emerson – highly experienced, dead tough and at his peak – the draw seemed to offer Laver few problems. By cruising through to the Final, then beating Emerson decisively, Laver demonstrated that he was still improving, and was by then more than a shade above the rest.

However, in the next leg of the Slam, the French Championship, arduously slugged out on the slow clay of Roland Garros, he struggled. Despite his apprenticeship on anthills, Laver admits that up to then he hadn't mastered slow courts. After some significant early scares, in the quarterfinals he found himself up against the tough scrambler Martin Mulligan, and a match point down on his own second serve. But, defiantly, he served to Mulligan's stronger backhand. Swiftly following in, he brilliantly anticipated the down-the-line return, and smacked a backhand volley for a clean winner.

At this point the Laver self-belief caught alight. After despatching Mulligan, in the semis he faced his old enemy – Fraser. The match reached the fifth set, but Rod now had joined the elite who could handle top left-handers, and was unstoppable. The Final, against his old Queensland mate Emerson, also went to the wire. Yet against one of the fastest and fittest athletes in tennis, Rod galloped away with the fifth set 6–2 — for the Championship and the second leg of the Slam.

This hard-won victory consolidated one of Laver's deepest beliefs. The highly experienced Fraser had, in the crunch, played safe against him — and lost. Against Mulligan, at match point, *The Rocket* had gone for it — and won. Laver thought: never in the future would he lose by 'scratching around'.

Despite all this, Laver allowed that the Slam's next leg, Wimbledon, made him 'very nervous'. Yet, after a bit of a scare in the form of the gifted Spaniard Manuel Santana in the quarters, by the time Laver reached the Final he was in ruthless form. On fast grass, he dispatched Mulligan in less than an hour.

Now only the US remained.

According to Laver's own account, as he headed off for New York he tried to dismiss any thought of taking out the Slam. But the media was hooked on Budge's favourite invention, and every day they were after him. Then came something that was glimpsed in an earlier chapter — the fortuitous intervention by another of our heroes.

For the first time, Laver managed a chat with none other than the only holder of the Grand Slam. Up stepped J. Donald Budge, portly, worldly and kind. Finding a shy young man caught up in a media frenzy, on a whim Budge whisked him out of New York and into the cool of the Catskill Mountains.

There they relaxed, talked, and played a couple of 'nonchalant' sets. Of these, the 46-year-old Budge took the second from the world amateur champion! But true modesty is a beautiful thing. In *Don Budge: A Tennis Memoir*, Budge mentions playing the sets, but not the result. Laver, in *The Education of a Tennis Player*, cites the loss of a set, and makes a point of saying how this shows what a marvel Budge was.

By the time they were to return, the old master's words to Laver were few: all he had to do was play his own way.

This is what Rod did. Nevertheless, the Final against Emerson provided the worst jitters of his tennis life. In the middle of the match he so lost his legendary cool that his 'racket felt foreign' to him – indeed so foreign that at one crucial instant he 'held it wrong and hit a volley [straight] into the ground'. But at once this elementary error seemed so comical to this unpretentious master that at once he started laughing, and this 'broke the tension'!

When he'd stopped laughing he held the racket correctly ... and once more beat Emerson to take the US Championships in four tough sets. Afterwards, he said he retained almost no memory of the last minutes of the match and its immediate aftermath.

Thus in 1962, after a quarter of a century Rodney George Laver joined John Donald Budge as the only winners of the Grand Slam. At the year's end he had also helped his country retain the Davis Cup, winning both singles. He was 24 years old, and indisputably the best player in the amateur world.

In a tennis world increasingly split between amateur and pro, there was one pinnacle left for Rod Laver to climb. He had to take on the 'vagabond rug beaters', as Bud Collins so colourfully described the pros. By then, the new holder of the Grand Slam wanted only one thing: to become the best of the lot.

For a record guarantee of $110,000 over three years, on January 4, 1963, he signed a contract with a group calling themselves the International Professional Tennis Association. This was the fragile group that Kramer had left running the pro show after he had decided to leave off being the boss.

Finally, the young champion from the bush could own up to what he'd been since he was fifteen: a professional tennis player.

Joining the circus – and starting all over

By the end of 1962, in the pristine world of the amateurs, Rod *The Rocket* Laver was the best by a Rockhampton country mile – and the pros needed him desperately.

Their circus was in one of its periodic holes. The cause was not a lack of top players. Champion Rosewall was at his peak, and the rest of the gang weren't too bad either. Despite chronic injury Hoad was still great, and occasionally sublime; and hanging on behind them was a superb bunch including the older masters Segura, Sedgman and Trabert. Pushing along the veterans came the vastly improved new boys Gimeno and Buchholz. Even the spear throwers were hardly pushovers: MacKay, Anderson, Cooper, Olmedo and Ayala had collared quite a few Wimbledon and individual Grand Slam titles.

Fortunately or unfortunately, the greatest of them all, *Big Pancho* Gonzales, was in one of his periodic 'retirements'. More than anyone, Rod Laver knew what this meant. Pancho had contacted him secretly during the Grand Slam year. Ever the recalcitrant loner, Gonzales was now well into his thirties and playing irregularly. Nonetheless, he still didn't acknowledge that Rosewall – not he, Pancho – reigned as the current Pro Champion. Further, he was under the pump for alimony from his growing clutch of ex-wives.

So for the first and only time in his career, *Gorgo* was aspiring to the role of promoter! For once he could forget about that control-freak Kramer! So Gonzales offered the amateur champion a lucrative contract to turn pro and play him in an old-style, hundred-match head-to-head. We can imagine what the ever-sour Pancho was thinking: *Come on, kid! You and me! Let's see which son-of-a-bitch is the real World Champion!*

Rod called up a few insiders, especially Rosewall and Hoad. *Don't trust the bastard* was the gist of what they said. (At least this is what Hoad could have said; his punctilious twin didn't swear.)

After that, Laver decided that he'd stick with his mates.

However, under the surface, the world of tennis was changing. 'Black' money in the amateur circuit had so burgeoned that the top amateurs could be both lionised and well rewarded. Worse, the pro ship was now without the skilful Kramer at its helm, and the players couldn't run the show and play as well. And, as ever, they continued to be ostracised.

With the help of Bud Collins, Rod Laver explains the pros' problems beautifully.

'There was just no way,' he writes in *The Education of a Tennis Player*, 'to change the public's feeling that [the pro] tour matches were meaningless exhibitions. Never mind the agonies and injuries that went into those matches. We left one place and travelled to another so quickly that nobody ever knew.' His next words are wonderfully apt: 'To the public, particularly the American public - for some reason I've never worked out - we were trained seals putting on a marvellous well-drilled act.' [14]

Laver and Collins found another fitting metaphor for the outcasts struggling through those times: the pros were 'lepers', and Wimbledon their 'Lourdes'. It appeared that when Laver joined the pros, they were so contagious that more than half a decade was required before the gates opened to let them in – and a further couple of years were needed before the lepers were sanitised sufficiently for 'open' tennis to become a reality.

Despite Laver's amateur supremacy and the disarray of the pro circus, his competitive blooding into this itinerant brotherhood was painful.

In *How to Play Winning Tennis*, he says that with the Slam completed, joining the pro band was inevitable. Yet, before he faced anyone on court, his trust in his future was tested. First came Gonzales' underhand offer. Then he discovered the travelling mercenaries were so parlous that Rosewall and Hoad had been forced to guarantee their offer to him with their own houses!

Even before his last amateur appearances at the end of 1962 – and by then he'd rebuffed Gonzales and contracted with the other pros – he had some idea of what he was going to be up against on court.

The pro leaders had told him that they were not intending to follow the format of the traditional head-to-head: contender Laver against champion Rosewall. With Laver's tour planned to start in Australia in January, they would put Laver on twice in each Australian capital city, and then swing to New Zealand. Finally they would make a tour through the US. In the Australia–New Zealand leg, Laver realised that 'twice' meant 'tough': in a dramatic series of confrontations between Australian world champions, he would have to play the famous 'twins' on consecutive days – Hoad one day, Rosewall the next.

Though the tyro pro knew a great deal about both Hoad and the current Pro Champion Rosewall, the knowledge came from a fair way off. Here's what Laver says about Hoad:

> Of all the great players I've met, I knew Hoad was the man who liked playing left-handers ... his enormous wrist development enabled him to take the ball very early ... [nullifying] the left-hander's natural advantage. He had my spin but ... power I could never hope to gain. He was ... admired by everyone who ... ever hacked a ball ... [15]

So it was that on January 5, 1963, in Lew's hometown of Sydney, one of Hoad's most fervent admirers came face to face with his boyhood idol. Laver described it this way: 'Lew had been training for weeks to get ready for the match and right away he made me understand that all the pros jealously defend their reputations.' Then Rod sharpens this statement with a graphic image: 'The whole pro group descend on a newcomer like eagles on lambs back home in central Queensland.'

For Laver, this first outing as pro brought mixed news.

The good part was that the tennis was great. It was four tough sets, and Laver played well, had his chances, and lost 8–6 in the final set. Further, Laver said that he 'enjoyed that match more than any I had played in years'. So, he thought, had the big crowd. Ten thousand had come out to watch! On this occasion, the two were neither lepers nor trained seals, but a pair of tennis legends, giving their all. Even the papers, notoriously anti-pro, raved about the match, saying that after years of dullness and division tennis had once more become exciting.

And the bad news?

'Lew and I played until after 11 pm,' said Laver, 'and by the time I got to bed ... it was 3 am. I woke about noon and at 2 pm I had to go out [against] Rosewall. It was tough all right.'

Laver, feeling stiff and let down after lifting himself for Hoad, was no match for the Pro Champion. Without Hoad's bravura, Rosewall, the delicate surgeon, took him apart. This time it was straight sets, and took less than an hour.

After the match, all he could say to the press was: 'Playing against Ken is like hitting against a brick wall.' Later, Rod said that when he played Hoad for the first time he saw that he was up against the best player he'd ever faced. Then it was Rosewall – who was 'a lot better' than Hoad ...

Then everything got worse.

Laver put it this way:

> Lew beat me in eight straight matches after that, and Ken did it in eleven out of thirteen. On the high level of the game, it was as though my tennis education was just beginning. The difference between pro and amateur tennis was so great it took me months to settle down. I felt the pressure ... [of being] the top amateur, the man who had equalled Budge's Grand Slam, and there was a psychological barrier to break through that the pros had created ... On some occasions the ease with which they beat me, the constant travelling, and hard matches night after night ... made me feel like quitting.

Then he would be consoled by the crowds and the money, and by his record in the world's great events. But, more, his game was improving.

By the time the US leg got under way in March, with the vulnerable Hoad mercifully absent through injury, Laver was establishing himself among the top three pros. Occasionally, his game would reach a new peak. Then he would have 'real hope that I would end up the world's best player like I had always planned'.

One night in April, four months after his debut, the troupe hit the pros' legendary venue at New York's Madison Square Garden. Suddenly it came together: he took Rosewall in straight sets, in the first of which he lost only nine points and not a single game. Then in June, Hoad came over for a pro tournament in Los Angeles. It was here that Laver beat Hoad for the first time – and without losing a set. Though he eventually lost a tough Final to Rosewall, Rod's win over Hoad had broken a crucial barrier.

But for most of the first 18 months as a pro life was harsh and big victories few.

In *The Education of a Tennis Player*, Laver encapsulates this period beautifully. 'We were gypsies,' he says, and the gypsy pros played 'anywhere money could be made'. At the very beginning of his first US tour, Laver had to play in Boston against the huge Barry MacKay. Laver was looking forward to it, admitting how nice it would be to 'get away from a menu of Hoad and Rosewall'. Surely here was a chance to take his 'head out of the cement mixer'.

But he soon found out that in certain conditions big Barry could be as bad as the legendary Australians. This was the first real winter for the boy from the tropics, and there was snow everywhere. The court consisted of rough planking over an ice rink. MacKay 'had one of the biggest serves going', says Laver, 'and trying to return it on that bumpy court was like trying to swat jackrabbits with a broom'.

So another beating. This time, from a player down from the top.

The US tour that followed in 1963 contained 60 *matches in 80 days*. We remember Kramer and his three fellow players scratching their way through the backblocks of Scotland in 1954. Now it's a decade later and little has changed. This time the six players – Rosewall, Gimeno, MacKay, Ayala, Buchholz and Laver – were packed into a couple of station wagons. They were 'on the run every minute, grabbing hot dogs, getting to bed about three every morning, driving, driving, driving'.

One dangerous and freezing night when the road was like grease, the car sliding and swerving, Laver caught himself wondering just 'what in the Hell' he was doing there. Right then, he could have been playing a swell little tourney in warm Jamaica, 'getting on nicely as an amateur'.

At this stage of his career, the neophyte pro was hardly alone. On confronting the pros, many other fine amateur players had felt the same. In his first tour as pro, again in the US in winter, a miserable Fred Stolle lamented: 'I can't beat anybody and I can't get warm.'

Though Laver might often have been frozen, usually he could beat somebody. And this sustained him. 'As I began to play better, I felt better,' he tells us simply.

Laver and collaborator Collins explain how easy it was for those new boys entering Open Tennis, and how unlike the trials of the old pro brotherhood. For example, those newcomers would never have had to 'risk their necks' playing on a converted ice rink in the English provinces, one which was so slippery that the two pros, Laver and Hoad, could hardly stand up. At one stage, Laver did the splits and – *ping!* – snapped his jockstrap! But soon after the completion of urgent sartorial repairs, the match had to be abandoned, at 27 games apiece in the first set!

Nor did the new boys of the Open Era have to experience another variety of tennis court.

On one occasion in the boondocks, Laver was up against Frank Sedgman. To his surprise Laver found that when he reached the net, Sedgman was passing him with ease. But Laver soon noted that when Sedg was at net, 'I was passing him pretty well too'. Suddenly, the two players twigged – maybe the court wasn't quite right. It wasn't. When they found a tape measure it was about a yard (a metre) wider, and nearly a yard longer than it should have been. With only this court at their disposal, they played on, if with sporadic forays netwards.

One time the pros got a call from someone in the Sudan. They were asked: What about a show over a few days in Khartoum? One of the players asked: 'Hey, isn't there a revolution going on?' The gist of the reply was: *No worries. There's still money about for tennis players like you.* So off they went.

When the pros arrived, they discovered there were soldiers everywhere, plus a curfew, so no publicity, newspapers or radio. Though they were all 'scared to death', the gypsies decided to stay when they were reassured by the promoter, who reckoned that folks might still hear about the tennis by word of mouth. 'For sure, someone will turn up,' he told them.

The next day the show got going.

Arriving at the courts, they found nobody there. Eventually a few people trickled in and, late in the afternoon, play started. They started on grass, but dusk soon descended. And so the four pros, with the spectators trickling along behind them, walked over to a nearby cement court with lights, and started up again.

They continued until any chance of further play vanished; so many insects arrived that it was impossible to see a thing, and they had to stop mid-match.

'The crowd realised this was a natural conclusion,' says Laver with the resigned sagacity of the veteran, 'and went away quietly and happily, having enjoyed some good tennis.'

And the rewards for all this? A purse of $1,000, split four ways.

However, recompense as lop-sided as this could not be relied upon! One day in La Paz – altitude 12,000 feet (3,600 metres) – with their noses streaming blood and the balls zooming everywhere as a consequence of the thin air, the finalists were not even playing for money. The first prize was a $600 watch.

Yet they never stopped playing and, as Laver says, never stopped trying: 'Personal pride pushed us, that's all ... I tried as hard at La Paz or Khartoum as I did at Wimbledon ... ' Though Laver admits he would choose to practise shots sometimes against the lesser players – and once in a while he would get beaten as a result – he swears that unless 'sick or injured', he never saw another pro 'tank' (give up) a match.

Despite such rigours, Charlie Hollis's perfectionist pupil kept studying his craft. From the outset he saw precisely what was needed to match Rosewall and Hoad. Concluding that his game didn't need radical change, he decided three aspects needed fine-tuning.

First, he had to cut out lapses that cost him easy points. Second, he had to harden his serve, particularly his second delivery, or the other pros would 'climb all over it'. Third, he had to improve his lob. He puts it this way: 'I soon found out in pro tennis that you were dead without a good lob – by far the most underrated shot in the game.' This was a must to enable him to maintain the pressure on his opponents, who were, to a man, expert commanders of the net. Soon Laver had mastered offensive as well as defensive lobs, and from the backhand as well as the forehand.

By watching the superlative lobber Segura at work, eventually Laver also came to learn the recondite art of 'rafter lobbing'. This was feeding the ball through the low-hanging beams of the little arenas that the pros were forced to frequent in the backblocks. Laver explains how one night, when playing at a particularly low-slung venue (a converted armoury), he beat Gimeno with such a beauty it 'wandered among the girders as though directed by radar'.

Though it had taken him two years, by about mid-1964 Laver was playing such an aggressive form of percentage tennis that the pro crown was looking close. McCauley quotes Frank Sedgman as saying at the time that Laver had made 'tremendous strides in a short time in the pro ranks'. Noting in particular that Laver now made far fewer errors than he had as an amateur, Sedgman said the relatively new boy was now ahead of the rest of the bunch and putting pressure on champion Rosewall. [16]

In September of that year of 1964, the two met in the British Professional Championships at Wembley. This was always a crucial tourney for the pros, a sort of pro Wimbledon. Rosewall, Vines, Budge and Kramer had cemented their supremacy by taking the British crown; Gonzales and Sedgman had also captured it in legendary style, and it was here that Jack Kramer had given his marvellous swansong.

This time the tournament was particularly important to Laver. Rosewall had won four times in a row, Gonzales had just returned from retirement, and Sedgman and Hoad were there to make a top field.

As it was to turn out, the British Professional Championship of 1964 was more than another in the line of splendid performances that the pros put on at Wembley: it passed on the baton. Two of the older masters and former titleholders, Gonzales and Sedgman, were still good enough to get through to the semifinal round. There, fittingly, they faced their successors, Laver and Rosewall. Gonzales, always a problem for Laver, pushed him to four tough sets. In a tense losing match against Rosewall, Sedgman also produced what one perceptive journalist called a 'minor classic'.

The Final between incumbent Rosewall and pretender Laver was more like a 'major classic'. Indeed, in his *History of Professional Tennis*, the veteran tennis writer and historian Joe McCauley counted it as one of the greatest matches he ever saw. Both Rosewall and Laver were masters near their peak, and they were playing for their reputations and for the top position in the tennis world. In just under three hours, despite Wembley's fast boards, the pair made hardly an error, and displayed every shot in the game.

Laver won the first set, then lost the next two. But after winning the fourth, in the final set he found himself down a break and 4–5, with Rosewall serving for the match. 'Suddenly,' says McCauley, '[going] all out to break back ... Rocket raised his game ... ' In the style that defied the possible – but was beginning to appear predictable – the challenger broke back with a stream of unplayable winners. Continuing to hit out, at 6–6 Laver again broke Rosewall's serve. Then he held his own for the championship.

Here was a changing of the guard. Yet, as reported by McCauley, this is what the unassuming winner had to say to the press after the match: 'I've still plenty of ambitions left and would like to be the world's No. 1. ... I am not that yet – Ken is .... [and] he has won the biggest tournaments except here. [And] I've lost to other people and Ken hasn't.'

Although such respectful modesty on the part of Laver may have provided some wry comfort to Champion Rosewall, at this point the second *Little Master* must have held no illusions. Once more Rosewall sensed that he was about to be upstaged – just as he had been as an amateur by Hoad, and again as a new pro by Gonzales. Yes, he was thirty, and he had had a good run at the top. But, except for the other pros and a few die-hard supporters, hardly a soul knew about it. Among a troupe of seals, no one knew who was Seal No.1.

When a reporter caught an exhausted Rosewall sitting alone courtside after his loss to Laver, he asked, 'How are you feeling?' Normally careful, fair and polite, this time Rosewall drew on the lonely reaches of his Aussie dialect. His head in his hands, he replied, 'Like a bastard on Father's Day.'

Thus, as McCauley informs us, 'Rosewall's long reign at the head of world tennis was finally brought to an end' and over the year of 1964 '*The Rockhampton Rocket* ... not only beat his close rival in 12 of their 17 meetings, but also won 15 tournaments to Rosewall's six'.

In the beginning of 1965, Rod Laver was officially declared the World Professional Champion.

Mastery at last and the end of the era: 1965–70

From the beginning of 1965 to the end of the Pro Era in 1968, Rod Laver remained unchallenged as World Pro Champion. He was also unquestionably the best player in the world. In the first two years of the Open Era that followed, this status was confirmed publicly and officially.

Again drawing on the Laver and Collins biography and McCauley's history, let's take a brief look at the last years of the Pro Era and the first of the Open Era, a period of half a decade through which our diminutive and freckle-faced hero strode like a colossus.

During the final years of the Pro Era – whether applauded by a good crowd in a famous venue, or by a handful of spectators in some forgotten basketball court or ice rink – these tatterdemalion outsiders produced tennis that was usually good, and sometimes sublime.

From 1965, Laver dominated, but Rosewall stayed on and was close enough to push his great rival, and lift the pair head and shoulders above the rest.

After Laver's marvellous win over Rosewall in the British Professional Championship at Wembley in 1964, Laver won it again the next year over Gimeno. The following two years, both in finals against Rosewall, he made it four in a row. Laver also won the second of the three traditional pro championships (the US) in 1966, '67 and '68. And in 1967 and '68, he also managed at last to extract the French pro crown from Rosewall, who had won it seven times between 1960 and 1966!

The transition to Open Tennis during Laver's reign becomes all the more meaningful when reviewed over time.

Forty years back, there been no pro troupe at all, only the 'club pros' of Western and Central Europe who occasionally gave up teaching to compete against each other in a tournament. Only, in 1926, when *Cash and Carry* Pyle and Vinnie Richards started the first play-for-pay show in the US did pro tennis take off.

During the next thirty years, the pros tried everything. For instance, after the war, *Big Bill* Tilden realised the pros needed a fresh image, and set up a series of prize money tournaments around the US. The idea was good, but premature, and before long it was back to the old format, warts and all, and *King* Kramer was running the show and doing his all to keep the pros alive and open tennis a possibility.

In the 1956 US Professional Championship, the struggling pros tried a radical ploy: the tourney was played under modified rules. Service games were not alternated, and points accumulated into 'sets' played until one player reached a designated number. This time *Big Pancho* Gonzales edged out an inspired *Little Pancho* Segura to the extraordinary score of 21–15, 13–21, 21–14, 22–20!

Although such tinkering was to produce the tie break, it was of little help to the pros. While the troupe did make tours of Europe, South America, and South Africa, during the whole year of 1956 there were only about ten tournaments, including the three national championships, in which more than four of the top players competed.

So we arrive in 1966, by which time Laver had become top dog. At least by then the numbers had grown: McCauley counted 54 events in that year in which most of the main pro players competed, and 10 were significant events.

By this time, things were so bleak, and open tennis seemed so far away, that the pros also had a go at emulating the Davis Cup: they set up a team event that was to become the Kramer Cup.

Though the American team was made up of the formidable Gonzales, Olmedo, Buchholz, and Segura, the team representing Australia was simply too strong. To the mighty trio of Laver, Rosewall and Hoad, the considerable Mal Anderson had been added to make up what was most probably the best tennis team representing any country in any era!

But despite displaying *three* of the finest tennis players ever to play the game, nobody noticed. By year's end, the whittled-down troupe was struggling through the African wilds of Abidjan and Dakar. And the pro troupe had one more set back: try as they might, they couldn't lure the two amateur kings, Santana of Spain and Emerson of Australia, into their fold – in the world of the amateurs, the pair were not only lauded as national heroes, but were making a killing on the side.

For the pros, then, in the whole period from 1926 to 1966 their circus had remained outside the gates – a troupe, a movable act – and in the eyes of the public, it appeared jaded, ever in need of freshening up. Though an irritant, the amateur bosses believed that the professionals held little power, and could be contained.

Yet by the early 1960s, few among the leaders of the amateur world believed in the charade. How could it be otherwise, when their system managed to hold the few remaining good players by paying them off in paper bags passed under the table?

Hugh Lunn's book on Ken Fletcher, another in the seemingly inexhaustible line of Aussie larrikins, provides a contemporary slant on this weird world of contemporary international tennis, and on the precarious life of an amateur who was a rung below the top.

Fletcher wasn't up to the level of Emerson or Santana, and so couldn't manage to snare the big deals. To make a living he was forced to emulate the pros, and become a gypsy – and in his case a pretty poor one. But unlike the pros, his livelihood had to be scraped together by shonky deals with the officials who led the amateur tennis associations and tournaments round the world. The Lawn Tennis Association of Australia held such absolute power, and executed it so erratically and unjustly, that the brilliant Aussie trio of Fletcher, Martin Mulligan and Bob Hewitt rebelled: to survive, they forsook their homeland to play for Hong Kong, France and South Africa respectively, and where they could more easily fiddle a better living.[17]

However, the beginning of the end arose from within the ruling elite itself. Why? Because by the middle of the 1960s, in the holiest watering hole of them all, Wimbledon, there was hardly a believer left. And some among that elite were prepared to say so. By 1967 the executives of the tournament that claimed the status of 'World Championship' decided that somebody had to tell the world that the emperor had no clothes. 'Open tennis', they thought, was inevitable.

The body ruling the amateur world, the International Lawn Tennis Federation (ILTF), didn't agree. Convening in July to consider the British proposal to start up the era of Open Tennis in 1968, they promptly threw it out.

In his fine book, *Open Tennis,* Richard Evans points out that in fact the ILTF had considered a similar proposal over half a decade earlier. His description of this event is so sharp that I give it here verbatim:

> Pancho Gonzales never won Wimbledon because, at a meeting of the ILTF ... in 1960, three delegates known to be in favour of Open Tennis failed to vote. One was in the toilet, one fell asleep, and, to complete the farce, a third was arranging ... [the delegates'] dinner ... [and] entertainment. The required two-thirds majority was missed by the narrowest of margins and while amateur delegates sipped champagne on the Seine that night, the game of tennis found itself anchored to the hypocrisy of amateurism for another eight years. [18]

But the Brits who'd wanted open tennis didn't give up. As noted in Chapter 4, the break-through came in mid-1967. They got together with Jack Kramer and BBC2 TV, and hatched a plan for a pro tourney at Wimbledon. In the words of the pros' historian, McCauley, the event was to be 'rather presumptuously entitled the "Wimbledon World Professional Championships"'. Limited to eight of the top pros, it was set to run over three days in August.

The experiment was a triumph. The players were made up of the top three pros: Laver, Rosewall and Gimeno, seeded one, two and three. To complete the eight were added the irrepressible Gonzales, and the tough quartet of Buchholz, Hoad, Ralston and Stolle. Each pro was champing at the bit. 'Near capacity crowds on all three days,' says McCauley, 'saw a standard [of play] far exceeding [that in] ... the traditional Wimbledon held some seven weeks earlier.'

Laver, banned since 1962, won the tournament from Rosewall, required to stand outside the ivied gates since 1956. As it turned out, it wasn't enough for the crowds to witness a Final of two hours of brilliant tennis from two of tennis's greatest masters close to their peak. On the opening day they had been given the chance to witness a match between the legends Hoad and Gonzales. This had turned out to be so charged with nostalgia, pathos and sheer staggering brilliance that the veteran BBC commentator,

Dan Maskell, stated it was the finest game he had seen at the famous club.

Though a worn-down Hoad lost to Rosewall in the Semifinal, McCauley notes that Hoad still managed to inspire an immortal epithet from *The Guardian*'s David Gray. The awestruck journalist wrote that, in exhausted defeat, Hoad remained 'splendidly imperfect'.

Thus, overnight, the paying public could see the best exponents of the game playing their hearts out. To the watchers they were prodigals. After a dark odyssey, the immortals – Hoad, Rosewall, Laver and Gonzales – had returned from oblivion more 'splendid' than ever.

Once the Wimbledon event got going, the TV producers checked their ratings – and grinned. At precisely that point, the nabobs who ran the amateur show around the world found their position altered – the media and its owners had swapped sides. When the renegade pros woke up the day after the Wimbledon pro tournament had ended, they discovered that they had newfound supporters, and from the big end of town.

Thereafter things were never the same.

In December of 1967, despite threats of expulsion from the ILTF, the British LTA endorsed Open Tennis. For the whole 1968 season, at least in Britain – including Wimbledon – it was decided there would be no references to 'amateurs' or 'professionals'.

What were the feelings of the unassuming little bloke who was expected to acquire the official – and true – title of World Champion? Rod Laver, the man who fervently believed that drama is best reserved for the tennis court, responded simply: 'I'm really pleased ... This will raise the quality of the game and clear it up a bit.'

As might be expected during the first stuttering year of Open Tennis, there was some confusion and upsets. But by 1969, the second year of the Open Era, Laver had extended his supremacy over all the other players. According to his fellow pros, this arose in no small measure from his elastic sense of what was possible.

His next decision seemed to fit with this. As an amateur, he had already won the Grand Slam in 1962, but now he saw a chance to become a first in the game's history. He planned to become the first winner of a second Grand Slam, with the difference that now it would be a first *Open* Grand Slam. With typical understatement, he tells us that if he won, he would have 'made an entry in the record books that was likely to stand for quite a while'.

Rod Laver knew that this time it would be much harder: the field was tougher and deeper. As it turned out, unlike 1962, he had no match points against him. Yet from beginning to end it was a battle, and one that required his Houdini escape act several times.

Here, in brief outline, is the Laver journey towards his grail: a second Grand Slam.

At the beginning, in Australia, the biggest hurdle turned out to be Tony Roche. Roche was another tough butcher's son from the outback, and another left-hander who could serve, volley and hit topspin from the ground. It took four and a half hours on a dreadful grass court in Brisbane's tropical heat, as well as a stroke of luck, for Rod to pull through. For the first time in years – after all he was back in boiling Queensland – to cool down he'd filled his hat with wet cabbage leaves.

On this occasion, the conditions were so bad and both players so exhausted that for once Laver admitted it was not *The Rocket* that got him through, but gutbucket defence – he won by 'hacking' his way out, scraping everything back, chipping and slicing, forcing his opponent to return yet another slithering ball. Afterwards he called it the hardest match he ever played.

After that marathon test, the Final against an in-form Gimeno was no trouble at all.

Next in line was the French, the tourney that journalist Rex Bellamy aptly called 'the great but cruel championships'.[19] This was, and still is, the only leg of the Slam played on clay, and slow clay at that. Although this looked 'the roughest' of the four legs of the Slam, Laver felt he had at long last worked out how to play on that demanding surface.

Despite such confidence, in Round Two he was down two sets to Love. But he pulled that match out of the fire, only to face real battles in the three final-round matches. In the quarters he had to face Gimeno, a clay-court master. Hell! If he won that match, he was likely to be up against the brilliant speedster Okker in the Semifinal ... And, if he won that, the Final – and most likely that killer-on-clay, Ken Rosewall!

Laver disposed of Gimeno, but appeared to be faltering against an inspired Okker in the Semifinal. But he suddenly lifted; later, Rod said that he felt as if he was 'hitting bullets'. And his opponent, one of the fastest players ever to have picked up a tennis racket, wasn't getting near them. Laver won the last three sets 6–0, 6–2, 6–4. After that, our ever-modest hero came to the conclusion: 'I wasn't just doing a lot right, I was doing *everything* right.'

In the French the year before, Rosewall had beaten Laver convincingly in the Final. (Rod joked that one day his old mate Kenny would be walking off with 'the great clay court championships in the sky'.) Nevertheless, in what he said was his finest demonstration of clay court tennis, Rod took heaven's clay court champion in straight sets.

This chapter began with a glimpse of Laver at the end of the next leg of the Slam, Wimbledon. But to get there he had needed to survive several extreme tests.

First, in an early round, he had been forced to the fifth set against Stan Smith, a serve-and-volleyer playing the game of his life on fast Wimbledon grass. After that he had to face a difficult challenge from Cliff Drysdale and an incendiary Arthur Ashe.

First came Drysdale. The South African was surprisingly confident: from the wily Gonzales and Rosewall, he'd learned to chip everything he could at Laver's feet, with the result that in the warm-up tournament to Wimbledon, this clever strategy had produced a Laver stumble and a Drysdale win.

But Laver broke the then almost inviolable rule of fast grass: to follow one's serve to net. Now, after Laver served, his feet weren't where Drysdale could take aim. When Drysdale woke up, the match was over.

In the Semifinal, Laver faced Ashe.

The tall American was a player capable of extraordinary streaks – and he was in one. Jack Kramer claimed that the first two sets of the match had been the most superlative tennis he had ever seen! With his opponent hitting 'out of his mind' the defending champion had at first fallen behind. But, after levelling the match in the second set, a brilliant Laver took the third, and at two sets to one, had his nose in front.

At the beginning of the fourth set, the match was still anybody's: at that point, out flashed another piece of Laver magic.

During a rally in the key first game, Ashe had forced Laver back and way out of court, and had moved in to intercept Laver's desperate forehand return. At net, the whole court open, Ashe made a sensible choice: a cross-court drop volley.

But 'sensible' is not always part of the vocabulary of the great.

'It was a good place for a drop volley,' admitted Laver later, 'because I was so far out ... about thirty feet [ten metres] from the ball when [Ashe's return] bounced softly on my side of the court.' But he had anticipated Ashe's shot. He tells us that he was 'already running forward ... in a mad dash like somebody trying to catch an egg rolling off the table'. Moving so fast that he thought he would split the net, he got to the ball 'just before it bounced again'. Then, off his backhand, he scooped up the dying ball – and flicked it over Ashe's head into an open court.

Against a now demoralised Ashe, Laver went on to win the set 6–0, and the match.

After that, came the triumphant Final against Newcombe, recounted earlier.

For Laver to win the fourth and last leg of the Slam, the US at Forest Hills, he needed to come up with more than great shots. Early in the tournament he struggled for five sets against Ralston, and then had to survive another battle against his old foe Emerson. But the Final turned out to be once more against Roche, who by then had clocked up an overall 5–3 match-advantage over Laver for the year.

The Forest Hills grass was always suspect, and conditions had been made worse by heavy rain. In response, Laver played smart. He tempered his aggression, and exploited his speed and wicked spin, made even more devilish on the uneven surface. At key moments Laver had reached tough shots, then found the balance to hit running lobs to strand his younger, but slower, opponent.

After losing a hard first set, the ruthless Laver took the next three, 6–1, 6–1, 6–2.

Unlike 1962, this victory hadn't required the nurturance of Don Budge, and Laver had got there without an attack of nerves like the one that had nearly downed him in the final match of the Slam seven years previously. So much had Laver learnt from these earlier trials that he had invited another generous soul, his friend John McDonald, to join him in New York, and emulate the spirit of Budge's retreat in the Catskills.

When it was all over, the winner of a second Slam stood facing Roche 'at the net and ... holding out his hand'. At this climactic moment, the victor did a crazy thing.

'Suddenly,' Laver tells us in *The Education of a Tennis Player*, 'I was in the air. What's this? I was leaping the net in classic fashion.'

Now this man felt a special aversion to 'show-offs', who were at the very bottom of his scale of values. These he called – in 'testimony to their egos' – 'bloody gloating high-jumpers'. But for once, Laver found that his 'built-in restrainers' had been released, and he was air-born.

In the big top, the high wire had been set higher than ever before. And on it he had performed his magic. But it took some moments for his heart and brain to take in what he had done.

When they did, he jumped the net.

By the end of the second Grand Slam, in greater and lesser tournaments, Rodney George Laver had won a record of 30 consecutive matches. Though he was then thirty-one, and was to keep the No. 1 world ranking for a further two years, he was never to win another Grand Slam title. [20]

In a most important way, he didn't need to.

Giving it a nudge – the style of Laver

If I have been given to elaboration in describing the Laver style, the excuse is that to many observers the unbridled virtuosity of the mature champion defied analysis. Even students of tennis as insightful as Elly Vines found Laver baffling. In his wonderful *Tennis: Myth and Method*, Vines explains: 'With Budge, Tilden, Gonzales, Kramer and the others in the pantheon ... experts could at least discern how they did it. But *Rocket* Rod was the ultimate magician; there is no way of explaining in rational terms ... the angles he achieved.' [21]

Since he rarely expressed emotion on court, Laver's dour mien compounded this perplexity. Typically, magic is performed with éclat. To many observers Laver performed his miracles with as much of that quality as shown by the average bush plumber.

Yet I believe that there was a sound basis to the extraordinary plays that Laver managed to create time and again, and his expressionless manner hid a sensitive and thoughtful soul.

Central to the Laver style was the whipping wrist, which allowed the ball to be struck at the end of his reach, with power and spin, and at astounding angles. And driving the workload that was crucial to his intricate style was a wizard's playfulness. To make up the 'full monty' were speed, strength, agility, a rock-like confidence, and courage in bucketfuls.

Technically, at maturity, his game was complete. John McEnroe has said: 'Laver [was] the first guy who had everything'. Certainly, by the time he was top pro, he owned a fine and reliable serve, a superb net game with a murderous overhead, and off the ground he was fearsome.

The balance of his ground strokes is beautifully demonstrated by one of Laver's own throwaway lines. After admitting that his backhand was 'more accurate' than his forehand, he noticed that the other pros never concentrated on his forehand!

In fact, the other pros found that serving to an in-form Laver was as intimidating as it had been to the generation facing Budge's bludgeon returns 30 years earlier. Because of Laver's variety, especially off the backhand, in some ways it was worse.

The sharp observer, John Alexander, notes: 'Serve wide to Laver's backhand in the deuce court ... not the best place to serve to Laver, and he has a perfect return – in six varieties.' He then specifies them: a full-swing topspin bullet rifled down the line or crosscourt; a sharply angled crosscourt chip; a moderately angled chip at the server's feet; a punishing slice, skimming the net, down the line; and a similarly straight, softer slice that sucks you in 'too close' to the net.[22]

But there's one that Alexander has forgotten! When feeling his oats, sometimes Laver would skip in, scoop up the serve on the rise, and confound the net-rushing server by arching it just over his reach into the backhand corner. Laver particularly enjoyed using this wicked play against big-serving Arthur Ashe. Poor Ashe! Even if he knew it was coming, he would be skewered by the shot – and perhaps even more by the dourness of the man finagling it.

The result? Laver beat Ashe sixteen times straight.

We have seen that the power and flair of his strokes were backed by a deceptive flexibility of game plan and a quiet – and often underrated – court intelligence. This allowed him to adjust his all court strategy when needed – in extremis, *The Rocket* could become a Rosewallian brick wall, and hack and scramble with the best of them.

Don Budge put it simply: the mature Laver had every shot and no weaknesses. However, in full flight Laver's game was even more than

Fig. 7.6. Explosive: the Laver smash. As great left-handers do, he leaps high to pluck the ball from over his right shoulder. Here Laver angles it to his opponent's left, but he could strike wide to the other side, or bang it down the middle.

Fig. 7.7. Laver serving at Wimbledon. For a small man, Laver came to own a fine serve arising from what Hollis called a 'Vines-type pendulum swing'. When he turned pro, he found an urgent need to improve his serve.

Budge's description implies: he also owned what I have named here *the eye*, and *the bolt-from-the-blue.*

The eye is a mysterious quality given to all great champions, but to Laver in bucket loads. It includes, but seems to go beyond, anticipation. Often Laver gave the impression that he knew more of what his opponents were doing, and thinking about doing, than they did themselves. This uncanny foresight resembles the capacity of the skilled defender in football or hockey. In some seemingly mystical way, they manage to 'read the play' and know in advance whether to go forward, go back, or stay put.[23]

Thus, in his account of the master stroke that turned the Wimbledon Final against Newcombe, Laver tells us that he not only knew that his

Fig. 7.8. Advanced tennis. Against John Newcombe at Wimbledon in 1969, Laver finesses a lob. Struck late with both under- and side-spin, the ball will curve away into his opponent's backhand corner.

opponent had come up to the net, but that he was 'tending to his left' to cover the alley. This visual processing occurred while Laver was on a dead run trying to catch the ball before it bounced. Such 'vision' allowed him to deduce that the last response his opponent expected was the crosscourt floater that the master contrived.

The bolt-from-the-blue emerges from the space created by *the eye*. Laver was unmatched in what one perceptive observer called 'hitting off the hesitation'. Because he could see – almost feel – his opponent hesitate or readjust in line or direction, he could respond by altering his own shot and confounding his opponent.

However, that last instant before he struck the ball held another kind of 'hesitation', one radically different from his opponent's. In that miniscule space-in-time before Laver hit the ball, his gigantic left arm withheld a bevy of potential retaliations! Like the more recent champion Roger Federer, in that split second before the ball was struck Laver appeared to be granted a peculiarly elongated fragment of freedom. From within that space he could check out his opponent – then surprise them.

There was yet another characteristic feature of Laver's play. Though stunning, it has been hardly noted in critiques of the Laver style.

An extrapolation of *the bolt-from-the-blue,* this was his ability to *hit winners off winners.* Here he resembled his hero, Hoad. When Hoad was 'on', he could dishearten even Gonzales by casually putting his racket on a huge Pancho smash ... and clinch a point apparently lost. Similarly, Laver would not only veer in to volley away the opponent's apparently decisive volleys, but frequently turn what looked like the opponent's winning shots, *including those that had almost passed him*, into winners of his own.

What must it have been like playing against a tennis god? Once, in the early 1970s, I attended a tournament in London and witnessed the Yugoslav Niki Pilić, in the best form of his life, face Laver in the finals.

After a savage defeat, a rueful if admiring Pilić told the press that after the first couple of games of the match, he had seen what he was up against. By then he had given up any chance of winning more than the odd point. In particular, he saw that 'the best shots I had ever played in my life were coming back as clean winners'.

He then added that apart from keeping up some sort of show by continuing to play his own best tennis, he had been glad of the opportunity to be on court with one of the game's greatest in full cry. He told the crowd that he had tried to register what he was seeing in order to remember some of his opponent's freakish play – for himself, and for his grandchildren.

The views of the taciturn Gonzales on Laver are also relevant. Said Pancho simply: the greatest difficulty in playing Laver was that he hit his best shots when you least expected them.

Back in Queensland, Charlie Hollis watched his old pupil as the triumphs multiplied. Certainly he was pleased and proud. But teachers like

Fig. 7.9. Another bolt-from-the-blue. *On indoor boards, Laver has got his racket to his opponent's near winner, and will probably make it into an angled winner of his own. Note the hugely developed left arm, and the extreme 'cradling' of the racket to give his shot 'feel'.*

Hollis are exceptional: their goal is an ideal, as sweet and elusive as a dream. After his second Grand Slam, Rod received a terse telegram from Charlie: 'Congratulations. Do it again.'

It is likely that Charlie had been reflecting on the hours spent alone in his room in the Rockhampton Hotel, where he had worked up a vision for his unprepossessing pupil. That vision dared fate, but the audacity of master and pupil had given it form.

Three sentences from John Newcombe illustrate the way Charlie

Fig. 7.10a and 7.10b. Two more bolts-from-the-blue. *Top, Laver has managed to catch a ball that has already nearly passed him – and will most probably return it offensively. His speed has lifted his Aussie floppy hat. Below, Laver has again moved fast to make an acute angled placement from an attempted passing shot. His Continental grip has allowed the racket head to 'lead around' the ball.*

Hollis's dream was realised, and add finish to this picture of tennis's most extravagant, exhilarating, influential, yet inimitable stylist:

> Everyone has seen Rocket's dramatic shots — the backhand winner down-the-line at 100 miles an hour or the crunching forehand volley. But the shot I like best is the forehand that he hits against a slow ball. He waits until the last

instant, holds the ball on the racket as long as possible, then puts the ball where his opponent isn't.[24]

To reproduce this lethal *bolt-from-the-blue* you have to possess all the attributes of style enumerated in these pages: the fitness, the speed, the wrist, the technique, and *the eye*.

However, as embodied in Rod Laver, there was one quality that seemed to unite them: a life-long passion for redeeming dry reality with a wicked touch of the imagination.

Curtain

We have noted that when Laver defeated Tony Roche to complete his second Grand Slam, he jumped the net. Apparently, never before had Rod displayed such extravagance. But this is not quite true. Laver himself provides an account of his one similar attempt at advertising his triumph.

In *The Education of a Tennis Player*, Laver says: '[Jumping the net] ... just wasn't me ... I thought it ... show-offish ... I feel humble about beating a man ... And possibly ... self-conscious, afraid to look a fool as I had that 1957 afternoon ... when I beat Herbie Flam.'

We ask: What *had* occurred over a decade earlier, and made him feel a fool? It was an occasion when he was 19 years old, and the first time he had beaten a world-ranked player. Rod remembers that at the moment of victory he was so elated that 'I didn't know where I was'. So he jumped the net.

But in doing so the young giant-killer caught his foot, and fell flat on his face! At once, lying on the ground, amidst the crowd roaring with laughter, he had a flash of understanding. And it was not just that he'd made a fool of himself.

By the time he'd picked himself up, and hobbled off the court, he understood that fate is a fickle master, and that in moments of triumph – especially in moments of triumph – even heroes can be undone.

Rod Laver never forgot this. Or it took a second Grand Slam to make him forget it, and then for only a few seconds

In *The Education of a Tennis Player* Rod also mentions his attitude, not to winning but to losing: 'Tell yourself to hit the ball. I mean by that hit through it. You can only lose, and losing isn't the worst thing that can happen to you.'

It was a short step for him to realise that the game he loved was just a game, and his ultimate challenge was to retain the humility with which he started playing it. In the strangest way his success at that task explains much of why he became just about the best player who picked up a tennis racket.

Whenever Rod Laver walked on to a tennis court, he felt that he'd nothing to lose.

Notes

1 Quoted by McCauley in *The History of Professional Tennis*. My main sources for this chapter are Laver and Collins, *The Education of a Tennis Player* and Laver's earlier book written with Jack Pollard, *How to Play Winning Tennis*, Pelham, London, 1964. Collins also collaborated with Laver in another useful book, *Rod Laver's Tennis Digest*, Digest Books, Northfield, Ill., 1973. A memorial publication for Australia Post provided further information on Laver's Queensland origins and on Charlie Hollis: Alan Trengove, *Advantage Australia: Rod Laver & Margaret Court, legends of the grand slam*, Australian Postal Corporation, Melbourne, 2003.

2 Laver and Collins, *The Education of a Tennis Player*.

3 The prejudice against the left-handed is neither new nor culture-specific. In French, for example, *gauche* means both 'left' and 'socially awkward'. And those preferring the left are unlikely to be *adroit*, derived from the French *à* (to) + *droit* (right), itself from the Latin *directum*, right. Indeed they might even be seen as *sinister* (from Latin: *sinistrum*, left). How fortunate that young Rodney found a coach who knew that true style comes from within.

4 Roger Federer, a recent champion with a sublime backhand, admitted to a degree of mixed handedness. If, among elite sportsmen, mixed handedness is more common, is this because it provides an advantage? A way to test this hypothesis would be to compare the handedness of champions in a sport played with one hand to one played with two.

5 This section is condensed from Laver and Collins, *The Education of a Tennis Player*, and Laver and Pollard, *How to Play Winning Tennis*.

6 It seems Charlie did that job well too. Laver has never been especially articulate, but he is well spoken – even if Aussies may be a little disappointed to hear something of an American accent.

7 Quoted by Alan Trengove in *Advantage Australia*.

8 Ashe and Stolle are quoted by Laver and Collins in *The Education of a Tennis Player*, and Scott by Laver and Pollard in *How to Play Winning Tennis*.

9 The Australian Davis Cupper Billy Sidwell provides further insight into the inventive Hollis and the more wooden Hopman. Sidwell tells us that once Hopman and Hollis watched the young Laver soar for a smash, and whack it miles out. 'Poor smasher', responded Hopman. 'Poor smasher be darned!' replied Charlie. 'He went up beautifully and... buried that ball? ... There's plenty of time to teach him to keep them in the court ...' Though Charlie acknowledged Hop's status, the proud coach from the bush quietly warned his young pupil, 'Do what Hop says, but don't listen to anyone but me.' Billy Sidwell, 'Kill that smash', Chapter 16 of *Lawn Tennis the Australian Way*.

10 Gordon Forbes, *A Handful of Summers*, HarperCollins, London, 1997.

11 However, if one is good enough, even in doubles the left-handed weakness so feared by Hollis can be exploited. In a key Davis Cup doubles against the US in 1958, Fraser, playing left court, and Mal Anderson were on top. Commentating was none other than Pancho Gonzales. Pancho sized up Fraser and, via Jack Kramer (advising the US team), got a message to the American pair. He suggested that they play tandem when serving against Fraser, and work the left-hander's backhand. (In tandem the server's partner stands near the net on the court's left side, the server moving to the right to cover the return.) The US team did so. Fraser, unable to make his ugly, but grooved and effective chip crosscourt,

and without a solid backhand drive, was mauled, and the match and the Cup lost. Good as Fraser was, if Gonzales or any of the other top pros had ever played Fraser in singles (it didn't happen, Fraser never turned pro), the left-hander would have been annihilated.

12 Budge, *Don Budge: A Tennis Memoir.*

13 LeCompte, *The Last Sure Thing.*

14 Laver and Collins, *The Education of a Tennis Player.*

15 Laver and Pollard, *How to Play Winning Tennis.*

16 McCauley in *The History of Professional Tennis.*

17 Lunn, *The Great Fletch.*

18 Evans, *Open Tennis.* It would be remiss not to mention three previous occasions in which the pro-amateur split might have crumbled. In the late 1930s, the tide seemed to be shifting towards moving tennis into the same (open) realm as golf. Then came World War II, first with no tennis, then with the pros pushed back into the situation they faced before the war. As outlined in Chapter 4, if the glamorous Hoad had defeated the great but less well-known Gonzales in their ill-fated tour of 1958, good sense buoyed by popular sentiment might have allowed the introduction of Open Tennis a decade earlier. This seems right, given Evans' sad tale of the distracted delegates a couple of years later. The studious Bowers has also discovered that as far back as 1929, near the very beginning of our tale, the International Lawn Tennis Federation voted decisively to consider open competition – then, under pressure, ditched the idea the next year.

19 Rex Belamy, *The Tennis Set*, Cassell, London, 1972.

20 In the ABC television programme, *Australian Story*, Laver was asked how he felt after completing a second Grand Slam. He replied with the astonishing remark that it 'wasn't that I thought I was the best – I just had a good year.' *Australian Story*, Episode 15 - The Slam - The Rod Laver Story, ABC, October 15, 2012.

21 Vines and Vier, *Tennis: Myth and Method.*

22 John Alexander, 'The Return of Service', Chapter 9 in *Tennis Strokes and Strategies*, Tennis Magazine.

23 In his brilliant Massey Lectures of 2011, Adam Gopnik highlighted a characteristic of the most gifted ice hockey players. Drawing on the literature in psychology, he named it 'spatial intelligence'. This is precisely what I have called 'the eye' with respect to Laver's tennis. See Adam Gopnik, Lecture 1, 'Romantic Winter - The Season in Sight', 2011 CBC Massey Lectures, broadcast on Big Ideas, ABC Radio National, February 27, 2012.

24 John Newcombe, 'What Makes a Champion', in Laver and Collins, eds, *Rod Laver's Tennis Digest.*

Fig. 8.0. The pros ham it up for a publicity shot during the 1947–8 tour. Top bill was Jack Kramer (right) and Bobby Riggs (2nd from left) playing for the Pro Title. Nimble Little Pancho Segura (left) and Dinny Pails (3rd from left) made up the preliminary bout.

EPILOGUE

A Golden Thread

We are merely the stars' tennis-balls, struck and bandied
Which way please them.

John Webster
The Duchess of Malfi

THIS book has drawn a picture of an almost forgotten era in tennis, and of eight of its masters. For over 40 years, through highs and lows, our band managed to hold its own through unruly times.

And unruly they were! John Sharnik has written a delightful memoir, *Remembrance of Games Past,* in which he describes his six-month-long odyssey travelling with a Grand Masters Tour during the 1980s. Sharnik explains that when he talked to those who had been on the old pro tour, he was shocked by the hardness of their recollections. They looked back on their pro days without a shred of sentimentality; for those times these veterans felt 'only a kind of fierce pride'. The ex-pros resembled old soldiers who had served at the front, and the front had involved trench warfare – down, dirty and drawn out. And we have seen how, as in all wars, the pro trenches saw casualties: these included the wondrously gifted Lew Hoad and the magnificent Don Budge, both of whom never recovered from a pro tour that they'd been forced to endure while injured.[1]

In telling the story of these eight men, I have attempted to answer two related questions: how did they become champions, and what made them end up in the pro trenches, sometimes for a decade or more? After all, these masters volunteered to their war, and were free to leave at any time.

The start of the long road might be called *finding a lineage.*

In different ways, at an early point of their development, most drew something unique from one older player. This connection enabled them to glimpse the gorgeous line of champions who'd come before them, and discover their own sense of history. Having uncovered a golden thread to the past, their imagination extended it to the future, into which they themselves might be spun.

Often this nexus occurred in a few moments.

For Jack Kramer it was as a 13-year-old boy, taking his first glimpse of World Pro Champion Ellsworth Vines in his shining white flannels. A few years later, the teenage Pancho Gonzales needed only one good look at the effortless serve of an unknown player in a public park in Los Angeles to stumble upon the spring to his own life force. And we caught the thrill of the young Rod Laver: invited to stay in the Hoad household, he found himself in Lew's bedroom swinging one of his hero's rackets – his mind leaping to scenes of future glory.

Sometimes the vision of a god in his tennis heaven occurred later in life, and was not in the shape of a beautiful other. Thus, for the twin souls of Bill Tilden and Bobby Riggs – quite different, yet in their own ways almost equally tormented – their glimpse was of the god within, of their own potentially transcendent self. The scene of their enlightenment could hardly have been more different: for Tilden, the Wimbledon Centre Court; for Riggs, a rubble court in the remote reaches of a world at war. But at that moment each knew that he was the best tennis player in the world.

Like Tilden and Riggs, Don Budge was well into his career before an alternative image of himself swung up into his mind's eye, and changed him. As Ellsworth Vines and Fred Perry slugged it out on court before him, it dawned that if he could integrate two apparent incompatibles – Perry's quickness and Vines' power – he might reach unthought-of perfection.

Rod Laver has provided us with a related kind of epiphany. During practice against his bush coach, Charlie Hollis, the unprepossessing 15-year-old passed his strapping teacher at net – for the first time and with a flick shot that confounded technique. At that moment he realised – as did Hollis – that here was the magic that would give him entry into the line of great champions set before him by his coach.

After these seminal visions of Kramer, Gonzales, Tilden, Riggs, Budge and Laver, there remain two of our eight champions – Vines and Rosewall. So far I have not provided a life-changing vision that served to drive these two on. However, at least for Rosewall, a recent article helps us to unearth a relevant jewel.

A few years ago, a section of *The Weekend Australian* called '10 Things You Didn't Know About ...' featured an interview with Rosewall. Inevitably, there came the old saw, 'Who was the best tennis player of all time?'

Rosewall didn't give his usual answer – his 'greatest' was not Laver, nor Hoad, Gonzales, or Kramer, all of whom he had previously acknowledged as titans. His answer appeared idiosyncratic, even oblique: 'That [question] is always difficult. It depends how far you go back. For me, it was John Bromwich. He was my idol. I was fortunate to play doubles with him when I was fourteen ... '[2]

So by the age of 73, the Rosewall memory has been focussed. His own 'greatest player ever' is a little known Australian who never turned pro and, as a singles player, scraped up only one Grand Slam tournament victory – the Australian Championships, then a relatively minor tournament. Figure 8.1 captures him in characteristic pose, hitting his devilish right-sided double-hander.

But to Rosewall, Bromwich was not just *the* best; he was his 'idol'.

Why? Fortunately for we moderns, the extraordinary study of tennis master Bill Talbert helps us understand the answer to this question.

Talbert provides a snapshot of Rosewall's guru just as he might have been observed from the left court by his 14-year-old partner.[3] Figure 8.2 reveals the pieces of a doubles rally recorded by Talbert, and allows us to picture the old spider Bromwich spinning his web. The experts call it 'crossing-up the opposition': Bromwich sets up his opponents by bamboozling them out of position, then he finds the space he's created, and finishes the point off.

In this case *Brom* himself provides the winner. However, as illustrated in Figure 4.4 in Chapter 4, more often than not the wily Bromwich would manipulate the play so that the clincher would be delivered by his 'straight man' partner in the left court. Usually, his offsiders were champs like Adrian Quist or Frank Sedgman, but from time to time he put an apprentice beside him, one being a little kid called Kenny Rosewall.

Fig. 8.1. John Bromwich's deceptive double-hander. Brom *could place this shot anywhere he wanted. The protruding tongue is typical, and in keeping with the relish with which he tortured his opponents. His student Ken Rosewall induced similar pain, but eschewed the gestures.*

Yet we must ask: How exactly could a man who played tennis with both hands – and was so eccentric in technique as to appear inimitable – become the lifelong inspiration to young Rosewall, an orthodox Tildenian stylist?

Crucially, Rosewall's newfound master was not much heavier in power than young Ken. Watching *Brom*, this slight boy realised that he could be a champion without pulverising the ball – he too could outmanoeuvre, not overpower his opponent.

We can now see that the Bromwich image that inspired Rosewall was wondrously entwined with Rosewall's own knowledge of himself. He was a little bloke, with not much strength, but quick, with nice moves. Already,

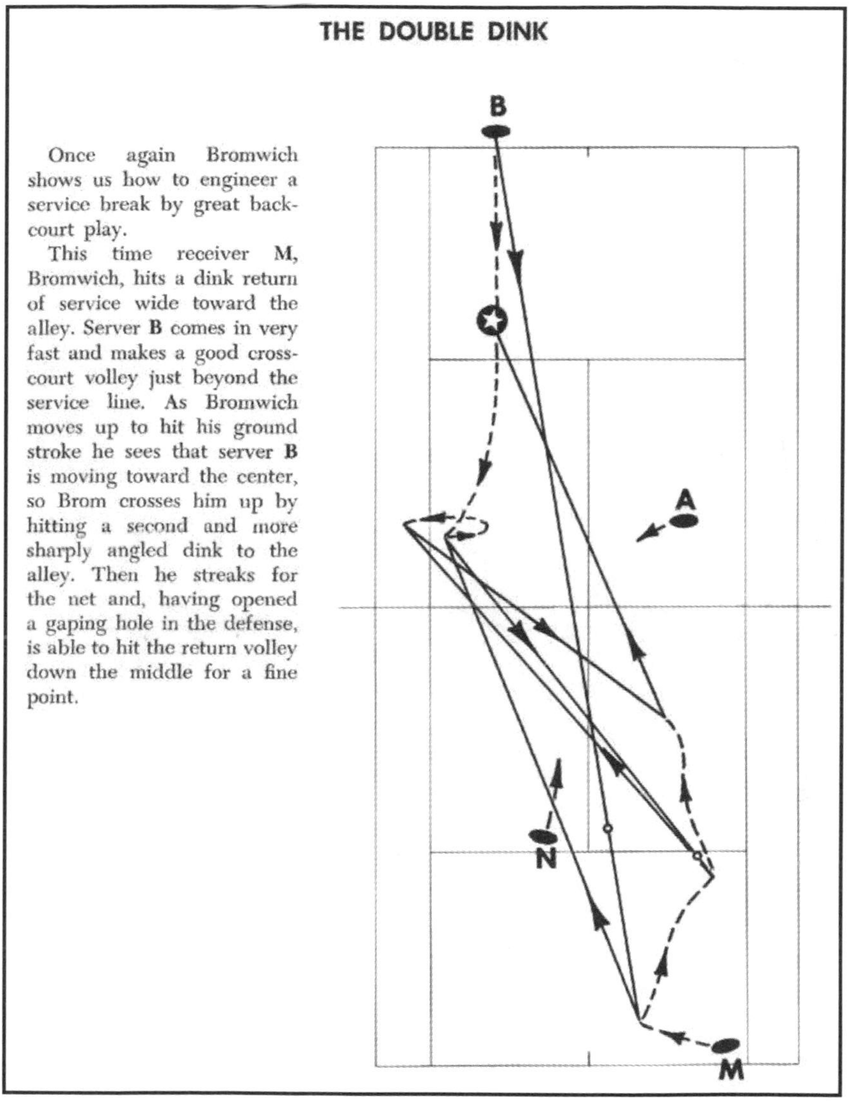

THE DOUBLE DINK

Once again Bromwich shows us how to engineer a service break by great back-court play.

This time receiver **M**, Bromwich, hits a dink return of service wide toward the alley. Server **B** comes in very fast and makes a good cross-court volley just beyond the service line. As Bromwich moves up to hit his ground stroke he sees that server **B** is moving toward the center, so Brom crosses him up by hitting a second and more sharply angled dink to the alley. Then he streaks for the net and, having opened a gaping hole in the defense, is able to hit the return volley down the middle for a fine point.

Fig. 8.2. As recorded by doubles master Bill Talbert, the wizard Bromwich mesmerises the opposition.

the 14-year-old possessed an acute understanding of his own possibilities and limitations; already, he understood the significance of *first know thyself.*

And how Rosewall learnt and followed through from that choice! A decade after young Ken first played beside Bromwich, Figure 8.3 shows Talbert again at work recording a doubles match. And this time one of the protagonists was the young Rosewall. At the end of a rally that seemed lost,

THE DESPERATION DRAW PLAY

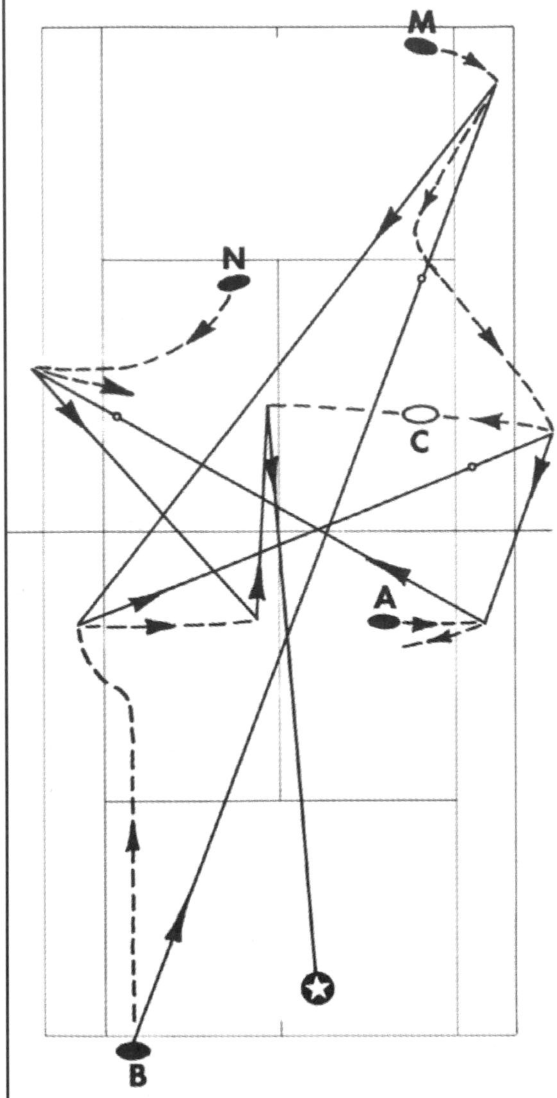

During the 1954 U. S. Nationals final this superb desperation draw play was made by the great little Rosewall.

Seixas, **B**, serves. At once he sees that the return of service by Rosewall, **M**, is high. So Seixas runs well in to the net and angles off a sharp volley that almost wins the point outright. But Rosewall guesses what's coming and, after a hard run, he retrieves the ball. He tries to slip his return down the line past net man **A**, Trabert, but Trabert has anticipated the shot so well that he is able to angle volley all the way cross-court for what looks like a winner. This time modified net man **N**, Hoad, saves the situation by running rapidly to the sideline. He tries to hit back through the middle between Seixas and Trabert. But Seixas has anticipated this shot and, with the Aussies hopelessly out of position, he moves over to pound the ball down the empty center of the court for a "sure winner." However, Rosewall, **M**, has other ideas. He had scrambled back as far as point C when he detected Seixas' intention. He hesitates at point C until Seixas is fully committed, then sprints to cover the shot and volley deep down the middle for the point!

Fig. 8.3. Sitting at the master's feet. Talbert and Old show one of the tricks Bromwich's former partner Rosewall imbibed from his teacher – and pulls out 'the desperation draw'.

Rosewall suckers Seixas into putting the ball exactly where his apparently struggling opponent wanted it! Rosewall pounces: end of point.

How *Old Brom* would have loved it!

On further scrutiny, this quality of self-understanding turns out to be common to all our eight. Sports psychologists suggest that this often distinguishes the champion from the dozens of supremely talented individuals who never quite make it to the top: the very best own a highly developed sense of their own capacity, mental and physical, their weaknesses and strengths.

With each of our eight champions, self-reflection seemed nascent when they first picked up a racket, was delivered alive and kicking by the time they began to hit a few shots, and persisted in concentrated form throughout their careers. Tilden provides a wonderful example. As a mature amateur player, he suddenly realised that his whole game was flawed by the absence of an attacking backhand: retiring from tournament play for a whole winter, he constructed one.

For the other seven, their raw moment of reality coincided with their arrival among the pros. Facing the pro masters for the first time hammered home a shocking truth: if they retained any significant weakness, it was as if they were poking their heads above the trenches – so would end up shot, sooner rather than later.

Thus they set about the laborious task of eliminating their weakness, and making their game as complete as they could make it. So we find Vines and Budge building consistency into their power, attackers Kramer, Gonzales and Laver learning defence, and defenders Rosewall and Riggs learning attack.

If these champions overcame their defects, some turned them into strengths. For instance, a couple of years into the pros, little defender Ken Rosewall had become an all-time great master of the net. [4] And it took only a few weeks in the pros for big-man serve-and-volleyer Jack Kramer to pull out a glorious backhand pass or an attacking lob. When Kramer began to unveil these skills against master defender Bobby Riggs, his previously indefatigable opponent decided it was time to throw in the towel.

The most breath-taking turn-around came from Pancho Gonzales. Well into a gruelling head-to-head tour that Gonzales was losing ('I had blisters under my blisters', he says) an unexpected change left his opponent, the majestic Lew Hoad, dumbfounded. By virtue of nothing other than a new grip, Pancho was suddenly passing him with a hard crosscourt backhand, a shot that a mere few weeks earlier he didn't possess at all.

Of course these champions also nurtured their strengths – the keystone of their game.

For Tilden it was his completeness of game and his court presence; for Vines, his serve and forehand; for Kramer, his serve, forehand and system; for Budge, his backhand and indestructible all court power; for Riggs, his consistency and omniscient cunning; for Gonzales, his serve and movement; for Rosewall his backhand, consistency and court-craft; and for Laver, his magician's mastery of spin.

Once they had reached their peak as pros, they could do more than use these big guns to wear down an opponent. As demonstrated several times by Rosewall in the luminous WCT Final against Laver – or by Laver himself when he flummoxed Newcombe in a Wimbledon Final – when at their best against the best, they knew the trick of unsheathing their treasured weapon at a crucial moment – and so the fatal thrust. [5]

In this way, by their maturity as pros these performers had honed their style to as close to perfection as they could manage. By then there was no place for the superfluous or the extravagant: each would have concurred with Cervantes' austere aphorism, '*toda afectacion es mala*' (all affectation is bad). They would also have applauded two related observations: Tilden's incisive description of form as 'the maximum result from the minimum of effort'; and racing car champion Nicki Lauda's comment: 'The point of Formula One is to win while driving as slowly as possible'.

By the time these men had reached the top of the slippery pro tennis pole, this process of distillation and internalisation helps to explain the depth of their confidence, a quality essential to all champions' capacity to lift their game at crucial moments.

Master coach Brad Gilbert highlights a related and even more remarkable gift: when champions like these get ahead, they rarely deteriorate or become loose, but play even better. [6]

Time and again, a situation arises where a fine player starts out well against the champion – might even get in front – but abruptly, the champion changes gear. He or she first comes back, then noses ahead. Before anyone notices, it's all over. Only afterwards we see that following the gear change the champion's play had reached another level, and then sustained until the opponent was disposed of – and the match won.

When Don Budge, Jack Kramer, Ken Rosewall, John McEnroe, Pete Sampras, Roger Federer and Rafael Nadal got ahead and were in form, their poor opponent soon realised a dismal truth: they wouldn't be given a chance to re-enter the match via any errors of the champion that arose from overconfidence or lack of concentration. Worse! From that moment on, the fearsome figure opposite was likely to play better!

In his aptly titled book, *Winning Ugly,* Gilbert graphically describes this particular experience: after the turning point, these champions 'first get one foot on your neck, then two feet, then, before you know it, they're jumping up and down ...'

Gilbert suggests that the reason for this defining quality is more than a concentrated competitive streak. These greats seem to hold an image of their own play at its best, and this ideal becomes as crucial a foil to them as the opposition on the other side of the net.

In his memoirs, John Newcombe provides a lovely example of the champion's search for perfection.

He explains that the first time he had a close look at Rosewall was when, as a young star, he had just got into the Australian Davis Cup team and faced the pro master in a practice game. For Newcombe's first five service points, Rosewall successively drilled each return for a clean winner on, or just inside, the line. Newcombe had never seen anything like it.

On the sixth serve, it looked like the same story, but this time Rosewall's return missed – by an inch.

To Newcombe's astonishment, the usually restrained maestro immediately began yelling and cursing himself.[7] For Rosewall, five bits of perfection in a row was insufficient.

In his brilliant – and at times chilling – introduction to the book *Winning Attitudes*, the champion middle-distance runner Herb Elliott says several things of relevance to this theme.[8]

Elliott, never beaten in a significant race, states explicitly that it is the mental edge that distinguishes the champion runner, and stresses that for him the real battle was with himself, not with his opponents. He explains that whether in a race or at training, inevitably he found 'a figure on [his] shoulder'. The 'little voice' of this perching homunculus would become at different times his spur, or his foil, or his tempter – but, one way or another, his well of energy.

We have no doubt that each of our heroes created, knew, and used, their own 'little voices' – and that such self-awareness helps to explain why there was a difference, if by a hair's breadth, between the great and the nearly great.[9]

If the stories of these champions highlight their capacity to imagine their own rich possibilities, what also emerges is their down-to-earth understanding of how to combine this imagining with the best competition, and with unending work. Yes, as shown in Figure 8.4, from time to time, as working pros they had to get out and play on the streets in order to steal a bit of attention.[10] Nonetheless, they felt they had to be down there with their fellows; how else could such driven men tell if they had reached the level of skill that they believed they were capable?

Of course, another ingredient in the makeup of the champion was years of intensively supervised practice, beginning in the early teens or younger. In modern terms, such virtuoso skill requires the laying down of crucial kinaesthetic patterns. As with master musicians, these had to be established well before adulthood.

In this foundation building, a good teacher was instrumental. With just two exceptions – mavericks Tilden and Gonzales – all the other pros were blessed with master teachers: for Vines, it was Mercer Beasley; for Budge, Tom Stow; for Riggs, Esther Bartosh; for Rosewall, Robert Rosewall; and for Laver, Charlie Hollis. These talented teachers built a rock-solid base to their student's game; moreover, they took up a lad's passion and, linking him into the larger game, transformed potential into marvellous reality. And how fertile was the clash between the studious femininity of Esther Bartosh and the rambunctious boysy ego of Bobby Riggs, or between the flamboyance of Charlie Hollis and the diffidence of Rod Laver!

And yet genius is in some way unteachable. In 1972, I watched Lew Hoad in a pro tournament in London. He'd been lured from comfortable retirement in sunny Spain, where Aussies might say that on occasions the fun-loving veteran had been known to 'bend the elbow' or 'have a shandy or two on a hot day'. Yet though unfit, overweight and injured, he made the quarter final – and gave the American Cliff Richey, then in the world's Top Ten, the fright of his life.

Early in the match, with the Australian at net, under pressure Richey threw up a lob over Hoad's backhand side. It was a little short. Hoad took three paces back, laid back his stonemason's wrist, and struck a backhand smash with such ferocity that Richey, a fleet-footed scrambler, didn't move. The ball thudded into the backstop for an untouchable winner.

Fig. 8.4a and 8.4b. On the streets. Above: Laver and Buchholz versus Rosewall and Gonzales are pushed out on the rutted streets of downtown St Louis in 1964. Below: By 1969, things hadn't changed much; bystanders on New York's Lexington Avenue catch Torben Ulrich and company spruiking the US Open.

Hoad glared at him. Richey, open-mouthed, stared back. It appeared that Richey had never witnessed a shot like this. Hoad knew that too.

The instant seemed to hold the difference between a fine player and a tennis genius.

Certainly, whatever else, being a touring pro was a job providing a living. But what a mess of contradiction!

Here were sublime skills derived from years of almost monkish study and practice, but displayed before an audience that often ignored and sometimes ridiculed them. If on occasion they played a great venue, at times the physical platform for their performance was so truncated that they had insufficient room to properly lay down the court they packed up and carried with them. And though at times there were good pickings to be had, on more than one occasion masters Rosewall and Laver provided a heroic performance for nothing – or for Rosewall, as runner up in one French Pro Championships, an eggcup.

And where were the bards who made men into heroes by telling their stories? Usually they were somewhere else.

Thus we are not surprised that the tennis public looked upon this little band not as the maestros they were, but as, in Rod Laver's words, 'performing seals'. More simply, to many tennis followers the pros were merely old stars vulgarly cashing in on the glorious reputations they'd once made in the great, green, fêted and infinitely more salubrious world of the amateurs. Well past being the nation's sporting heroes, our band of pros seemed to have been hatched on the margins of respectable society and got stuck there, brothers to the itinerant boxing troupes whose gnarled fighters fought each other for shonky purses, or to the clowns and stuntmen of the tatty circus that had hit town a few weeks before.

To complete our story, I wish to single out one of the countless performances in the history of the pros.

●●●

Once upon a time, buried in a pro tour, was a doubles match.

So far in this story, the doubles matches of the pro era have been mentioned only in passing, but they must have provided the lover of tennis with the most exuberant displays of skill they'd ever seen. In the four-man contests, the crucial stakes were put aside – not just the money, but also the pecking order on which rested the chance to win it. Here the pros could play for their own enjoyment, and for their unalloyed pride, and direct their performance to those in the audience who appreciated the finer points of the game.

It must also be said that if in the singles the contestants nearly always played their hearts out, in the doubles they sometimes fiddled the performance for their own ends.

For much of the pro era, the performance began with the so-called 'animal act' between the two lesser pros. Then came the main championship clash, followed by the doubles, featured as the third and final part of the pros' evening bill.

As Jack Kramer explains in his autobiography, *The Game*, a night of three long matches might easily have gone until three in the morning. To shorten the night, often the four doubles players would make a private agreement. In the doubles, billed as 'the best of three sets', they would play only 'the first set fair and square.' Then the winner would get a free ride in the second.

But the performers wanted to give the crowd its money's worth. So, though they would play that second set hard too, after a good tussle the first-set losers would contrive to hand over a service break, and the set. In short, the promoter might have billed 'best of three', but as Kramer says, 'sure as hell [the players] didn't want to play three sets'.[11]

One exceptional occasion was on a winter's night in 1953. It was the Sedgman–Kramer tour, and the pros were in Pittsburgh.

The bill consisted of Pancho aka *Seegoo* Segura versus the Australian Ken McGregor in the preliminary, followed by Kramer against Sedgman as top feature. Finally, Segura and Kramer took on the two Aussies in the doubles. Kramer says simply: 'This was the finest sustained doubles competition I was ever in.'

In this company, in singles, McGregor might have been a journeyman. But the champion Aussie Rules footballer was a master at doubles. Indeed, he and the superb Sedgman formed an all-time great team. *Macca* and *Sedg,* as the popular pair was often called, had won the Grand Slam of doubles in 1951, and nearly repeated it the year after that.

Figure 8.5 shows their glorious smashes. If tennis gurus Vines and Segura regarded the leaping McGregor smash as, simply, the best they'd ever seen,

Fig. 8.5a and 8.5b. In the air: the phenomenal smashes of McGregor and Sedgman. Left: Although Macca's smash was one of tennis's greatest shots, and here the power seems to have bent his racket, partner Sedg still looks worried. Right: This time Sedgman, also airborne and scissor-kicking, also a master smasher, induces such confidence in partner McGregor, he jumps for joy.

Fig. 8.6. After flying lessons. In Wimbledon in 1952, teenager Rosewall emulates McGregor's spring heels, and Sedgman's concerns, as partner Hoad soars. By then aged 18, the brilliant youngsters had confronted the older pair of Sedgman and McGregor several times, extended them, and received advanced tutoring on court.

they also noted that partner Sedgman was hardly a slouch in the air! As Figure 8.6 shows, earlier in their stellar careers the pair had been able to pass on some tips to a couple of youngsters called Hoad and Rosewall.

But surprise! Superlative as the Sedgman–McGregor pairing was, as the tour unfolded their opponents – awesome master Kramer in his beloved left court, nimble Segura playing the right – were but a whisker behind them.

This time, as the match progressed, something unexpected turned up: the pros' little fix to shorten the night seemed in danger. The first set went to Kramer and Segura: but as the second got going, the shocked Kramer and Segura found that they were about to be 'double-crossed'.

With most of the night and most of the crowd gone, the American team – believing that their rules were bound by their prior agreement – were more or less coasting along in the second, waiting for their gift of a service break. But they became aware that the opposition was not yielding them the expected break! In fact, the Australians 'broke us, the dirty rascals'.

Kramer continues: 'my first reaction was that they had forgotten who had won the first set'. But when, in emphatic terms, their opponents were reminded of the score and the agreement, they merely replied that 'no, they just wanted to win'.

This was betrayal. He and *Segoo* were infuriated. They 'told the Aussies that if that was the way they wanted to play it', then best of three it might have to be.

So it turned out.

But it was the Aussies who won the second set, then the third. By the end of the match, there were but a handful of spectators remaining, and it was past one o'clock in the morning. Since McGregor and Segura had walked onto the court to begin the evening's performance, six hours had elapsed – and much professional pride staked.

One can easily slip into the shoes of Sedgman and McGregor. OK, this might have been doubles, and this tough finale to a hard night wasn't contributing one extra dime to their payout. But something *was* on the line: their pride!

Especially McGregor's.

Over the last couple of months, this superb athlete, winner of one Grand Slam singles title and a swathe of Grand Slam doubles titles, was being skewered in the first singles. Night after night, an unknown, bandy-legged Ecuadorian named Pancho Segura, a near midget of well over 30 years, had been giving *Mac* the tennis lesson of his life! Now, by courtesy of Kramer and his infuriating little mate (the very same Segura), McGregor's last chance on the tour for a bit of truncated glory was close to vanishing.

In brief, though the world might have forgotten, McGregor believed that he and Sedgman – not Kramer and Segura – were the best doubles team on earth. And they intended to remain so.

As for the agreement? In Australian slang, 'it could go to buggery'.

If only there were a chance to turn back the clock and join that trickle of spectators on that icy night in Pittsburgh! The evening's final performance must have been a masterpiece.

Here were four supreme masters at their peak – surpassing themselves in their chosen vocation, using everything they had learned about a game they loved, giving no quarter and asking for none. *Macca* soared and smashed his thunderbolts. The legendary hands of *Sedg* were stealing volleys from mid-air. Quicksilver *Segoo* was flashing all over the court, contriving impossible angles and lobs. And ever-commanding *Big Jake* Kramer seemed like an impenetrable wall.

Then, past 1.00 am, it was all over.

Two sets to one, the Aussie masters had, for a time, made their point.

Though we cannot be there, luckily we are still able to catch something of their artistry: Talbert, the master student of doubles, recorded a few of the marvellous matches between Kramer–Segura and Sedgman–McGregor on this 1953 tour. In Figure 8.7 he reveals a moment in one of these: the playmaking, with its seductive mixture of power and finesse, offers us a reminder of the delights these four must have been showing the spectators night after night.

It is tempting to leave the pros there. Perhaps we can imagine bidding farewell to them at the very instant captured in Talbert's snapshot when McGregor pounces, and joyfully terminates the rally.

As it happened, when the players left the court that evening, their night turned out to be far from over – and far from joyful. On this occasion, the pros had to play their next gig the following night, and way over the Canadian border in Quebec. So, after their marathon doubles had ended,

THE OLD COLLEGE TRY, PRO STYLE

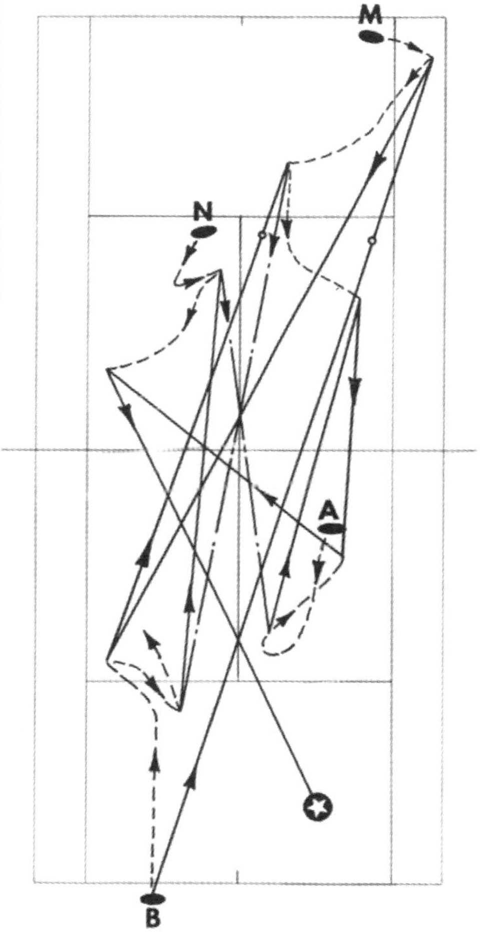

This play shows how, by pure fight and determination, a thrice-lost point can be won from even the best of players.

Server Kramer, **B**, plays a fine first volley low to the middle, which receiver Sedgman, **M**, decides to play as a ground stroke. Sedgman lobs, but not deep enough, and the point appears lost as Kramer moves back and hits a tremendous overhead smash. However, modified net man McGregor, **N**, is watching carefully and is rewarded by being able to stick out his racquet at the last second and save the point temporarily with a weak, high lob volley return. Net man Segura, **A**, drops back and powders a second overhead down the line for a second apparent winner. But Sedgman, **M**, is in no mood to give up the ship. He moves over rapidly and just manages to return a weak volley. Segura is almost smiling cockily at this moment as he moves in for a sure winner this time—the cross-court angle volley area is wide open. But as Segura, **A**, makes the shot, McGregor anticipates beautifully and roars in to blast a deep volley between Kramer and Segura for an incredible point!

Fig.8.7. Masters don't rollover. Talbert and Old record how, three times, the sheer class of Sedgman and McGregor defy another brilliant pair, Kramer and Segura – and a point is saved.

the net and the other support equipment needed to be packed up, and then long-hauled by truck to make it in time for the next evening's play.

In *The Game*, Kramer tells us that the person driving the truck for them was 'a nice kid named Billy Sullivan'.

'It was a tough overnight trip,' says Kramer, 'and Billy crashed and was killed, going too fast trying to make up time.'

He continues: 'But you know, the show went on the next night [in Canada]. We got a relief truck and driver, and they picked up the court and the rest of the stuff out of the wreck ... and got it ... in time for us to play, right on schedule as advertised: Ken McGregor versus Pancho Segura in the opener.'

The man behind it all concludes with the following rueful reflection: 'But I've always thought if we hadn't started playing the doubles out, if we hadn't played so late that night in Pittsburgh, Billy Sullivan wouldn't have been going so fast ... and the kid might be alive today.'

Kramer reminds us that come what may, when their performance ended, and the last spectator shuffled off home, the little band needed to pack up their stuff, and hit the road for the next show.

And though no one knows who won the doubles between Kramer–Segura and Sedgman–McGregor that next freezing night in Canada following their marathon in Pittsburgh, it must have been a pretty good show – if decided in two sets.

●●●

We are now ready to leave the pros and our story.

My hope is that these men have emerged from this book as the masters they were. And as the heroes they were. For as heroes must be, they were brave, resourceful and capable of dreaming our dreams and singing them up. Yet they were also one more band of humble players, drawing out the settled folk to see them play, and to pay them something for the privilege. In many ways they were closer to their distant forebears, the travelling players of the Middle Ages, than to their immediate heirs, the stars of today's industrialised, commercialised, technologised pro circuit.

In telling of eight men and their long and lonely path to mastery, I have sung a song in praise of the great champions they became, and I have tried to put a few things to rights. In parting with them, the image I wish to leave is that last contrary scene in Pittsburgh, and its sequel. Here they are, reduced to a tiny troupe, hardly noticed, hardly rewarded, but majestically fighting out their doubles before hitting the hardest of roads. How brave and skilful – yet how ordinary and vulnerable – were our pros.

After all, our masters' example, arising from a near-empty hall one faraway, freezing and fatal night, reminds us that to create beauty is always a precious task, no matter how fleeting.

One old pro, Torben Ulrich, put it: 'The scoreboard? That's just a painting on the wall.'[12]

Notes

1 John Sharnik, *Remembrance of Games Past.* I have again quoted extensively from Kramer and Deford, *The Game.*

2 'Ten Things You Didn't Know about ... ', *The Weekend Australian*, April 7, 2007.

3 Talbert and Old, *The Game of Doubles in Tennis.*

4 Writing in an instruction book, Frank Sedgman makes a hilarious but significant aside: Rosewall became so razor-sharp at net that the other pros attributed his exceptional vision to some esoteric eye exercises, which he secreted from their gaze! Sedgman's chapter is in Trengove, *The Art of Tennis.*

5 Study of our eight champions, all of whom had directly or indirectly learnt from Tilden, also shows that they deployed another tactic of which Tilden was a master. They would make their opponent's strength the point of their attack but, at a crucial moment, switch the attack to their weakness.

6 Brad Gilbert and Steve Jamison, *Winning Ugly*, Fireside Books, New York, 1993.

7 John Newcombe, *Newk: Life On and Off the Court*, Macmillan, Sydney, 2002.

8 Herb Elliott in his Introduction to *Winning Attitudes*, Ian Heads and Geoff Armstrong, eds, Hardie Grant Books, Sydney, 2000.

9 One player who exemplifies the difference between the great and the near-great was Australian Rex Hartwig, who briefly joined the pros. Hartwig was one of those gifted one-in-a-million who could beat anyone on the day – or during the hours – when he was 'on'. Once at Queen's Club, Hartwig demolished the South African Davis Cupper, Gordon Forbes, 6–0, 6–0. Afterwards, Hartwig apologised to Forbes, confessing that he'd played the whole match 'with his eyes shut'. Once at Wimbledon, Hartwig had been equally blind against Rosewall, and led 6–0, 5–1 – but lost the match. However, on the 1955 head-to-head pro tour when Hartwig took on Segura in the prelude to the highwire of Gonzales versus Trabert, Segura and the pro grind nearly killed the easy-going Australian. Questioned during this tour, where he was being taken apart by the genial, aging master, the forlorn Hartwig replied: 'There are only two good things about being a pro, Segura and the money.' Hartwig never developed the mental qualities required to handle the top pros. Gonzales, with a kind of stunned amazement, reports that Hartwig had once confessed to him that he (Hartwig) 'never knew what he was doing on court'. Poor Hartwig! On the pro tour he was facing the two Panchos, who knew exactly what *they* were doing, and pretty well what their opponents were doing as well.

10 To the survivors of the old pro tour, even such stunts as these were relatively tame: once in the mid-fifties, one of them had to play the first round of a pro tournament against an opponent fully dressed and billed as *The Masked Marvel.*

11 The description and narrative that follows draws on Kramer, *The Game.*

12 Torben Ulrich was a marvellous Dane who joined the pros in the 1960s. Figure 8.4b. shows him, bearded, with a hippie headband, hitting a lovely topspin backhand. This student of Zen was famed for his philosophical twist. When asked about his key to learning tennis, Ulrich replied, 'Watch the ball. But remember there is suffering in the world.' On another occasion, leaving the court following a gruelling five-set loss to the inflammatory Gonzales in the US Open, Ulrich was moved to remark, 'Pancho gives great happiness.'

AFTERWORD

by John Clarke

WRITING an Afterword is like walking home with friends after seeing a play or a film, reflecting on what we have seen and which aspects of it will stay with us.

To describe this book as a history of tennis would be like describing Dickens as a travel writer. Although it is true Dickens' novels are set in different places, what makes them work is the characters. Like a novelist, Peter Underwood has composed a sequence of sometimes overlapping character studies in order to describe the modernisation of an international sporting code by its own elite.

The eight players are very different from one another and their careers collectively span nearly 50 years. Peter's knowledge of his subject is extraordinary and he's also very perceptive. He explains their physical abilities, their coaching and their psychology and he outlines the broader social and economic factors that were driving change at the time. Every now and again two of these legendary figures played one another and we find ourselves court-side with Peter, watching a match which we imagine either of them can win even though it was played in 1947. While we are sometimes transported by hope and whatever else we're projecting onto the story, we are also presented with non-fiction: actual photographs of the shots, the techniques, the different body and arm positions needed when rackets were nearly twice the weight they are today and court surfaces were organised along the lines of a raffle.

Peter often focuses on carefully selected and very telling incidents. The more particular these are and the more specific to the moment and to the individuals involved, the more we recognise them in our own experience. Consider, for example, Harry Hopman's reaction when he first saw the kid from Rockhampton who would grow up to conquer the world: 'Gee' said Harry on seeing Rod Laver, 'He's so small.'

Everyone starts somewhere. Laver was called *Rocket* not because he was fast but because when Hopman first saw him he was slow. Ken Rosewall was called *Muscles* not because he had muscles but because he didn't.

We learn very early in the book about Peter's deadly eye for psychological turning points. He describes beautifully, for example, the look of magic that Peggy Wood saw in Bill Tilden's eyes when he was a set down and in all sorts of trouble in the Wimbledon final against Patterson in 1920. Again, it is a private and secret moment, but we all recognise it. We're not always in front when we glimpse the prospect of success.

The history by which these events and people are connected is not only a story about tennis. It is the story of the twentieth century. When professional tennis got going in the late 1920s, the Great Depression had begun and for millions of people, including many in this book, there was no work, education was cut short and families struggled to survive.

One of the activities that held society together was sport. It was free, it was a way of meeting people, it kept you fit, and tennis was an individual sport so you could turn up with a racket and get a game.

A few years later came the Second World War and there was war service for Don Budge, Jack Kramer, Bobby Riggs and Pancho Gonzales. Sixty million people were killed and Europe and Russia and parts of Asia were devastated.

Throughout the 1950s and '60s when those economies were still recovering, Australia and the United States both did very well at sport and this was particularly evident in tennis. In the 25 years between the war and 1970, Australia won the Davis Cup 15 times and the US 10 times. By 1968 when the Open Era arrived, there was greater prosperity, free tertiary education and Wimbledon was broadcast live on television. World-class tennis players are now like film stars, there are professional tennis circuits all over the world, and it seems that the attempt to prevent people from making a living playing sport has not been entirely successful.

There is also a sense of loss in the story Peter tells. In those very tough years, when the world's best players were outcasts and were struggling to make a living, they produced some of the finest tennis ever played.

They were masters, not just of tennis but of themselves.

I hope a lot of young people read this very impressive and beautifully written book.

John Clarke
July 2015

Endpiece. *A wounded hero: the battle and its cost. Lew Hoad just before his last Wimbledon Final in 1957. Hoad went out and triumphed. But during the exacting pro tour that followed, the frailty, captured here by photographer David Moore, resurfaced.*

ACKNOWLEDGEMENTS

WHILE many have helped me with this book, one is owed special thanks.

My brother, Roger, has been there from the first. At the beginning, he was a co-author, but withdrew to let me make it my project. However, he believed in the book, and abetted its creation at every stage. My debt to him is incalculable.

I am also most grateful to the person who began the editing of this book, Michèle Drouart. Michèle understood what I was trying to do, and her suggestions were on the button. Since then, I have greatly benefitted from the lucid professionalism of my second editor, Janine Drakeford.

My writers' group has been meeting for over fifteen years, and members have heard parts of this book from the earliest to the final versions. Only one of the seven is a sports fan, and I was dismayed when at first they appeared to have little idea of what I was trying to achieve. Since then I have found the group's feedback generous and useful. Even more valuable has been their comradeship, a foil to the isolated world of the writer.

Robert Drewe once recommended to me that one should never give one's writing to friends – good advice, which I have at times broken. Here, two old comrades, Brian Roberman and Perpetua Durack Clancy, were crucial: when the whole project seemed worthless, they saw something in it and urged me to keep going.

This is a book about eight great tennis players, and it has been my good fortune to be in touch with three of them.

Jack Kramer was nearing the end of his life when, through the generosity of his son David, I could seek his advice. He knew exactly what was needed, and encouraged me to tell a story that he believed was important and was being fast forgotten. 'Why', said Jack over the phone to me, 'the kids these days have never heard of Rod Laver, let alone Don Budge!'

On another occasion, when Jack had just left hospital and I asked how he was, his reply would warm the heart of every tennis aficionado: 'Well, Peter, not great, but at least I'm holding my serve!'

Jack had agreed to write the Foreword to the book, and had started on the task. Alas, before completing it he was to join the great tournament in the sky.

By reviewing earlier drafts of the book Ken Rosewall and Rod Laver have also gone out of their way to help, and Ken in particular has been most generous to me in a number of ways. Another great champion, Frank Sedgman – who just missed out on becoming World Pro Champion – was also of special assistance at the start of the project. Like Jack Kramer, Frank told me how keenly he wanted what he called 'our' story – that is, the pros' story – to be made public.

I can assure the reader that each of the four tennis masters I have come to know a little – and John Newcombe who has so kindly written the Foreword – seem far from the common perception of the egotistical superstar, and their self-effacing engagement and enthusiasm for this project has inspired me from the beginning.

I am also most grateful to John Clarke. Besides contributing an Afterword of wit, insight and originality, he has passed on some of his boundless knowledge of sports and those who play them.

With any long-term and demanding project, most of us agree that without our family we are goners: in this case my sons Crispin and Jim, and their extraordinarily wise partners, Galatée de Laubadère and Katie Bewley, not only know my eccentricities (such as spending years submerged in things marginal and long forgotten), sometimes they seem to enjoy them.

Loyalty and intelligence, what more can one ask from one's intimates?

PHOTO CREDITS

Author's note: In good faith I have attempted to seek permission for illustrations likely to remain in copyright. Since many are now over fifty years old, it was not possible to trace and secure the permissions of some copyright owners. Further, a good many of the photos taken from published tennis books did not provide attribution, so their source could not always be identified. If any copyright owners who have not so far been reached by me wish to do so, I am happy to provide further acknowledgement and appropriate reimbursement if required.

The following listing provides the sources of all illustrations used. References not given in full are found at the end of respective chapters.

Front Cover – Collins and Hollander's *Modern Encyclopaedia of Tennis,* photo referenced to UPI.

Back Cover – Scott, *Tennis: Game of Motion,* photo referenced to Melchior DiGiacomo

Inside Back Cover – Photo by the author.

Frontispiece – Metzler, *Tennis Styles and Stylists,* photo referenced to *Sydney Morning Herald.*

Prologue – Fig. 0.1: LeCompte, *The Last Sure Thing,* photo referenced to the Riggs Family Estate.

Chapter 1 – Fig. 1.0: John Haylett and Richard Evans, ed., *The Illustrated Encyclopaedia of World Tennis,* Marshall Cavendish, London, 1989, photo referenced to The Photo Source (now Getty Images); Fig. 1.1: Clerici, *Tennis,* photo sources not referenced; Fig. 1.2: Deford, *Big Bill Tilden,* photo referenced to *New York Daily News;* Fig. 1.3a: Tilden, *The Art of Lawn Tennis,* photo referenced to Sport and General Press; Fig. 1.3b: A Wallis Myers, *Lawn Tennis: Its Principles and Practice,* Seeley, Service and Co., London, 1930, photo referenced to Sport and General Press; Fig. 1.4: Clerici, *Tennis,* photo source not referenced; Fig. 1.5: Bill Shannon, ed., *USTA Official Encyclopaedia of Tennis,* Harper and Row, New York, 1979, photo referenced to USTA; Fig. 1.6: Clerici, Tennis, photo source not referenced; Fig. 1.7: Collins and Hollander's *Modern Encyclopaedia of Tennis,* photo referenced to UPI; Fig. 1.8: Quist, *Tennis: the Greats 1920–1960,* photo source Quist/Egan; Fig. 1.9: Clerici, *Tennis,* photo source not referenced; Fig. 1.10: Eugene Scott, *Tennis: Game of Motion,* Crown Publishing, New York, 1973, photo referenced to Bettmann Archive Inc. (now Getty Images).; Fig. 1.11: Deford, *Big Bill Tilden,* photo referenced to *New York Daily News;* Fig. 1.12: Shannon, ed., *USTA Official Encyclopaedia of Tennis,* photo referenced to USTA.

Chapter 2 – Fig. 2.0a: Metzler, *Tennis Styles and Stylists,* photo referenced to M Phillipe Chartrier; Fig.2.0b: Metzler, *Tennis Styles and Stylists,* photo source J D Budge; Fig. 2.1: Grimsley, *Tennis: Its History, People and Events,* photo referenced to USLTA; Fig. 2.2: Quist, *Tennis: the Greats 1920–1960,* photo source Quist/Egan; Fig. 2.3: Richard Schikel, *The World of Tennis,* Random House, New York, 1975, photo referenced to Underwood and Underwood; Fig. 2.4: L Buchanan, *The Story of Tennis,* Vanguard, New York, 1951, photo source not referenced; Fig. 2.5: Clerici, *Tennis,* photo referenced to *Sports Illustrated;* Fig. 2.6: Quist, *Tennis: the Greats 1920–1960,* photo source Quist/Egan; Fig. 2.7: Budge, *Don*

Budge: A Tennis Memoir, photo referenced to Sports Illustrated; Fig. 2.8: Buchanan, The Story of Tennis, source not referenced; Fig. 2.9: Budge, Don Budge: A Tennis Memoir, photo referenced to US Department of Defense; Fig. 2.10: Vines, *Tennis: Myth and Method,* photo source not referenced.

Chapter 3 – Fig. 3.0: Riggs, *Tennis is My Racket,* photo source not referenced; Fig. 3.1: LeCompte, *The Last Sure Thing,* photo referenced to US Department of Defense; Fig. 3.2: Riggs, *Tennis is My Racket,* photo source not referenced; Fig. 3.3: Riggs, *Tennis is My Racket,* photo source not referenced; Fig. 3.4 LeCompte, *The Last Sure Thing,* photo referenced to Otto Rothschild/LA Public Library; Fig. 3.5: Riggs, *Tennis is My Racket,* photo source not referenced; Fig. 3.6: Robertson and Kramer, eds, *The Encyclopaedia of Tennis,* Allen and Unwin, London, 1974, photo referenced to UPI; Figs 3.7a and Fig. 3.7b: Riggs, *Court Hustler,* photos referenced to *Sports Illustrated* and *Time* Inc.

Chapter 4 – Fig. 4.0: Metzler, *Tennis Styles and Stylists,* photo referenced to Melbourne *Herald-Sun*; Fig. 4.1 Quist, *Tennis: the Greats 1920–1960,* photo source Quist/Egan; Fig. 4.2: Metzler, *Tennis Styles and Stylists,* photo referenced to *Melbourne Herald-Sun*; Fig. 4.3: From author's collection, source not known; Fig. 4.4: Quist, *Tennis: the Greats 1920–1960,* photo source Quist/Egan; Fig. 4.5: Grimsley, *Tennis: Its History, People and Events,* photo referenced to Max P Haas; Fig. 4.6: Alan Trengove, ed., *The Art of Tennis,* photo referenced to Le-Roye Productions (now Wimbledon Archives); Fig. 4.7: Quist, *Tennis: the Greats 1920–1960,* photo source Quist/Egan.

Chapter 5 – Fig. 5.0: LeCompte, *The Last Sure Thing,* photo referenced to International Tennis Hall of Fame; Fig. 5.1: Quist, *Tennis: the Greats 1920–1960,* photo source Quist/ Egan; Fig. 5.2: Budge Patty, *Tennis My Way,* Hutchison, London, 1951, photo source not referenced; Fig. 5.3: Gonzales with Dick Hawk, *How to Play and Win at Tennis,* photo source not referenced; 5.4: Graph designed by the author from accounts of the tour, particularly Gonzales' *Man with a Racket* and Kramer's *The Game*; Fig. 5.5: Clerici, *Tennis,* photo source not referenced; Fig. 5.6: Clerici, *Tennis,* photo sources not referenced; Fig. 5.7: Grimsley, *Tennis: Its History, People and Events,* photo referenced to E D Lacey; Fig. 5.8: Clerici, *Tennis,* photo sources not referenced; Fig. 5.9: Clerici, *Tennis,* photo sources not referenced;

Chapter 6 – Fig. 6.0: Scott, *Tennis: Game of Motion,* photo referenced to Melchior DiGiacomo; Fig. 6.1a and Fig. 6.1b: Clerici, *Tennis,* photo sources not referenced; Fig 6.1c.

: Rosewall, *Play Tennis with Rosewall,* photo source Rosewall; Fig. 6.2: Quist, *Tennis: the Greats 1920–1960,* photo source Quist/Egan; Fig. 6.3: Evans, *Open Tennis,* photo referenced to Jenny Hoad; Fig. 6.4: Quist, *Tennis: the Greats 1920–1960,* photo source Quist/Egan; Fig. 6.5: Quist, *Tennis: the Greats 1920–1960,* photo source Quist/Egan; Fig. 6.6: Laver and Collins, *Rod Laver's Tennis Digest,* photo referenced to Digest Books; Fig. 6.7: Clerici, *Tennis,* photo sources not referenced; Fig. 6.8a: Laver and Collins, *Rod Laver's Tennis Digest,* photo referenced to Digest Books; Fig. 6.8b: *Match Point, the Nestlé Book of Tennis,* Stanley Paul and Co, London, 1963, source not referenced; Fig. 6.9: Clerici, *Tennis,* photo sources not referenced; Fig. 6.10: Scott, *Tennis: Game of Motion,* photo referenced to Fred Kaplan;

Chapter 7 – Fig. 7.0: Laver and Collins, *Rod Laver's Tennis Digest,* cover photo referenced to Digest Books; Fig. 7.1: Trengove, *Advantage Australia: Rod Laver and Margaret Court, legends of the grand slam,* photos referenced to Australia Post; Fig. 7.2: Trengove, *Advantage Australia: Rod Laver and Margaret Court, legends of the grand slam,* photos referenced to Australia Post; Fig. 7.3: Trengove, *The Art of Tennis,* photo referenced to Le-Roye Productions (now

Wimbledon Archives); Fig.7.4: Clerici, *Tennis*, photo sources not referenced; Fig. 7.5: Laver and Pollard, *How to Play Winning Tennis*, photo source not referenced; Fig. 7.6: Haylett and Evans, *The Illustrated Encyclopaedia of World Tennis*, Marshall Cavendish, London 1989, photo referenced to Michael Cole Camerawork (now Wimbledon Archives); Fig. 7.7: Clerici, *Tennis*, photo source not referenced; Fig. 7.8: Davidson and Jones, *Lawn Tennis: the great ones*, cover photo referenced to Press Association; Fig. 7.9: Laver and Collins, *Rod Laver's Tennis Digest*, photo referenced to Digest Books Fig. 7.10a: Sedgman, *How to Play Tennis*, Pollard Publishing Company, Wollstonecraft, 1972, photo source not referenced; Fig. 7.10b: Douglas, *The Handbook of Tennis*, Pelham Books, London, 1982, photo referenced to Gerry Cranham FIIP.

Epilogue – Fig. 8.0: Collins and Hollander's *Modern Encyclopaedia of Tennis*, photo referenced to UPI; Fig. 8.1: Metzler, *Tennis Styles and Stylists*, photo referenced to Melbourne Herald Sun; Fig, 8.2: Talbert and Old, *The Game of Doubles in Tennis*, photos referenced to the publishers, Lippincott; Fig. 8.3: Talbert and Old, *The Game of Doubles in Tennis*, photos referenced to the publishers, Lippincott; Fig. 8.4a: Laver and Collins, *The Education of a Tennis Player*, photo referenced to Wide World Photos; Fig. 8.4b: Sharnik, *Remembrance of Games Past*, referenced to UPI; Fig. 8.5a: Patty, *Tennis My Way*, source not referenced; Fig. 8.5b: Clerici, *Tennis*, source not referenced; Fig. 8.6: Hoad, *My Game*, source referenced to Reuters Photos; Fig. 8.7: Talbert and Old, *The Game of Doubles in Tennis*, photos referenced to the publishers, Lippincott.

Endpiece – Conrad, *At Home in Australia*, photo referenced to Estate of David Moore.

Index

Page numbers in **bold** indicate photographs.